The Essence of Christianity

LUDWIG FEUERBACH
Translated by George Eliot

COSIMOCLASSICS

NEW YORK

The Essence of Christianity
Cover Copyright © 2008 by Cosimo, Inc.

The Essence of Christianity was originally published in 1902.

For information, address:
P.O. Box 416, Old Chelsea Station
New York, NY 10011

or visit our website at:
www.cosimobooks.com

Ordering Information:
Cosimo publications are available at online bookstores. They may
also be purchased for educational, business or promotional use:
- *Bulk orders:* special discounts are available on bulk orders for reading
groups, organizations, businesses, and others. For details contact
Cosimo Special Sales at the address above or at info@cosimobooks.com.
- *Custom-label orders:* we can prepare selected books with your cover or
logo of choice. For more information, please contact Cosimo at
info@cosimobooks.com.

Cover Design by www.popshopstudio.com

ISBN: 978-1-60520-443-7

As man in his utmost remoteness from himself, in God, always returns upon himself, always revolves round himself; so in his utmost remoteness from the world, he always at last comes back to it. The more extra- and supra-human God appears at the commencement, the more human does he show himself to be in the subsequent course of things, or at the close: and just so, the more supernatural the heavenly life looks in the beginning or at a distance, the more clearly does it, in the end or when viewed closely, exhibit its identity with the natural life...

—from Chapter XVIII: "The Christian Heaven, or Personal Immortality"

CONTENTS

x CONTENTS.

PART II.

THE FALSE OR THEOLOGICAL ESSENCE OF RELIGION

APPENDIX

CONTENTS.

PREFACE TO THE SECOND EDITION.*

THE clamour excited by the present work has not surprised me, and hence it has not in the least moved me from my position. On the contrary, I have once more, in all calmness, subjected my work to the severest scrutiny, both historical and philosophical; I have, as far as possible, freed it from its defects of form, and enriched it with new developments, illustrations, and historical testimonies,—testimonies in the highest degree striking and irrefragable. Now that I have thus verified my analysis by historical proofs, it is to be hoped that readers whose eyes are not sealed will be convinced and will admit, even though reluctantly, that my work contains a faithful, correct translation of the Christian religion out of the Oriental language of imagery into plain speech. And it has no pretension to be anything more than a close translation, or, to speak literally, an empirical or historico-philosophical analysis, a solution of the enigma of the Christian religion. The general propositions which I premise in the Introduction are no *à priori*, excogitated propositions, no products of speculation; they have arisen out of the analysis of religion; they are only, as indeed are all the fundamental ideas of the work, generalisations from the known manifestations of human nature, and in particular of the religious consciousness,—facts converted into thoughts, *i.e.*, expressed in general terms, and thus made the property of the understanding. The ideas of my work are only conclusions, *consequences*, drawn from premisses which are not themselves mere ideas, but objective facts either actual or historical—facts which had not their place

* The opening paragraphs of this Preface are omitted, as having too specific a reference to transient German polemics to interest the English reader.

in my head simply in virtue of their ponderous existence in folio. I unconditionally repudiate *absolute*, immaterial, self-sufficing speculation,—that speculation which draws its material from within. I differ *toto cœlo* from those philosophers who pluck out their eyes that they may see better; for *my* thought I require the senses, especially sight; I found my ideas on materials which can be appropriated only through the activity of the senses. I do not generate the object from the thought, but the thought from the object; and I hold *that* alone to be an object which has an existence beyond one's own brain. I am an idealist only in the region of *practical* philosophy, that is, I do not regard the limits of the past and present as the limits of humanity, of the future; on the contrary, I firmly believe that many things—yes, many things—which with the short-sighted, pusillanimous practical men of to-day, pass for flights of imagination, for ideas never to be realised, for mere chimeras, will to-morrow, *i.e.*, in the next century,—centuries in individual life are days in the life of humanity,—exist in full reality. Briefly, the "Idea" is to me only faith in the historical future, in the triumph of truth and virtue; it has for me only a political and moral significance; for in the sphere of strictly theoretical philosophy, I attach myself, in direct opposition to the Hegelian philosophy, only to *realism*, to materialism in the sense above indicated. The maxim hitherto adopted by speculative philosophy: All that is mine I carry with me, the old *omnia mea mecum porto*, I cannot, alas! appropriate. I have many things outside myself, which I cannot convey either in my pocket or my head, but which nevertheless I look upon as belonging to me, not indeed as a mere man—a view not now in question—but as a philosopher. I am nothing but a *natural philosopher in the domain of mind;* and the natural philosopher can do nothing without instruments, without material means. In this character I have written the present work, which consequently contains nothing else than the principle of a new philosophy verified practically, *i.e., in concreto*, in application to a special object, but an object which has a universal significance: namely, to religion, in which this principle is exhibited, developed, and thoroughly carried out. This philosophy is essentially distinguished from the systems hitherto prevalent, in that it corresponds to the real, complete nature of man; but for that very reason it is antagonistic to minds perverted and crippled by a superhuman, *i.e.*, anti-human, anti-natural religion and speculation. It does not, as I have already said elsewhere, regard the *pen* as the only fit organ for the revelation of truth, but the eye and ear, the hand and foot; it does not identify the *idea* of the fact with the fact itself, so as to reduce real existence to an existence on paper, but it separates the two, and precisely by this separation attains to the *fact itself;* it recognises as the true thing, not the thing as it is an object of the abstract reason, but as it is an object of the real, complete man, and hence as it is itself a real, complete thing. This philosophy does not rest on an Understanding *per se*, on an absolute, nameless understanding, belonging one knows not to whom, but on the understanding of man;—though not, I grant, on that of man enervated by speculation and dogma;—and it speaks the language of men, not an empty, unknown tongue. Yes, both in substance and in speech, it places philosophy in *the negation of philosophy*, *i.e.*, it declares *that* alone to be the true philosophy which is converted *in succum et sanguinem*, which is incarnate in Man; and hence it finds its highest triumph in the fact that to all dull and pedantic minds, which place the *essence* of philosophy in the *show* of philosophy, it appears to be no philosophy at all.

This philosophy has for its principle, not the Substance of Spinoza, not the *ego* of Kant and Fichte, not the Absolute Identity of Schelling, not the Absolute Mind of Hegel, in short, no abstract, merely conceptional being, but a *real* being, the true *Ens realissimum*—man; its principle, therefore, is in the highest degree positive and real. It generates thought from the *opposite* of thought, from Matter, from existence, from the senses; it has relation to its object first through the senses, *i.e.*, passively, before defining it in thought. Hence my work, as a specimen of this philosophy, so far from being a production to be placed in the category of Speculation,—although in another point of view it is the true, the incarnate result of prior philosophical systems,—is the direct opposite of speculation, nay, puts an end to it by explaining it. Speculation makes religion say only what it has *itself* thought, and expressed far better than religion; it assigns a meaning to religion without any reference to the *actual* meaning of religion; it does not look beyond itself. I, on the contrary, let religion itself speak: I constitute myself only its listener and interpreter, not its prompter. Not to invent, but to discover, " to unveil existence," has been my sole object; to *see* correctly, my sole endeavour. It is not I, but religion that worships man, although religion, or rather theology, denies this; it is not I, an insignificant individual, but religion itself that says: God is man, man is God; it is not I, but religion that denies the God who is *not* man, but only an *ens rationis*, — since it makes God become man, and then constitutes this God, not distinguished from man, having a human form, human feelings, and human thoughts, the object of its worship and veneration. I have only found the key to the cipher of the Christian religion, only extricated its true meaning from the web of contradictions and delusions called theology;—but in doing so I have certainly committed a sacrilege. If therefore my work is negative, irreligious, atheistic, let it be remembered that atheism—at least in the sense of this work—is the secret of religion itself; that religion itself, not indeed on the surface, but fundamentally, not in intention or according to its own supposition, but in its heart, in its essence, believes in nothing else than the truth and divinity of human nature. Or let it be *proved* that the historical as well as the rational arguments of my work are false; let them be refuted—not, however, I entreat, by judicial denunciations, or theological jeremiads, by the trite phrases of speculation, or other pitiful expedients for which I have no name, but by *reasons*, and such reasons as I have not already thoroughly answered.

Certainly, my work is negative, destructive; but, be it observed, only in relation to the *un*human, not to the human elements of religion. It is therefore divided into two parts, of which the first is, as to its main idea, *positive*, the second, including the Appendix, not wholly, but in the main, *negative;* in both, however, the same positions are proved, only in a different or rather opposite manner. The first exhibits religion in its *essence*, its *truth*, the second exhibits it in its *contradictions;* the first is development, the second polemic; thus the one is, according to the nature of the case, calmer, the other more vehement. Development advances gently, contest impetuously, for development is self-contented at every stage, contest only at the last blow. Development is deliberate, but contest resolute. Development is *light*, contest *fire*.. Hence results a difference between the two parts even as to their form. Thus in the first part I show that the true sense of Theology is Anthropology, that there is no distinction between the *predicates* of the divine and human nature, and, consequently, no distinction between the divine and human *subject*: I say *consequently*, for wherever, as is especially the case in theology, the predicates are not accidents, but express the essence of the subject, there is no distinction between subject and predicate, the one can be put in the place of the other; on which point I refer the reader to the Analytics of Aristotle, or even merely to the Introduction of Porphyry. In the second part, on the other hand, I show that the distinction which is made, or rather supposed to be made, between the theological and anthropological predicates resolves itself into an absurdity. Here is a striking example. In the first part I prove that the Son of God is *in religion* a real son, the son of God in the same sense in which man is the son of man, and I find therein the *truth*, the *essence* of religion, that it conceives and affirms a profoundly human relation as a divine relation; on the other hand, in the second part I show that the Son of God—not indeed in religion, but in theology, which is the reflection of religion upon itself,— is not a son in the natural, human sense, but in an entirely different manner, contradictory to Nature and reason, and therefore absurd, and I find in this negation of human sense and the human understanding, the negation of religion. Accordingly the first part is the *direct*, the second the *indirect* proof, that theology is anthropology: hence the second part necessarily has reference to the first; it has no independent significance; its only aim is to show that the sense in which religion is interpreted in the previous part of the work *must* be the true one, because the contrary is absurd. In brief, in the first part I am chiefly concerned with *religion*, in the second with *theology*: I say *chiefly*, for it was impossible to exclude theology from the first part, or religion from the second. A mere glance will show that my investigation includes *speculative* theology or philosophy, and not, as has been here and there erroneously supposed, *common* theology only, a kind of trash from which I rather keep as clear as possible, (though, for the rest, I am sufficiently well acquainted with it), confining myself always to the most essential, strict and necessary definition of the object,* and hence to that definition which gives to an object the most general interest, and raises it above the sphere of theology. But it is with theology that I have to do, not with theologians; for I can only undertake to characterise what is *primary*,—the *original*, not the copy, *principles*, not persons, *species*, not individuals, *objects of history*, not objects of the *chronique scandaleuse*.

If my work contained only the second part, it would be perfectly just to accuse it of a negative tendency, to represent the proposition : Religion is nothing, is an absurdity, as its essential purport. But I by no means say (that were an easy task!): God is nothing, the Trinity is nothing, the Word of God is nothing, &c. I only show that they are not *that* which the illusions of theology make them,—not foreign. but native mysteries, the mysteries of human nature; I show that religion takes the apparent, the superficial in Nature and humanity for the essential, and hence conceives their true essence as a separate, special existence : that consequently, religion, in the definitions which it gives of God, *e.g.*, of the Word of God,—at least in those definitions which are not negative in the sense above alluded to,—only defines or makes objective the true nature of the human word. The reproach that according to my book religion is an absurdity, a nullity, a pure illusion, would be well founded only if, according to it, that into which I resolve religion, which I prove to be its true object and substance, namely, *man,—anthropology*, were an absurdity, a nullity, a pure illusion. But so far from giving a trivial or even a subordinate significance to anthropology,—a significance which is assigned to it only just so long as a theology stands above it and in opposition to it,—I, on the contrary, while reducing theology to anthropology, exalt anthropology into theology, very much as Christianity, while lowering God into man, made man into God; though, it is true, this human God was by a further process made a transcendental, imaginary God, remote from man. Hence it is obvious that I do not take the word anthropology in the sense of the Hegelian or of any

---

* For example, in considering the sacraments, I limit myself to two ; for, in the strictest sense (see Luther, T. xvii. p. 558), there are no more.

other philosophy, but in an infinitely higher and more general sense.

Religion is the dream of the human mind. But even in dreams we do not find ourselves in emptiness or in heaven, but on earth, in the realm of reality; we only see real things in the entrancing splendour of imagination and caprice, instead of in the simple daylight of reality and necessity. Hence I do nothing more to religion—and to speculative philosophy and theology also—than to open its eyes, or rather to turn its gaze from the internal towards the external, *i.e.*, I change the object as it is in the imagination into the object as it is in reality.

But certainly for the present age, which prefers the sign to the thing signified, the copy to the original, fancy to reality, the appearance to the essence, this change, inasmuch as it does away with illusion, is an absolute annihilation, or at least a reckless profanation; for in these days *illusion* only is *sacred, truth profane.* Nay, sacredness is held to be enhanced in proportion as truth decreases and illusion increases, so that the highest degree of illusion comes to be the highest degree of sacredness. Religion has disappeared, and for it has been substituted, even among Protestants, the *appearance* of religion—the Church—in order at least that "the faith" may be imparted to the ignorant and indiscriminating multitude; *that* faith being still the Christian, because the Christian churches stand now as they did a thousand years ago, and now, as formerly, the *external signs* of the faith are in vogue. That which has no longer any existence in faith (the faith of the modern world is only an ostensible faith, a faith which does not believe what it fancies that it believes, and is only an undecided, pusillanimous unbelief) is still to pass current as *opinion:* that which is no longer sacred in itself and in truth is still at least to *seem* sacred. Hence the simulated religious indignation of the present age, the age of shows and illusion, concerning my analysis, especially of the Sacraments. But let it not be demanded of an author who proposes to himself as his goal not the favour of his contemporaries, but only the truth, the unveiled, naked truth, that he should have or feign respect towards an empty appearance, especially as the object which underlies this appearance is in itself the culminating‑point of religion, *i.e.*, the point at

which the religious slides into the irreligious. Thus much
in justification, not in excuse, of my analysis of the Sacraments.

With regard to the true bearing of my analysis of the
Sacraments, especially as presented in the concluding chapter, I only remark, that I therein illustrate by a palpable
and visible example the essential purport, the peculiar theme
of my work ; that I therein call upon the senses themselves to witness to the truth of my analysis and my ideas,
and demonstrate *ad oculos, ad tactum, ad gustum,* what I
have taught *ad captum* throughout the previous pages. As,
namely, the water of Baptism, the wine and bread of the
Lord's Supper, taken in their natural power and significance,
are and effect infinitely more than in a supernaturalistic,
illusory significance ; so the object of religion in general,
conceived in the sense of this work, *i.e.,* the anthropological sense, is infinitely more productive and real, both in
theory and practice, than when accepted in the sense of theology.   For as that which is or is supposed to be imparted
in the water, bread, and wine, over and above these natural
substances themselves, is something in the imagination only,
but in truth, in reality, nothing ; so also the object of religion in general, the Divine essence, in distinction from
the essence of Nature and Humanity,—that is to say, if
its attributes, as understanding, love, &c., are and signify
something else than these attributes as they belong to man
and Nature,—is only something in the imagination, but in
truth and reality nothing.   Therefore—this is the moral of
the fable—we should not, as is the case in theology and
speculative philosophy, make real beings and things into
arbitrary signs, vehicles, symbols, or predicates of a distinct,
transcendant, absolute, *i.e.,* abstract being ; but we should
accept and understand them in the significance which they
have in themselves, which is identical with their qualities,
with those conditions which make them what they are:—
thus only do we obtain the key to a *real theory and practice.*
I, in fact, put in the place of the barren baptismal water,
the beneficent effect of real water.   How " watery," how
trivial !   Yes, indeed, very trivial.   But so Marriage, in its
time, was a *very trivial truth,* which Luther, on the ground
of his natural good sense, maintained in opposition to the
seemingly holy illusion of celibacy.   But while I thus view

water as a real thing, I at the same time intend it as a vehicle, an image, an example, a symbol, of the "unholy" spirit of my work, just as the water of Baptism—the object of my analysis—is at once literal and symbolical water. It is the same with bread and wine. Malignity has hence drawn the conclusion that bathing, eating, and drinking are the *summa summarum*, the positive result of my work. I make no other reply than this: If the whole of religion is contained in the Sacraments, and there are consequently no other religious acts than those which are performed in Baptism and the Lord's Supper; *then* I grant that the entire purport and positive result of my work are bathing, eating, and drinking, since this work is nothing but a faithful, rigid, historico-philosophical analysis of religion—the revelation of religion to itself, the *awakening of religion to self-consciousness.*

I say an *historico-philosophical* analysis, in distinction from a merely *historical* analysis of Christianity. The historical critic—such a one, for example, as Daumer or Ghillany—shows that the Lord's Supper is a rite lineally descended from the ancient cultus of human sacrifice ; that once, instead of bread and wine, real human flesh and blood were partaken. I, on the contrary, take as the object of my analysis and reduction only the Christian significance of the rite, that view of it which is *sanctioned* in Christianity, and I proceed on the supposition that only *that significance* which a dogma or institution has in Christianity (of course in ancient Christianity, not in modern), whether it may present itself in other religions or not, is also the *true origin* of that dogma or institution *in so far* as it is *Christian.* Again, the historical critic, as, for example, Lützelberger, shows that the narratives of the miracles of Christ resolve themselves into contradictions and absurdities, that they are later fabrications, and that consequently Christ was no miracle-worker, nor, in general, that which he is represented to be in the Bible. I, on the other hand, do not inquire what the real, natural Christ was or may have been in distinction from what he has been made or has become in Supernaturalism; on the contrary, I accept the Christ of religion, but I show that this superhuman being is nothing else than a product and reflex of the supernatural human mind. I do not ask whether this or that, or any miracle can happen or not; I only show *what* miracle *is*, and I show it not *à priori*, but by examples of miracles narrated in the Bible as real events; in doing so, however, I answer or rather preclude the question as to the possibility or reality of necessity of miracle. Thus much concerning the distinction between me and the historical critics who have attacked Christianity. As regards my relation to Strauss and Bruno Bauer, in company with whom I am constantly named, I merely point out here that the distinction between our works is sufficiently indicated by the distinction between their objects, which is implied even in the title-page. Bauer takes for the object of his criticism the evangelical history, *i.e.*, biblical Christianity, or rather biblical theology; Strauss, the System of Christian Doctrine and the Life of Jesus (which may also be included under the title of Christian Doctrine), *i.e.*, dogmatic Christianity, or rather dogmatic theology; I, Christianity in general, *i.e.*, the Christian *religion*, and consequently only Christian philosophy or theology. Hence I take my citations chiefly from men in whom Christianity was not merely a theory or a dogma, not merely theology, but religion. My principal theme is Christianity, is Religion, as it is the *immediate object*, the *immediate nature*, of man. Erudition and philosophy are to me only the *means* by which I bring to light the treasure hid in man.

I must further mention that the circulation which my work has had amongst the public at large was neither desired nor expected by me. It is true that I have always taken as the standard of the mode of teaching and writing, not the abstract, particular, professional philosopher, but universal man, that I have regarded *man* as the criterion of truth, and not this or that founder of a system, and have from the first placed the highest excellence of the philosopher in this, that he abstains, both as a man and as an author, from the ostentation of philosophy, *i.e.*, that he is a philosopher only in reality, not formally, that he is a quiet philosopher, not a loud and still less a brawling one. Hence, in all my works, as well as in the present one, I have made the utmost clearness, simplicity, and definiteness a law to myself, so that they may be understood, at least in the main, by every cultivated and thinking man. But notwithstanding this, my work can be appreciated and fully understood only by the scholar, that is to say, by the scholar who loves truth, who is capable of forming a judgment, who is above the notions and prejudices of the learned and unlearned vulgar; for although a thoroughly independent production, it has yet its necessary logical basis in history. I very frequently refer to this or that historical phenomenon without expressly designating it, thinking this superfluous; and such references can be understood by the scholar alone. Thus, for example, in the very first chapter, where I develop the necessary consequences of the standpoint of Feeling, I allude to Jacobi and Schleiermacher; in the second chapter I allude chiefly to Kantism, Scepticism, Theism, Materialism and Pantheism; in the chapter on the "Standpoint of Religion," where I discuss the contradictions between the religious or theological and the physical or natural-philosophical view of Nature, I refer to philosophy in the age of orthodoxy, and especially to the philosophy of Descartes and Leibnitz, in which this contradiction presents itself in a peculiarly characteristic manner. The reader, therefore, who is unacquainted with the historical facts and ideas presupposed in my work, will fail to perceive on what my arguments and ideas hinge; no wonder if my positions often appear to him baseless, however firm the footing on which they stand. It is true that the subject of my work is of universal human interest; moreover, its fundamental ideas, though not in the form in which they are here expressed, or in which they could be expressed under existing circumstances, will one day become the common property of mankind: for nothing is opposed to them in the present day but empty, powerless illusions and prejudices in contradiction with the true nature of man. But in considering this subject in the first instance, I was under the necessity of treating it as a matter of science, of philosophy; and in rectifying the aberrations of Religion, Theology, and Speculation, I was naturally obliged to use their expressions, and even to appear to speculate, or—which is the same thing—to turn theologian myself, while I nevertheless only analyse speculation, *i.e.*, reduce theology to anthropology. My work, as I said before, contains, and applies in the concrete, the principle of a new philosophy suited—not to the schools, but—to man. Yes, it contains that principle, but only by *evolving* it out of the very core of religion; hence, be it said in passing, the new philosophy can no longer, like the old Catholic and modern Protestant scholasticism, fall into the temptation to prove its agreement with religion by its agreement with Christian dogmas; on the contrary, being evolved from the nature of religion, it has in itself the true essence of religion,—is, in its very quality as a philosophy, a religion also. But a work which considers ideas in their genesis and explains and demonstrates them in strict sequence, is, by the very form which this purpose imposes upon it, unsuited to popular reading.

Lastly, as a supplement to this work with regard to many apparently unvindicated positions, I refer to my articles in the *Deutsches Jahrbuch,* January and February 1842, to my critiques and *Charakteristiken des modernen After-christenthums,* in previous numbers of the same periodical, and to my earlier works, especially the following: — *P. Bayle. Ein Beitrag zur Geschichte der Philosophie und Menschheit,* Ausbach, 1838, and *Philosophie und Christenthum,* Mannheim, 1839. In these works I have sketched, with a few sharp touches, the historical solution of Christianity, and have shown that Christianity has in fact long vanished, not only from the reason but from the life of mankind, that it is nothing more than a *fixed idea,* in flagrant contradiction with our fire and life assurance companies, our railroads and steam-carriages, our picture and sculpture galleries, our military and industrial schools, our theatres and scientific museums.

LUDWIG FEUERBACH.

BRUCKBERG, *Feb.* 14, 1843.

CHAPTER I.

INTRODUCTION.

§ 1. *The Essential Nature of Man.*

RELIGION has its basis in the essential difference between man and the brute—the brutes have no religion. It is true that the old uncritical writers on natural history attributed to the elephant, among other laudable qualities, the virtue of religiousness; but the religion of elephants belongs to the realm of fable. Cuvier, one of the greatest authorities on the animal kingdom, assigns, on the strength of his personal observations, no higher grade of intelligence to the elephant than to the dog.

But what is this essential difference between man and the brute? The most simple, general, and also the most popular answer to this question is—consciousness:—but consciousness in the strict sense; for the consciousness implied in the feeling of self as an individual, in discrimination by the senses, in the perception and even judgment of outward things according to definite sensible signs, cannot be denied to the brutes. Consciousness in the strictest sense is present only in a being to whom his species, his essential nature, is an object of thought. The brute is indeed conscious of himself as an individual—and he has accordingly the feeling of self as the common centre of successive sensations—but not as a species: hence, he is without that consciousness which in its nature, as in its name, is akin to science. Where there is this higher consciousness there is a capability of science. Science is the cognisance of species. In practical life we have to do with individuals; in science, with species. But only a being to whom his own species, his own nature, is an object of thought, can make the essential nature of other things or beings an object of thought.

Hence the brute has only a simple, man a twofold life: in the brute, the inner life is one with the outer; man has both an inner and an outer life. The inner life of man is the life which has relation to his species, to his general, as distinguished from his individual, nature. Man thinks— that is, he converses with himself. The brute can exercise no function which has relation to its species without another individual external to itself; but man can perform the functions of thought and speech, which strictly imply such a relation, apart from another individual. Man is himself at once I and thou; he can put himself in the place of another, for this reason, that to him his species, his essential nature, and not merely his individuality, is an object of thought.

Religion being identical with the distinctive characteristic of man, is then identical with self-consciousness—with the consciousness which man has of his nature. But religion, expressed generally, is consciousness of the infinite; thus it is and can be nothing else than the consciousness which man has of his own—not finite and limited, but infinite nature. A really finite being has not even the faintest adumbration, still less consciousness, of an infinite being, for the limit of the nature is also the limit of the consciousness. The consciousness of the caterpillar, whose life is confined to a particular species of plant, does not extend itself beyond this narrow domain. It does, indeed, discriminate between this plant and other plants, but more it knows not. A consciousness so limited, but on account of that very limitation so infallible, we do not call consciousness, but instinct. Consciousness, in the strict or proper sense, is identical with consciousness of the infinite; a limited consciousness is no consciousness; consciousness is essentially infinite in its nature.[1] The consciousness of the

---

[1] "Objectum intellectus esse illimitatum sive omne verum ac, ut loquuntur, omne ens ut ens, ex eo constat, quod ad nullum non genus rerum extenditur, nullumque est, cujus cognoscendi capax non sit, licet ob varia obstacula multa sint, quæ re ipsa non norit."—Gassendi (Opp. Omn. Phys.).

infinite is nothing else than the consciousness of the infinity of the consciousness; or, in the consciousness of the infinite, the conscious subject has for his object the infinity of his own nature.

What, then, *is* the nature of man, of which he is conscious, or what constitutes the specific distinction, the proper humanity of man?[1] Reason, Will, Affection. To a complete man belong the power of thought, the power of will, the power of affection. The power of thought is the light of the intellect, the power of will is energy of character, the power of affection is love. Reason, love, force of will, are perfections—the perfections of the human being—nay, more, they are absolute perfections of being. To will, to love, to think, are the highest powers, are the absolute nature of man as man, and the basis of his existence. Man exists to think, to love, to will. Now that which is the end, the ultimate aim, is also the true basis and principle of a being. But what is the end of reason? Reason. Of love? Love. Of will? Freedom of the will. We think for the sake of thinking; love for the sake of loving; will for the sake of willing—*i.e.*, that we may be free. True existence is thinking, loving, willing existence. That alone is true, perfect, divine, which exists for its own sake. But such is love, such is reason, such is will. The divine trinity in man, above the individual man, is the unity of reason, love, will. Reason, Will, Love, are not powers which man possesses, for he is nothing without them, he is what he is only by them; they are the constituent elements of his nature, which he neither has nor makes, the animating, determining, governing powers — divine, absolute powers—to which he can oppose no resistance.[2]

How can the feeling man resist feeling, the loving one love, the rational one reason? Who has not experienced the overwhelming power of melody? And what else is the power of melody but the power of feeling? Music is the

---

[1] The obtuse Materialist says: "Man is distinguished from the brute *only* by consciousness—he is an animal with consciousness superadded;" not reflecting, that in a being which awakes to consciousness, there takes place a qualitative change, a differentiation of the entire nature. For the rest, our words are by no means intended to depreciate the nature of the lower animals. This is not the place to enter further into that question.

[2] "Toute opinion est assez forte pour se faire exposer au prix de la vie."—Montaigne.

language of feeling; melody is audible feeling—feeling communicating itself. Who has not experienced the power of love, or at least heard of it? Which is the stronger—love or the individual man? Is it man that possesses love, or is it not much rather love that possesses man? When love impels a man to suffer death even joyfully for the beloved one, is this death-conquering power his own individual power, or is it not rather the power of love? And who that ever truly thought has not experienced that quiet, subtle power—the power of thought? When thou sinkest into deep reflection, forgetting thyself and what is around thee, dost thou govern reason, or is it not reason which governs and absorbs thee? Scientific enthusiasm—is it not the most glorious triumph of intellect over thee? The desire of knowledge—is it not a simply irresistible, and all-conquering power? And when thou suppressest a passion, renouncest a habit, in short, achievest a victory over thyself, is this victorious power thy own personal power, or is it not rather the energy of will, the force of morality, which seizes the mastery of thee, and fills thee with indignation against thyself and thy individual weaknesses?

Man is nothing without an object. The great models of humanity, such men as reveal to us what man is capable of, have attested the truth of this proposition by their lives. They had only one dominant passion—the realisation of the aim which was the essential object of their activity. But the object to which a subject essentially, necessarily relates, is nothing else than this subject's own, but objective, nature. If it be an object common to several individuals of the same species, but under various conditions, it is still, at least as to the form under which it presents itself to each of them according to their respective modifications, their own, but objective, nature.

Thus the Sun is the common object of the planets, but it is an object to Mercury, to Venus, to Saturn, to Uranus, under other conditions than to the Earth. Each planet has its own sun. The Sun which lights and warms Uranus has no physical (only an astronomical, scientific) existence for the Earth; and not only does the Sun appear different, but it really is *another* sun on Uranus than on the Earth. The relation of the Sun to the Earth is therefore at the

same time a relation of the Earth to itself, or to its own
nature, for the measure of the size and of the intensity of
light which the Sun possesses as the object of the Earth is
the measure of the distance which determines the peculiar
nature of the Earth. Hence each planet has in its sun the
mirror of its own nature.

In the object which he contemplates, therefore, man
becomes acquainted with himself; consciousness of the
objective is the self-consciousness of man. We know the
man by the object, by his conception of what is external to
himself; in it his nature becomes evident; this object is
his manifested nature, his true objective *ego*. And this is
true not merely of spiritual, but also of sensuous objects.
Even the objects which are the most remote from man, *because*
they are objects to him, and to the extent to which they
are so, are revelations of human nature. Even the moon,
the sun, the stars, call to man Γνῶθι σεαυτόν. That he
sees them, and so sees them, is an evidence of his own
nature. The animal is sensible only of the beam which
immediately affects life; while man perceives the ray, to
him physically indifferent, of the remotest star. Man alone
has purely intellectual, disinterested joys and passions; the
eye of man alone keeps theoretic festivals. The eye which
looks into the starry heavens, which gazes at that light,
alike useless and harmless, having nothing in common with
the earth and its necessities—this eye sees in that light its
own nature, its own origin. The eye is heavenly in its
nature. Hence man elevates himself above the earth only
with the eye; hence theory begins with the contemplation
of the heavens. The first philosophers were astronomers.
It is the heavens that admonish man of his destination,
and remind him that he is destined not merely to action,
but also to contemplation.

The *absolute* to man is his own nature. The power of
the object over him is therefore the power of his own
nature. Thus the power of the object of feeling is the
power of feeling itself; the power of the object of the
intellect is the power of the intellect itself; the power of
the object of the will is the power of the will itself. The
man who is affected by musical sounds is governed by
feeling; by the feeling, that is, which finds its corresponding element in musical sounds. But it is not melody as

such, it is only melody pregnant with meaning and emotion, which has power over feeling. Feeling is only acted on by that which conveys feeling, *i.e.*, by itself, its own nature. Thus also the will; thus, and infinitely more, the intellect. Whatever kind of object, therefore, we are at any time conscious of, we are always at the same time conscious of our own nature; we can affirm nothing without affirming ourselves. And since to will, to feel, to think, are perfections, essences, realities, it is impossible that intellect, feeling, and will should feel or perceive themselves as limited, finite powers, *i.e.*, as worthless, as nothing. For finiteness and nothingness are identical; finiteness is only a euphemism for nothingness. Finiteness is the metaphysical, the theoretical—nothingness the pathological, practical expression. What is finite to the understanding is nothing to the heart. But it is impossible that we should be conscious of will, feeling, and intellect, as finite powers, because every perfect existence, every original power and essence, is the immediate verification and affirmation of itself. It is impossible to love, will, or think, without perceiving these activities to be perfections —impossible to feel that one is a loving, willing, thinking being, without experiencing an infinite joy therein. Consciousness consists in a being becoming objective to itself; hence it is nothing apart, nothing distinct from the being which is conscious of itself. How could it otherwise become conscious of itself? It is therefore impossible to be conscious of a perfection as an imperfection, impossible to feel feeling limited, to think thought limited.

Consciousness is self-verification, self-affirmation, self-love, joy in one's own perfection. Consciousness is the characteristic mark of a perfect nature; it exists only in a self-sufficing, complete being. Even human vanity attests this truth. A man looks in the glass; he has complacency in his appearance. This complacency is a necessary, involuntary consequence of the completeness, the beauty of his form. A beautiful form is satisfied in itself; it has necessarily joy in itself—in self-contemplation. This complacency becomes vanity only when a man piques himself on his form as being his individual form, not when he admires it as a specimen of human beauty in general. It is fitting that he should admire it thus: he can conceive no form more beautiful, more sublime than the human.[1] Assuredly every being loves itself, its existence—and fitly so. To exist is a good. *Quidquid essentia dignum est, scientia dignum est.* Everything that exists has value, is a being of distinction—at least this is true of the species : hence it asserts, maintains itself. But the highest form of self-assertion, the form which is itself a superiority, a perfection, a bliss, a good, is consciousness.

Every limitation of the reason, or in general of the nature of man, rests on a delusion, an error. It is true that the human being, as an individual, can and must—herein consists his distinction from the brute—feel and recognise himself to be limited; but he can become conscious of his limits, his finiteness, only because the perfection, the infinitude of his species, is perceived by him, whether as an object of feeling, of conscience, or of the thinking consciousness. If he makes his own limitations the limitations of the species, this arises from the mistake that he identifies himself immediately with the species—a mistake which is intimately connected with the individual's love of ease, sloth, vanity, and egoism. For a limitation which I know to be merely mine humiliates, shames, and perturbs me. Hence to free myself from this feeling of shame, from this state of dissatisfaction, I convert the limits of my individuality into the limits of human nature in general. What is incomprehensible to me is incomprehensible to others; why should I trouble myself further? It is no fault of mine; my understanding is not to blame, but the understanding of the race. But it is a ludicrous and even culpable error to define as finite and limited what constitutes the essence of man, the nature of the species, which is the absolute nature of the individual. Every being is sufficient to itself. No being can deny itself, *i.e.*, its own nature; no being is a limited one to itself. Rather, every being is in and by itself infinite—has its God, its highest conceivable being, in itself. Every limit of a being is cognisable only by another being out of and above him.

[1] Homini homine nihil pulchrius. (Cic. de Nat. D. l. i.) And this is no sign of limitation, for he regards other beings as beautiful besides himself ; he delights in the beautiful forms of animals, in the beautiful forms of plants, in the beauty of nature in general. But only the absolute, the perfect form, can delight without envy in the forms of other beings.

The life of the ephemera is extraordinarily short in comparison with that of longer-lived creatures; but nevertheless, for the ephemera this short life is as long as a life of years to others. The leaf on which the caterpillar lives is for it a world, an infinite space.

That which makes a being what it is, is its talent, its power, its wealth, its adornment. How can it possibly hold its existence non-existence, its wealth poverty, its talent incapacity? If the plants had eyes, taste, and judgment, each plant would declare its own flower the most beautiful; for its comprehension, its taste, would reach no farther than its natural power of production. What the productive power of its nature has brought forth as the highest, that must also its taste, its judgment, recognise and affirm as the highest. What the nature affirms, the understanding, the taste, the judgment, cannot deny; otherwise the understanding, the judgment, would no longer be the understanding and judgment of this particular being, but of some other. The measure of the nature is also the measure of the understanding. If the nature is limited, so also is the feeling, so also is the understanding. But to a limited being its limited understanding is not felt to be a limitation; on the contrary, it is perfectly happy and contented with this understanding; it regards it, praises and values it, as a glorious, divine power; and the limited understanding, on its part, values the limited nature whose understanding it is. Each is exactly adapted to the other; how should they be at issue with each other? A being's understanding is its sphere of vision. As far as thou seest, so far extends thy nature; and conversely. The eye of the brute reaches no farther than its needs, and its nature no farther than its needs. And so far as thy nature reaches, so far reaches thy unlimited self-consciousness, so far art thou God. The discrepancy between the understanding and the nature, between the power of conception and the power of production in the human consciousness, on the one hand, is merely of individual significance and has not a universal application; and, on the other hand, it is only apparent. He who, having written a bad poem, knows it to be bad, is in his intelligence, and therefore in his nature, not so limited as he who, having written a bad poem, admires it and thinks it good.

It follows that if thou thinkest the infinite, thou perceivest and affirmest the infinitude of the power of thought; if thou feelest the infinite, thou feelest and affirmest the infinitude of the power of feeling. The object of the intellect is intellect objective to itself; the object of feeling is feeling objective to itself. If thou hast no sensibility, no feeling for music, thou perceivest in the finest music nothing more than in the wind that whistles by thy ear, or than in the brook which rushes past thy feet. What, then, is it which acts on thee when thou art affected by melody? What dost thou perceive in it? What else than the voice of thy own heart? Feeling speaks only to feeling; feeling is comprehensible only by feeling, that is, by itself—for this reason, that the object of feeling is nothing else than feeling. Music is a monologue of emotion. But the dialogue of philosophy also is in truth only a monologue of the intellect; thought speaks only to thought. The splendours of the crystal charm the sense, but the intellect is interested only in the laws of crystallisation. The intellectual only is the object of the intellect.[1]

All therefore which, in the point of view of metaphysical, transcendental speculation and religion, has the significance only of the secondary, the subjective, the medium, the organ—has in truth the significance of the primary, of the essence, of the object itself. If, for example, feeling is the essential organ of religion, the nature of God is nothing else than an expression of the nature of feeling. The true but latent sense of the phrase, " Feeling is the organ of the divine," is, feeling is the noblest, the most excellent, *i.e.*, the divine, in man. How couldst thou perceive the divine by feeling, if feeling were not itself divine in its nature? The divine assuredly is known only by means of the divine—God is known only by himself. The divine nature which is discerned by feeling is in truth nothing else than feeling enraptured, in ecstasy with itself—feeling intoxicated with joy, blissful in its own plenitude.

It is already clear from this that where feeling is held to be the organ of the infinite, the subjective essence of religion,—the external data of religion lose their objective value. And thus, since feeling has been held the cardinal

---

[1] " The understanding is percipient only of understanding, and what proceeds thence."—Reimarus (Wahrh. der Natürl. Religion, iv. Abth. § 8).

principle in religion, the doctrines of Christianity, formerly so sacred, have lost their importance. If, from this point of view, some value is still conceded to Christian ideas, it is a value springing entirely from the relation they bear to feeling; if another object would excite the same emotions, it would be just as welcome. But the object of religious feeling is become a matter of indifference, only because when once feeling has been pronounced to be the subjective essence of religion, it in fact is also the objective essence of religion, though it may not be declared, at least directly, to be such. I say directly; for indirectly this is certainly admitted, when it is declared that feeling, as such, is religious, and thus the distinction between specifically religious and irreligious, or at least non-religious, feelings is abolished—a necessary consequence of the point of view in which feeling only is regarded as the organ of the divine. For on what other ground than that of its essence, its nature, dost thou hold feeling to be the organ of the infinite, the divine being? And is not the nature of feeling in general also the nature of every special feeling, be its object what it may? What, then, makes this feeling religious? A given object? Not at all; for this object is itself a religious one only when it is not an object of the cold understanding or memory, but of feeling. What then? The nature of feeling—a nature of which every special feeling, without distinction of objects, partakes. Thus, feeling is pronounced to be religious, simply because it is feeling; the ground of its religiousness is its own nature—lies in itself. But is not feeling thereby declared to be itself the absolute, the divine? If feeling in itself is good, religious, *i.e.*, holy, divine, has not feeling its God in itself?

But if, notwithstanding, thou wilt posit an object of feeling, but at the same time seekest to express thy feeling truly, without introducing by thy reflection any foreign element, what remains to thee but to distinguish between thy individual feeling and the general nature of feeling;—to separate the universal in feeling from the disturbing, adulterating influences with which feeling is bound up in thee, under thy individual conditions? Hence what thou canst alone contemplate, declare to be the infinite, and define as its essence, is merely the nature of feeling. Thou hast thus no other definition of God than this: God is pure, unlimited, free Feeling. Every other God, whom thou supposest, is a God thrust upon thy feeling from without. Feeling is atheistic in the sense of the orthodox belief, which attaches religion to an external object; it denies an objective God—it is itself God. In this point of view only the negation of feeling is the negation of God. Thou art simply too cowardly or too narrow to confess in words what thy feeling tacitly affirms. Fettered by outward considerations, still in bondage to vulgar empiricism, incapable of comprehending the spiritual grandeur of feeling, thou art terrified before the religious atheism of thy heart. By this fear thou destroyest the unity of thy feeling with itself, in imagining to thyself an objective being distinct from thy feeling, and thus necessarily sinking back into the old questions and doubts—is there a God or not?—questions and doubts which vanish, nay, are impossible, where feeling is defined as the essence of religion. Feeling is thy own inward power, but at the same time a power distinct from thee, and independent of thee ; it is in thee, above thee; it is itself that which constitutes the objective in thee—thy own being which impresses thee as another being; in short, thy God. How wilt thou, then, distinguish from this objective being within thee another objective being? how wilt thou get beyond thy feeling ?

But feeling has here been adduced only as an example. It is the same with every other power, faculty, potentiality, reality, activity—the name is indifferent—which is defined as the essential organ of any object. Whatever is a subjective expression of a nature is simultaneously also its objective expression. Man cannot get beyond his true nature. He may indeed by means of the imagination conceive individuals of another so-called higher kind, but he can never get loose from his species, his nature ; the conditions of being, the positive final predicates which he gives to these other individuals, are always determinations or qualities drawn from his own nature—qualities in which he in truth only images and projects himself. There may certainly be thinking beings besides men on the other planets of our solar system. But by the supposition of such beings we do not change our standing point—we extend our conceptions *quantitatively* not *qualitatively*. For as surely as on the other planets there are the same laws of motion, so

surely are there the same laws of perception and thought
as here.   In fact, we people the other planets, not that we
may place there different beings from ourselves, but *more*
beings of our own or of a similar nature.[1]

§ 2. *The Essence of Religion Considered Generally.*

What we have hitherto been maintaining generally, even
with regard to sensational impressions, of the relation between subject and object, applies especially to the relation
between the subject and the religious object.

In the perceptions of the senses consciousness of the
object is distinguishable from consciousness of self; but in
religion, consciousness of the object and self-consciousness
coincide.   The object of the senses is out of man, the
religious object is within him, and therefore as little forsakes him as his self-consciousness or his conscience; it is
the intimate, the closest object.   "God," says Augustine,
for example, "is nearer, more related to us, and therefore
more easily known by us, than sensible, corporeal things."[2]
The object of the senses is in itself indifferent—independent
of the disposition or of the judgment; but the object of
religion is a selected object; the most excellent, the first,
the supreme being; it essentially presupposes a critical
judgment, a discrimination between the divine and the non-
divine, between that which is worthy of adoration and that
which is not worthy.[3]   And here may be applied, without
any limitation, the proposition : the object of any subject
is nothing else than the subject's own nature taken objectively.   Such as are a man's thoughts and dispositions,
such is his God; so much worth as a man has, so much
and no more has his God.   Consciousness of God is self-
consciousness, knowledge of God is self-knowledge.   By his
God thou knowest the man, and by the man his God; the
two are identical.   Whatever is God to a man, that is his heart
and soul; and conversely, God is the manifested inward

[1] " Verisimile est, non minus quam geometriæ, etiam musicæ oblectationem
ad plures quam ad nos pertinere.   Positis enim aliis terris atque animalibus
ratione et auditu pollentibus, cur tantum his nostris contigisset ea voluptas,
quæ sola ex sono percipi potest ?"—Christ. Hugenius (Cosmotheor., l. i.).
[2] De Genesi ad litteram, l. v. c. 16.
[3] " Unusquisque vestrum non cogitat, *prius* se debere Deum *nosse*, quam
colere."—M. Minucii Felicis Octavianus, c. 24.

nature, the expressed self of a man,—religion the solemn unveiling of a man's hidden treasures, the revelation of his intimate thoughts, the open confession of his love-secrets.

But when religion—consciousness of God—is designated as the self-consciousness of man, this is not to be understood as affirming that the religious man is directly aware of this identity; for, on the contrary, ignorance of it is fundamental to the peculiar nature of religion. To preclude this misconception, it is better to say, religion is man's earliest and also indirect form of self-knowledge. Hence, religion everywhere precedes philosophy, as in the history of the race, so also in that of the individual. Man first of all sees his nature as if *out of* himself, before he finds it in himself. His own nature is in the first instance contemplated by him as that of another being. Religion is the childlike condition of humanity; but the child sees his nature—man—out of himself; in childhood a man is an object to himself, under the form of another man. Hence the historical progress of religion consists in this: that what by an earlier religion was regarded as objective, is now recognised as subjective; that is, what was formerly contemplated and worshipped as God is now perceived to be something *human.* What was at first religion becomes at a later period idolatry; man is seen to have adored his own nature. Man has given objectivity to himself, but has not recognised the object as his own nature: a later religion takes this forward step; every advance in religion is therefore a deeper self-knowledge. But every particular religion, while it pronounces its predecessors idolatrous, excepts itself—and necessarily so, otherwise it would no longer be religion—from the fate, the common nature of all religions: it imputes only to other religions what is the fault, if fault it be, of religion in general. Because it has a different object, a different tenor, because it has transcended the ideas of preceding religions, it erroneously supposes itself exalted above the necessary eternal laws which constitute the essence of religion—it fancies its object, its ideas, to be superhuman. But the essence of religion, thus hidden from the religious, is evident to the thinker, by whom religion is viewed objectively, which it cannot be by its votaries. And it is our task to show that the antithesis of divine and human is altogether illusory, that it is nothing else than the antithesis between the human nature in general and the human individual; that, consequently, the object and contents of the Christian religion are altogether human.

Religion, at least the Christian, is the relation of man to himself, or more correctly to his own nature (*i.e.*, his subjective nature);[1] but a relation to it, viewed as a nature apart from his own. The divine being is nothing else than the human being, or, rather, the human nature purified, freed from the limits of the individual man, made objective —*i.e.*, contemplated and revered as another, a distinct being. All the attributes of the divine nature are, therefore, attributes of the human nature.[2]

In relation to the attributes, the predicates, of the Divine Being, this is admitted without hesitation, but by no means in relation to the subject of these predicates. The negation of the subject is held to be irreligion, nay, atheism; though not so the negation of the predicates. But that which has no predicates or qualities, has no effect upon me; that which has no effect upon me has no existence for me. To deny all the qualities of a being is equivalent to denying the being himself. A being without qualities is one which cannot become an object to the mind, and such a being is virtually non-existent. Where man deprives God of all qualities, God is no longer anything more to him than a negative being. To the truly religious man, God is not a being without qualities, because to him he is a positive, real being. The theory that God cannot be defined, and consequently cannot be known by man, is therefore the offspring of recent times, a product of modern unbelief.

As reason is and can be pronounced finite only where man regards sensual enjoyment, or religious emotion, or æsthetic contemplation, or moral sentiment, as the absolute, the true; so the proposition that God is unknowable or un-

---

[1] The meaning of this parenthetic limitation will be clear in the sequel.

[2] "Les perfections de Dieu sont celles de nos âmes, mais il les possede sans bornes—il y a en nous quelque puissance, quelque connaissance, quelque bonté, mais elles sont toutes entières en Dieu."—Leibnitz (Théod. Preface). "Nihil in anima esse putemus eximium, quod non etiam divinæ naturæ proprium sit—Quidquid a Deo alienum extra definitionem animæ."—St. Gregorius Nyss. "Est ergo, ut videtur, disciplinarum omnium pulcherrima et maxima se ipsum nosse; si quis enim se ipsum norit, Deum cognoscet." —Clemens Alex. (Pæd. l. iii. c. 1).

definable, can only be enunciated and become fixed as a dogma, where this object has no longer any interest for the intellect; where the real, the positive, alone has any hold on man, where the real alone has for him the significance of the essential, of the absolute, divine object, but where at the same time, in contradiction with this purely worldly tendency, there yet exist some old remains of religiousness. On the ground that God is unknowable, man excuses himself to what is yet remaining of his religious conscience for his forgetfulness of God, his absorption in the world : he denies God practically by his conduct,—the world has possession of all his thoughts and inclinations,—but he does not deny him theoretically, he does not attack his existence ; he lets that rest. But this existence does not affect or incommode him; it is a merely negative existence, an existence without existence, a self-contradictory existence,—a state of being which, as to its effects, is not distinguishable from non-being. The denial of determinate, positive predicates concerning the divine nature is nothing else than a denial of religion, with, however, an appearance of religion in its favour, so that it is not recognised as a denial ; it is simply a subtle, disguised atheism. The alleged religious horror of limiting God by positive predicates is only the irreligious wish to know nothing more of God, to banish God from the mind. Dread of limitation is dread of existence. All real existence, *i.e.*, all existence which is truly such, is qualitative, determinative existence. He who earnestly believes in the Divine existence is not shocked at the attributing even of gross sensuous qualities to God. He who dreads an existence that may give offence, who shrinks from the grossness of a positive predicate, may as well renounce existence altogether. A God who is injured by determinate qualities has not the courage and the strength to exist. Qualities are the fire, the vital breath, the oxygen, the salt of existence. An existence in general, an existence without qualities, is an insipidity, an absurdity. But there can be no more in God than is supplied by religion. Only where man loses his taste for religion, and thus religion itself becomes insipid, does the existence of God become an insipid existence—an existence without qualities.

There is, however, a still milder way of denying the divine predicates than the direct one just described. It is admitted that the predicates of the divine nature are finite, and, more particularly, human qualities, but their rejection is rejected; they are even taken under protection, because it is necessary to man to have a definite conception of God, and since he is man he can form no other than a human conception of him. In relation to God, it is said, these predicates are certainly without any objective validity; but to me, if he is to exist for me, he cannot appear otherwise than as he does appear to me, namely, as a being with attributes analogous to the human. But this distinction between what God is in himself, and what he is for me destroys the peace of religion, and is besides in itself an unfounded and untenable distinction. I cannot know whether God is something else in himself or for himself than he is for me; what he is to me is to me all that he is. For me, there lies in these predicates under which he exists for me, what he is in himself, his very nature; he is for me what he can alone ever be for me. The religious man finds perfect satisfaction in that which God is in relation to himself; of any other relation he knows nothing, for God is to him what he can alone be to man. In the distinction above stated, man takes a point of view above himself, *i.e.*, above his nature, the absolute measure of his being; but this transcendentalism is only an illusion; for I can make the distinction between the object as it is in itself, and the object as it is for me, only where an object can really appear otherwise to me, not where it appears to me such as the absolute measure of my nature determines it to appear—such as it must appear to me. It is true that I may have a merely subjective conception, *i.e.*, one which does not arise out of the general constitution of my species; but if my conception is determined by the constitution of my species, the distinction between what an object is in itself, and what it is for me ceases; for this conception is itself an absolute one. The measure of the species is the absolute measure, law, and criterion of man. And, indeed, religion has the conviction that its conceptions, its predicates of God, are such as every man ought to have, and must have, if he would have the true ones—that they are the conceptions necessary to human nature; nay, further, that they are objectively true, representing God as he is. To every religion the gods of *other* religions are only notions concerning God, but its own conception of God is to it God himself, the true God — God such as he is in himself. Religion is satisfied only with a complete Deity, a God without reservation; it will not have a mere phantasm of God; it demands God himself. Religion gives up its own existence when it gives up the nature of God; it is no longer a truth when it renounces the possession of the true God. Scepticism is the arch-enemy of religion; but the distinction between object and conception—between God as he is in himself, and God as he is for me—is a sceptical distinction, and therefore an irreligious one.

That which is to man the self-existent, the highest being, to which he can conceive nothing higher—that is to him the Divine Being. How then should he inquire concerning this being, what he is in himself? If God were an object to the bird, he would be a winged being: the bird knows nothing higher, nothing more blissful, than the winged condition. How ludicrous would it be if this bird pronounced: To me God appears as a bird, but what he is in himself I know not. To the bird the highest nature is the bird-nature; take from him the conception of this, and you take from him the conception of the highest being. How, then, could he ask whether God in himself were winged? To ask whether God is in himself what he is for me, is to ask whether God is God, is to lift oneself above one's God, to rise up against him.

Wherever, therefore, this idea, that the religious predicates are only anthropomorphisms, has taken possession of a man, there has doubt, has unbelief, obtained the mastery of faith. And it is only the inconsequence of faint-heartedness and intellectual imbecility which does not proceed from this idea to the formal negation of the predicates, and from thence to the negation of the subject to which they relate. If thou doubtest the objective truth of the predicates, thou must also doubt the objective truth of the subject whose predicates they are. If thy predicates are anthropomorphisms, the subject of them is an anthropomorphism too. If love, goodness, personality, &c., are human attributes, so also is the subject which thou presupposest, the existence of God, the belief that there is a God, an anthropomorphism—a presupposition purely human. Whence knowest thou that the belief in a God

at all is not a limitation of man's mode of conception?
Higher beings—and thou supposest such—are perhaps so
blest in themselves, so at unity with themselves, that they
are not hung in suspense between themselves and a yet
higher being. To know God and not oneself to be God, to
know blessedness and not oneself to enjoy it, is a state of
disunity, of unhappiness. Higher beings know nothing of
this unhappiness; they have no conception of that which
they are not.

Thou believest in love as a divine attribute because thou
thyself lovest; thou believest that God is a wise, benevolent being because thou knowest nothing better in thyself than benevolence and wisdom; and thou believest that
God exists, that therefore he is a subject—whatever exists
is a subject, whether it be defined as substance, person,
essence, or otherwise—because thou thyself existest, art
thyself a subject. Thou knowest no higher human good
than to love, than to be good and wise; and even so thou
knowest no higher happiness than to exist, to be a subject;
for the consciousness of all reality, of all bliss, is for thee
bound up in the consciousness of being a subject, of existing. God is an existence, a subject to thee, for the same
reason that he is to thee a wise, a blessed, a personal being.
The distinction between the divine predicates and the
divine subject is only this, that to thee the subject, the
existence, does not appear an anthropomorphism, because
the conception of it is necessarily involved in thy own
existence as a subject, whereas the predicates do appear
anthropomorphisms, because their necessity—the necessity
that God should be conscious, wise, good, &c.,—is not an
immediate necessity, identical with the being of man, but
is evolved by his self-consciousness, by the activity of his
thought. I am a subject, I exist, whether I be wise or
unwise, good or bad. To exist is to man the first datum;
it constitutes the very idea of the subject; it is presupposed by the predicates. Hence man relinquishes the
predicates, but the existence of God is to him a settled,
irrefragable, absolutely certain, objective truth. But,
nevertheless, this distinction is merely an apparent one.
The necessity of the subject lies only in the necessity of
the predicate. Thou art a subject only in so far as thou
art a human subject; the certainty and reality of thy

existence lie only in the certainty and reality of thy human attributes. What the subject is lies only in the predicate; the predicate is the *truth* of the subject—the subject only the personified, existing predicate, the predicate conceived as existing. Subject and predicate are distinguished only as existence and essence. The negation of the predicates is therefore the negation of the subject. What remains of the human subject when abstracted from the human attributes ? Even in the language of common life the divine predicates—Providence, Omniscience, Omnipotence — are put for the divine subject.

The certainty of the existence of God, of which it has been said that it is as certain, nay, more certain to man than his own existence, depends only on the certainty of the qualities of God—it is in itself no immediate certainty. To the Christian the existence of the Christian God only is a certainty; to the heathen that of the heathen God only. The heathen did not doubt the existence of Jupiter, because he took no offence at the nature of Jupiter, because he could conceive of God under no other qualities, because to him these qualities were a certainty, a divine reality. The reality of the predicate is the sole guarantee of existence.

Whatever man conceives to be true, he immediately conceives to be real (that is, to have an objective existence), because, originally, only the real is true to him— true in opposition to what is merely conceived, dreamed, imagined. The idea of being, of existence, is the original idea of truth; or, originally, man makes truth dependent on existence, subsequently, existence dependent on truth. Now God is the nature of man regarded as absolute truth, —the truth of man; but God, or, what is the same thing, religion, is as various as are the conditions under which man conceives this his nature, regards it as the highest being. These conditions, then, under which man conceives God, are to him the truth, and for that reason they are also the highest existence, or rather they are existence itself; for only the emphatic, the highest existence, is existence, and deserves this name. Therefore, God is an existent, real being, on the very same ground that he is a particular, definite being; for the qualities of God are nothing else than the essential qualities of man

himself, and a particular man is what he is, has his existence, his reality, only in his particular conditions. Take
away from the Greek the quality of being Greek, and you
take away his existence. On this ground it is true that
for a definite positive religion—that is, relatively—the
certainty of the existence of God is *immediate;* for just as
involuntarily, as necessarily, as the Greek was a Greek, so
necessarily were his gods Greek beings, so necessarily were
they real, existent beings. Religion is that conception of
the nature of the world and of man which is essential to,
i.e., identical with, a man's nature. But man does not
stand above this his necessary conception; on the contrary,
it stands above him; it animates, determines, governs him.
The necessity of a proof, of a middle term to unite qualities
with existence, the possibility of a doubt, is abolished.
Only that which is apart from my own being is capable of
being doubted by me. How then can I doubt of God, who
is my being? To doubt of God is to doubt of myself.
Only when God is thought of abstractly, when his predicates are the result of philosophic abstraction, arises the
distinction or separation between subject and predicate,
existence and nature—arises the fiction that the existence
or the subject is something else than the predicate, something immediate, indubitable, in distinction from the predicate, which is held to be doubtful. But this is only a
fiction. A God who has abstract predicates has also an
abstract existence. Existence, being, varies with varying
qualities.

The identity of the subject and predicate is clearly evi-
denced by the progressive development of religion, which
is identical with the progressive development of human
culture. So long as man is in a mere state of nature,
so long is his god a mere nature-god—a personification
of some natural force. Where man inhabits houses, he
also encloses his gods in temples. The temple is only a
manifestation of the value which man attaches to beautiful buildings. Temples in honour of religion are in truth
temples in honour of architecture. With the emerging of
man from a state of savagery and wildness to one of culture,
with the distinction between what is fitting for man and
what is not fitting, arises simultaneously the distinction
between that which is fitting and that which is not fitting

for God. God is the idea of majesty, of the highest dignity: the religious sentiment is the sentiment of supreme fitness. The later more cultured artists of Greece were the first to embody in the statues of the gods the ideas of dignity, of spiritual grandeur, of imperturbable repose and serenity. But why were these qualities in their view attributes, predicates of God? Because they were in themselves regarded by the Greeks as divinities. Why did those artists exclude all disgusting and low passions? Because they perceived them to be unbecoming, unworthy, unhuman, and consequently ungodlike. The Homeric gods eat and drink;—that implies eating and drinking is a divine pleasure. Physical strength is an attribute of the Homeric gods: Zeus is the strongest of the gods. Why? Because physical strength, in and by itself, was regarded as something glorious, divine. To the ancient Germans the highest virtues were those of the warrior; therefore their supreme god was the god of war, Odin,—war, "the original or oldest law." Not the attribute of the divinity, but the divineness or deity of the attribute, is the first true Divine Being. Thus what theology and philosophy have held to be God, the Absolute, the Infinite, is not God; but that which they have held not to be God is God: namely, the attribute, the quality, whatever has reality. Hence he alone is the true atheist to whom the predicates of the Divine Being,— for example, love, wisdom, justice,—are nothing; not he to whom merely the subject of these predicates is nothing. And in no wise is the negation of the subject necessarily also a negation of the predicates considered in themselves. These have an intrinsic, independent reality; they force their recognition upon man by their very nature; they are self-evident truths to him; they prove, they attest themselves. It does not follow that goodness, justice, wisdom, are chimæras because the existence of God is a chimæra, nor truths because this is a truth. The idea of God is dependent on the idea of justice, of benevolence; a God who is not benevolent, not just, not wise, is no God; but the converse does not hold. The fact is not that a quality is divine because God has it, but that God has it because it is in itself divine: because without it God would be a defective being. Justice, wisdom, in general every quality which constitutes the divinity of God, is determined and known by itself independently, but the idea of God is determined by the qualities which have thus been previously judged to be worthy of the divine nature; only in the case in which I identify God and justice, in which I think of God immediately as the reality of the idea of justice, is the idea of God self-determined. But if God as a subject is the determined, while the quality, the predicate, is the determining, then in truth the rank of the godhead is due not to the subject, but to the predicate.

Not until several, and those contradictory, attributes are united in one being, and this being is conceived as personal —the personality being thus brought into especial prominence—not until then is the origin of religion lost sight of, is it forgotten that what the activity of the reflective power has converted into a predicate distinguishable or separable from the subject, was originally the true subject. Thus the Greeks and Romans deified accidents as substances; virtues, states of mind, passions, as independent beings. Man, especially the religious man, is to himself the measure of all things, of all reality. Whatever strongly impresses a man, whatever produces an unusual effect on his mind, if it be only a peculiar, inexplicable sound or note, he personifies as a divine being. Religion embraces all the objects of the world: everything existing has been an object of religious reverence; in the nature and consciousness of religion there is nothing else than what lies in the nature of man and in his consciousness of himself and of the world. Religion has no material exclusively its own. In Rome even the passions of fear and terror had their temples. The Christians also made mental phenomena into independent beings, their own feelings into qualities of things, the passions which governed them into powers which governed the world, in short, predicates of their own nature, whether recognised as such or not, into independent subjective existences. Devils, cobolds, witches, ghosts, angels, were sacred truths as long as the religious spirit held undivided sway over mankind.

In order to banish from the mind the identity of the divine and human predicates, and the consequent identity of the divine and human nature, recourse is had to the idea that God, as the absolute, real Being, has an infinite fulness of various predicates, of which we here know only

a part, and those such as are analogous to our own ; while
the rest, by virtue of which God must thus have quite a
different nature from the human or that which is analogous
to the human, we shall only know in the future—that is,
after death. But an infinite plenitude or multitude of
predicates which are really different, so different that the
one does not immediately involve the other, is realised
only in an infinite plenitude or multitude of different
beings or individuals. Thus the human nature presents
an infinite abundance of different predicates, and for that
very reason it presents an infinite abundance of different
individuals. Each new man is a new predicate, a new
phasis of humanity. As many as are the men, so many are
the powers, the properties of humanity. It is true that
there are the same elements in every individual, but under
such various conditions and modifications that they appear new and peculiar. The mystery of the inexhaustible
fulness of the divine predicates is therefore nothing else
than the mystery of human nature considered as an
infinitely varied, infinitely modifiable, but, consequently,
phenomenal being. Only in the realm of the senses, only
in space and time, does there exist a being of really infinite
qualities or predicates. Where there are really different
predicates there are different times. One man is a distinguished musician, a distinguished author, a distinguished
physician ; but he cannot compose music, write books,
and perform cures in the same moment of time. Time,
and not the Hegelian dialectic, is the medium of uniting
opposites, contradictories, in one and the same subject. But
distinguished and detached from the nature of man, and
combined with the idea of God, the infinite fulness of
various predicates is a conception without reality, a mere
phantasy, a conception derived from the sensible world, but
without the essential conditions, without the truth of sensible existence, a conception which stands in direct contradiction with the Divine Being considered as a spiritual,
i.e., an abstract, simple, single being ; for the predicates of
God are precisely of this character, that one involves all the
others, because there is no real difference between them.
If, therefore, in the present predicates I have not the future,
in the present God not the future God, then the future God

is not the present, but they are two distinct beings.[1]   But
this distinction is in contradiction with the unity and simplicity of the theological God.   Why is a given predicate
a predicate of God?   Because it is divine in its nature, *i.e.*,
because it expresses no limitation, no defect.   Why are other
predicates applied to him?   Because, however various in
themselves, they agree in this, that they all alike express
perfection, unlimitedness.   Hence I can conceive innumerable predicates of God, because they must all agree with
the abstract idea of the Godhead, and must have in common
that which constitutes every single predicate a divine attribute.   Thus it is in the system of Spinoza.   He speaks of
an infinite number of attributes of the divine substance, but
he specifies none except Thought and Extension.   Why?
Because it is a matter of indifference to know them ; nay,
Because they are in themselves indifferent, superfluous ; for
with all these innumerable predicates, I yet always mean
to say the same thing as when I speak of Thought and
Extension.   Why is Thought an attribute of substance?
Because, according to Spinoza, it is capable of being conceived by itself, because it expresses something indivisible,
perfect, infinite.   Why Extension or Matter?   For the
same reason.   Thus, substance can have an indefinite
number of predicates, because it is not their specific
definition, their difference, but their identity, their equi-
valence, which makes them attributes of substance.   Or
rather, substance has innumerable predicates only because
(how strange!) it has properly no predicate ; that is, no
definite, real predicate.   The indefinite unity which is
the product of thought, completes itself by the indefinite
multiplicity which is the product of the imagination.
Because the predicate is not *multum*, it is *multa*.   In
truth, the positive predicates are Thought and Extension.
In these two infinitely more is said than in the nameless
innumerable predicates ; for they express something definite—in them I have something.   But substance is too
indifferent, too apathetic to be *something ;* that is, to have

---

[1] For religious faith there is no other distinction between the present and
future God than that the former is an object of faith, of conception, of
imagination, while the latter is to be an object of immediate, that is, personal, sensible perception.   In this life and in the next he ﹕s the same
God ; but in the one he is incomprehensible, in the other comprehensible.

qualities and passions; that it may not be something, it is rather nothing.

Now, when it is shown that what the subject is lies entirely in the attributes of the subject; that is, that the predicate is the true subject; it is also proved that if the divine predicates are attributes of the human nature, the subject of those predicates is also of the human nature. But the divine predicates are partly general, partly personal. The general predicates are the metaphysical, but these serve only as external points of support to religion ; they are not the characteristic definitions of religion. It is the personal predicates alone which constitute the essence of religion— in which the Divine Being is the object of religion. Such are, for example, that God is a Person, that he is the moral Lawgiver, the Father of mankind, the Holy One, the Just, the Good, the Merciful. It is, however, at once clear, or it will at least be clear in the sequel, with regard to these and other definitions, that, especially as applied to a personality, they are purely human definitions, and that consequently man in religion—in his relation to God—is in relation to his own nature ; for to the religious sentiment these predicates are not mere conceptions, mere images, which man forms of God, to be distinguished from that which God is in himself, but truths, facts, realities. Religion knows nothing of anthropomorphisms; to it they are not anthropomorphisms. It is the very essence of religion, that to it these definitions express the nature of God. They are pronounced to be images only by the understanding, which reflects on religion, and which while defending them yet before its own tribunal denies them. But to the religious sentiment God is a real Father, real Love and Mercy ; for to it he is a real, living, personal being, and therefore his attributes are also living and personal. Nay, the definitions which are the most sufficing to the religious sentiment are precisely those which give the most offence to the understanding, and which in the process of reflection on religion it denies. Religion is essentially emotion; hence, objectively also, emotion is to it necessarily of a divine nature. Even anger appears to it an emotion not unworthy of God, provided only there be a religious motive at the foundation of this anger.

But here it is also essential to observe, and this phenomenon is an extremely remarkable one, characterising the very core of religion, that in proportion as the divine subject is in reality human, the greater is the apparent difference between God and man; that is, the more, by reflection on religion, by theology, is the identity of the divine and human denied, and the human, considered as such, is depreciated.[1] The reason of this is, that as what is positive in the conception of the divine being can only be human, the conception of man, as an object of consciousness, can only be negative. To enrich God, man must become poor; that God may be all, man must be nothing. But he desires to be nothing in himself, because what he takes from himself is not lost to him, since it is preserved in God. Man has his being in God; why then should he have it in himself? Where is the necessity of positing the same thing twice, of having it twice? What man withdraws from himself, what he renounces in himself, he only enjoys in an incomparably higher and fuller measure in God.

The monks made a vow of chastity to God; they mortified the sexual passion in themselves, but therefore they had in heaven, in the Virgin Mary, the image of woman —an image of love. They could the more easily dispense with real woman in proportion as an ideal woman was an object of love to them. The greater the importance they attached to the denial of sensuality, the greater the importance of the heavenly virgin for them : she was to them in the place of Christ, in the stead of God. The more the sensual tendencies are renounced, the more sensual is the God to whom they are sacrificed. For whatever is made an offering to God has an especial value attached to it; in it God is supposed to have especial pleasure. That which is the highest in the estimation of man is naturally the highest in the estimation of his God; what pleases man pleases God also. The Hebrews did not offer to Jehovah unclean, ill-conditioned animals; on the contrary, those which they most highly prized, which they themselves ate, were also the food of God (*Cibus Dei*, Lev. iii.

[1] Inter creatorem et creaturam non potest tanta similitudo notari, quin inter eos major sit dissimilitudo notanda.—Later. Conc. can. 2. (Summa Omn. Conc. Carranza. Antw. 1559. p. 326.) The last distinction between man and God, between the finite and infinite nature, to which the religious speculative imagination soars, is the distinction between Something and Nothing, Ens and Non-Ens ; for only in Nothing is all community with other beings abolished.

2). Wherever, therefore, the denial of the sensual delights is made a special offering, a sacrifice well-pleasing to God, there the highest value is attached to the senses, and the sensuality which has been renounced is unconsciously restored, in the fact that God takes the place of the material delights which have been renounced. The nun weds herself to God; she has a heavenly bridegroom, the monk a heavenly bride. But the heavenly virgin is only a sensible presentation of a general truth, having relation to the essence of religion. Man denies as to himself only what he attributes to God. Religion abstracts from man, from the world; but it can only abstract from the limitations, from the phenomena; in short, from the negative, not from the essence, the positive, of the world and humanity : hence, in the very abstraction and negation it must recover that from which it abstracts, or believes itself to abstract. And thus, in reality, whatever religion consciously denies— always supposing that what is denied by it is something essential, true, and consequently incapable of being ultimately denied—it unconsciously restores in God. Thus, in religion man denies his reason ; of himself he knows nothing of God, his thoughts are only worldly, earthly ; he can only believe what God reveals to him. But on this account the thoughts of God are human, earthly thoughts : like man, he has plans in his mind, he accommodates himself to circumstances and grades of intelligence, like a tutor with his pupils ; he calculates closely the effect of his gifts and revelations ; he observes man in all his doings ; he knows all things, even the most earthly, the commonest, the most trivial. In brief, man in relation to God denies his own knowledge, his own thoughts, that he may place them in God. Man gives up his personality ; but in return, God, the Almighty, infinite, unlimited being, is a person ; he denies human dignity, the human *ego;* but in return God is to him a selfish, egoistical being, who in all things seeks only himself, his own honour, his own ends; he represents God as simply seeking the satisfaction of his own selfishness, while yet he frowns on that of every other being; his God is the very luxury of egoism.[1] Religion further denies goodness

---

[1] Gloriam suam plus amat Deus quam omnes creaturas. "God can only love himself, can only think of himself, can only work for himself. In creating man, God seeks his own ends, his own glory," &c.—Vide P. Bayle, Ein Beitrag zur Geschichte der Philos. u. Menschh., pp. 104-107.

as a quality of human nature; man is wicked, corrupt, incapable of good; but, on the other hand, God is only good —the Good Being. Man's nature demands as an object goodness, personified as God; but is it not hereby declared that goodness is an essential tendency of man? If my heart is wicked, my understanding perverted, how can I perceive and feel the holy to be holy, the good to be good? Could I perceive the beauty of a fine picture if my mind were æsthetically an absolute piece of perversion? Though I may not be a painter, though I may not have the power of producing what is beautiful myself, I must yet have æsthetic feeling, æsthetic comprehension, since I perceive the beauty that is presented to me externally. Either goodness does not exist at all for man, or, if it does exist, therein is revealed to the individual man the holiness and goodness of human nature. That which is absolutely opposed to my nature, to which I am united by no bond of sympathy, is not even conceivable or perceptible by me. The holy is in opposition to me only as regards the modifications of my personality, but as regards my fundamental nature it is in unity with me. The holy is a reproach to my sinfulness; in it I recognise myself as a sinner; but in so doing, while I blame myself, I acknowledge what I am not, but ought to be, and what, for that very reason, I, according to my destination, can be; for an "ought" which has no corresponding capability does not affect me, is a ludicrous chimæra without any true relation to my mental constitution. But when I acknowledge goodness as my destination, as my law, I acknowledge it, whether consciously or unconsciously, as my own nature. Another nature than my own, one different in quality, cannot touch me. I can perceive sin as sin, only when I perceive it to be a contradiction of myself with myself—that is, of my personality with my fundamental nature. As a contradiction of the absolute, considered as another being, the feeling of sin is inexplicable, unmeaning.

The distinction between Augustinianism and Pelagianism consists only in this, that the former expresses after the manner of religion what the latter expresses after the manner of Rationalism. Both say the same thing, both vindicate the goodness of man; but Pelagianism does it directly, in a rationalistic and moral form; Augustinianism

indirectly, in a mystical, that is, a religious form.[1] For
that which is given to man's God is in truth given to man
himself; what a man declares concerning God, he in truth
declares concerning himself. Augustinianism would be a
truth, and a truth opposed to Pelagianism, only if man had
the devil for his God, and, with the consciousness that he
was the devil, honoured, reverenced, and worshipped him
as the highest being. But so long as man adores a good
being as his God, so long does he contemplate in God the
goodness of his own nature.

As with the doctrine of the radical corruption of human
nature, so is it with the identical doctrine, that man can
do nothing good, *i.e.*, in truth, nothing of himself—by his
own strength. For the denial of human strength and
spontaneous moral activity to be true, the moral activity
of God must also be denied; and we must say, with the
Oriental nihilist or pantheist: the Divine being is absolutely
without will or action, indifferent, knowing nothing of the
discrimination between evil and good. But he who defines
God as an active being, and not only so, but as morally
active and morally critical,—as a being who loves, works,
and rewards good, punishes, rejects, and condemns evil,—
he who thus defines God only in appearance denies human
activity, in fact, making it the highest, the most real activity.
He who makes God act humanly, declares human activity
to be divine; he says: A god who is not active, and not
morally or humanly active, is no god; and thus he makes
the idea of the Godhead dependent on the idea of activity,
that is, of human activity, for a higher he knows not.

Man—this is the mystery of religion—projects his being

---

[1] Pelagianism denies God, religion—isti tantam tribuunt potestatem
voluntati, ut pietati auferant orationem. (Augustin de Nat. et Grat. cont.
Pelagium, c. 58.) It has only the Creator, *i.e.*, Nature, as a basis, not the
Saviour, the true God of the religious sentiment—in a word, it denies God;
but, as a consequence of this, it elevates man into a God, since it makes
him a being not needing God, self-sufficing, independent. (See on this
subject Luther against Erasmus and Augustine, l. c. c. 33.) Augustinianism denies man; but, as a consequence of this, it reduces God to the level
of man, even to the ignominy of the cross, for the sake of man. The former
puts man in the place of God, the latter puts God in the place of man;
both lead to the same result—the distinction is only apparent, a pious
illusion. Augustinianism is only an inverted Pelagianism; what to the
latter is a subject, is to the former an object.

into objectivity,[1] and then again makes himself an object
to this projected image of himself thus converted into a
subject; he thinks of himself is an object to himself, but
as the object of an object, of another being than himself.
Thus here. Man is an object to God. That man is good
or evil is not indifferent to God; no! He has a lively,
profound interest in man's being good; he wills that man
should be good, happy—for without goodness there is no
happiness. Thus the religious man virtually retracts the
nothingness of human activity, by making his dispositions
and actions an object to God, by making man the end of
God—for that which is an object to the mind is an end in
action; by making the divine activity a means of human
salvation. God acts, that man may be good and happy.
Thus man, while he is apparently humiliated to the lowest
degree, is in truth exalted to the highest. Thus, in and
through God, man has in view himself alone. It is true
that man places the aim of his action in God, but God has
no other aim of action than the moral and eternal salvation
of man: thus man has in fact no other aim than himself.
The divine activity is not distinct from the human.

How could the divine activity work on me as its object,
nay, work in me, if it were essentially different from me;
how could it have a human aim, the aim of ameliorating
and blessing man, if it were not itself human? Does not
the purpose determine the nature of the act? When man
makes his moral improvement an aim to himself, he has
divine resolutions, divine projects; but also, when God
seeks the salvation of man, he has human ends and a
human mode of activity corresponding to these ends.
Thus in God man has only his own activity as an object.
But for the very reason that he regards his own activity
as objective, goodness only as an object, he necessarily
receives the impulse, the motive not from himself, but
from this object. He contemplates his nature as external
to himself, and this nature as goodness; thus it is self-

---

[1] The religious, the original mode in which man becomes objective to
himself, is (as is clearly enough explained in this work) to be distinguished
from the mode in which this occurs in reflection and speculation; the latter
is voluntary, the former involuntary, necessary—as necessary as art, as
speech. With the progress of time, it is true, theology coincides with
religion.

evident, it is mere tautology to say that the impulse to good comes only from thence where he places the good.

God is the highest subjectivity of man abstracted from himself; hence man can do nothing of himself, all goodness comes from God. The more subjective God is, the more completely does man divest himself of his subjectivity, because God is, *per se*, his relinquished self, the possession of which he however again vindicates to himself. As the action of the arteries drives the blood into the extremities, and the action of the veins brings it back again, as life in general consists in a perpetual systole and diastole; so is it in religion. In the religious systole man propels his own nature from himself, he throws himself outward; in the religious diastole he receives the rejected nature into his heart again. God alone is the being who acts of himself,— this is the force of repulsion in religion ; God is the being who acts in me, with me, through me, upon me, for me, is the principle of my salvation, of my good dispositions and actions, consequently my own good principle and nature,— this is the force of attraction in religion.

The course of religious development which has been generally indicated consists specifically in this, that man abstracts more and more from God, and attributes more and more to himself. This is especially apparent in the belief in revelation. That which to a later age or a cultured people is given by nature or reason, is to an earlier age, or to a yet uncultured people, given by God. Every tendency of man, however natural—even the impulse to cleanliness, was conceived by the Israelites as a positive divine ordinance. From this example we again see that God is lowered, is conceived more entirely on the type of ordinary humanity, in proportion as man detracts from himself. How can the self-humiliation of man go further than when he disclaims the capability of fulfilling spontaneously the requirements of common decency?[1] The Christian religion, on the other hand, distinguished the impulses and passions of man according to their quality, their character; it represented only good emotions, good dispositions, good thoughts, as revelations, operations—that is, as dispositions, feelings, thoughts,—of God; for what God reveals is a quality of God himself: that of which the heart is full overflows the

[1] Deut. xxiii. 12, 13.

lips; as is the effect such is the cause; as the revelation, such the being who reveals himself. A God who reveals himself in good dispositions is a God whose essential attribute is only moral perfection. The Christian religion distinguishes inward moral purity from external physical purity; the Israelites identified the two.[1] In relation to the Israelitish religion, the Christian religion is one of criticism and freedom. The Israelite trusted himself to do nothing except what was commanded by God; he was without will even in external things; the authority of religion extended itself even to his food. The Christian religion, on the other hand, in all these external things made man dependent on himself, *i.e.*, placed in man what the Israelite placed out of himself in God. Israel is the most complete presentation of Positivism in religion. In relation to the Israelite, the Christian is an *esprit fort*, a free-thinker. Thus do things change. What yesterday was still religion is no longer such to-day; and what to-day is atheism, to-morrow will be religion.

---

[1] See, for example, Gen. xxxv. 2 ; Levit. xi. 44 ; xx. 26 ; and the Commentary of Le Clerc on these passages.

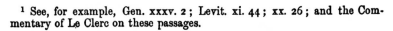

PART I.

___

THE TRUE OR ANTHROPOLOGICAL ESSENCE OF RELIGION.

___

CHAPTER II.

GOD AS A BEING OF THE UNDERSTANDING.

RELIGION is the disuniting of man from himself; he sets God before him as the antithesis of himself. God is not what man is—man is not what God is. God is the infinite, man the finite being; God is perfect, man imperfect; God eternal, man temporal; God almighty, man weak; God holy, man sinful. God and man are extremes: God is the absolutely positive, the sum of all realities; man the absolutely negative, comprehending all negations.

But in religion man contemplates his own latent nature. Hence it must be shown that this antithesis, this differencing of God and man, with which religion begins, is a differencing of man with his own nature.

The inherent necessity of this proof is at once apparent from this,—that if the divine nature, which is the object of religion, were really different from the nature of man, a division, a disunion could not take place. If God is really a different being from myself, why should his perfection trouble me? Disunion exists only between beings who are at variance, but who ought to be one, who can be one, and who consequently in nature, in truth, are one. On this general ground, then, the nature with which man feels himself in disunion must be inborn, immanent in himself, but at the same time it must be of a different character from that nature or power which gives him the feeling, the consciousness of reconciliation, of union with God, or, what is the same thing, with himself.

This nature is nothing else than the intelligence—the reason or the understanding. God as the antithesis of man, as a being not human, *i.e.,* not personally human, is the objective nature of the understanding. The pure, perfect divine nature is the self-consciousness of the understanding, the consciousness which the understanding has of its own perfection. The understanding knows nothing of the sufferings of the heart; it has no desires, no passions, no wants, and, for that reason, no deficiencies and weaknesses, as the heart has. Men in whom the intellect predominates, who, with one-sided but all the more characteristic definiteness, embody and personify for us the nature of the understanding, are free from the anguish of the heart, from the passions, the excesses of the man who has strong emotions; they are not passionately interested in any finite, *i.e.,* particular object; they do not give themselves in pledge; they are free. "To want nothing, and by this freedom from wants to become like the immortal gods;"—"not to subject ourselves to things, but things to us;"—"all is vanity;"—these and similar sayings are the mottoes of the men who are governed by abstract understanding. The understanding is that part of our nature which is neutral, impassible, not to bribed, not subject to illusions—the pure, passionless light of the intelligence. It is the categorical, impartial consciousness of the fact as fact, because it is itself of an objective nature. It is the consciousness of the uncontradictory, because it is itself the uncontradictory unity, the source of logical identity. It is the consciousness of law, necessity, rule, measure, because it is itself the activity of law, the necessity of the nature of things under the form of spontaneous activity, the rule of rules, the absolute measure, the measure of measures. Only by the understanding can man judge and act in contradiction with his dearest human, that is, personal feelings, when the God of the understanding,—law, necessity, right,—commands it. The father who, as a judge, condemns his own son to death because he knows him to be guilty, can do this only as a rational, not as an emotional being. The understanding shows us the faults and weaknesses even of our beloved ones; it shows us even our own. It is for this reason that it so often throws us into painful collision with ourselves, with our own hearts. We do not like to give reason the upper hand: we are too tender to ourselves to carry out the true, but hard, relentless verdict of the understanding. The understanding is the power which has relation to species: the heart represents particular circumstances, individuals,—the understanding, general circumstances, universals; it is the superhuman, *i.e.*, the impersonal power in man. Only by and in the understanding has man the power of abstraction from himself, from his subjective being, —of exalting himself to general ideas and relations, of distinguishing the object from the impressions which it produces on his feelings, of regarding it in and by itself without reference to human personality. Philosophy, mathematics, astronomy, physics, in short, science in general, is the practical proof, because it is the product of this truly infinite and divine activity. Religious anthropomorphisms, therefore, are in contradiction with the understanding; it repudiates their application to God; it denies them. But this God, free from anthropomorphisms, impartial, passionless, is nothing else than the nature of the understanding itself regarded as objective.

God as God, that is, as a being not finite, not human, not materially conditioned, not phenomenal, is only an object of thought. He is the incorporeal, formless, incomprehensible—the abstract, negative being: he is known, *i.e.*, becomes an object, only by abstraction and negation (*viâ negationis*). Why? Because he is nothing but the objective nature of the thinking power, or in general of the power or activity, name it what you will, whereby man is conscious of reason, of mind, of intelligence. There is no other spirit, that is (for the idea of spirit is simply the idea of thought, of intelligence, of understanding, every other spirit being a spectre of the imagination), no other intelligence which man can believe in or conceive than that intelligence which enlightens him, which is active in him. He can do nothing more than separate the intelligence from the limitations of his own individuality. The "infinite spirit," in distinction from the finite, is therefore nothing else than the intelligence disengaged from the limits of individuality and corporeality, —for individuality and corporeality are inseparable,—intelligence posited in and by itself. God, said the schoolmen, the Christian fathers, and long before them the heathen philosophers,—God is immaterial essence, intelligence, spirit, pure understanding. Of God as God no image can be made;

but canst thou frame an image of mind? Has mind a
form? Is not its activity the most inexplicable, the most
incapable of representation? God is incomprehensible;
but knowest thou the nature of the intelligence? Hast thou
searched out the mysterious operation of thought, the hidden
nature of self-consciousness? Is not self-consciousness the
enigma of enigmas? Did not the old mystics, schoolmen,
and fathers, long ago compare the incomprehensibility of the
divine nature with that of the human intelligence, and thus,
in truth, identify the nature of God with the nature of
man?* God as God—as a purely thinkable being, an object
of the intellect—is thus nothing else than the reason in its
utmost intensification become objective to itself. It is asked
what is the understanding or the reason? The answer is
found in the idea of God. Everything must express itself,
reveal itself, make itself objective, affirm itself. God is the
reason expressing, affirming itself as the highest existence.
To the imagination, the reason is the revelation of God; but
to the reason, God is the revelation of the reason; since
what reason is, what it can do, is first made objective in
God. God is a need of the intelligence, a necessary thought
—the highest degree of the thinking power. "The reason
cannot rest in sensuous things;" it can find contentment only
when it penetrates to the highest, first necessary being, which
can be an object to the reason alone. Why? Because with
the conception of this being it first completes itself, because
only in the idea of the highest nature is the highest nature
of reason existent, the highest step of the thinking power
attained: and it is a general truth, that we feel a blank, a
void, a want in ourselves, and are consequently unhappy and
unsatisfied, so long as we have not come to the last degree
of a power, to that *quo nihil majus cogitari potest,*—so long
as we cannot bring our inborn capacity for this or that art,
this or that science, to the utmost proficiency. For only in
the highest proficiency is art truly art; only in its highest
degree is thought truly thought, reason. Only when thy

* Augustine, in his work *Contra Academicos*, which he wrote when he was
still in some measure a heathen, says (l. iii. c. 12) that the highest good of
man consists in the mind or in the reason. On the other hand, in his *Libr.
Retractationum*, which he wrote as a distinguished Christian and theologian, he
revises (l. i. c. 1) this declaration as follows :—Verius dixissem in Deo. Ipso
enim mens fruitur, ut beata sit. tanquam summo bono suo. But is there any
distinction here? Where my highest good is, is not there my nature also?

thought is God dost thou truly think, rigorously speaking; for only God is the realised, consummate, exhausted thinking power. Thus in conceiving God, man first conceives reason as it truly is, though by means of the imagination he conceives this divine nature as distinct from reason, because as a being affected by external things he is accustomed always to distinguish the object from the conception of it. And here he applies the same process to the conception of the reason, thus for an existence in reason, in thought, substituting an existence in space and time, from which he had, nevertheless, previously abstracted it. God, as a metaphysical being, is the intelligence satisfied in itself, or rather, conversely, the intelligence, satisfied in itself, thinking itself as the absolute being, is God as a metaphysical being. Hence all metaphysical predicates of God are *real* predicates only when they are recognised as belonging to thought, to intelligence, to the understanding.

The understanding is that which conditionates and co-ordinates all things, that which places all things in reciprocal dependence and connection, because it is itself immediate and unconditioned; it inquires for the cause of all things, because it has its own ground and end in itself. Only that which itself is nothing deduced, nothing derived, can deduce and construct, can regard all besides itself as derived; just as only that which exists for its own sake can view and treat other things as means and instruments. The understanding is thus the original, primitive being. The understanding derives all things from God as the first cause; it finds the world, without an intelligent cause, given over to senseless, aimless chance; that is, it finds only in itself, in its own nature, the efficient and the final cause of the world—the existence of the world is only then clear and comprehensible when it sees the expla nation of that existence in the source of all clear and intelligible ideas, *i.e.*, in itself. The being that works with design towards certain ends, *i.e.*, with understanding, is alone the being that to the understanding has immediate certitude, self-evidence. Hence that which of itself has no designs, no purpose, must have the cause of its existence in the design of another, and that an intelligent being. And thus the understanding posits its own nature as the causal, first, premundane existence—*i.e.*, being in rank the first but in time the last, it makes itself the first in time also.

The understanding is to itself the criterion of all reality.

That which is opposed to the understanding, that which is self-contradictory, is nothing; that which contradicts reason contradicts God. For example, it is a contradiction of reason to connect with the idea of the highest reality the limitations of definite time and place; and hence reason denies these of God as contradicting his nature. The reason can only believe in a God who is accordant with its own nature, in a God who is not beneath its own dignity, who, on the contrary, is a realisation of its own nature: *i.e.,* the reason believes only in itself, in the absolute reality of its own nature. The reason is not dependent on God, but God on the reason. Even in the age of miracles and faith in authority, the understanding constitutes itself, at least formally, the criterion of divinity. God is all and can do all, it was said, by virtue of his omnipotence; but nevertheless he is nothing and he can do nothing which contradicts himself, *i.e.,* reason. Even omnipotence cannot do what is contrary to reason. Thus above the divine omnipotence stands the higher power of reason; above the nature of God the nature of the understanding, as the criterion of that which is to be affirmed and denied of God, the criterion of the positive and negative. Canst thou believe in a God who is an unreasonable and wicked being? No, indeed; but why not? Because it is in contradiction with thy understanding to accept a wicked and unreasonable being as divine. What then dost thou affirm, what is an object to thee, in God? Thy own understanding. God is thy highest idea, the supreme effort of thy understanding, thy highest power of thought. God is the sum of all realities, *i.e.,* the sum of all affirmations of the understanding. That which I recognise in the understanding as essential I place in God as existent: God *is* what the understanding thinks as the highest. But in what I perceive to be essential is revealed the nature of my understanding, is shown the power of my thinking faculty.

Thus the understanding is the *ens realissimum*, the most real being of the old onto-theology. "Fundamentally," says onto-theology, "we cannot conceive God otherwise than by attributing to him without limit all the real qualities which we find in ourselves."* Our positive, essential qualities, our realities, are therefore the realities of God, but in us they exist with, in God without, limits. But what then withdraws

---

* Kant, Vorles. über d. philos. Religionsl., Leipzig, 1817, p. 39.

the limits from the realities, what does away with the limits? The understanding. What, according to this, is the nature conceived without limits, but the nature of the understanding releasing, abstracting itself from all limits? As thou thinkest God, such is thy thought;—the measure of thy God is the measure of thy understanding. If thou conceivest God as limited, thy understanding is limited; if thou conceivest God as unlimited, thy understanding is unlimited; If, for example, thou conceivest God as a corporeal being, corporeality is the boundary, the limit of thy understanding; thou canst conceive nothing without a body. If, on the contrary, thou deniest corporeality of God, this is a corroboration and proof of the freedom of thy understanding from the limitation of corporeality. In the unlimited divine nature thou representest only thy unlimited understanding. And when thou declarest this unlimited being the ultimate essence, the highest being, thou sayest in reality nothing else than this: the *être suprême*, the highest being, is the understanding.

The understanding is further the self-subsistent and independent being. That which has no understanding is not self-subsistent, is dependent. A man without understanding is a man without will. He who has no understanding allows himself to be deceived, imposed upon, used as an instrument by others. How shall he whose understanding is the tool of another have an independent will? Only he who thinks is free and independent. It is only by the understanding that man reduces the things around and beneath him to mere means of his own existence. In general, that only is self-subsistent and independent which is an end to itself, an object to itself. That which is an end and object to itself is for that very reason—in so far as it is an object to itself—no longer a means and object for another being. To be without understanding is, in one word, to exist for another,—to be an object: to have understanding is to exist for oneself,—to be a subject. But that which no longer exists for another, but for itself, rejects all dependence on another being. It is true we, as physical beings, depend on the beings external to us, even as to the modifications of thought; but in so far as we think, in the activity of the understanding as such, we are dependent on no other being. Activity of thought is spontaneous activity. "When I think, I am conscious that my *ego* in me thinks, and not some other thing.

I conclude, therefore, that this thinking in me does not inhere in another thing outside of me, but in myself, consequently that I am a substance, *i.e.*, that I exist by myself, without being a predicate of another being." * Although we always need the air, yet as natural philosophers we convert the air from an object of our physical need into an object of the self-sufficing activity of thought, *i.e.*, into a mere thing for us. In breathing I am the object of the air, the air the subject; but when I make the air an object of thought, of investigation, when I analyse it, I reverse this relation,—I make myself the subject, the air an object. But that which is the object of another being is dependent. Thus the plant is dependent on air and light, that is, it is an object for air, and light, not for itself. It is true that air and light are reciprocally an object for the plant. Physical life in general is nothing else than this perpetual interchange of the objective and subjective relation. We consume the air and are consumed by it; we enjoy and are enjoyed. The understanding alone enjoys all things without being itself enjoyed; it is the self-enjoying, self-sufficing existence—the absolute subject—the subject which cannot be reduced to the object of another being, because it makes all things objects, predicates of itself,—which comprehends all things in itself, because it is itself not a thing, because it is free from all things.

That is dependent the possibility of whose existence lies out of itself; that is independent which has the possibility of its existence in itself. Life therefore involves the contradiction of an existence at once dependent and independent,— the contradiction that its possibility lies both in itself and out of itself. The understanding alone is free from this and other contradictions of life; it is the essence perfectly self-subsistent, perfectly at one with itself, perfectly self-existent.† Thinking is existence in self; life, as differenced from thought, existence out of self: life is to give from oneself; thought is to take into oneself. Existence out of self is the world; existence in self is God. To think is to be God.

* Kant, l. c., p. 80.
† To guard against mistake, I observe that I do not apply to the understanding the expression self-subsistent essence, and other terms of a like character, in my own sense, but that I am here placing myself on the standpoint of onto-theology, of metaphysical theology in general, in order to show that metaphysics is resolvable into psychology, that the onto-theological predicates are merely predicates of the understanding.

The act of thought, as such, is the freedom of the immortal gods from all external limitations and necessities of life. The unity of the understanding is the unity of God. To the understanding the consciousness of its unity and universality is essential ; the understanding is itself nothing else than the consciousness of itself as absolute identity, *i.e.*, that which is accordant with the understanding is to it an absolute, universally valid, law ; it is impossible to the understanding to think that what is self-contradictory, false, irrational, can anywhere be true, and, conversely, that what is true, rational, can anywhere be false and irrational. "There may be intelligent beings who are not like me, and yet I am certain that there are no intelligent beings who know laws and truths different from those which I recognise ; for every mind necessarily sees that two and two make four, and that one must prefer one's friend to one's dog.* Of an essentially different understanding from that which affirms itself in man, I have not the remotest conception, the faintest adumbration. On the contrary, every understanding which I posit as different from my own, is only a position of my own understanding, *i.e.*, an idea of my own, a conception which falls within my power of thought, and thus expresses my understanding. What I think, that I myself do, of course only in purely intellectual matters ; what I think of as united, I unite ; what I think of as distinct, I distinguish ; what I think of as abolished, as negatived, that I myself abolish and negative. For example, if I conceive an understanding in which the intuition or reality of the object is immediately united with the thought of it, I actually unite it ; my understanding or my imagination is itself the power of uniting these distinct or opposite ideas. How would it be possible for me to conceive them united—whether this conception be clear or confused—if I did not unite them in myself ? But whatever may be the conditions of the understanding which a given human individual may suppose as distinguished from his own, this other understanding is only the understanding which exists in man in general—the understanding conceived apart from the limits of this particular indi-

---

* Malebranche. (See the author's Geschichte der Philos., 1 Bd. p. 322.) "Exstaretne alibi diversa ab hac ratio? censereturque injustum aut scelestum in Jove aut Marte, quod apud nos justum ac præclarum habetur ? Certe nec verisimile nec omnino possibile."—Chr. Hugenii (Cosmotheoros, lib. i.).

vidual. Unity is involved in the idea of the understanding. The impossibility for the understanding to think two supreme beings, two infinite substances, two Gods, is the impossibility for the understanding to contradict itself, to deny its own nature, to think of itself as divided.

The understanding is the infinite being. Infinitude is immediately involved in unity, and finiteness in plurality. Finiteness—in the metaphysical sense—rests on the distinction of the existence from the essence, of the individual from the species; infinitude, on the unity of existence and essence. Hence, that is finite which can be compared with other beings of the same species; that is infinite which has nothing like itself, which consequently does not stand as an individual under a species, but is species and individual in one, essence and existence in one. But such is the understanding; it has its essence in itself, consequently it has nothing, together with or external to itself, which can be ranged beside it; it is incapable of being compared, because it is itself the source of all combinations and comparisons; immeasurable, because it is the measure of all measures,— we measure all things by the understanding alone; it can be circumscribed by no higher generalisation, it can be ranged under no species, because it is itself the principle of all generalising, of all classification, because it circumscribes all things and beings. The definitions which the speculative philosophers and theologians give of God, as the being in whom existence and essence are not separable, who himself *is* all the attributes which he *has*, so that predicate and subject are with him identical,—all these definitions are thus ideas drawn solely from the nature of the understanding.

Lastly, the understanding or the reason is the necessary being. Reason exists because only the existence of the reason is reason; because, if there were no reason, no consciousness, all would be nothing; existence would be equivalent to non-existence. Consciousness first founds the distinction between existence and non-existence. In consciousness is first revealed the value of existence, the value of nature. Why, in general, does something exist? why does the world exist? on the simple ground that if something did not exist, nothing would exist; if reason did not exist, there would be only unreason; thus the world exists

because it is an absurdity that the world should not exist.
In the absurdity of its non-existence is found the true
reason of its existence, in the groundlessness of the supposition that it were not the reason that it is. Nothing, non-
existence, is aimless, nonsensical, irrational. Existence
alone has an aim, a foundation, rationality; existence is,
because only existence is reason and truth; existence is
the absolute necessity. What is the cause of conscious
existence, of life? The need of life. But to whom is it a
need? To that which does not live. It is not a being who
saw that made the eye: to one who saw already, to what
purpose would be the eye? No! only the being who saw
not needed the eye. We are all come into the world without the operation of knowledge and will; but we are come
that knowledge and will may exist. Whence, then, came
the world? Out of necessity; not out of a necessity which
lies in another being distinct from itself—that is a pure
contradiction,—but out of its own inherent necessity; out
of the necessity of necessity; because without the world
there would be no necessity; without necessity, no reason,
no understanding. The nothing, out of which the world
came, is nothing without the world. It is true that thus,
negativity, as the speculative philosophers express themselves—*nothing* is the cause of the world;—but a nothing
which abolishes itself, *i e.*, a nothing which could not have
existed if there had been no world. It is true that the
world springs out of a want, out of privation, but it is false
speculation to make this privation an ontological being:
this want is simply *the* want which lies in the supposed
non-existence of the world. Thus the world is only necessary out of itself and through itself. But the necessity of
the world is the necessity of reason. The reason, as the
sum of all realities,—for what are all the glories of the
world without light, much more external light without
internal light?—the reason is the most indispensable being
—the profoundest and most essential necessity. In the
reason first lies the self-consciousness of existence, self-
conscious existence; in the reason is first revealed the end,
the meaning of existence. Reason is existence objective
to itself as its own end; the ultimate tendency of things.
That which is an object to itself is the highest, the final
being; that which has power over itself is almighty.

CHAPTER III.

GOD AS A MORAL BEING, OR LAW.

GOD as God—the infinite, universal, non-anthropomorphic being of the understanding, has no more significance for religion than a fundamental general principle has for a special science; it is merely the ultimate point of support,—as it were, the mathematical point of religion. The consciousness of human limitation or nothingness which is united with the idea of this being, is by no means a religious consciousness; on the contrary, it characterises sceptics, materialists, and pantheists. The belief in God—at least in the God of religion—is only lost where, as in scepticism, pantheism, and materialism, the belief in man is lost, at least in man such as he is presupposed in religion. As little then as religion has any influential belief in the nothingness of man,* so little has it any influential belief in that abstract being with which the consciousness of this nothingness is united. The vital elements of religion are those only which make man an object to man. To deny man is to deny religion.

It certainly is the interest of religion that its object should be distinct from man; but it is also, nay, yet more, its interest that this object should have human attributes. That he should be a distinct being concerns his existence only; but that he should be human concerns his essence. If he be of a different nature, how can his existence or non-existence be of any importance to man? How can he take so profound an interest in an existence in which his own nature has no participation?

To give an example. "When I believe that the human nature alone has suffered for me, Christ is a poor Saviour to

---

* In religion, the representation or expression of the nothingness of man before God is the anger of God ; for as the love of God is the affirmation, his anger is the negation of man. But even this anger is not taken in earnest. "God . . . is not really angry. He is not thoroughly in earnest even when we think that he is angry, and punishes."—Luther (Th. viii. p. 208).

me : in that case, he needs a Saviour himself." And thus, out
of the need for salvation is postulated something transcending human nature, a being different from man. But no
sooner is this being postulated than there arises the yearning
of man after himself, after his own nature, and man is immediately re-established. " Here is God, who is not man
and never yet became man. But this is not a God for me.
. . . That would be a miserable Christ to me, who . . .
should be nothing but a purely separate God and divine
person . . . without humanity. No, my friend ; where thou
givest me God, thou must give me humanity too." *

In religion man seeks contentment ; religion is his highest
good. But how could he find consolation and peace in God
if God were an essentially different being ? How can I share
the peace of a being if I am not of the same nature with him ?
If his nature is different from mine, his peace is essentially
different,—it is no peace for me. How then can I become a
partaker of his peace if I am not a partaker of his nature ?
but how can I be a partaker of his nature if I am really of a
different nature ? Every being experiences peace only in its
own element, only in the conditions of its own nature. Thus,
if man feels peace in God, he feels it only because in God he
first attains his true nature, because here, for the first time,
he is with himself, because everything in which he hitherto
sought peace, and which he hitherto mistook for his nature,
was alien to him. Hence, if man is to find contentment in
God, he must find himself in God. " No one will taste of
God but as he wills, namely—in the humanity of Christ ;
and if thou dost not find God thus, thou wilt never have
rest." † " Everything finds rest on the place in which it was
born. The place where I was born is God. God is my
fatherland. Have I a father in God ? Yes, I have not only
a father, but I have myself in him ; before I lived in myself,
I lived already in God." ‡

A God, therefore, who expresses only the nature of the understanding does not satisfy religion, is not the God of religion.
The understanding is interested not only in man, but in the

---

* Luther, Concordienbuch, Art. 8, Erklär.
† Luther, Sämmtliche Schriften und Werke, Leipzig, 1729, fol. Th. iii.
p. 589. It is according to this edition that references are given throughout
the present work.
‡ Predigten etzlicher Lehrer vor und zu Tauleri Zeiten, Hamburg, 1621,
p. 81.

things out of man, in universal nature. The intellectual man forgets even himself in the contemplation of nature. The Christians scorned the pagan philosophers because, instead of thinking of themselves, of their own salvation, they had thought only of things out of themselves. The Christian thinks only of himself. By the understanding an insect is contemplated with as much enthusiasm as the image of God—man. The understanding is the absolute indifference and identity of all things and beings. It is not Christianity, not religious enthusiasm, but the enthusiasm of the understanding that we have to thank for botany, mineralogy, zoology, physics, and astronomy. The understanding is universal, pantheistic, the love of the universe; but the grand characteristic of religion, and of the Christian religion especially, is that it is thoroughly anthropotheistic, the exclusive love of man for himself, the exclusive self-affirmation of the human nature, that is, of subjective human nature; for it is true that the understanding also affirms the nature of man, but it is his objective nature, which has reference to the object for the sake of the object, and the manifestation of which is science. Hence it must be something entirely different from the nature of the understanding which is an object to man in religion, if he is to find contentment therein, and this something will necessarily be the very kernel of religion.

Of all the attributes which the understanding assigns to God, that which in religion, and especially in the Christian religion, has the pre-eminence, is moral perfection. But God as a morally perfect being is nothing else than the realised idea, the fulfilled law of morality, the moral nature of man posited as the absolute being; man's own nature, for the moral God requires man to be as he himself is: Be ye holy for I am holy; man's own conscience, for how could he otherwise tremble before the Divine Being, accuse himself before him, and make him the judge of his inmost thoughts and feelings?

But the consciousness of the absolutely perfect moral nature, especially as an abstract being separate from man, leaves us cold and empty, because we feel the distance, the chasm between ourselves and this being;—it is a dispiriting consciousness, for it is the consciousness of our personal nothingness, and of the kind which is the most acutely felt

—moral nothingness. The consciousness of the divine omnipotence and eternity in opposition to my limitation in space
and time does not afflict me : for omnipotence does not command me to be myself omnipotent, eternity, to be myself
eternal. But I cannot have the idea of moral perfection
without at the same time being conscious of it as a law
for me. Moral perfection depends, at least for the moral
consciousness, not on the nature, but on the will—it is a
perfection of will, perfect will. I cannot conceive perfect
will, the will which is in unison with law, which is itself
law, without at the same time regarding it is an object of
will, *i.e.*, as an obligation for myself. The conception of the
morally perfect being is no merely theoretical, inert conception, but a practical one, calling me to action, to imitation, throwing me into strife, into disunion with myself;
for while it proclaims to me what I ought to be, it also tells
me to my face, without any flattery, what I am not.* And
religion renders this disunion all the more painful, all the
more terrible, that it sets man's own nature before him as a
separate nature, and moreover as a personal being, who hates
and curses sinners, and excludes them from his grace, the
source of all salvation and happiness.

Now, by what means does man deliver himself from this
state of disunion between himself and the perfect being,
from the painful consciousness of sin, from the distressing
sense of his own nothingness ? How does he blunt the fatal
sting of sin ? Only by this ; that he is conscious of *love* as
the highest, the absolute power and truth, that he regards
the Divine Being not only as a law, as a moral being, as a
being of the understanding; but also as a loving, tender, even
subjective human being (that is, as having sympathy with
individual man).

The understanding judges only according to the stringency
of law ; the heart accommodates itself, is considerate, lenient,
relenting, κατ' ἄνθρωπον. No man is sufficient for the law
which moral perfection sets before us ; but, for that reason,
neither is the law sufficient for man, for the heart. The law
condemns ; the heart has compassion even on the sinner. The

* "That which, in our own judgment, derogates from our self-conceit,
humiliates us. Thus the moral law inevitably humiliates every man when
he compares with it the sensual tendency of his nature."—Kant, Kritik der
prakt. Vernunft, 4th edition, p. 132.

law affirms me only as an abstract being,—love, as a real being. Love gives me the consciousness that I am a man; the law only the consciousness that I am a sinner, that I am worthless.* The law holds man in bondage; love makes him free.

Love is the middle term, the substantial bond, the principle of reconciliation between the perfect and the imperfect, the sinless and sinful being, the universal and the individual, the divine and the human. Love is God himself, and apart from it there is no God. Love makes man God and God man. Love strengthens the weak and weakens the strong, abases the high and raises the lowly, idealises matter and materialises spirit. Love it the true unity of God and man, of spirit and nature. In love common nature is spirit, and the preeminent spirit is nature. Love is to deny spirit from the point of view of spirit, to deny matter from the point of view of matter. Love is materialism; immaterial love is a chimæra. In the longing of love after the distant object, the abstract idealist involuntarily confirms the truth of sensuousness. But love is also the idealism of nature—love is also spirit, *esprit.* Love alone makes the nightingale a songstress; love alone gives the plant its corolla. And what wonders does not love work in our social life! What faith, creed, opinion separates, love unites. Love even, humorously enough, identifies the high noblesse with the people. What the old mystics said of God, that he is the highest and yet the commonest being, applies in truth to love, and that not a visionary, imaginary love—no! a real love, a love which has flesh and blood, which vibrates as an almighty force through all living.

Yes, it applies only to the love which has flesh and blood, for only this can absolve from the sins which flesh and blood commit. A merely moral being cannot forgive what is contrary to the law of morality. That which denies the law is denied by the law. The moral judge, who does not infuse human blood into his judgment judges the sinner relentlessly, inexorably. Since, then, God is regarded as a sin-pardoning being, he is posited, not indeed as an unmoral, but as more than a moral being—in a word, as a human

---

* "Omnes peccavimus. . . . Parricide cum lega cæperunt et illis facinus pœna monstravit."—Seneca. "The law destroys us."—Luther (Th. xvi. a. 320).

being. The negation or annulling of sin is the negation of abstract moral rectitude,—the positing of love, mercy, sensuous life. Not abstract beings—no! only sensuous, living beings are merciful. Mercy is the *justice of sensuous life.* Hence God does not forgive the sins of men as the abstract God of the understanding, but as man, as the God made flesh, the visible God. God as man sins not, it is true, but he knows, he takes on himself, the sufferings, the wants, the needs of sensuous beings. The blood of Christ cleanses us from our sins in the eyes of God; it is only his human blood that makes God merciful, allays his anger; that is, our sins are forgiven us because we are no abstract beings, but creatures of flesh and blood.†

* "Das Rechtsgefühl der Sinnlichkeit."
† "This, my God and Lord, has taken upon him my nature, flesh and blood such as I have, and has been tempted and has suffered in all things like me, but without sin; therefore he can have pity on my weakness.— Hebrews v. Luther (Th. xvi. s. 533). "The deeper we can bring Christ into the flesh the better."—(Ibid. s. 565.) "God himself, when he is dealt with out of Christ, is a terrible God, for no consolation is found in him, but pure anger and disfavour."—(Th. xv. s. 298.)

CHAPTER IV.

THE MYSTERY OF THE INCARNATION; OR, GOD AS LOVE, AS A BEING OF THE HEART.

IT is the consciousness of love by which man reconciles himself with God, or rather with his own nature as represented in the moral law. The consciousness of the divine love, or what is the same thing, the contemplation of God as human, is the mystery of the Incarnation. The Incarnation is nothing else than the practical, material manifestation of the human nature of God. God did not become man for his own sake; the need, the want of man—a want which still exists in the religious sentiment—was the cause of the Incarnation. God became man out of mercy : thus he was in himself already a human God before he became an actual man ; for human want, human misery, went to his heart. The Incarnation was a tear of the divine compassion, and hence it was only the visible advent of a Being having human feelings, and therefore essentially human.

If in the Incarnation we stop short at the fact of God becoming man, it certainly appears a surprising, inexplicable, marvellous event. But the incarnate God is only the apparent manifestation of deified man ; for the descent of God to man is necessarily preceded by the exaltation of man to God. Man was already in God, was already God himself, before God became man, *i.e.*, showed himself as man.* How otherwise could God have become man ? The old maxim, *ex nihilo nihil fit*, is applicable here also. A king who has not the welfare of his subjects at heart, who, while seated on his throne, does not mentally live with them in their dwellings, who, in feeling, is not, as the people say, " a common man,"

---

* " Such descriptions as those in which the Scriptures speak of God as of a man, and ascribe to him all that is human, are very sweet and comforting —namely, that he talks with us as a friend, and of such things as men are wont to talk of with each other ; that he rejoices, sorrows, and suffers, like a man, for the sake of the mystery of the future humanity of Christ."—Luther (Th. ii. p. 334).

such a king will not descend bodily from his throne to make his people happy by his personal presence. Thus, has not the subject risen to be a king before the king descends to be a subject? And if the subject feels himself honoured and made happy by the personal presence of his king, does this feeling refer merely to the bodily presence, and not rather to the manifestation of the disposition, of the philanthropic nature which is the cause of the appearance? But that which in the truth of religion is the cause, takes in the consciousness of religion the form of a consequence; and so here the raising of man to God is made a consequence of the humiliation or descent of God to man. God, says religion, made himself human that he might make man divine.*

That which is mysterious and incomprehensible, *i.e.*, contradictory, in the proposition, "God is or becomes a man," arises only from the mingling or confusion of the idea or definitions of the universal, unlimited, metaphysical being with the idea of the religious God, *i.e.*, the conditions of the understanding with the conditions of the heart, the emotive nature; a confusion which is the greatest hindrance to the correct knowledge of religion. But, in fact, the idea of the Incarnation is nothing more than the human *form* of a God, who already in his nature, in the profoundest depths of his soul, is a merciful and therefore a human God.

The form given to this truth in the doctrine of the Church is, that it was not the first person of the Godhead who was incarnate, but the second, who is the representative of man in and before God; the second person being however in reality, as will be shown, the sole, true, first person in religion. And it is only apart from this distinction of persons that the God-man appears mysterious, incomprehensible, "speculative;" for, considered in connection with it, the Incarnation is a necessary, nay, a self-evident consequence. The allegation, therefore, that the Incarnation is a purely empirical fact, which could be made known only by means of a revelation in the theological sense, betrays the most crass religious materialism; for the Incarnation is a conclusion which rests

* "Deus homo factus est, ut homo Deus fieret."—Augustinus (Serm. ad Pop. p. 371, c. 1). In Luther, however (Th. i. p. 334), there is a passage which indicates the true relation. When Moses called man "the image of God, the likeness of God," he meant, says Luther, obscurely to intimate that "God was to become man." Thus here the incarnation of God is clearly enough represented as a consequence of the deification of man.

on a very comprehensible premiss. But it is equally perverse to attempt to deduce the Incarnation from purely speculative, *i.e.*, metaphysical, abstract grounds; for metaphysics apply only to the first person of the Godhead, who does not become incarnate, who is not a dramatic person. Such a deduction would at the utmost be justifiable if it were meant consciously to deduce from metaphysics the negation of metaphysics.

This example clearly exhibits the distinction between the method of our philosophy and that of the old speculative philosophy. The former does not philosophise concerning the Incarnation, as a peculiar, stupendous mystery, after the manner of speculation dazzled by mystical splendour; on the contrary, it destroys the illusive supposition of a peculiar supernatural mystery; it criticises the dogma and reduces it to its natural elements, immanent in man, to its originating principle and central point—love.

The dogma presents to us two things—God and love. God is love: but what does that mean? Is God something besides love? a being distinct from love? Is it as if I said of an affectionate human being, he is love itself? Certainly; otherwise I must give up the name God, which expresses a special personal being, a subject in distinction from the predicate. Thus love is made something apart. God out of love sent his only-begotten Son. Here love recedes and sinks into insignificance in the dark background—God. It becomes merely a personal, though an essential, attribute; hence it receives both in theory and in feeling, both objectively and subjectively, the rank simply of a predicate, not that of a subject, of the substance; it shrinks out of observation as a collateral, an accident; at one moment it presents itself to me as something essential, at another, it vanishes again. God appears to me in another form besides that of love; in the form of omnipotence, of a severe power not bound by love; a power in which, though in a smaller degree, the devils participate.

So long as love is not exalted into a substance, into an essence, so long there lurks in the background of love a subject who even without love is something by himself, an unloving monster, a diabolical being, whose personality, separable and actually separated from love, delights in the blood of heretics and unbelievers,—the phantom of religious

fanaticism. Nevertheless the essential idea of the Incarnation, though enveloped in the night of the religious consciousness, is love. Love determined God to the renunciation of
his divinity.* Not because of his Godhead as such, according to which he is the *subject* in the proposition, God is
love, but because of his love, of the *predicate*, is it that he renounced his Godhead; thus love is a higher power and truth
than deity. Love conquers God. It was love to which
God sacrificed his divine majesty. And what sort of love
was that? another than ours? than that to which we sacrifice life and fortune? Was it the love of himself? of himself
as God? No! it was love to man. But is not love to man
human love? Can I love man without loving him humanly,
without loving him as he himself loves, if he truly loves?
Would not love be otherwise a devilish love? The devil
too loves. man, but not for man's sake—for his own; thus
he loves man out of egotism, to aggrandise himself, to extend
his power. But God loves man for man's sake, *i.e.*, that he
may make him good, happy, blessed. Does he not then
love man as the true man loves his fellow? Has love a
plural? Is it not everywhere like itself? What then is
the true unfalsified import of the Incarnation but absolute,
pure love, without adjunct, without a distinction between
divine and human love? For though there is also a self-
interested love among men, still the true human love, which
is alone worthy of this name, is that which impels the
sacrifice of self to another. Who then is our Saviour and
Redeemer? God or Love? Love; for God as God has not
saved us, but Love, which transcends the difference between
the divine and human personality. As God has renounced
himself out of love, so we, out of love, should renounce
God; for if we do not sacrifice God to love, we sacrifice love
to God, and, in spite of the predicate of love, we have the
God—the evil being—of religious fanaticism.

* It was in this sense that the old uncompromising enthusiastic faith
celebrated the Incarnation. " Amor triumphat de Deo," says St. Bernard.
And only in the sense of a real self-renunciation, self-negation of the Godhead, lies the reality, the *vis* of the Incarnation; although this self-negation is in itself merely a conception of the imagination, for, looked at in
broad daylight, God does not negative himself in the Incarnation, but he
shows himself as that which he is, as a human being. The fabrications
which modern rationalistic orthodoxy and pietistic rationalism have advanced concerning the Incarnation, in opposition to the rapturous conceptions and expressions of ancient faith, do not deserve to be mentioned, still
less controverted.

While, however, we have laid open this nucleus of truth in the Incarnation, we have at the same time exhibited the dogma in its falsity ; we have reduced the apparently supernatural and super-rational mystery to a simple truth inherent in human nature:—a truth which does not belong to the Christian religion alone, but which, implicitly at least, belongs more or less to every religion as such. For every religion which has any claim to the name presupposes that God is not indifferent to the beings who worship him, that therefore what is human is not alien to him, that, as an object of human veneration, he is a human God. Every prayer discloses the secret of the Incarnation, every prayer is in fact an incarnation of God. In prayer I involve God in human distress, I make him a participator in my sorrows and wants. God is not deaf to my complaints ; he has compassion on me; hence he renounces his divine majesty, his exaltation above all that is finite and human ; he becomes a man with man ; for if he listens to me, and pities me, he is affected by my sufferings. God loves man —*i.e.,* God suffers from man. Love does not exist without sympathy, sympathy does not exist without suffering in common. Have I any sympathy for a being without feeling? No! I feel only for that which has feeling, only for that which partakes of my nature, for that in which I feel myself, whose sufferings I myself suffer. Sympathy presupposes a like nature. The Incarnation, Providence, prayer, are the expression of this identity of nature in God and man.*

It is true that theology, which is pre-occupied with the metaphysical attributes of eternity, unconditionedness, unchangeableness, and the like abstractions, which express the nature of the understanding,—theology denies the possibility that God should suffer, but in so doing it denies the truth of religion.† For religion—the religious man in the

---

* "Nos scimus affici Deum misericordia nostri et non solum respicere lacrymas nostras, sed etiam numerare stillulas, sicut scriptum in Psalmo LVI. Filius Dei vere afficitur sensu miseriarum nostrarum."—Melancthonis et aliorum (Declam. Th. iii. p. 286, p. 450).

† St. Bernard resorts to a charmingly sophistical play of words :— "*Impassibilis* est Deus, sed non *incompassibilis,* cui proprium est misereri semper et parcere."—(Sup. Cant. Sermo 26.) As if compassion were not suffering—the suffering of love, it is true, the suffering of the heart. But what does suffer if not thy sympathising heart? No love, no suffering. The material, the source of suffering, is the universal heart, the common bond of all beings.

act of devotion believes in a real sympathy of the divine being in his sufferings and wants, believes that the will of God can be determined by the fervour of prayer, *i.e.*, by the force of feeling, believes in a real, present fulfilment of his desire, wrought by prayer. The truly religious man unhesitatingly assigns his own feelings to God; God is to him a heart susceptible to all that is human. The heart can betake itself only to the heart; feeling can appeal only to feeling; it finds consolation in itself, in its own nature alone.

The notion that the fulfilment of prayer has been determined from eternity, that it was originally included in the plan of creation, is the empty, absurd fiction of a mechanical mode of thought, which is in absolute contradiction with the nature of religion. "We need," says Lavater somewhere, and quite correctly according to the religious sentiment, "an arbitrary God." Besides, even according to this fiction, God is just as much a being determined by man, as in the real, present fulfilment consequent on the power of prayer; the only difference is, that the contradiction with the unchangeableness and unconditionedness of God—that which constitutes the difficulty—is thrown back into the deceptive distance of the past or of eternity. Whether God decides on the fulfilment of my prayer now, on the immediate occasion of my offering it, or whether he did decide on it long ago, is fundamentally the same thing.

It is the greatest inconsequence to reject the idea of a God who can be determined by prayer, that is, by the force of feeling, as an unworthy anthropomorphic idea. If we once believe in a being who is an object of veneration, an object of prayer, an object of affection, who is providential, who takes care of man,—in a Providence, which is not conceivable without love,—in a being, therefore, who is loving, whose motive of action is love; we also believe in a being, who has, if not an anatomical, yet a psychical human heart. The religious mind, as has been said, places everything in God, excepting that alone which it despises. The Christians certainly gave their God no attributes which contradicted their own moral ideas, but they gave him without hesitation, and of necessity, the emotions of love, of compassion. And the love which the religious mind places in God is not an illusory, imaginary love, but a real, true love. God is loved and loves again; the divine love is only human love made objective, affirming itself. In God love is absorbed in itself as its own ultimate truth.

It may be objected to the import here assigned to the Incarnation, that the Christian Incarnation is altogether peculiar, that at least it is different (which is quite true in certain respects, as will hereafter be apparent) from the incarnations of the heathen deities, whether Greek or Indian. These latter are mere products of men or deified men; but in Christianity is given the idea of the true God; here the union of the divine nature with the human is first significant and "speculative." Jupiter transforms himself into a bull; the heathen incarnations are mere fancies. In paganism there is no more in the nature of God than in his incarnate manifestation; in Christianity, on the contrary, it is God, a separate, superhuman being, who appears as man. But this objection is refuted by the remark already made, that even the premiss of the Christian Incarnation contains the human nature. God loves man; moreover God has a Son; God is a father; the relations of humanity are not excluded from God; the human is not remote from God, not unknown to him. Thus here also there is nothing more in the nature of God than in the incarnate manifestation of God. In the Incarnation religion only confesses, what in reflection on itself, as theology, it will not admit; namely, that God is an altogether human being. The Incarnation, the mystery of the "God-man," is therefore no mysterious composition of contraries, no synthetic fact, as it is regarded by the speculative religious philosophy, which has a particular delight in contradiction; it is an analytic fact,—a human word with a human meaning. If there be a contradiction here, it lies before the incarnation and out of it; in the union of providence, of love, with deity; for if this love is a real love, it is not essentially different from our love,—there are only our limitations to be abstracted from it; and thus the Incarnation is only the strongest, deepest, most palpable, open-hearted expression of this providence, this love. Love knows not how to make its object happier than by rejoicing it with its personal presence, by letting itself be seen. To see the invisible benefactor face to face is the most ardent desire of love. To see is a divine act. Happiness lies in the mere sight of the beloved one. The glance is the certainty of love. And the Incarnation has no other significance, no other effect, than the indubitable certitude of the love of God to man. Love remains, but the Incarnation upon the earth passes away : the appearance was limited by time and place, accessible to few; but the essence, the nature which was manifested, is eternal and universal. We can no longer believe in the manifestation for its own sake, but only for the sake of the thing manifested; for to us there remains no immediate presence but that of love.

The clearest, most irrefragable proof that man in religion contemplates himself as the object of the Divine Being, as the end of the divine activity, that thus in religion he has relation only to his own nature, only to himself,—the clearest, most irrefragable proof of this is the love of God to man, the basis and central point of religion. God, for the sake of man, empties himself of his Godhead, lays aside his Godhead. Herein lies the elevating influence of the Incarnation ; the highest, the perfect being humiliates, lowers himself for the sake of man. Hence in God I learn to estimate my own nature; I have value in the sight of God ; the divine significance of my nature is become evident to me. How can the worth of man be more strongly expressed than when God, for man's sake, becomes a man, when man is the end, the object of the divine love ? The love of God to man is an essential condition of the Divine Being : God is a God who loves me—who loves man in general. Here lies the emphasis, the fundamental feeling of religion. The love of God makes me loving; the love of God to man is the cause of man's love to God ; the divine love causes, awakens human love. "We love God because he first loved us." What, then, is it that I love in God ? Love: love to man. But when I love and worship the love with which God loves man, do I not love man ; is not my love of God, though indirectly, love of man ? If God loves man, is not man, then, the very substance of God ? That which I love, is it not my inmost being ? Have I a heart when I do not love ? No! love only is the heart of man. But what is love without the thing loved ? Thus what I love is my heart, the substance of my being, my nature. Why does man grieve, why does he lose pleasure in life when he has lost the beloved object ? Why ? because with the beloved object he has lost his heart, the activity of his affections, the principle of life. Thus if God loves man, man is the heart of God—the welfare of man his deepest anxiety. If man, then, is the object of God, is not man, in God, an object to himself? is not the content of the divine nature the human nature? If God is love, is not the essential content of this love man? Is not the love of God to man—the basis and central point of religion—the love of man to himself made an object, contemplated as the highest objective truth, as the highest being to man? Is not then the proposition, "God loves man" an orientalism (religion is essentially oriental), which in plain speech means, the highest is the love of man?

The truth to which, by means of analysis, we have here reduced the mystery of the Incarnation, has also been recognised even in the religious consciousness. Thus Luther, for example, says, "He who can truly conceive such a thing (namely, the incarnation of God) in his heart, should, for the sake of the flesh and blood which sits at the right hand of God, bear love to all flesh and blood here upon the earth, and never more be able to be angry with any man. The gentle manhood of Christ our God should at a glance fill all hearts with joy, so that never more could an angry, unfriendly thought come therein—yea, every man ought, out of great joy, to be tender to his fellow-man for the sake of that our flesh and blood." This is a fact which should move us to great joy and blissful hope that we are thus honoured above all creatures, even above the angels, so that we can with truth boast, My own flesh and blood sits at the right hand of God and reigns over all. Such honour has no creature, not even an angel. This ought to be a furnace that should melt us all into one heart, and should create such a fervour in us men that we should heartily love each other." But that which in the truth of religion is the essence of the fable, the chief thing, is to the religious consciousness only the moral of the fable, a collateral thing.

CHAPTER V.

AN essential condition of the incarnate, or, what is the same thing, the human God, namely, Christ, is the Passion. Love attests itself by suffering. All thoughts and feelings which are immediately associated with Christ concentrate themselves in the idea of the Passion. God as God is the sum of all human perfection; God as Christ is the sum of all human misery. The heathen philosophers celebrated activity, especially the spontaneous activity of the intelligence, as the highest, the divine; the Christians consecrated passivity, even placing it in God. If God as *actus purus*, as pure activity, is the God of abstract philosophy; so, on the other hand, Christ, the God of the Christians, is the *passio pura*, pure suffering—the highest metaphysical thought, the *être suprême* of the heart. For what makes more impression on the heart than suffering? especially the suffering of one who considered in himself is free from suffering, exalted above it;—the suffering of the innocent, endured purely for the good of others, the suffering of love,—self-sacrifice? But for the very reason that the history of the Passion is the history which most deeply affects the human heart, or let us rather say the heart in general—for it would be a ludicrous mistake in man to attempt to conceive any other heart than the human,—it follows undeniably that nothing else is expressed in that history, nothing else is made an object in it, but the nature of the heart,—that it is not an invention of the understanding or the poetic faculty, but of the heart. The heart, however, does not invent in the same way as the free imagination or intelligence; it has a passive, receptive relation to what it produces; all that proceeds from it seems to it given from without, takes it by violence, works with the force of irresistible necessity. The heart overcomes, masters man; he who is once in its power is possessed as it were by his demon, by his God. The heart knows no other God, no

59

more excellent being than itself, than a God whose name may indeed be another, but whose nature, whose substance is the nature of the heart. And out of the heart, out of the inward impulse to do good, to live and die for man, out of the divine instinct of benevolence which desires to make all happy, and excludes none, not even the most abandoned and abject, out of the moral duty of benevolence in the highest sense, as having become an inward necessity, *i.e.*, a movement of the heart,—out of the human nature, therefore, as it reveals itself through the heart, has sprung what is best, what is true in Christianity—its essence purified from theological dogmas and contradictions.

For, according to the principles which we have already developed, that which in religion is the predicate we must make the subject, and that which in religion is a subject we must make a predicate, thus inverting the oracles of religion; and by this means we arrive at the truth. God suffers—suffering is the predicate—but for men, for others, not for himself. What does that mean in plain speech? Nothing else than this: to suffer for others is divine; he who suffers for others, who lays down his life for them, acts divinely, is a God to men.*

The Passion of Christ, however, represents not only moral, voluntary suffering, the suffering of love, the power of sacrificing self for the good of others; it represents also suffering as such, suffering in so far as it is an expression of passibility in general. The Christian religion is so little superhuman that it even sanctions human weakness. The heathen philosopher, on hearing tidings of the death of his child exclaims: "I knew that he was mortal." Christ, on the contrary,—at least in the Bible,—sheds tears over the death of Lazarus, a death which he nevertheless knew to be only an apparent one. While Socrates empties the cup of poison with unshaken soul, Christ exclaims, "If it be possible,

---

* Religion speaks by example. Example is the law of religion. What Christ did is law. Christ suffered for others; therefore, we should do likewise. "Quæ necessitas fuit ut sic exinaniret se, sic humiliaret se, sic abbreviaret se Dominus majestatis; nisi ut vos similiter faciatis?"—Bernardus (in Die nat. Domini). "We ought studiously to consider the example of Christ. . . . That would move us and incite us, so that we from our hearts should willingly help and serve other people, even though it might be hard, and we must suffer on account of it."—Luther (Th. xv. p. 40).

let this cup pass from me." * Christ is in this respect the
self-confession of human sensibility. In opposition to the
heathen, and in particular the stoical principle, with its
rigorous energy of will and self-sustainedness, the Christian
involves the consciousness of his own sensitiveness and
susceptibility in the consciousness of God; he finds it, if
only it be no sinful weakness, not denied, not condemned
in God.

To suffer is the highest command of Christianity—the
history of Christianity is the history of the Passion of
Humanity. While amongst the heathens the shout of sensual
pleasure mingled itself in the worship of the gods, amongst
the Christians, we mean of course the ancient Christians,
God is served with sighs and tears.† But as where sounds
of sensual pleasure make a part of the cultus, it is a sensual
God, a God of life, who is worshipped, as indeed these shouts
of joy are only a symbolical definition of the nature of the
gods to whom this jubilation is acceptable; so also the
sighs of Christians are tones which proceed from the inmost
soul, the inmost nature of their God. The God expressed
by the cultus, whether this be an external, or, as with the
Christians, an inward spiritual worship,—not the God of
sophistical theology,—is the true God of man. But the
Christians, we mean of course the ancient Christians, believed that they rendered the highest honour to their God
by tears, the tears of repentance and yearning. Thus tears
are the light-reflecting drops which mirror the nature of
the Christian's God. But a God who has pleasure in tears,
expresses nothing else than the nature of the heart. It is
true that the theory of the Christian religion says: Christ
has done all for us, has redeemed us, has reconciled us with
God; and from hence the inference may be drawn: Let us
be of a joyful mind and disposition; what need have we
to trouble ourselves as to how we shall reconcile ourselves
with God? we are reconciled already. But the imperfect
tense in which the fact of suffering is expressed makes a

* "Hærent plerique hoc loco. Ego autem non solum excusandum non
puto, sed etiam nusquam magis pietatem ejus majestatemque demiror.
Minus enim contulerat mihi, nisi meum suscepisset affectum. Ergo pro
me doluit, qui pro se nihil habuit, quod doleret."—Ambrosius (Exposit. in
Lucæ Ev. l. x. c. 22).

† "Quando enim illi (Deo) appropinquare auderemus in sua impassi-
bilitate manenti?"—Bernardus (Tract. de xii. Grad. Humil. et Superb.).

deeper, a more enduring impression, than the perfect tense which expresses the fact of redemption. The redemption is only the result of the suffering; the suffering is the cause of the redemption. Hence the suffering takes deeper root in the feelings; the suffering makes itself an object of imitation;—not so the redemption. If God himself suffered for my sake, how can I be joyful, how can I allow myself any gladness, at least on this corrupt earth, which was the theatre of his suffering?* Ought I to fare better than God? Ought I not, then, to make his sufferings my own? Is not what God my Lord does my model? Or shall I share only the gain and not the cost also? Do I know merely that he has redeemed me? Do I not also know the history of his suffering? Should it be an object of cold remembrance to me, or even an object of rejoicing, because it has purchased my salvation? Who can think so—who can wish to be exempt from the sufferings of his God?

The Christian religion is the religion of suffering.† The images of the crucified one which we still meet with in all churches, represent not the Saviour, but only the crucified, the suffering Christ. Even the self-crucifixions among the Christians are, psychologically, a deep-rooted consequence of their religious views. How should not he who has always the image of the crucified one in his mind, at length contract the desire to crucify either himself or another? At least we have as good a warrant for this conclusion as Augustine and other fathers of the Church for their reproach against the heathen religion, that the licentious religious images of the heathens provoked and authorised licentiousness.

God suffers, means in truth nothing else than: God is a heart. The heart is the source, the centre of all suffering. A being without suffering is a being without a heart. The mystery of the suffering God is therefore the mystery of feeling, sensibility. A suffering God is a feeling, sensitive God.‡ But the proposition: God is a feeling Being, is only

---

* "Deus meus pendet in patibulo et ego voluptati operam dabo?"— (Form. Hon. Vitæ. Among the spurious writings of St. Bernard.) "Memoria crucifixi crucifigat in te carnem tuam."—Joh. Gerhard (Medit. Sacræ, M. 37).

† "It is better to suffer evil than to do good."—Luther (Th. iv. s. 15).

‡ "Pati voluit, ut compati disceret, miser fieri, ut misereri disceret."—Bernhard (de Grad.). "Miserere nostri, quoniam carnis imbecillitatem, tu ipse eam passus, expertus es."—Clemens Alex. Pædag. l. i. c. 8.

the religious periphrase of the proposition : feeling is absolute, divine in its nature.

Man has the consciousness not only of a spring of activity, but also of a spring of suffering in himself.   I feel ; and I feel feeling (not merely will and thought, which are only too often in opposition to me and my feelings), as belonging to my essential being, and, though the source of all sufferings and sorrows, as a glorious, divine power and perfection.   What would man be without feeling ?   It is the musical power in man.   But what would man be without music ?   Just as man has a musical faculty and feels an inward necessity to breathe out his feelings in song ; so, by a like necessity, he in religious sighs and tears streams forth the nature of feeling as an objective, divine nature.

Religion is human nature reflected, mirrored in itself. That which exists has necessarily a pleasure, a joy in itself, loves itself, and loves itself justly ; to blame it because it loves itself is to reproach it because it exists.   To exist is to assert oneself, to affirm oneself, to love oneself ; he to whom life is a burthen rids himself of it.   Where, therefore, feeling is not depreciated and repressed, as with the Stoics, where existence is awarded to it, there also is religious power and significance already conceded to it, there also is it already exalted to that stage in which it can mirror and reflect itself, in which it can project its own image as God.   God is the mirror of man.

That which has essential value for man, which he esteems the perfect, the excellent, in which he has true delight,— that alone is God to him.   If feeling seems to thee a glorious attribute, it is then, *per se*, a divine attribute to thee.   Therefore, the feeling, sensitive man believes only in a feeling, sensitive God, *i.e.*, he believes only in the truth of his own existence and nature, for he can believe in nothing else than that which is involved in his own nature.   His faith is the consciousness of that which is holy to him ; but that alone is holy to man which lies deepest within him, which is most peculiarly his own, the basis, the essence of his individuality.   To the feeling man a God without feeling is an empty, abstract, negative God, *i.e.*, nothing ; because that is wanting to him which is precious and sacred to man. God is for man the commonplace book where he registers his highest feelings and thoughts, the genealogical tree on which are entered the names that are dearest and most sacred to him.

It is a sign of an undiscriminating good-nature, a womanish instinct, to gather together and then to preserve tenaciously all that we have gathered, not to trust anything to the waves of forgetfulness, to the chance of memory, in short not to trust ourselves and learn to know what really has value for us. The freethinker is liable to the danger of an unregulated, dissolute life. The religious man who binds together all things in one, does not lose himself in sensuality; but for that reason he is exposed to the danger of illiberality, of spiritual selfishness and greed. Therefore, to the religious man at least, the irreligious or un-religious man appears lawless, arbitrary, haughty, frivolous; not because that which is sacred to the former is not also in itself sacred to the latter, but only because that which the unreligious man holds in his head merely, the religious man places out of and above himself as an object, and hence recognises in himself the relation of a formal subordination. The religious man having a commonplace book, a nucleus of aggregation, has an aim, and having an aim he has firm standing-ground. Not mere will as such, not vague knowledge—only activity with a purpose, which is the union of theoretic and practical activity, gives man a moral basis and support, *i.e.*, character. Every man, therefore, must place before himself a God, *i.e.*, an aim, a purpose. The aim is the conscious, voluntary, essential impulse of life, the glance of genius, the focus of self-knowledge,—the unity of the material and spiritual in the individual man. He who has an aim has a law over him; he does not merely guide himself; he is guided. He who has no aim, has no home, no sanctuary; aimlessness is the greatest unhappiness. Even he who has only common aims gets on better, though he may not be better, than he who has no aim. An aim sets limits; but limits are the mentors of virtue. He who has an aim, an aim which is in itself true and essential, has, *eo ipso*, a religion, if not in the narrow sense of common pietism, yet—and this is the only point to be considered— in the sense of reason, in the sense of the universal, the only true love.

CHAPTER VI.

THE MYSTERY OF THE TRINITY AND THE MOTHER OF GOD.

IF a God without feeling, without a capability of suffering, will not suffice to man as a feeling, suffering being, neither will a God with feeling only, a God without intelligence and will. Only a being who comprises in himself the whole man can satisfy the whole man. Man's consciousness of himself in his totality is the consciousness of the Trinity. The Trinity knits together the qualities or powers which were before regarded separately into unity, and thereby reduces the universal being of the understanding, *i.e.*, God as God, to a special being, a special faculty.

That which theology designates as the image, the similitude of the Trinity, we must take as the thing itself, the essence, the archetype, the original ; by this means we shall solve the enigma. The so-called images by which it has been sought to illustrate the Trinity, and make it comprehensible, are principally : mind, understanding, memory, will, love— *mens, intellectus, memoria, voluntas, amor* or *caritas.*

God thinks, God loves ; and, moreover, he thinks, he loves himself ; the object thought, known, loved, is God himself. The objectivity of self-consciousness is the first thing we meet with in the Trinity. Self-consciousness necessarily urges itself upon man as something absolute. Existence is for him one with self-consciousness ; existence with self-consciousness is for him existence simply. If I do not know that I exist, it is all one whether I exist or not. Self-consciousness is for man—is, in fact, in itself—absolute. A God who knows not his own existence, a God without consciousness, is no God. Man cannot conceive himself as without consciousness ; hence he cannot conceive God as without it. The divine self-consciousness is nothing else than the consciousness of consciousness as an absolute or divine essence.

But this explanation is by no means exhaustive. On the contrary, we should be proceeding very arbitrarily if we sought to reduce and limit the mystery of the Trinity to the proposition just laid down. Consciousness, understanding, will, love, in the sense of abstract essences or qualities, belong only to abstract philosophy. But religion is man's consciousness of himself in his concrete or living totality, in which the identity of self-consciousness exists only as the pregnant, complete unity of *I* and *thou*.

Religion, at least the Christian, is abstraction from the world; it is essentially inward. The religious man leads a life withdrawn from the world, hidden in God, still, void of worldly joy. He separates himself from the world, not only in the ordinary sense, according to which the renunciation of the world belongs to every true, earnest man, but also in that wider sense which science gives to the word, when it calls itself world-wisdom (*welt-weisheit*); but he thus separates himself only because God is a being separate from the world, an extra and supramundane being,—*i.e.*, abstractly and philosophically expressed, the non-existence of the world. God, as an extramundane being, is however nothing else than the nature of man withdrawn from the world and concentrated in itself, freed from all worldly ties and entanglements, transporting itself above the world, and positing itself in this condition as a real objective being; or, nothing else than the consciousness of the power to abstract oneself from all that is external, and to live for and with oneself alone, under the form which this power takes in religion, namely, that of a being distinct, apart from man.* God as God, as a simple being, is the being absolutely alone, solitary—absolute solitude and self-sufficingness; for that only can be solitary which is self-sufficing. To be able to be solitary is a sign of character and thinking power. Solitude is the want of the thinker,

---

* "Dei essentia est extra omnes·creaturas, sicut ab æterno fuit Deus in se ipso ; ab omnibus ergo creaturis amorem tuum abstrahas."—John Gerhard (Medit. Sacræ, M. 31). "If thou wouldst have the Creator, thou must do without the creature. The less of the creature, the more of God. Therefore, abjure all creatures, with all their consolations."—J. Tauler (Postilla. Hamburg, 1621, p. 312). "If a man cannot say in his heart with truth : God and I are alone in the world—there is nothing else,—he has no peace in himself."—G. Arnold (Von Verschmähung der Welt. Wahre Abbild der Ersten Christen, L. 4, c. 2, § 7).

society the want of the heart. We can think alone, but we can love only with another. In love we are dependent, for it is the need of another being; we are independent only in the solitary act of thought. Solitude is self-sufficingness. But from a solitary God the essential need of duality, of love, of community, of the real, completed self-consciousness, of the *alter ego*, is excluded. This want is therefore satisfied by religion thus: in the still solitude of the Divine Being is placed another, a second, different from God as to personality, but identical with him in essence,—God the Son, in distinction from God the Father. God the Father is *I*, God the Son *Thou*. The *I* is understanding, the *Thou* love. But love with understanding and understanding with love is mind, and mind is the totality of man as such—the total man.

Participated life is alone true, self-satisfying, divine life: —this simple thought, this truth, natural, immanent in man, is the secret, the supernatural mystery of the Trinity. But religion expresses this truth, as it does every other, in an indirect manner, *i.e.*, inversely, for it here makes a general truth into a particular one, the true subject into a predicate, when it says: God is a participated life, a life of love and friendship. The third Person in the Trinity expresses nothing further than the love of the two divine Persons towards each other; it is the unity of the Son and the Father, the idea of community, strangely enough regarded in its turn as a special personal being.

The Holy Spirit owes its personal existence only to a name, a word. The earliest Fathers of the Church are well known to have identified the Spirit with the Son. Even later, its dogmatic personality wants consistency. He is the love with which God loves himself and man, and, on the other hand, he is the love with which man loves God and men. Thus he is the identity of God and man, made objective according to the usual mode of thought in religion, namely, as in itself a distinct being. But for us this unity or identity is already involved in the idea of the Father, and yet more in that of the Son. Hence we need not make the Holy Spirit a separate object of our analysis. Only this one remark further. In so far as the Holy Spirit represents the subjective phase, he is properly the representation of the religious sentiment to itself, the representation of religious emotion, of religious enthusiasm, or the personification, the rendering objective of religion in religion. The Holy Spirit is therefore the sighing creature, the yearning of the creature after God.

But that there are in fact only two Persons in the Trinity, the third representing, as has been said, only love, is involved in this, that to the strict idea of love two suffice. With two we have the principle of multiplicity and all its essential results. Two is the principle of multiplicity, and can therefore stand as its complete substitute. If several Persons were posited, the force of love would only be weakened—it would be dispersed. But love and the heart are identical; the heart is no special power; it is the man who loves, and in so far as he loves. The second Person is therefore the self-assertion of the human heart as the principle of duality, of participated life,—it is warmth; the Father is light, although light was chiefly a predicate of the Son, because in him the Godhead first became clear, comprehensible. But notwithstanding this, light as a superterrestrial element may be ascribed to the Father, the representative of the Godhead as such, the cold being of the intelligence; and warmth, as a terrestrial element, to the Son. God as the Son first gives warmth to man ; here God, from an object of the intellectual eye, of the indifferent sense of light, becomes an object of feeling, of affection, of enthusiasm, of rapture ; but only because the Son is himself nothing else than the glow of love, enthusiasm.* God as the Son is the primitive incarnation, the primitive self-renunciation of God, the negation of God in God; for as the Son he is a finite being, because he exists *ab alio,* he has a source, whereas the Father has no source, he exists *à se.* Thus in the second Person the essential attribute of the Godhead, the attribute of self-existence, is given up. But God the Father himself begets the Son; thus he renounces his rigorous, exclusive divinity; he humiliates, lowers himself, evolves within himself the principle of finiteness, of dependent existence; in the Son he becomes man, not indeed, in the first instance, as to the outward form, but as to the inward nature. And for this reason it is as the Son that God first becomes the object of man, the object of feeling, of the heart.

* "Exigit ergo Deus timeri ut Dominus, honorari ut pater, ut sponsus amari. Quid in his præstat, quid eminet ?—Amor." Bernardus (Sup. Cant. Serm. 83).

The heart comprehends only what springs from the heart. From the character of the subjective disposition and impressions the conclusion is infallible as to the character of the object. The pure, free understanding denies the Son,—not so the understanding determined by feeling, overshadowed by the heart; on the contrary, it finds in the Son the depths of the Godhead, because in him it finds feeling, which in and by itself is something dark, obscure, and therefore appears to man a mystery. The Son lays hold on the heart, because the *true* Father of the Divine Son is the human heart,* and the Son himself nothing else than the divine heart, *i.e.*, the human heart become objective to itself as a Divine Being.

A God who has not in himself the quality of finiteness, the principle of concrete existence, the essence of the feeling of dependence, is no God for a finite, concrete being. The religious man cannot love a God who has not the essence of love in himself, neither can man, or, in general, any finite being, be an object to a God who has not in himself the ground, the principle of finiteness. To such a God there is wanting the sense, the understanding, the sympathy for finiteness. How can God be the Father of men, how can he love other beings subordinate to himself, if he has not in himself a subordinate being, a Son, if he does not know what love is, so to speak, from his own experience, in relation to himself? The single man takes far less interest in the family sorrows of another than he who himself has family ties. Thus God the Father loves men only in the Son and for the sake of the Son. The love to man is derived from the love to the Son.

The Father and Son in the Trinity are therefore father and son not in a figurative sense, but in a strictly literal sense. The Father is a real father in relation to the Son, the Son is a real son in relation to the Father, or to God as the Father. The essential personal distinction between them consists only in this, that the one begets, the other is begotten. If this natural empirical condition is taken away, their personal existence and reality are annihilated. The Christians—we mean of course the Christians of former days, who would with difficulty recognise the worldly,

* Just as the *feminine* spirit of Catholicism—in distinction from Protestantism, whose principle is the masculine God, the masculine spirit—is the *Mother* of God.

frivolous, pagan Christians of the modern world as their brethren in Christ—substituted for the natural love and unity immanent in man a purely religious love and unity; they rejected the real life of the family, the intimate bond of love which is naturally moral, as an undivine, unheavenly, *i.e.,* in truth, a worthless thing. But in compensation they had a Father and Son in God, who embraced each other with heartfelt love, with that intense love which natural relationship alone inspires. On this account the mystery of the Trinity was to the ancient Christians an object of unbounded wonder, enthusiasm, and rapture, because here the satisfaction of those profoundest human wants which in reality, in life, they denied, became to them an object of contemplation in God.*

It was therefore quite in order that, to complete the divine family, the bond of love between Father and Son, a third, and that a feminine person, was received into heaven; for the personality of the Holy Spirit is a too vague and precarious, a too obviously poetic personification of the mutual love of the Father and Son, to serve as the third complementary being. It is true that the Virgin Mary was not so placed between the Father and Son as to imply that the Father had begotten the Son through her, because the sexual relation was regarded by the Christians as something unholy and sinful; but it is enough that the maternal principle was associated with the Father and Son.

It is, in fact, difficult to perceive why the Mother should be something unholy, *i.e.,* unworthy of God, when once God is Father and Son. Though it is held that the Father is not a father in the natural sense—that, on the contrary, the divine generation is quite different from the natural and human—still he remains a Father, and a real, not a nominal or symbolical Father in relation to the Son. And the idea of the Mother of God, which now appears so strange to us, is therefore not really more strange or paradoxical, than the idea of the Son of God, is not more in contradiction with the general, abstract definition of God than the Sonship. On the contrary, the Virgin Mary fits in perfectly with the relations of the Trinity, since she conceives without man the

---

* "Dum Patris et Filii proprietates communionemque delectabilem intueor, nihil delectabilius in illis invenio, quam mutuum amoris affectum." —Anselmus (in Rixner's Gesch. d. Phil. II. B. Anh. p. 18).

Son whom the Father begets without woman; * so that thus the Holy Virgin is a necessary, inherently requisite antithesis to the Father in the bosom of the Trinity. Moreover we have, if not *in concreto* and explicitly, yet *in abstracto* and implicitly, the feminine principle already in the Son. The Son is the mild, gentle, forgiving, conciliating being—the womanly sentiment of God. God, as the Father, is the generator, the active, the principle of masculine spontaneity; but the Son is begotten without himself begetting, *Deus genitus*, the passive, suffering, receptive being; he receives his existence from the Father. The Son, as a son, of course not as God, is dependent on the Father, subject to his authority. The Son is thus the feminine feeling of dependence in the Godhead; the Son implicity urges upon us the need of a real feminine being.†

The son—I mean the natural, human son—considered as such, is an intermediate being between the masculine nature of the father and the feminine nature of the mother; he is, as it were, still half a man, half a woman, inasmuch as he has not the full, rigorous consciousness of independence which characterises the man, and feels himself drawn rather to the mother than to the father. The love of the son to the mother is the first love of the masculine being for the feminine. The love of man to woman, the love of the youth for the maiden, receives its religious—its sole truly religious consecration in the love of the son to the mother; the son's love for his mother is the first yearning of man towards woman—his first humbling of himself before her.

Necessarily, therefore, the idea of the Mother of God is associated with the idea of the Son of God,—the same heart that needed the one needed the other also. Where the Son is, the Mother cannot be absent; the Son is the only-begotten of the Father, but the Mother is the concomitant of the Son. The Son is a substitute for the Mother to the Father, but not so the Father to the Son. To the

---

* "Natus est de Patre semper et matre semel; de Patre sine sexu, de matre sine usu. Apud patrem quippe defuit concipientis uterus; apud matrem defuit seminantis amplexus."—Augustinus (Serm. ad Pop. p. 372, c. 1, ed. Bened. Antw. 1701).

† In Jewish mysticism, God, according to one school, is a masculine, the Holy Spirit a feminine principle, out of whose intermixture arose the Son, and with him the world. Gfrörer, Jahrb. d. H. i. Abth. pp. 332-334. The Herrnhuters also called the Holy Spirit the mother of the Saviour.

Son the Mother is indispensable; the heart of the Son is
the heart of the Mother. Why did God become man only
through woman? Could not the Almighty have appeared
as a man amongst men in another manner—immediately?
Why did the Son betake himself to the bosom of the
Mother?* For what other reason than because the Son is
the yearning after the Mother, because his womanly, tender
heart found a corresponding expression only in a feminine
body? It is true that the Son, as a natural man, dwells
only temporarily in the shrine of this body, but the impressions which he here receives are inextinguishable; the
Mother is never out of the mind and heart of the Son. If
then the worship of the Son of God is no idolatry, the
worship of the Mother of God is no idolatry. If herein
we perceive the love of God to us, that he gave us his
only-begotten Son, *i.e.*, that which was dearest to him, for
our salvation,—we can perceive this love still better when
we find in God the beating of a mother's heart. The highest
and deepest love is the mother's love. The father consoles
himself for the loss of his son; he has a stoical principle
within him. The mother, on the contrary, is inconsolable;
she is the sorrowing element, that which cannot be indem-
nified—the true in love.

Where faith in the Mother of God sinks, there also sinks
faith in the Son of God, and in God as the Father. The
Father is a truth only where the Mother is a truth. Love
is in and by itself essentially feminine in its nature. The
belief in the love of God is the belief in the feminine principle as divine.* Love apart from living nature is an
anomaly, a phantom. Behold in love the holy necessity
and depth of Nature!

Protestantism has set aside the Mother of God; but this
deposition of woman has been severely avenged.† The
arms which it has used against the Mother of God have
turned against itself, against the Son of God, against the
whole Trinity. He who has once offered up the Mother of

* "For it could not have been difficult or impossible to God to bring his
Son into the world without a mother; but it was his will to use the
woman for that end."—Luther (Th. ii. p. 348).

† In the Concordienbuch, Erklär. Art. 8, and in the Apol. of the Augsburg Confession, Mary is nevertheless still called the "Blessed Virgin, who
was truly the Mother of God, and yet remained a virgin,"—"worthy of all
honour."

God to the understanding, is not far from sacrificing the mystery of the Son of God as an anthropomorphism. The anthropomorphism is certainly veiled when the feminine being is excluded, but only veiled—not removed. It is true that Protestantism had no need of the heavenly bride, because it received with open arms the earthly bride. But for that very reason it ought to have been consequent and courageous enough to give up not only the Mother, but the Son and the Father. Only he who has no earthly parents needs heavenly ones. The triune God is the God of Catholicism; he has a profound, heartfelt, necessary, truly religious significance, only in antithesis to the negation of all substantial bonds, in antithesis to the life of the anchorite, the monk, and the nun.* The triune God has a substantial meaning only where there is an abstraction from the substance of real life. The more empty life is, the fuller, the more concrete is God. The impoverishing of the real world and the enriching of God is one act. Only the poor man has a rich God. God springs out of the feeling of a want; what man is in need of, whether this be a definite and therefore conscious, or an unconscious need,—that is God. Thus the disconsolate feeling of a void, of loneliness, needed a God in whom there is society, a union of beings fervently loving each other.

Here we have the true explanation of the fact that the Trinity has in modern times lost first its practical, and ultimately its theoretical significance.

---

* "Sit monachus quasi Melchisedec sine patre, sine matre, sine genealogia : neque patrem sibi vocet super terram. Imo sic existimet, quasi ipse sit solus et Deus. (Specul. Monach. Pseudo-Bernard.) Melchisedec . . . refertur ad exemplum, ut tanquam sine patre et sine matre sacerdos esse debeat."—Ambrosius.

CHAPTER VII.

THE MYSTERY OF THE LOGOS AND DIVINE IMAGE.

THE essential significance of the Trinity is, however, concentrated in the idea of the second Person. The warm interest of Christians in the Trinity has been, in the main, only an interest in the Son of God.* The fierce contention concerning the *Homousios* and *Homoiousios* was not an empty one, although it turned upon a letter. The point in question was the co-equality and divine dignity of the second Person, and therefore the honour of the Christian religion itself; for its essential, characteristic object is the second Person; and that which is essentially the object of a religion is truly, essentially its God. The real God of any religion is the so-called Mediator, because he alone is the immediate object of religion. He who, instead of applying to God, applies to a saint, does so only on the assumption that the saint has all power with God, that what he prays for, *i.e.*, wishes and wills, God readily performs; that thus God is entirely in the hands of the saint. Supplication is the means, under the guise of humility and submission, of exercising one's power and superiority over another being. That to which my mind first turns is also, in truth, the first being to me. I turn to the saint, not because the saint is dependent on God, but because God is dependent on the saint, because God is determined and ruled by the prayers, *i.e.*, by the wish or heart of the saint. The distinctions which the Catholic theologians made between *latreia, doulia,* and *hyperdoulia*, are absurd, groundless sophisms. The God in the background of the Mediator is only an abstract, inert conception, the conception or idea of the Godhead in general; and it is not to reconcile us with this idea, but to remove it to a distance, to negative it, because it is no

* "Negas ergo Deum, si non omnia filio, quæ Dei sunt, deferentur."—Ambrosius de Fide ad Gratianum, l. iii. c. 7. On the same ground the Latin Church adhered so tenaciously to the dogma that the Holy Spirit proceeded not from the Father alone, as the Greek Church maintained, but from the Son also. See on this subject J. G. Walchii, Hist. Contr. Gr. et Lat. de Proc. Spir. S. Jenæ, 1751.

object for religion, that the Mediator interposes.* God above the Mediator is nothing else than the cold understanding above the heart, like Fate above the Olympic gods. Man, as an emotional and sensuous being, is governed and made happy only by images, by sensible representations. Mind presenting itself as at once type-creating, emotional, and sensuous, is the imagination. The second Person in God, who is in truth the first person in religion, is the nature of the imagination made objective. The definitions of the second Person are principally images or symbols; and these images do not proceed from man's incapability of conceiving the object otherwise than symbolically,—which is an altogether false interpretation,—but the thing cannot be conceived otherwise than symbolically because the thing itself is a symbol or image. The Son is, therefore, expressly called the Image of God; his essence is that he is an image —the representation of God, the visible glory of the invisible God. The Son is the satisfaction of the need for mental images, the nature of the imaginative activity in man made objective as an absolute, divine activity. Man makes to himself an image of God, *i.e.*, he converts the abstract being of the reason, the being of the thinking power, into an object of sense or imagination.† But he places this image in God himself, because his want would not be satisfied if he did not regard this image as an objective reality, if it were nothing more for him than a subjective image, separate from God,—a mere figment devised by man. And it is in fact no devised, no arbitrary image; for it expresses the necessity of the imagination, the necessity of affirming the imagination as a divine power. The Son is the reflected splendour of the imagination, the image dearest to the heart; but for the very reason that he is only an object of the imagination, he is only the nature of the imagination made objective.‡

---

* This is expressed very significantly in the Incarnation. God renounces, denies his majesty, power, and affinity, in order to become a man ; *i.e.*, man denies the God who is not himself a man, and only affirms the God who affirms man. *Exinanivit*, says St. Bernard, *majestate et potentia, non bonitate et misericordia.* That which cannot be renounced, cannot be denied, is thus the Divine goodness and mercy, *i.e.*, the self-affirmation of the human heart.

† It is obvious that the Image of God has also another signification, namely, that the personal, visible man is God himself. But here the image is considered simply as an image.

‡ Let the reader only consider, for example, the Transfiguration, the Resurrection, and the Ascension of Christ.

It is clear from this how blinded by prejudice dogmatic speculation is, when, entirely overlooking the inward genesis of the Son of God as the Image of God, it demonstrates the Son as a metaphysical *ens*, as an object of thought, whereas the Son is a declension, a falling off from the metaphysical idea of the Godhead;—a falling off, however, which religion naturally places in God himself, in order to justify it, and not to feel it as a falling off. The Son is the chief and ultimate principle of image-worship, for he is the image of God; and the image necessarily takes the place of the thing. The adoration of the saint in his image is the adoration of the image as the saint. Wherever the image is the essential expression, the organ of religion, there also it is the essence of religion.

The Council of Nice adduced, amongst other grounds for the religious use of images, the authority of Gregory of Nyssa, who said that he could never look at an image which represented the sacrifice of Isaac without being moved to tears, because it so vividly brought before him that event in sacred history. But the effect of the represented object is not the effect of the object as such, but the effect of the representation. The holy object is simply the haze of holiness in which the image veils its mysterious power. The religious object is only a pretext, by means of which art or imagination can exercise its dominion over men unhindered. For the religious consciousness, it is true, the sacredness of the image is associated, and necessarily so, only with the sacredness of the object; but the religious consciousness is not the measure of truth. Indeed, the Church itself, while insisting on the distinction between the image and the object of the image, and denying that the worship is paid to the image, has at the same time made at least an indirect admission of the truth, by itself declaring the sacredness of the image.*

But the ultimate, highest principle of image-worship is the worship of the Image of God in God. The Son, who is the "brightness of his glory, the express image of his person," is the entrancing splendour of the imagination, which only manifests itself in visible images. Both to inward and outward contemplation the representation of

* "Sacram imaginem Domini nostri Jesu Christi et omnium Salvatoris æquo honore cum libro sanctorum evangeliorum adorari decernimus . . . Dignum est enim ut . . . propter honorem qui ad principia refertur, etiam derivative imagines honorentur et adorentur."—Gener. Const. Conc. viii. Art. 10, Can. 3.

Christ, the Image of God, was the image of images. The images of the saints are only optical multiplications of one and the same image. The speculative deduction of the Image of God is therefore nothing more than an unconscious deduction and establishing of image-worship: for the sanction of the principle is also the sanction of its necessary consequences; the sanction of the archetype is the sanction of its semblance. If God has an image of himself, why should not I have an image of God? If God loves his Image as himself, why should not I also love the Image of God as I love God himself? If the Image of God is God himself, why should not the image of the saint be the saint himself? If it is no superstition to believe that the image which God makes of himself is no image, no mere conception, but a substance, a person, why should it be a superstition to believe that the image of the saint is the sensitive substance of the saint? The Image of God weeps and bleeds; why then should not the image of a saint also weep and bleed? Does the distinction lie in the fact that the image of the saint is a product of the hands? Why, the hands did not make this image, but the mind which animated the hands, the imagination; and if God makes an image of himself, that also is only a product of the imagination. Or does the distinction proceed from this, that the Image of God is produced by God himself, whereas the image of the saint is made by another? Why, the image of the saint is also a product of the saint himself: for he appears to the artist; the artist only represents him as he appears.

Connected with the nature of the image is another definition of the second Person, namely, that he is the Word of God.

A word is an abstract image, the imaginary thing, or, in so far as everything is ultimately an object of the thinking power, it is the imagined thought: hence men, when they know the word, the name for a thing, fancy that they know the thing also. Words are a result of the imagination. Sleepers who dream vividly and invalids who are delirious speak. The power of speech is a poetic talent. Brutes do not speak because they have no poetic faculty. Thought expresses itself only by images; the power by which thought expresses itself is the imagination; the imagination expressing itself is speech. He who speaks, lays under a spell, fascinates those to whom he speaks; but the power of words is the power of the imagination.

Therefore to the ancients, as children of the imagination, the Word was a being—a mysterious, magically powerful being. Even the Christians, and not only the vulgar among them, but also the learned, the Fathers of the Church, attached to the mere *name* Christ, mysterious powers of healing.* And in the present day the common people still believe that it is possible to bewitch men by mere words. Whence comes this ascription of imaginary influences to words? Simply from this, that words themselves are only a result of the imagination, and hence have the effect of a narcotic on man, imprison him under the power of the imagination. Words possess a revolutionising force; words govern mankind. Words are held sacred; while the *things* of reason and truth are decried.

The affirming or making objective of the nature of the imagination is therefore directly connected with the affirming or making objective of the nature of speech, of the word. Man has not only an instinct, an internal necessity, which impels him to think, to perceive, to imagine; he has also the impulse to speak, to utter, impart his thoughts. A divine impulse this—a divine power, the power of words. The word is the imaged, revealed, radiating, lustrous, enlightening thought. The word is the light of the world. The word guides to all truth, unfolds all mysteries, reveals the unseen, makes present the past and the future, defines the infinite, perpetuates the transient. Men pass away, the word remains; the word is life and truth. All power is given to the word: the word makes the blind see and the lame walk, heals the sick, and brings the dead to life;— the word works miracles, and the only rational miracles. The word is the gospel, the paraclete of mankind. To convince thyself of the divine nature of speech, imagine thyself alone and forsaken, yet acquainted with language; and imagine thyself further hearing for the first time the word of a human being: would not this word seem to thee angelic? would it not sound like the voice of God himself, like heavenly music? Words are not really less rich, less pregnant than music, though music seems to say more, and appears deeper and richer than words, for this reason simply, that it is invested with that prepossession, that illusion.

* " Tanta certe vis nomini Jesu inest contra dæmones, ut nonnunquam etiam a malis nominatum sit efficax."—Origenes adv. Celsum, l. i. ; see also l. iii.

The word has power to redeem, to reconcile, to bless, to make free. The sins which we confess are forgiven us by virtue of the divine power of the word. The dying man who gives forth in speech his long-concealed sins departs reconciled. The forgiveness of sins lies in the confession of sins. The sorrows which we confide to our friend are already half healed. Whenever we speak of a subject, the passions which it has excited in us are allayed ; we see more clearly ; the object of anger, of vexation, of sorrow, appears to us in a light in which we perceive the unworthiness of those passions. If we are in darkness and doubt on any matter, we need only speak of it ;—often in the very moment in which we open our lips to consult a friend, the doubts and difficulties disappear. The word makes man free. He who cannot express himself is a slave. Hence, excessive passion, excessive joy, excessive grief, are speechless. To speak is an act of freedom ; the word is freedom. Justly therefore is language held to be the root of culture ; where language is cultivated, man is cultivated. The barbarism of the Middle Ages disappeared before the revival of language.

As we can conceive nothing else as a Divine Being than the Rational which we think, the Good which we love, the Beautiful which we perceive ; so we know no higher spiritually operative power and expression of power than the power of the Word.* God is the sum of all reality. All that man feels or knows as a reality he must place in God or regard as God. Religion must therefore be conscious of the power of the word as a divine power. The Word of God is the divinity of the word, as it becomes an object to man within the sphere of religion,—the true nature of the human word. The Word of God is supposed to be distinguished from the human word in that it is no transient breath, but an imparted being. But does not the word of man also contain the being of man, his imparted self,—at least when it is a true word ? Thus religion takes the *appearance* of the human word for its essence ; hence it necessarily conceives the true nature of the Word to be a special being, distinct from the human word.

* "God reveals himself to us, as the Speaker, who has, in himself, an eternal uncreated Word, whereby he created the world and all things, with slight labour, namely, with speech, so that to God it is not more difficult to create than it is to us to name."—Luther, Th. i. p. 302.

CHAPTER VIII.

THE MYSTERY OF THE COSMOGONICAL PRINCIPLE IN GOD.

THE second Person, as God revealing, manifesting, declaring himself (*Deus se dicit*), is the world-creating principle in God. But this means nothing else than that the second Person is intermediate between the noumenal nature of God and the phenomenal nature of the world, that he is the divine principle of the finite, of that which is distinguished from God. The second Person as begotten, as not *à se*, not existing of himself, has the fundamental condition of the finite in himself.* But at the same time, he is not yet a real finite Being, posited out of God; on the contrary, he is still identical with God,—as identical as the son is with the father, the son being indeed another person, but still of like nature with the father. The second Person, therefore, does not represent to us the pure idea of the Godhead, but neither does he represent the pure idea of humanity, or of reality in general : he is an intermediate Being between the two opposites. The opposition of the noumenal or invisible divine nature and the phenomenal or visible nature of the world, is, however, nothing else than the opposition between the nature of abstraction and the nature of perception; but that which connects abstraction with perception is the imagination : consequently, the transition from God to the world by means of the second Person, is only the form in which religion makes objective the transition from abstraction to perception by means of the imagination. It is the imagination alone by which man neutralises the opposition between God and the world. All religious cosmogonies are products of the' imagination. Every being, intermediate between God and the world, let it be defined

* " Hylarius . . . Si quis innascibilem et sine initio dicat filium, quasi duo sine principio et duo innascibilia, et duo innata dicens, duos faciat Deos, anathema sit. Caput autem quod est principium Christi, Deus. . . . Filium innascibilem confiteri impiissimum est."—Petrus Lomb. Sent. l. i. dist. 31, c. 4.

how it may, is a being of the imagination. The psychological truth and necessity which lies at the foundation of all these theogonies and cosmogonies is the truth and necessity of the imagination as a middle term between the abstract and concrete. And the task of philosophy in investigating this subject is to comprehend the relation of the imagination to the reason,—the genesis of the image by means of which an object of thought becomes an object of sense, of feeling.

But the nature of the imagination is the complete, exhaustive truth of the cosmogonic principle, only where the antithesis of God and the world expresses nothing but the indefinite antithesis of the noumenal, invisible, incomprehensible being, God, and the visible, tangible existence of the world. If, on the other hand, the cosmogonic being is conceived and expressed abstractly, as is the case in religious speculation, we have also to recognise a more abstract psychological truth as its foundation.

The world is not God ; it is other than God, the opposite of God, or at least that which is different from God. But that which is different from God cannot have come immediately from God, but only from a distinction of God in God. The second Person is God distinguishing himself from himself in himself, setting himself opposite to himself, hence being an object to himself. The self-distinguishing of God from himself is the ground of that which is different from himself, and thus self-consciousness is the origin of the world. God first thinks the world in thinking himself : to think oneself is to beget oneself, to think the world is to create the world. Begetting precedes creating. The idea of the production of the world, of another being who is *not* God, is attained through the idea of the production of another being who is *like* God.

This cosmogonical process is nothing else than the mystic paraphrase of a psychological process, nothing else than the unity of consciousness and self-consciousness made objective. God thinks himself :—thus he is self-conscious. God is self-consciousness posited as an object, as a being ; but inasmuch as he knows himself, thinks himself, he also thinks another than himself ; for to know oneself is to distinguish oneself from another, whether this be a possible, merely conceptional, or a real being. Thus the world—at least the possibility, the idea of the world—is posited with consciousness, or rather conveyed in it. The Son, *i.e.*, God thought by himself, objective to himself, the original reflection of God, the other God, is the principle of creation. The truth which lies at the foundation of this is the nature of man : the identity of his self-consciousness with his consciousness of another who is identical with himself, and of another who is not identical with himself. And the second, the other who is of like nature, is necessarily the middle term between the first and third. The idea of another in general, of one who is essentially different from me, arises to me first through the idea of one who is essentially like me.

Consciousness of the world is the consciousness of my limitation : if I knew nothing of a world, I should know nothing of limits ; but the consciousness of my limitation stands in contradiction with the impulse of my egoism towards unlimitedness. Thus from egoism conceived as absolute (God is the absolute Self) I cannot pass immediately to its opposite; I must introduce, prelude, moderate this contradiction by the consciousness of a being who is indeed another, and in so far gives me the perception of my limitation, but in such a way as at the same time to affirm my own nature, make my nature objective to me. The consciousness of the world is a humiliating consciousness; the creation was an " act of humility;" but the first stone against which the pride of egoism stumbles is the *thou*, the *alter ego*. The *ego* first steels its glance in the eye of a *thou* before it endures the contemplation of a being which does not reflect its own image. My fellow-man is the bond between me and the world. I am, and I feel myself, dependent on the world, because I first feel myself dependent on other men. If I did not need man, I should not need the world. I reconcile myself with the world only through my fellow-man. Without other men, the world would be for me not only dead and empty, but meaningless. Only through his fellow does man become clear to himself and self-conscious ; but only when I am clear to myself does the world become clear to me. A man existing absolutely alone would lose himself without any sense of his individuality in the ocean of Nature ; he would neither comprehend himself as man nor Nature as Nature. The first object of man is man. The sense of Nature, which opens to us the consciousness of the world as a world, is a later product; for it first arises through the distinction of man from himself. The natural philosophers of Greece were preceded by the so-called seven Sages, whose wisdom had immediate reference to human life only.

The *ego*, then, attains to consciousness of the world through consciousness of the *thou*. Thus man is the God of man. That he is, he has to thank Nature; that he is man, he has to thank man; spiritually as well as physically he can achieve nothing without his fellow-man. Four hands can do more than two, but also four eyes can see more than two. And this combined power is distinguished not only in quantity but also in quality from that which is solitary. In isolation human power is limited, in combination it is infinite. The knowledge of a single man is limited, but reason, science, is unlimited, for it is a common act of mankind; and it is so, not only because innumerable men co-operate in the construction of science, but also in the more profound sense, that the scientific genius of a particular age comprehends in itself the thinking powers of the preceding age, though it modifies them in accordance with its own special character. Wit, acumen, imagination, feeling as distinguished from sensation, reason as a subjective faculty,—all these so-called powers of the soul are powers of humanity, not of man as an individual; they are products of culture, products of human society. Only where man has contact and friction with his fellow-man are wit and sagacity kindled; hence there is more wit in the town than in the country, more in great towns than in small ones. Only where man suns and warms himself in the proximity of man arise feeling and imagination. Love, which requires mutuality, is the spring of poetry; and only where man communicates with man, only in speech, a social act, awakes reason. To ask a question and to answer are the first acts of thought. Thought originally demands two. It is not until man has reached an advanced stage of culture that he can double himself, so as to play the part of another within himself. To think and to speak are therefore, with all ancient and sensuous nations, identical; they think only in speaking; their thought is only conversation. The common people, *i.e.*, people in whom the power of abstraction has not been developed, are still incapable of understanding what is written if they do not read it audibly, if they do not pronounce what they read. In this point of view Hobbes correctly enough derives the understanding of man from his ears !

Reduced to abstract logical categories, the creative principle in God expresses nothing further than the tautological proposition : the different can only proceed from a principle of difference, not from a simple being. However the Christian philosophers and theologians insisted on the creation of the world out of nothing, they were unable altogether to evade the old axiom—" Nothing comes ·from nothing," because it expresses a law of thought. It is true that they supposed no real matter as the principle of the diversity of material things, but they made the divine understanding (and the Son is the wisdom, the science, the understanding of the Father)—as that which comprehends within itself all things as *spiritual matter*—the principle of real matter. The distinction between the heathen eternity of matter and the Christian creation in this respect is only that the heathens ascribed to the world a real, objective eternity, whereas the Christians gave it an invisible, immaterial eternity. Things were before they existed positively, —not, indeed, as an object of sense, but of the subjective understanding. The Christians, whose principle is that of absolute subjectivity, conceive all things as effected only through this principle. The matter posited by their subjective thought, conceptional, subjective matter, is therefore to them the first matter,—far more excellent than real, objective matter. Nevertheless, this distinction is only a distinction in the mode of existence. The world is eternal in God. Or did it spring up in him as a sudden idea, a caprice ? Certainly man can conceive this too ; but, in doing so, he deifies nothing but his own irrationality. If, on the contrary, I abide by reason, I can only derive the world from its essence, its idea, *i.e.*, one mode of its existence from another mode ; in other words, I can derive the world only from itself. The world has its basis in itself, as has everything in the world which has a claim to the name of species. The *differentia specifica*, the peculiar character, that by which a given being is what it is, is always in the ordinary sense inexplicable, undeducible, is through itself, has its cause in itself.

The distinction between the world and God as the creator of the world is therefore only a formal one. The nature of God—for the divine understanding, that which comprehends

within itself all things, is the divine nature itself; hence
God, inasmuch as he thinks and knows himself, thinks and
knows at the same time the world and all things—the
nature of God is nothing else than the abstract, *thought*
nature of the world; the nature of the world nothing else
than the real, concrete, perceptible nature of God. Hence
creation is nothing more than a formal act; for that which,
before the creation, was an object of thought, of the understanding, is by creation simply made an object of sense, its
ideal contents continuing the same; although it remains
absolutely inexplicable how a real material thing can spring
out of a pure thought.*

So it is with plurality and difference—if we reduce the
world to these abstract categories—in opposition to the
unity and identity of the Divine nature. Real difference
can be derived only from a being which has a principle of
difference in itself. But I posit difference in the original
being, because I have originally found difference as a positive
reality. Wherever difference is in itself nothing, there also
no difference is conceived in the principle of things. I posit
difference as an essential category, as a truth, where I derive
it from the original being, and *vice versâ*: the two propositions are identical. The rational expression is this: Difference lies as necessarily in the reason as identity.

But as difference is a positive condition of the reason, I
cannot deduce it without presupposing it; I cannot explain
it except by itself, because it is an original, self-luminous,
self-attesting reality. Through what means arises the
world, that which is distinguished from God? through the
distinguishing of God from himself in himself. God thinks
himself, he is an object to himself; he distinguishes himself
from himself. Hence this distinction, the world, arises
only from a distinction of another kind, the external distinction from an internal one, the static distinction from a
dynamic one,—from an *act* of distinction: thus I establish
difference only through itself, *i.e.*, it is an original concept,
a *ne plus ultra* of my thought, a law, a necessity, a truth.
The last distinction that I can think is the distinction of a
being from and in itself. The distinction of one being from

---

* It is therefore mere self-delusion to suppose that the hypothesis of a
creation explains the existence of the world.

another is self-evident, is already implied in their existence, is a palpable truth : they are two. But I first establish difference for thought when I discern it in one and the same being, when I unite it with the law of identity. Herein lies the ultimate truth of difference. The cosmogonic principle in God, reduced to its last elements, is nothing else than the act of thought in its simplest forms made objective. If I remove difference from God, he gives me no material for thought ; he ceases to be an object of thought ; for difference is an essential principle of thought. And if I consequently place difference in God, what else do I establish, what else do I make an object, than the truth and necessity of this principle of thought ?

CHAPTER IX.

THE MYSTERY OF MYSTICISM, OR OF NATURE IN GOD.

INTERESTING material for the criticism of cosmogonic and theogonic fancies is furnished in the doctrine—revived by Schelling and drawn from Jacob Böhme—of eternal Nature in God.

God is pure spirit, clear self-consciousness, moral personality; Nature, on the contrary, is, at least partially, confused, dark, desolate, immoral, or to say no more, unmoral. But it is self-contradictory that the impure should proceed from the pure, darkness from light. How then can we remove these obvious difficulties in the way of assigning a divine origin to Nature ? Only by positing this impurity, this darkness in God, by distinguishing in God himself a principle of light and a principle of darkness. In other words, we can only explain the origin of darkness by renouncing the idea of origin, and presupposing darkness as existing from the beginning.*

But that which is dark in Nature is the irrational, the material, Nature strictly, as distinguished from intelligence. Hence the simple meaning of this doctrine is, that Nature, Matter, cannot be explained as a result of intelligence ; on the contrary, it is the basis of intelligence, the basis of personality, without itself having any basis ; spirit without Nature is an unreal abstraction ; consciousness develops itself only out of Nature. But this materialistic doctrine is veiled in a mystical yet attractive obscurity, inasmuch as it is not expressed in the clear, simple language of reason, but emphatically enunciated in that consecrated word of the emotions—God. If the light in God springs out of the

---

* It is beside our purpose to criticise this crass mystical theory. We merely remark here, that darkness can be explained only when it is derived from light; that the derivation of the darkness in Nature from light appears an impossibility only when it is not perceived that even in darkness there is a residue of light, that the darkness in Nature is not an absolute, but a modified darkness, tempered by light.

darkness in God, this is only because it is involved in the idea of light in general, that it illuminates darkness, thus presupposing darkness, not making it. If then God is once subjected to a general law,—as he must necessarily be unless he be made the arena of conflict for the most senseless notions,—if self-consciousness in God as well as in itself, as in general, is evolved from a principle in Nature, why is not this natural principle abstracted from God? That which is a law of consciousness in itself is a law for the consciousness of every personal being, whether man, angel, demon, God, or whatever else thou mayest conceive to thyself as a being. To what then, seen in their true light, do the two principles in God reduce themselves? The one to Nature, at least to Nature as it exists in the conception, abstracted from its reality ; the other to mind, consciousness, personality. The one half, the reverse side, thou dost not name God, but only the obverse side, on which he presents to thee mind, consciousness : thus his specific essence, that whereby he is *God*, is mind, intelligence, consciousness. Why then dost thou make that which is properly the subject in God as God, *i.e.*, as mind, into a mere predicate, as if God existed as God apart from mind, from consciousness? Why, but because thou art enslaved by mystical religious speculation, because the primary principle in thee is the imagination, thought being only secondary and serving but to throw into formulæ the products of the imagination,—because thou feelest at ease and at home only in the deceptive twilight of mysticism.

Mysticism is deuteroscopy—a fabrication of phrases having a double meaning. The mystic speculates concerning the essence of Nature or of man, but under, and by means of, the supposition that he is speculating concerning another, a personal being, distinct from both. The mystic has the same objects as the plain, self-conscious thinker ; but the real object is regarded by the mystic, not as itself, but as an imaginary being, and hence the imaginary object is to him the real object. Thus here, in the mystical doctrine of the two principles in God, the real object is pathology, the imaginary one, theology ; *i.e.*, pathology is converted into theology. There would be nothing to urge against this, if consciously real pathology were recognised and expressed as theology ; indeed, it is precisely our task to show that theology is nothing else than an unconscious, esoteric pathology, anthropology, and psychology, and that therefore real anthropology, real pathology, and real psychology have far more claim to the name of theology than has theology itself, because this is nothing more than an imaginary psychology and anthropology. But this doctrine or theory is supposed—and for this reason it is mystical and fantastic—to be not pathology, but theology, in the old or ordinary sense of the word; it is supposed that we have here unfolded to us the life of a Being distinct from us, while nevertheless it is only our own nature which is unfolded, though at the same time again shut up from us by the fact that this nature is represented as inhering in another being. The mystic philosopher supposes that in God, not in us human individuals,—that would be far too trivial a truth,—reason first appears after the Passion of Nature ;—that not man, but God, has wrestled himself out of the obscurity of confused feelings and impulses into the clearness of knowledge ; that not in our subjective, limited mode of conception, but in God himself, the nervous tremors of darkness precede the joyful consciousness of light; in short, he supposes that his theory presents not a history of human throes, but a history of the development, *i.e.*, the throes of God—for developments (or transitions) are birth-struggles. But, alas! this supposition itself belongs only to the pathological element.

If, therefore, the cosmogonic process presents to us the Light of the power of distinction as belonging to the divine essence; so, on the other hand, the Night or Nature in God represents to us the *Pensées confuses* of Leibnitz as divine powers. But the *Pensées confuses*—confused, obscure conceptions and thoughts, or more correctly images—represent the flesh, matter ;—a pure intelligence, separate from matter, has only clear, free thoughts, no obscure, *i.e.*, fleshly ideas, no material images, exciting the imagination and setting the blood in commotion. The Night in God, therefore, implies nothing else than this : God is not only a spiritual, but also a material, corporeal, fleshly being ; but as man is man, and receives his designation, in virtue not of his fleshly nature, but of his mind, so is it with God.

But the mystic philosopher expresses this only in obscure, mystical, indefinite, dissembling images. Instead of the rude, but hence all the more precise and striking expression, *flesh,* it substitutes the equivocal, abstract words *nature* and *ground.* "As nothing is before or out of God, he must have the ground of his existence in himself. This all philosophies say, but they speak of this ground as a mere idea, without making it something real. This ground of his existence which God has in himself, is not God considered absolutely, *i.e.,* in so far as he exists; it is only the ground of his existence. It is Nature—in God; an existence inseparable from him, it is true, but still distinct. Analogically (?), this relation may be illustrated by gravitation and light in Nature." But this ground is the *non-intelligent* in God. "That which is the commencement of an intelligence (in itself) cannot also be intelligent." "In the strict sense, intelligence is born of this unintelligent principle. Without this antecedent darkness there is no reality of the Creator." "With abstract ideas of God as *actus purissimus,* such as were laid down by the older philosophy, or such as the modern, out of anxiety to remove God far from Nature, is always reproducing, we can effect nothing. God is something more real than a mere moral order of the world, and has quite another and a more living motive power in himself than is ascribed to him by the jejune subtilty of abstract idealists. Idealism, if it has not a living realism as its basis, is as empty and abstract a system as that of Leibnitz or Spinoza, or as any other dogmatic system." "So long as the God of modern theism remains the simple, supposed purely essential, but in fact non-essential Being that all modern systems make him, so long as a real duality is not recognised in God, and a limiting, negativing force, opposed to the expansive affirming force, so long will the denial of a personal God be scientific honesty." "All consciousness is concentration, is a gathering together, a collecting of oneself. This negativing force, by which a being turns back upon itself, is the true force of personality, the force of egoism." "How should there be a fear of God if there were no strength in him? But that there should be something in God which is mere force and strength cannot be held astonishing if only it be not maintained that he is this alone and nothing besides."*

* Schelling, Ueber das Wesen der Menschlichen Freiheit, 429, 432, 427. Denkmal Jacobi's, s. 82, 97–99.

But what then is force and strength which is merely such, if not corporeal force and strength? Dost thou know any power which stands at thy command, in distinction from the power of kindness and reason, besides muscular power? If thou canst effect nothing through kindness and the arguments of reason, force is what thou must take refuge in. But canst thou "effect" anything without strong arms and fists? Is there known to thee, in distinction from the power of the moral order of the world, "another and more living motive power" than the lever of the criminal court? Is not Nature without body also an "empty, abstract" idea, a "jejune subtilty"? Is not the mystery of Nature the mystery of corporeality? Is not the system of a "living realism" the system of the organised body? Is there, in general, any other force, the opposite of intelligence, than the force of flesh and blood,—any other strength of Nature than the strength of the fleshly impulses? And the strongest of the impulses of Nature, is it not the sexual feeling? Who does not remember the old proverb: "*Amare et sapere vix Deo competit?*" So that if we would posit in God a nature, an existence opposed to the light of intelligence,—can we think of a more living, a more real antithesis, than that of *amare* and *sapere*, of spirit and flesh, of freedom and the sexual impulse?

Personality, individuality, consciousness, without Nature, is nothing; or, which is the same thing, an empty, unsubstantial abstraction. But Nature, as has been shown and is obvious, is nothing without corporeality. The body alone is that negativing, limiting, concentrating, circumscribing force, without which no personality is conceivable. Take away from thy personality its body, and thou takest away that which holds it together. The body is the basis, the subject of personality. Only by the body is a real personality distinguished from the imaginary one of a spectre. What sort of abstract, vague, empty personalities should we be, if we had not the property of impenetrability,—if in the same place, in the same form in which we are, others might stand at the same time? Only by the exclusion of others from the space it occupies does personality prove itself to be real. But a body does not exist without flesh and blood. Flesh and blood is life, and life alone is corporeal reality. But flesh and blood is nothing without the oxygen of sexual distinction. The distinction of sex is not superficial, or limited to certain parts of the body; it is an essential one: it penetrates bones and marrow. The substance of man is manhood; that of woman, womanhood. However spiritual and supersensual the man may be, he remains always a man; and it is the same with the woman. Hence personality is nothing without distinction of sex; personality is essentially distinguished into masculine and feminine. Where there is no *thou*, there is no *I;* but the distinction between *I* and *thou*, the fundamental condition of all personality, of all consciousness, is only real, living, ardent, when felt as the distinction between man and woman. The *thou* between man and woman has quite another sound than the monotonous *thou* between friends.

Nature in distinction from personality can signify nothing else than difference of sex. A personal being apart from Nature is nothing else than a being without sex, and conversely. Nature is said to be predicated of God, "in the sense in which it is said of a man that he is of a strong, healthy nature." But what is more feeble, what more insupportable, what more contrary to Nature, than a person without sex, or a person who in character, manners, or feelings denies sex? What is virtue, the excellence of man as man? Manhood. Of man as woman? Womanhood. But man exists only as man and woman. The strength, the healthiness of man consists therefore in this: that as a woman, he be truly woman; as man, truly man. Thou repudiatest "the horror of all that is real, which supposes the spiritual to be polluted by contact with the real." Repudiate then, before all, thy own horror for the distinction of sex. If God is not polluted by Nature, neither is he polluted by being associated with the idea of sex. In renouncing sex, thou renouncest thy whole principle. A moral God apart from Nature is without basis; but the basis of morality is the distinction of sex. Even the brute is capable of self-sacrificing love in virtue of the sexual distinction. All the glory of Nature, all its power, all its wisdom and profundity, concentrates and individualises itself in distinction of sex. Why then dost thou shrink from naming the nature of God by its true name? Evidently, only because thou hast a general horror of things in their truth and reality; because thou lookest at all things through the deceptive vapours of mysticism. For this very reason then, because Nature in God is only a delusive, unsubstantial appearance, a fantastic ghost of Nature,—for it is based, as we have said, not on flesh and blood, not on a real ground,—this attempt to establish a personal God is once more a failure, and I, too, conclude with the words, " The denial of a personal God will be scientific honesty :"—and, I add, scientific truth, so long as it is not declared and shown in unequivocal terms, first *à priori*, on speculative grounds, that form, place, corporeality, and sex do not contradict the idea of the Godhead; and secondly, *à posteriori*,—for the reality of a personal being is sustained only on empirical grounds,—what sort of form God has, where he exists,—in heaven,—and lastly, of what sex he is.

Let the profound, speculative religious philosophers of Germany courageously shake off the embarrassing remnant of rationalism which yet clings to them, in flagrant contradiction with their true character; and let them complete their system, by converting the mystical " potence " of Nature in God into a really powerful, generating God.

The doctrine of Nature in God is borrowed from Jacob Böhme. But in the original it has a far deeper and more interesting significance than in its second modernised and emasculated edition. Jacob Böhme has a profoundly religious mind. Religion is the centre of his life and thought. But at the same time, the significance which has been given to Nature in modern times—by the study of natural science, by Spinozism, materialism, empiricism—has taken possession of his religious sentiment. He has opened his senses to Nature, thrown a glance into her mysterious being ; but it alarms him, and he cannot harmonise this terror at Nature with his religious conceptions. " When I looked into the great depths of this world, and at the sun and stars, also at the clouds, also at the rain and snow, and considered in my mind the whole creation of this world ; then I found in all things evil and good, love and anger,—in unreasoning things, such as wood, stone, earth, and the elements, as well as in men and beasts. . . . But because I found that in all things there was good and evil, in the elements as well as in the creatures, and that it goes as well in the world with the godless as with the pious, also that the barbarous nations possess the best lands, and have more prosperity than the godly; I was therefore altogether melancholy and extremely troubled, and the Scriptures could not console me, though almost all well known to me; and therewith assuredly the devil was not idle, for he often thrust upon me heathenish thoughts, of which I will here be silent." * But while his mind seized with fearful earnestness the dark side of Nature, which did not harmonise with the religious idea of a heavenly Creator, he was on the other hand rapturously affected by her resplendent aspects. Jacob Böhme has a sense for Nature. He preconceives, nay, he feels the joys of the mineralogist, of the botanist, of the chemist—the joys of "godless natural science." He is enraptured by the splendour of jewels, the tones of metals, the hues and odours of plants, the beauty and gentleness of many animals. In another place, speaking of the revelation of God in the phenomena of light, the process by which "there arises in the Godhead the wondrous and beautiful structure of the heavens in various colours and kinds, and every spirit shows itself in its form specially," he says, "I can compare it with nothing but with the noblest precious stones, such as the ruby, emerald, epidote, onyx, sapphire, diamond, jasper, hyacinth, amethyst, beryl, sardine, carbuncle, and the like." Elsewhere: "But regarding the precious stones, such as the carbuncle, ruby, emerald, epidote, onyx, and the like, which are the very best, these have the very same origin—the flash of light in love. For that flash is born in tenderness, and is the heart in the centre of the Fountain-spirit, wherefore those stones also are mild, powerful, and lovely." It is evident that Jacob Böhme had no bad taste in mineralogy; that he had delight in flowers also, and consequently a faculty for botany, is proved by the following passages among others: —"The heavenly powers gave birth to heavenly joy-giving fruits and colours, to all sorts of trees and shrubs, whereupon grows the beauteous and lovely fruit of life: also there spring up in these powers all sorts of flowers with beauteous heavenly colours and scents. Their taste is various, in each according to its quality and kind, altogether holy, divine, and joy-giving." "If thou desirest to contemplate the heavenly, divine pomp and glory, as they are, and to know what sort of products, pleasure, or joys there are

* Kernhafter Auszug . . . J. Böhme : Amsterdam, 1718, p. 58.

above: look diligently at this world, at the varieties of fruits and plants that grow upon the earth,—trees, shrubs, vegetables, roots, flowers, oils, wines, corn, and everything that is there, and that thy heart can search out. All this is an image of the heavenly pomp." *

A despotic fiat could not suffice as an explanation of the origin of Nature to Jacob Böhme; Nature appealed too strongly to his senses, and lay too near his heart; hence he sought for a natural explanation of Nature; but he necessarily found no other ground of explanation than those qualities of Nature which made the strongest impression on him. Jacob Böhme—this is his essential character—is a mystical natural philosopher, a theosophic Vulcanist and Neptunist,† for according to him "all things had their origin in fire and water." Nature had fascinated Jacob's religious sentiments,—not in vain did he receive his mystical light from the shining of tin utensils; but the religious sentiment works only within itself; it has not the force, not the courage, to press forward to the examination of things in their reality; it looks at all things through the medium of religion, it sees all in God, *i.e.*, in the entrancing, soul-possessing splendour of the imagination, it sees all in images and as an image. But Nature affected his mind in an opposite manner; hence he must place this opposition in God himself,—for the supposition of two independently existing, opposite, original principles would have afflicted his religious sentiment;—he must distinguish in God himself a gentle, beneficent element, and a fierce consuming one. Everything fiery, bitter, harsh, contracting, dark, cold, comes from a divine harshness and bitterness; everything mild, lustrous, warming, tender, soft, yielding, from a mild, soft, luminous quality in God. "Thus are the creatures on the earth, in the water, and in the air, each creature out of its own science, out of good and evil. . . . As one sees before one's eyes that there are good and evil creatures; as venomous beasts and serpents from the centre of the nature of darkness, from the power of the fierce quality, which only want to dwell in darkness, abiding in caves and hiding

---

* L. c. pp. 480, 338, 340, 323.

† The *Philosophus teutonicus* walked physically as well as mentally on volcanic ground. "The town of Görlitz is paved throughout with pure basalt."—Charpentier, Mineral. Geographie der Chursächsischen Lande, p. 19.

themselves from the sun. By each animal's food and dwelling we see whence they have sprung, for every creature needs to dwell with its mother, and yearns after her, as is plain to the sight." " Gold, silver, precious stones, and all bright metal, has its origin in the light, which appeared before the times of anger," &c. " Everything which in the substance of this world is yielding, soft, and thin, is flowing, and gives itself forth, and the ground and origin of it is in the eternal Unity, for unity ever flows forth from itself; for in the nature of things not dense, as water and air, we can understand no susceptibility or pain, they being one in themselves.* In short, heaven is as rich as the earth. Everything that is on this earth is in heaven,† all that is in Nature is in God. But in the latter it is divine, heavenly; in the former, earthly, visible, external, material, but yet the same." " When I write of trees, shrubs and fruits, thou must not understand me of earthly things, such as are in this world ; for it is not my meaning that in heaven there grows a dead, hard, wooden tree, or a stone of earthly qualities. No: my meaning is heavenly and spiritual, but yet truthful and literal ; thus, I mean no other things than what I write in the letters of the alphabet ;" *i.e.*, in heaven there are the same trees and flowers, but the trees in heaven are the trees which bloom and exhale in my imagination, without making coarse material impressions upon me; the trees on earth are the trees which I perceive through my senses. The distinction is the distinction between imagination and perception. "It is not my undertaking," says Jacob Böhme himself, " to describe the course of all stars, their place and name, or how they have yearly their conjunction or opposition, or quadrate, or the like,—what they do yearly and hourly,—which through long years has been discovered by wise, skilful, ingenious men, by diligent contemplation and observation, and deep thought and calculation. I have not learned and studied these things, and leave scholars to treat of them, but my undertaking is to

---

* L. c. pp. 468, 617, 618.

† According to Swedenborg, the angels in heaven have clothes and dwellings. "Their dwellings are altogether such as the dwellings or houses on earth, but far more beautiful ; there are apartments, rooms, and sleeping chambers therein in great number, and entrance-courts, and round about gardens, flowers, meadows, and fields." (E.* v. S. Auserlesene Schriften, 1 Th. Frankf. a. M. 1776, p. 190, and 96.) Thus to the mystic this world is the other world ; but for that reason the other world is this world.

write according to the spirit and thought, not according to sight." *

The doctrine of Nature in God aims, by naturalism, to establish theism, especially the theism which regards the Supreme Being as a personal being. But personal theism conceives God as a personal being, separate from all material things; it excludes from him all development, because that is nothing else than the self-separation of a being from circumstances and conditions which do not correspond to its true idea. And this does not take place in God, because in him beginning, end, middle, are not to be distinguished,—because he is at once what he is, is from the beginning what he is to be, what he can be; he is the pure unity of existence and essence, reality and idea, act and will. *Deus suum Esse est.* Herein theism accords with the essence of religion. All religions, however positive they may be, rest on abstraction; they are distinguished only in that from which the abstraction is made. Even the Homeric gods, with all their living strength and likeness to man, are abstract forms; they have bodies, like men, but bodies from which the limitations and difficulties of the human body are eliminated. The idea of a divine being is essentially an abstracted, distilled idea. It is obvious that this abstraction is no arbitrary one, but is determined by the essential stand-point of man. As he is, as he thinks, so does he make his abstraction.

The abstraction expresses a judgment,—an affirmative and a negative one at the same time, praise and blame. What man praises and approves, that is God to him;† what he blames, condemns, is the non-divine. Religion is a *judgment.* The most essential condition in religion—in the idea of the divine being—is accordingly the discrimination of the praiseworthy from the blameworthy, of the perfect from the imperfect; in a word, of the positive from the negative. The cultus itself consists in nothing else than in the continual renewal of the origin of religion—a solemnising of the critical discrimination between the divine and the non-divine.

The Divine Being is the human being glorified by the

---

* L. c. p. 339, p. 69.
† "Quidquid enim unus quisque super cætera colit : hoc illi Deus est."— Origines Explan. in Epist. Pauli ad Rom. c. l.

death of abstraction; it is the departed spirit of man. In religion man frees himself from the limits of life; he here lets fall what oppresses him, obstructs him, affects him repulsively; God is the self-consciousness of man freed from all discordant elements; man feels himself free, happy, blessed in his religion, because he only here lives the life of genius, and keeps holiday. The basis of the divine idea lies for him outside of that idea itself; its truth lies in the prior *judgment*, in the fact that all which he excludes from God is previously judged by him to be non-divine, and what is non-divine to be worthless, nothing. If he were to include the attaining of this idea in the idea itself, it would lose its most essential significance, its true value, its beatifying charm. The divine being is the pure subjectivity of man, freed from all else, from everything objective, having relation only to itself, enjoying only itself, reverencing only itself—his most subjective, his inmost self. The process of discrimination, the separating of the intelligent from the non-intelligent, of personality from Nature, of the perfect from the imperfect, necessarily therefore takes place in the subject, not in the object, and the idea of God lies not at the beginning but at the end of sensible existence, of the world, of Nature. "Where Nature ceases, God begins," because God is the *ne plus ultra*, the last limit of abstraction. That from which I can no longer abstract is God, the last thought which I am capable of grasping—the last, *i.e.*, the highest. *Id quo nihil majus cogitari potest, Deus est.* That this Omega of sensible existence becomes an Alpha also, is easily comprehensible; but the essential point is, that he is the Omega. The Alpha is primarily a consequence; because God is the last or highest, he is also the first. And this predicate—the first Being, has by no means immediately a cosmogonic significance, but only implies the highest rank. The creation in the Mosaic religion has for its end to secure to Jehovah the predicate of the highest and first, the true and exclusive God in opposition to idols.

The effort to establish the personality of God through Nature has therefore at its foundation an illegitimate, profane mingling of philosophy and religion, a complete absence of criticism and knowledge concerning the genesis of the personal God. Where personality is held the essential attribute of God, where it is said—an impersonal God is no

God; there personality is held to be in and by itself the highest and most real thing, there it is presupposed that everything which is not a person is dead, is nothing, that only personal existence is real, absolute existence, is life and truth—but Nature is impersonal, and is therefore a trivial thing. The truth of personality rests only on the untruth of Nature. To predicate personality of God is nothing else than to declare personality as the absolute essence; but personality is only conceived in distinction, in abstraction from Nature. Certainly a merely personal God is an abstract God; but so he ought to be—that is involved in the idea of him; for he is nothing else than the personal nature of man positing itself out of all connection with the world, making itself free from all dependence on nature. In the personality of God man consecrates the supernaturalness, immortality, independence, unlimitedness of his own personality.

In general, the need of a personal God has its foundation in this, that only in the attribute of personality does the personal man meet with himself, find himself. Substance, pure spirit, mere reason, does not satisfy him, is too abstract for him, *i.e.*, does not express himself, does not lead him back to himself. And man is content, happy, only when he is with himself, with his own nature. Hence, the more personal a man is, the stronger is his need of a personal God. The free, abstract thinker knows nothing higher than freedom; he does not need to attach it to a personal being; for him freedom in itself, as such, is a real positive thing. A mathematical, astronomical mind, a man of pure understanding, an objective man, who is not shut up in himself, who feels free and happy only in the contemplation of objective rational relations, in the reason which lies in things in themselves—such a man will regard the substance of Spinoza, or some similar idea, as his highest being, and be full of antipathy towards a personal, *i.e.*, subjective God. Jacobi therefore was a classic philosopher, because (in this respect, at least) he was consistent, he was at unity with himself; as was his God, so was his philosophy—personal, subjective. The personal God cannot be established otherwise than as he is established by Jacobi and his disciples. Personality is proved only in a personal manner.

Personality may be, nay, must be, founded on a natural

basis; but this natural basis is attained only when I cease to grope in the darkness of mysticism, when I step forth into the clear daylight of real Nature, and exchange the idea of the personal God for the idea of personality in general. But into the idea of the personal God, the positive idea of whom is liberated, disembodied personality, released from the limiting force of Nature, to smuggle again this very Nature, is as perverse as if I were to mix Brunswick mum with the nectar of the gods, in order to give the ethereal beverage a solid foundation. Certainly the ingredients of animal blood are not to be derived from the celestial juice which nourishes the gods. But the flower of sublimation arises only through the evaporation of matter; why, then, wilt thou mix with the sublimate that very matter from which thou hast disengaged it? Certainly, the impersonal existence of Nature is not to be explained by the idea of personality; but where personality is a truth, or, rather, the absolute truth, Nature has no positive significance, and consequently no positive basis. The literal creation out of nothing is here the only sufficient ground of explanation; for it simply says this: Nature is nothing;—and this precisely expresses the significance which Nature has for absolute personality.

CHAPTER X.

THE MYSTERY OF PROVIDENCE, AND CREATION OUT OF NOTHING.

CREATION is the spoken word of God; the creative, cosmogonic fiat is the tacit word, identical with the thought. To speak is an act of the will; thus, creation is a product of the Will: as in the Word of God man affirms the divinity of the human word, so in creation he affirms the divinity of the Will: not, however, the will of the reason, but the will of the imagination—the absolutely subjective, unlimited will. The culminating point of the principle of subjectivity is creation out of nothing.* As the eternity of the world or of matter imports nothing further than the essentiality of matter, so the creation of the world out of nothing imports simply the non-essentiality, the nothingness of the world. The commencement of a thing is immediately connected, in idea if not in time, with its end. "Lightly come, lightly go." The will has called it into existence—the will calls it back again into nothing. When? The time is indifferent: its existence or non-existence depends only on the will. But this will is not its own will:—not only because a thing cannot will its non-existence, but for the prior reason that the world is itself destitute of will. Thus the nothingness of the world expresses the power of the will. The will that it should exist is, at the same time, the will —at least the possible will—that it should not exist. The existence of the world is therefore a momentary, arbitrary, unreliable, *i.e.*, unreal existence.

Creation out of nothing is the highest expression of omnipotence: but omnipotence is nothing else than subjectivity exempting itself from all objective conditions and limita-

---

* "Quare fecit Deus coelum et terram? Quia voluit. Voluntas enim Dei causa est coeli et terræ et ideo major est voluntas Dei quam coelum et terra. Qui autem dicit: quare voluit facere coelum et terram? majus aliquid quærit, quam est voluntas Dei, nihil enim majus invenire potest."—Augustinus (de Genesi adv. Manich. l. i. c. 2).

tions, and consecrating this exemption as the highest power and reality: nothing else than the ability to posit everything real as unreal—everything conceivable as possible: nothing else than the power of the imagination, or of the will as identical with the imagination, the power of self-will.* The strongest and most characteristic expression of subjective arbitrariness is, " it has pleased ; "—the phrase, " it has pleased God to call the world of bodies and spirits into existence," is the most undeniable proof that individual subjectivity, individual arbitrariness, is regarded as the highest essence—the omnipotent world-principle. On this ground, creation out of nothing as a work of the Almighty Will falls into the same category with miracle, or rather it is the first miracle, not only in time but in rank also ;—the principle of which all further miracles are the spontaneous result. The proof of this is history itself ; all miracles have been vindicated, explained, and illustrated by appeal to the omnipotence which created the world out of nothing. Why should not He who made the world out of nothing, make wine out of water, bring human speech from the mouth of an ass, and charm water out of a rock ? But miracle is, as we shall see further on, only a product and object of the imagination, and hence creation out of nothing, as the primitive miracle, is of the same character. For this reason the doctrine of creation out of nothing has been pronounced a supernatural one, to which reason of itself could not have attained; and in proof of this, appeal has been made to the fact that the pagan philosophers represented the world to have been formed by the Divine Reason out of already existing matter. But this supernatural principle is no other than the principle of subjectivity, which in Christianity exalted itself to an unlimited, universal monarchy; whereas the ancient philosophers were not subjective enough to regard the absolutely subjective being as the exclusively absolute being, because they limited subjectivity by the contemplation of the world or reality—because to them the world was a truth.

Creation out of nothing, as identical with miracle, is one

* A more profound origin of the creation out of nothing lies in the emotional nature, as is both directly and indirectly declared in this work. But arbitrariness is, in fact, the will of the emotions, their external manifestation of force.

with Providence; for the idea of Providence—originally, in its true religious significance, in which it is not yet infringed upon and limited by the unbelieving understanding—is one with the idea of miracle. The proof of Providence is miracle.* Belief in Providence is belief in a power to which all things stand at command to be used according to its pleasure, in opposition to which all the power of reality is nothing. Providence cancels the laws of Nature; it interrupts the course of necessity, the iron bond which inevitably binds effects to causes; in short, it is the same unlimited, all-powerful will, that called the world into existence out of nothing. Miracle is a *creatio ex nihilo.* He who turns water into wine, makes wine out of nothing, for the constituents of wine are not found in water; otherwise, the production of wine would not be a miraculous, but a natural act. The only attestation, the only proof of Providence is miracle. Thus Providence is an expression of the same idea as creation out of nothing. Creation out of nothing can only be understood and explained in connection with Providence; for miracle properly implies nothing more than that the miracle worker is the same as he who brought forth all things by his mere will—God the Creator.

But Providence has relation essentially to man. It is for man's sake that Providence makes of things whatever it pleases: it is for man's sake that it supersedes the authority and reality of a law otherwise omnipotent. The admiration of Providence in Nature, especially in the animal kingdom, is nothing else than an admiration of Nature, and therefore belongs merely to naturalism, though to a religious naturalism; † for in Nature is revealed only natural, not divine Providence—not Providence as it is an object to religion. Religious Providence reveals itself only in miracles—especially in the miracle of the Incarnation, the central point of religion. But we nowhere read that God, for the sake of

* " Certissimum divinæ providentiæ testimonium præbent miracula."— H. Grotius (de Verit. Rel. Christ. l. i. § 13).

† It is true that religious naturalism, or the acknowledgment of the Divine in Nature, is also an element of the Christian religion, and yet more of the Mosaic, which was so friendly to animals. But it is by no means the characteristic, the Christian tendency of the Christian religion. The Christian, the religious Providence, is quite another than that which clothes the lilies and feeds the ravens. The natural Providence lets a man sink in the water, if he has not learned to swim; but the Christian, the religious Providence, leads him with the hand of omnipotence over the water unharmed.

brutes, became a brute—the very idea of this is, in the eyes of religion, impious and ungodly; or that God ever performed a miracle for the sake of animals or plants. On the contrary, we read that a poor fig-tree, because it bore no fruit at a time when it could not bear it, was cursed, purely in order to give men an example of the power of faith over Nature;— and again, that when the tormenting devils were driven out of men, they were driven into brutes. It is true we also read: "No sparrow falls to the ground without your Father;" but these sparrows have no more worth and importance than the hairs on the head of a man, which are all numbered.

Apart from instinct, the brute has no other guardian spirit, no other Providence, than its senses or its organs in general. A bird which loses its eyes has lost its guardian angel; it necessarily goes to destruction if no miracle happens. We read indeed that a raven brought food to the prophet Elijah, but not (at least to my knowledge) that an animal was supported by other than natural means. But if a man believes that he also has no other Providence than the powers of his race—his senses and understanding,—he is in the eyes of religion, and of all those who speak the language of religion, an irreligious man; because he believes only in a natural Providence, and a natural Providence is in the eyes of religion as good as none. Hence Providence has relation essentially to men, and even among men only to the religious. "God is the Saviour of all men, but especially of them that believe." It belongs, like religion, only to man; it is intended to express the essential distinction of man from the brute, to rescue man from the tyranny of the forces of Nature. Jonah in the whale, Daniel in the den of lions, are examples of the manner in which Providence distinguishes (religious) men from brutes. If therefore the Providence which manifests itself in the organs with which animals catch and devour their prey, and which is so greatly admired by Christian naturalists, is a truth, the Providence of the Bible, the Providence of religion, is a falsehood; and *vice versâ.* What pitiable and at the same time ludicrous hypocrisy is the attempt to do homage to *both,* to Nature, and the Bible at once! How does Nature contradict the Bible! How does the Bible contradict Nature! The God of Nature reveals himself by giving to the lion strength and appropriate organs in order that, for the preservation of his life, he may in case of necessity kill and devour even a human being; the God of the Bible reveals himself by interposing his own aid to rescue the human being from the jaws of the lion!*

Providence is a privilege of man. It expresses the value of man, in distinction from other natural beings and things; it exempts him from the connection of the universe. Providence is the conviction of man of the infinite value of his existence,—a conviction in which he renounces faith in the reality of external things; it is the idealism of religion. Faith in Providence is therefore identical with faith in personal immortality; save only, that in the latter the infinite value of existence is expressed in relation to time, as infinite duration. He who prefers no special claims, who is indifferent about himself, who identifies himself with the world, who sees himself as a part merged in the whole,—such a one believes in no Providence, *i.e.*, in no special Providence; but only special Providence is Providence in the sense of religion. Faith in Providence is faith in one's own worth, the faith of man in himself; hence the beneficent consequences of this faith, but hence also false humility, religious arrogance, which, it is true, does not rely on itself, but only because it commits the care of itself to the blessed God. God concerns himself about me; he has in view my happiness, my salvation; he wills that I shall be blest; but that is my will also: thus, my interest is God's interest, my own will is God's will, my own aim is God's aim,—God's love for me nothing else than my self-love deified. Thus when I believe in Providence, in what do I believe but in the divine reality and significance of my own being?

But where Providence is believed in, belief in God is made dependent on belief in Providence. He who denies that there is a Providence, denies that there is a God, or—what is the same thing—that God is God; for a God who is not the Providence of man, is a contemptible God, a God who is wanting in the divinest, most adorable attribute. Consequently, the belief in God is nothing but the belief in human dignity,† the belief in the absolute reality and signi-

---

* In this contrast of the religious, or biblical, and the natural Providence, the author had especially in view the vapid, narrow theology of the English natural philosophers.

† "Qui Deos negant, nobilitatem generis humani destruunt."—Bacon (Serm. Fidel. 16).

ficance of the human nature. But belief in a (religious) Providence is belief in creation out of nothing, and *vice versâ*; the latter, therefore, can have no other significance than that of Providence as just developed, and it has actually no other. Religion sufficiently expresses this by making man the end of creation. All things exist, not for their own sake, but for the sake of man. He who, like the pious Christian naturalists, pronounces this to be pride, declares Christianity itself to be pride; for to say that the material world exists for the sake of man, implies infinitely less than to say that God—or at least, if we follow Paul, a being who is almost God, scarcely to be distinguished from God—becomes man for the sake of men.

But if man is the end of creation, he is also the true cause of creation, for the end is the principle of action. The distinction between man as the end of creation, and man as its cause, is only that the cause is the latent, inner man, the essential man, whereas the end is the self-evident, empirical, individual man,—that man recognises himself as the end of creation, but not as the cause, because he distinguishes the cause, the essence from himself as another personal being.* But this other being, this creative principle, is in fact nothing else than his subjective nature separated from the limits of individuality and materiality, *i.e.*, of objectivity, unlimited will, personality posited out of all connection with the world,—which by creation, *i.e.*, the positing of the world, of objectivity, of another, as a dependent, finite, nonessential existence, gives itself the certainty of its exclusive reality. The point in question in the Creation is not the truth and reality of the world, but the truth and reality of personality, of subjectivity in distinction from the world. The point in question is the personality of God; but the personality of

* In Clemens Alex. (Coh. ad Gentes) there is an interesting passage. It runs in the Latin translation (the bad Augsburg edition, 1778) thus:—"At nos ante mundi constitutionem fuimus, ratione futuræ nostræ productionis, in ipso Deo quodammodo tum præexistentes. Divini igitur Verbi sive Rationis, nos creaturæ rationales sumus, et per eum primi esse dicimur, quoniam in principio erat verbum." Yet more decidedly, however, has Christian mysticism declared the human nature to be the creative principle, the ground of the world. "Man, who, before time was, existed in eternity, works with God all the works that God wrought a thousand years ago, and now, after a thousand years, still works." "All creatures have sprung forth through man."—Predigten, vor u. zu Tauleri Zeiten (Ed. c. p. 5, p. 119).

God is the personality of man freed from all the conditions
and limitations of Nature. Hence the fervent interest in
the Creation, the horror of all pantheistic cosmogonies.
The Creation, like the idea of a personal God in general,
is not a scientific, but a personal matter; not an object of
the free intelligence, but of the feelings; for the point on
which it hinges is only the guarantee, the last conceivable
proof and demonstration of personality or subjectivity as
an essence quite apart, having nothing in common with
Nature, a supra- and extra-mundane entity.*

Man distinguishes himself from Nature. This distinction
of his is his God: the distinguishing of God from Nature
is nothing else than the distinguishing of man from Nature.
The antithesis of pantheism and personalism resolves itself
into the question: Is the nature of man transcendental or
immanent, supranaturalistic or naturalistic? The speculations and controversies concerning the personality or
impersonality of God are therefore fruitless, idle, uncritical,
and odious; for the speculatists, especially those who maintain the personality, do not call the thing by the right
name; they put the light under a bushel. While they
in truth speculate only concerning themselves, only in the
interest of their own instinct of self-preservation; they yet
will not allow that they are splitting their brains only about
themselves; they speculate under the delusion that they
are searching out the mysteries of another being. Pantheism
identifies man with Nature, whether with its visible appearance, or its abstract essence. Personalism isolates, separates,
him from Nature; converts him from a part into the whole,
into an absolute essence by himself. This is the distinction.
If, therefore, you would be clear on these subjects, exchange
your mystical, perverted anthropology, which you call
theology, for real anthropology, and speculate in the light
of consciousness and Nature concerning the difference or
identity of the human essence with the essence of Nature.
You yourselves admit that the essence of the pantheistical
God is nothing but the essence of Nature. Why, then, will

---

* Hence is explained why all attempts of speculative theology and of its
kindred philosophy to make the transition from God to the world, or to
derive the world from God, have failed and must fail. Namely, because
they are fundamentally false, from being made in ignorance of the idea on
which the Creation really turns.

you only see the mote in the eyes of your opponents, and not observe the very obvious beam in your own eyes? why make yourselves an exception to a universally valid law? Admit that your personal God is nothing else than your own personal nature, that while you believe in and construct your supra- and extra-natural God, you believe in and construct nothing else than the supra- and extra-naturalism of your own self.

In the Creation, as everywhere else, the true principle is concealed by the intermingling of universal, metaphysical, and even pantheistic definitions. But one need only be attentive to the closer definitions to convince oneself that the true principle of creation is the self-affirmation of subjectivity in distinction from Nature. God produces the world outside himself; at first it is only an idea, a plan, a resolve; now it becomes an act, and therewith it steps forth out of God as a distinct and, relatively at least, a self-subsistent object. But just so subjectivity in general, which distinguishes itself from the world, which takes itself for an essence distinct from the world, posits the world out of itself as a separate existence, indeed, this positing out of self, and the distinguishing of self, is one act. When therefore the world is posited outside of God, God is posited by himself, is distinguished from the world. What else then is God but your subjective nature, when the world is separated from it? *   It is true that when astute reflection intervenes, the distinction between *extra* and *intra* is disavowed as a finite and human (?) distinction. But to the disavowal by the understanding, which in relation to religion is pure misunderstanding, no credit is due. If it is meant seriously, it destroys the foundation of the religious consciousness; it does away with the possibility, the very principle of the creation, for this rests solely on the reality

* It is not admissible to urge against this the omnipresence of God, the existence of God in all things, or the existence of things in God. For, apart from the consideration that the future destruction of the world expresses clearly enough its existence outside of God, *i.e.*, its non-divineness, God is in a *special* manner only in man; but I am at home only where I am *specially* at home. "Nowhere is God properly God, but in the soul. In all creatures there is something of God; but in the soul God exists completely, for it is his resting-place."—Predigten etzlicher Lehrer, &c., p. 19. And the existence of things in God, especially where it has no pantheistic significance, and any such is here excluded, is equally an idea without reality, and does not express the special sentiments of religion.

of the above-mentioned distinction. Moreover, the effect of the creation, all its majesty for the feelings and the imagination, is quite lost, if the production of the world out of God is not taken in the real sense. What is it to make, to create, to produce, but to make that which in the first instance is only subjective, and so far invisible, non-existent, into something objective, perceptible, so that other beings besides me may know and enjoy it, and thus to put something out of myself, to make it distinct from myself? Where there is no reality or possibility of an existence external to me, there can be no question of making or creating. God is eternal, but the world had a commencement; God was, when as yet the world was not; God is invisible, not cognisable by the senses, but the world is visible, palpable, material, and therefore outside of God; for how can the material as such, body, matter, be in God? The world exists outside of God, in the same sense in which a tree, an animal, the world in general, exists outside of my conception, outside of myself, is an existence distinct from subjectivity. Hence, only when such an external existence is admitted, as it was by the older philosophers and theologians, have we the genuine, unmixed doctrine of the religious consciousness. The speculative theologians and philosophers of modern times, on the contrary, foist in all sorts of pantheistic definitions, although they deny the principle of pantheism; and the result of this process is simply an absolutely self-contradictory, insupportable fabrication of their own.

Thus the creation of the world expresses nothing else than subjectivity, assuring itself of its own reality and infinity through the consciousness that the world is created, is a product of will, *i.e.*, a dependent, powerless, unsubstantial existence. The "nothing" out of which the world was produced, is a still inherent nothingness. When thou sayest the world was made out of nothing, thou conceivest the world itself as nothing, thou clearest away from thy head all the limits to thy imagination, to thy feelings, to thy will, for the world is the limitation of thy will, of thy desire; the world alone obstructs thy soul; it alone is the wall of separation between thee and God,—thy beatified, perfected nature. Thus, subjectively, thou annihilatest the world; thou thinkest God by himself, *i.e.*, absolutely unlimited subjectivity, the subjectivity or soul which enjoys itself alone, which needs not the world, which knows nothing of the painful bonds of matter. In the inmost depths of thy soul thou wouldest rather there were no world, for where the world is, there is matter, and where there is matter there is weight and resistance, space and time, limitation and necessity. Nevertheless, there *is* a world, there *is* matter. How dost thou escape from the dilemma of this contradiction? How dost thou expel the world from thy consciousness, that it may not disturb thee in the beatitude of the unlimited soul? Only by making the world itself a product of will, by giving it an arbitrary existence always hovering between existence and non-existence, always awaiting its annihilation. Certainly the act of creation does not suffice to explain the existence of the world or matter (the two are not separable), but it is a total misconception to demand this of it, for the fundamental idea of the creation is this: there is to be no world, no matter; and hence its end is daily looked forward to with longing. The world in its truth does not here exist at all, it is regarded only as the obstruction, the limitation of subjectivity; how could the world in its truth and reality be deduced from a principle which denies the world?

In order to recognise the above developed significance of the creation as the true one, it is only necessary seriously to consider the fact, that the chief point in the creation is not the production of earth and water, plants and animals, for which indeed there is no God, but the production of personal beings—of spirits, according to the ordinary phrase. God is the idea of personality as itself a person, subjectivity existing in itself apart from the world, existing for self alone, without wants, posited as absolute existence, the *me* without a *thee*. But as absolute existence for self alone contradicts the idea of true life, the idea of love; as self-consciousness is essentially united with the consciousness of a *thee*, as solitude cannot, at least in perpetuity, preserve itself from tedium and uniformity; thought immediately proceeds from the divine Being to other conscious beings, and expands the idea of personality which was at first condensed in one being to a plurality of persons.* If the

---

* Here is also the point where the Creation represents to us not only the Divine power, but also the Divine love. " Quia bonus est (Deus), sumus "

person is conceived physically, as a real man, in which form
he is a being with wants, he appears first at the end of the
physical world, when the conditions of his existence are
present,—as the goal of creation. If, on the other hand,
man is conceived abstractly as a person, as is the case in
religious speculation, this circuit is dispensed with, and the
task is the direct deduction of the person, *i.e.*, the self-
demonstration, the ultimate self-verification of the human
personality. It is true that the divine personality is distinguished in every possible way from the human in order
to veil their identity; but these distinctions are either
purely fantastic, or they are mere assertions, devices which
exhibit the invalidity of the attempted deduction. All
positive grounds of the creation reduce themselves only to
the conditions, to the grounds, which urge upon the *me* the
consciousness of the necessity of another personal being.
Speculate as much as you will, you will never derive your
personality from God, if you have not beforehand introduced
it, if God himself be not already the idea of your personality, your own subjective nature.

(Augustin). In the beginning, before the world, God was alone. " Ante
omnia Deus erat solus, ipsi sibi et mundus et locus et omnia. Solus autem ;
quia nihil extrinsecus præter ipsum " (Tertullian). But there is no higher
happiness than to make another happy, bliss lies in the act of imparting.
And only joy, only love imparts. Hence man conceives imparting love as the
principle of existence. "Extasis bono non sinit ipsum manere in se ipso "
(Dionysius A.). Everything positive establishes, attests itself, only by itself.
The divine love is the joy of life, establishing itself, affirming itself. But
the highest self-consciousness of life, the supreme joy of life is the love which
confers happiness. God is the bliss of existence.

CHAPTER XI.

THE doctrine of the Creation sprang out of Judaism; indeed, it is the characteristic, the fundamental doctrine of the Jewish religion. The principle which lies at its foundation is, however, not so much the principle of subjectivity as of egoism. The doctrine of the Creation in its characteristic significance arises only on that stand-point where man in practice makes Nature merely the servant of his will and needs, and hence in thought also degrades it to a mere machine, a product of the will. *Now* its existence is intelligible to him, since he explains and interprets it out of himself, in accordance with his own feelings and notions. The question, Whence is Nature or the world? presupposes wonder that it exists, or the question, Why does it exist? But this wonder, this question, arises only where man has separated himself from Nature and made it a mere object of will. The author of the Book of Wisdom says truly of the heathens, that, "for admiration of the beauty of the world they did not raise themselves to the idea of the Creator." To him who feels that Nature is lovely, it appears an end in itself, it has the ground of its existence in itself: in him the question, Why does it exist? does not arise. Nature and God are identified in his consciousness, his perception, of the world. Nature, as it impresses his senses, has indeed had an origin, has been produced, but not created in the religious sense, is not an arbitrary product. And by this origin he implies nothing evil; originating involves for him nothing impure, undivine; he conceives his gods themselves as having had an origin. The generative force is to him the primal force: he posits, therefore, as the ground of Nature, a force of Nature,—a real, present, visibly active force, as the ground of reality. Thus does man think where his relation to the world is æsthetic or theoretic (for the theoretic view was originally the æsthetic view, the

112

prima philosophia), where the idea of the world is to him the idea of the cosmos, of majesty, of deity itself. Only where such a theory was the fundamental principle could there be conceived and expressed such a thought as that of Anaxagoras :—Man is born to behold the world.* The standpoint of theory is the standpoint of harmony with the world. The subjective activity, that in which man contents himself, allows himself free play, is here the sensuous imagination alone. Satisfied with this, he lets Nature subsist in peace, and constructs his castles in the air, his poetical cosmogonies, only out of natural materials. When, on the contrary, man places himself only on the practical standpoint and looks at the world from thence, making the practical standpoint the theoretical one also, he is in disunion with Nature ; he makes Nature the abject vassal of his selfish interest, of his practical egoism. The theoretic expression of this egoistical, practical view, according to which Nature is in itself nothing, is this : Nature or the world is made, created, the product of a command. God said, Let the world be, and straightway the world presented itself at his bidding.†

Utilism is the essential theory of Judaism. The belief in a special Divine Providence is the characteristic belief of Judaism ; belief in Providence is belief in miracle ; but belief in miracle exists where Nature is regarded only as an object of arbitrariness, of egoism, which uses Nature only as an instrument of its own will and pleasure. Water divides or rolls itself together like a firm mass, dust is changed into lice, a staff into a serpent, rivers into blood, a rock into a fountain ; in the same place it is both light and dark at once, the sun now stands still, now goes backward. And all these contradictions of Nature happen for the welfare of Israel, purely at the command of Jehovah, who troubles himself about nothing but Israel, who is nothing

---

* In Diogenes (L. l. ii. c. iii. § 6), it is literally, "for the contemplation of the sun, the moon and the heavens." Similar ideas were held by other philosophers. Thus the Stoics also said :—" Ipse autem homo ortus est ad mundum contemplandum et imitandum."—Cic. (de Nat.).

† "Hebræi numen verbo quidquid videtur efficiens describunt et quasi imperio omnia creata tradunt, ut facilitatem in eo quod vult efficiendo, summamque ejus in omnia potentiam ostendant."—Ps. xxxiii. 6. "Verbo Jehovæ cœli facti sunt."—Ps. cxlviii. 5. " Ille jussit eaque creata sunt."—J. Clericus (Comment. in Mosem. Genes. i. 3).

but the personified selfishness of the Israelitish people, to the exclusion of all other nations,—absolute intolerance, the secret essence of monotheism. The Greeks looked at Nature with the theoretic sense; they heard heavenly music in the harmonious course of the stars ; they saw Nature rise from the foam of the all-producing ocean as Venus Anadyomene. The Israelites, on the contrary, opened to Nature only the gastric sense; their taste for Nature lay only in the palate ; their consciousness of God in eating manna. The Greek addicted himself to polite studies, to the fine arts, to philosophy ; the Israelite did not rise above the alimentary view of theology. " At even ye shall eat flesh, and in the morning ye shall be filled with bread ; and ye shall know that I am the Lord your God." * " And Jacob vowed a vow, saying, If God will be with me, and will keep me in this way that I go, and will give me bread to eat and raiment to put on, so that I come again to my father's house in peace, then shall the Lord be my God." † Eating is the most solemn act or the initiation of the Jewish religion. In eating, the Israelite celebrates and renews the act of creation; in eating, man declares Nature to be an insignificant object. When the seventy elders ascended the mountain with Moses, " they saw God ; and when they had seen God, they ate and drank." ‡ Thus with them what the sight of the Supreme Being heightened was the appetite for food.

The Jews have maintained their peculiarity to this day. Their principle, their God, is the most practical principle in the world,—namely, egoism ; and moreover egoism in the form of religion. Egoism is the God who will not let his servants come to shame. Egoism is essentially monotheistic, for it has only one, only self, as its end. Egoism strengthens cohesion, concentrates man on himself, gives him a consistent principle of life ; but it makes him theoretically narrow, because indifferent to all which does not relate to the wellbeing of self. Hence science, like art, arises only out of polytheism, for polytheism is the frank, open, unenvying sense of all that is beautiful and good without distinction, the sense of the world, of the universe. The Greeks looked

---

* Exod. xvi. 12.   † Gen. xxviii. 20.
‡ Exod. xxiv. 10, 11. "Tantum abest ut mortui sint, ut contra convivium hilares celebrarint."—Clericus.

abroad into the wide world that they might extend their sphere of vision ; the Jews to this day pray with their faces turned towards Jerusalem. In the Israelites, monotheistic egoism excluded the free theoretic tendency. Solomon, it is true, surpassed " all the children of the East " in understanding and wisdom, and spoke (treated, *agebat*) moreover " of trees, from the cedar that is in Lebanon, even unto the hyssop that springeth out of the wall," and also of " beasts and of fowl, and of creeping things and of fishes " (1 Kings iv. 30, 34). But it must be added that Solomon did not serve Jehovah with his whole heart; he did homage to strange gods and strange women; and thus he had the polytheistic sentiment and taste. The polytheistic sentiment, I repeat, is the foundation of science and art.

The significance which Nature in general had for the Hebrews is one with their idea of its origin. The mode in which the genesis of a thing is explained is the candid expression of opinion, of sentiment respecting it. If it be thought meanly of, so also is its origin. Men used to suppose that insects, vermin, sprang from carrion and other rubbish. It was not because they derived vermin from so uninviting a source that they thought contemptuously of them, but, on the contrary, because they thought thus, because the nature of vermin appeared to them so vile, they imagined an origin corresponding to this nature, a vile origin. To the Jews Nature was a mere means towards achieving the end of egoism, a mere object of will. But the ideal, the idol of the egoistic will is that Will which has unlimited command, which requires no means in order to attain its end, to realise its object, which immediately by itself, *i.e.*, by pure will, calls into existence whatever it pleases. It pains the egoist that the satisfaction of his wishes and need is only to be attained immediately, that for him there is a chasm between the wish and its realisation, between the object in the imagination and the object in reality. Hence, in order to relieve this pain, to make himself free from the limits of reality, he supposes as the true, the highest being, One who brings forth an object by the mere I WILL. For this reason, Nature, the world, was to the Hebrews the product of a dictatorial word, of a categorical imperative, of a magic fiat.

To that which has no essential existence for me in theory

I assign no theoretic, no positive ground. By referring it to Will I only enforce its theoretic nullity. What we despise we do not honour with a glance : that which is observed has importance : contemplation is respect. Whatever is looked at fetters by secret forces of attraction, overpowers by the spell which it exercises upon the eye, the criminal arrogance of that Will which seeks only to subject all things to itself. Whatever makes an impression on the theoretic sense, on the reason, withdraws itself from the dominion of the egoistic Will : it reacts, it presents resistance. That which devastating egoism devotes to death, benignant theory restores to life.

The much-belied doctrine of the heathen philosophers concerning the eternity of matter, or the world, thus implies nothing more than that Nature was to them a theoretic reality.* The heathens were idolaters, that is, they contemplated Nature; they did nothing else than what the profoundly Christian nations do at this day when they make Nature an object of their admiration, of their indefatigable investigation. "But the heathens actually worshipped natural objects." Certainly; for worship is only the childish, the religious form of contemplation. Contemplation and worship are not essentially distinguished. That which I contemplate I humble myself before, I consecrate to it my noblest possession, my heart, my intelligence, as an offering. The natural philosopher also falls on his knees before Nature when, at the risk of his life, he snatches from some precipice a lichen, an insect, or a stone, to glorify it in the light of contemplation, and give it an eternal existence in the memory of scientific humanity. The study of Nature is the worship of Nature—idolatry in the sense of the Israelitish and Christian God; and idolatry is simply man's primitive contemplation of Nature; for religion is nothing else than man's primitive, and therefore childish, popular, but prejudiced, unemancipated consciousness of himself and of Nature. The Hebrews, on the other hand, raised themselves from the worship of idols to the worship of God, from the creature to the Creator; *i.e.,* they raised

---

* It is well known, however, that their opinions on this point were various. (See *e.g.* Aristoteles de Cœlo, l. i. c. 10.) But their difference is a subordinate one, since the creative agency itself is with them a more or less cosmical being.

themselves from the theoretic view of Nature, which fascinated the idolaters, to the purely practical view which subjects Nature only to the ends of egoism. "And lest thou
lift up thine eyes unto heaven, and when thou seest the
sun, the moon, and the stars, even all the host of heaven,
shouldst be driven to worship them and serve them, which
the Lord thy God hath divided unto (*i.e.*, bestowed upon,
largitus est) all nations under the whole heaven." * Thus
the creation out of nothing, *i.e.*, the creation as a purely
imperious act, had its origin only in the unfathomable depth
of Hebrew egoism.

On this ground, also, the creation out of nothing is no
object of philosophy;—at least in any other way than it is
so here;—for it cuts away the root of all true speculation,
presents no grappling-point to thought, to theory; theoretically considered, it is a baseless air-built doctrine, which
originated solely in the need to give a warrant to utilism,
to egoism, which contains and expresses nothing but the
command to make Nature—not an object of thought, of
contemplation, but—an object of utilisation. The more
empty it is, however, for natural philosophy, the more profound is its "speculative" significance; for just because it
has no theoretic fulcrum, it allows to the speculatist infinite
room for the play of arbitrary, groundless interpretation.

It is in the history of dogma and speculation as in the
history of states. World-old usages, laws, and institutions
continue to drag out their existence long after they have
lost their true meaning. What has once existed will not
be denied the right to exist for ever; what was once good,
claims to be good for all times. At this period of super-
annuation come the interpreters, the speculatists, and talk
of the profound sense, because they no longer know the
true one.† Thus religious speculation deals with the dogmas torn from the connection in which alone they have any

* Deut. iv. 19. "Licet enim ea, quæ sunt in cœlo, non sint hominum
artificia, at hominum tamen gratia condita fuerunt. Ne quis igitur solem
adoret, sed solis effectorem desideret."—Clemens Alex. (Coh. ad Gentes).

† But of course they only do this in the case of the "absolute religion;"
for with regard to other religions they hold up the ideas and customs which
are foreign to us, and of which we do not know the original meaning and
purpose, as senseless and ludicrous. And yet, in fact, to worship the urine
of cows, which the Parsees and Hindoos drink that they may obtain forgiveness of sins, is not more ludicrous than to worship the comb or a shred
of the garment of the Mother of God.

true meaning; instead of tracing them back critically to their true origin, it makes the secondary primitive, and the primitive secondary. To it God is the first, man the second. Thus it inverts the natural order of things. In reality, the first is man, the second the nature of man made objective, namely, God. Only in later times, in which religion is already become flesh and blood, can it be said—As God is, so is man; although, indeed, this proposition never amounts to anything more than tautology. But in the origin of religion it is otherwise; and it is only in the origin of a thing that we can discern its true nature. Man first unconsciously and involuntarily creates God in his own image, and after this God consciously and voluntarily creates man in his own image. This is especially confirmed by the development of the Israelitish religion. Hence the position of theological one-sidedness, that the revelation of God holds an even pace with the development of the human race. Naturally; for the revelation of God is nothing else than the revelation, the self-unfolding of human nature. The supranaturalistic egoism of the Jews did not proceed from the Creator, but conversely, the latter from the former; in the creation the Israelite justified his egoism at the bar of his reason.

It is true, and it may be readily understood on simply practical grounds, that even the Israelite could not, as a man, withdraw himself from the theoretic contemplation and admiration of Nature. But in celebrating the power and greatness of Nature, he celebrates only the power and greatness of Jehovah. And the power of Jehovah has exhibited itself with the most glory in the miracles which it has wrought in favour of Israel. Hence, in the celebration of this power, the Israelite has always reference ultimately to himself; he extols the greatness of Nature only for the same reason that the conqueror magnifies the strength of his opponent, in order thereby to heighten his own self-complacency, to make his own fame more illustrious. Great and mighty is Nature, which Jehovah has created, but yet mightier, yet greater, is Israel's self-estimation. For his sake the sun stands still; for his sake, according to Philo, the earth quaked at the delivery of the law; in short, for his sake all Nature alters its course. "For the whole creature in his proper kind was fashioned again anew, serving the peculiar commandments that were given unto them, that thy children might be kept without hurt."* According to Philo, God gave Moses power over the whole of Nature; all the elements obeyed him as the Lord of Nature.† Israel's requirement is the omnipotent law of the world, Israel's need the fate of the universe. Jehovah is Israel's consciousness of the sacredness and necessity of his own existence,— a necessity before which the existence of Nature, the existence of other nations, vanishes into nothing; Jehovah is the *salus populi*, the salvation of Israel, to which everything that stands in its way must be sacrificed; Jehovah is exclusive, monarchical arrogance, the annihilating flash of anger in the vindictive glance of destroying Israel; in a word, Jehovah is the *ego* of Israel, which regards itself as the end and aim, the Lord of Nature. Thus, in the power of Nature the Israelite celebrates the power of Jehovah, and in the power of Jehovah the power of his own self-consciousness. "Blessed be God! God is our help, God is our salvation."— "Jehovah is my strength."—"God himself hearkened to the word of Joshua, for Jehovah himself fought for Israel."— "Jehovah is a God of war."

If, in the course of time, the idea of Jehovah expanded itself in individual minds, and his love was extended, as by the writer of the Book of Jonah, to man in general, this does not belong to the essential character of the Israelitish religion. The God of the fathers, to whom the most precious recollections are attached, the ancient historical God, remains always the foundation of a religion.‡

---

* Wisd. xix. 6.   † See Gfrörer's Philo.

‡ We may here observe, that certainly the admiration of the power and glory of God in general, and so of Jehovah, as manifested in Nature, is in fact, though not in the consciousness of the Israelite, only admiration of the power and glory of Nature. (See, on this subject, *P. Bayle, Ein Beitrag*, &c., pp. 25–29.) But to prove this formally lies out of our plan, since we here confine ourselves to Christianity, *i.e.*, the adoration of God in man (Deum colimus per Christum. 'Tertullian, Apolog. c. 21). Nevertheless, the principle of this proof is stated in the present work.

CHAPTER XII.

THE OMNIPOTENCE OF FEELING, OR THE MYSTERY OF PRAYER.

ISRAEL is the historical definition of the specific nature of the religious consciousness, save only that here this consciousness was circumscribed by the limits of a particular, a national interest. Hence, we need only let these limits fall, and we have the Christian religion. Judaism is worldly Christianity; Christianity, spiritual Judaism. The Christian religion is the Jewish religion purified from national egoism, and yet at the same time it is certainly another, a new religion; for every reformation, every purification, produces—especially in religious matters, where even the trivial becomes important —an essential change. To the Jew, the Israelite was the mediator, the bond between God and man; in his relation to Jehovah he relied on his character of Israelite; Jehovah himself was nothing else than the self-consciousness of Israel made objective as the absolute being, the national conscience, the universal law, the central point of the political system.* If we let fall the limits of nationality, we obtain—instead of the Israelite—*man*. As in Jehovah the Israelite personified his national existence, so in God the Christian personified his subjective human nature, freed from the limits of nationality. As Israel made the wants of his national existence the law of the world, as, under the dominance of these wants, he deified even his political vindictiveness; so the Christian made the requirements of human feeling the absolute powers and laws of the world. The miracles of Christianity, which belong just as essentially to its characterisation as the miracles of the Old Testament to that of Judaism, have not the welfare of a nation for their object, but the welfare of man :—that is, indeed, only of man considered as Christian; for Christianity, in contradiction with the genuine universal

* "The greater part of Hebrew poetry, which is often held to be only spiritual, is political."—Herder.

120

human heart, recognised man only under the condition, the limitation, of belief in Christ. But this fatal limitation will be diseussed further on. Christianity has spiritualïsed the egoism of Judaism into subjectivity (though even within Christianity this subjectivity is again expressed as pure egoism), has changed the desire for earthly happiness, the goal of the Israelitish religion, into the longing for heavenly bliss, which is the goal of Christianity.

The highest idea, the God of a political community, of a people whose political system expresses itself in the form of religion, is Law, the consciousness of the law as an absolute divine power; the highest idea, the God of unpolitical, unworldly feeling is Love; the love which brings all the treasures and glories in heaven and upon earth as an offering to the beloved, the love whose law is the wish of the beloved one, and whose power is the unlimited power of the imagination, of intellectual miracle-working.

God is the Love that satisfies our wishes, our emotional wants; he is himself the realised wish of the heart, the wish exalted to the certainty of its fulfilment, of its reality, to that undoubting certainty before which no contradiction of the understanding, no difficulty of experience or of the external world, maintains its ground. Certainty is the highest power for man; that which is certain to him is the essential, the divine. "God is love:" this, the supreme dictum of Christianity, only expresses the certainty which human feeling has of itself, as the alone essential, *i.e.,* absolute divine power, the certainty that the inmost wishes of the heart have objective validity and reality, that there are no limits, no positive obstacles to human feeling, that the whole world, with all its pomp and glory, is nothing weighed against human feeling. God is love: that is, feeling is the God of man, nay, God absolutely, the Absolute Being. God is the nature of human feeling, unlimited, pure feeling, made objective. God is the optative of the human heart transformed into the *tempus finitum,* the certain, blissful "IS,"— the unrestricted omnipotence of feeling, prayer hearing itself, feeling perceiving itself, the echo of our cry of anguish. Pain must give itself utterance; involuntarily the artist seizes the lute that he may breathe out his sufferings in its tones. He soothes his sorrow by making it audible to himself, by making it objective; he lightens the burden which weighs upon his heart by communicating it to the air, by making his sorrow a general existence. But nature listens not to the plaints of man, it is callous to his sorrows. Hence man turns away from Nature, from all visible objects. He turns within, that here, sheltered and hidden from the inexorable powers, he may find audience for his griefs. Here he utters his oppressive secrets; here he gives vent to his stifled sighs. This open-air of the heart, this outspoken secret, this uttered sorrow of the soul, is God. God is a tear of love, shed in the deepest concealment over human misery. "God is an unutterable sigh, lying in the depths of the heart;"* this saying is the most remarkable, the profoundest, truest expression of Christian mysticism.

The ultimate essence of religion is revealed by the simplest act of religion—prayer; an act which implies at least as much as the dogma of the Incarnation, although religious speculation stands amazed at this, as the greatest of mysteries. Not, certainly, the prayer before and after meals, the ritual of animal egoism, but the prayer pregnant with sorrow, the prayer of disconsolate love, the prayer which expresses the power of the heart that crushes man to the ground, the prayer which begins in despair and ends in rapture.

In prayer, man addresses God with the word of intimate affection—*Thou;* he thus declares articulately that God is his *alter ego;* he confesses to God, as the being nearest to him, his most secret thoughts, his deepest wishes, which otherwise he shrinks from uttering. But he expresses these wishes in the confidence, in the certainty that they will be fulfilled. How could he apply to a being that had no ear for his complaints? Thus what is prayer but the wish of the heart expressed with confidence in its fulfilment?† what else is the being that fulfils these wishes

---

* Sebastian Frank von Wörd in Zinkgrefs Apophthegmata deutscher Nation.

† It would be an imbecile objection to say that God fulfils only those wishes, those prayers, which are uttered in his name, or in the interest of the Church of Christ, in short, only the wishes which are accordant with his will; for the will of God is the will of man, or rather God has the power, man the will: God makes men happy, but man wills that he may be happy. A particular wish may not be granted; but that is of no consequence, if only the species, the essential tendency is accepted. The pious soul whose prayer has failed consoles himself, therefore, by thinking that its fulfilment would not have been salutary for him. "Nullo igitur modo vota

but human affection, the human soul, giving ear to itself, approving itself, unhesitatingly affirming itself? The man who does not exclude from his mind the idea of the world, the idea that everything here must be sought intermediately, that every effect has its natural cause, that a wish is only to be attained when it is made an end and the corresponding means are put into operation—such a man does not pray: he only works; he transforms his attainable wishes into objects of real activity; other wishes which he recognises as purely subjective he denies, or regards as simply subjective, pious aspirations. In other words, he limits, he conditionates his being by the world, as a member of which he conceives himself; he bounds his wishes by the idea of necessity. In prayer, on the contrary, man excludes from his mind the world, and with it all thoughts of intermediateness and dependence; he makes his wishes—the concerns of his heart, objects of the independent, omnipotent, absolute being, *i.e.*, he affirms them without limitation. God is the affirmation * of human feeling; prayer is the unconditional confidence of human feeling in the absolute identity of the subjective and objective, the certainty that the power of the heart is greater than the power of Nature, that the heart's need is absolute necessity, the fate of the world. Prayer alters the course of Nature; it determines God to bring forth an effect in contradiction with the laws of Nature. Prayer is the absolute relation of the human heart to itself, to its own nature; in prayer, man forgets that there exists a limit to his wishes, and is happy in this forgetfulness.

Prayer is the self-division of man into two beings,—a dialogue of man with himself, with his heart. It is essential to the effectiveness of prayer that it be audibly, intelligibly, energetically expressed. Involuntarily prayer wells forth in sound; the struggling heart bursts the barrier of the closed lips. But audible prayer is only prayer revealing its nature; prayer is virtually, if not actually, speech,— the Latin word *oratio* signifies both: in prayer, man speaks undisguisedly of that which weighs upon him, which affects him closely; he makes his heart objective;—hence the

aut preces sunt irritæ aut infrugiferæ et recte dicitur, in petitione rerum corporalium aliquando Deum exaudire nos, non ad voluntatem nostram, sed ad salutem."—Oratio de Precatione, in Declamat. Melancthonis, Th. iii.
* Ja-wort.

moral power of prayer. Concentration, it is said, is the condition of prayer; but it is more than a condition; prayer is itself concentration,—the dismissal of all distracting ideas, of all disturbing influences from without, retirement within oneself, in order to have relation only with one's own being. Only a trusting, open, hearty, fervent prayer is said to help; but this help lies in the prayer itself. As everywhere in religion the subjective, the secondary, the conditionating, is the *prima causa*, the objective fact; so here, these subjective qualities are the objective nature of prayer itself.*

It is an extremely superficial view of prayer to regard it as an expression of the sense of dependence. It certainly expresses such a sense, but the dependence is that of man on his own heart, on his own feeling. He who feels himself only dependent, does not open his mouth in prayer; the sense of dependence robs him of the desire, the courage for it, for the sense of dependence is the sense of need. Prayer has its root rather in the unconditional trust of the heart, untroubled by all thought of compulsive need, that its concerns are objects of the Absolute Being, that the almighty, infinite nature of the Father of men is a sympathetic, tender, loving nature, and that thus the dearest, most sacred emotions of man are divine realities. But the child does not feel itself dependent on the father as a father; rather, he has in the father the feeling of his own strength, the consciousness of his own worth, the guarantee of his existence, the certainty of the fulfilment of his wishes; on the father rests the burden of care; the child, on the contrary, lives careless and happy in reliance on the father, his visible guardian spirit, who desires nothing but the child's welfare and happiness. The father makes the child an end, and himself the means of its existence. The child, in asking something of its father, does not apply to him as a being distinct from itself, a master, a person in general, but it

---

* Also, on subjective grounds, social prayer is more effectual than isolated prayer. Community enhances the force of emotion, heightens confidence. What we are unable to do alone we are able to do with others. The sense of solitude is the sense of limitation : the sense of community is the sense of freedom. Hence it is that men, when threatened by the destructive powers of Nature, crowd together. "Multorum preces impossibile est, ut non impetrent, inquit Ambrosius. . . . Sanctæ orationis fervor quanto inter plures collectior tanto ardet diutius ac intensius cor divinum penetrat. . . . Negatur singularitati, quod conceditur charitati."—Sacra Hist. de Gentis Hebr. ortu. P. Paul. Mezger. Aug. Vind. 1700, pp. 668, 669.

applies to him in so far as he is dependent on, and determined by his paternal feeling, his love for his child.* The entreaty is only an expression of the force which the child exercises over the father; if, indeed, the word force is appropriate here, since the force of the child is nothing more than the force of the father's own heart. Speech has the same form both for entreaty and command, namely, the imperative. And the imperative of love has infinitely more power than that of despotism. Love does not command; love needs but gently to intimate its wishes to be certain of their fulfilment; the despot must throw compulsion even into the tones of his voice in order to make other beings, in themselves uncaring for him, the executors of his wishes. The imperative of love works with electro-magnetic power; that of despotism with the mechanical power of a wooden telegraph. The most intimate epithet of God in prayer is the word "Father;" the most intimate, because in it man is in relation to the absolute nature as to his own; the word "Father" is the expression of the closest, the most intense identity,—the expression in which lies the pledge that my wishes will be fulfilled, the guarantee of my salvation. The omnipotence to which man turns in prayer is nothing but the Omnipotence of Goodness, which, for the sake of the salvation of man, makes the impossible possible;—is, in truth, nothing else than the omnipotence of the heart, of feeling, which breaks through all the limits of the understanding, which soars above all the boundaries of Nature, which wills that there be nothing else than feeling, nothing that contradicts the heart. Faith in omnipotence is faith in the unreality of the external world, of objectivity,—faith in the absolute reality of man's emotional nature: the essence of omnipotence is simply the essence of feeling. Omnipotence is the power before which no law, no external condition, avails or subsists; but this power is the emotional nature, which feels every determination, every law, to be a limit, a restraint, and for that reason dismisses it. Omnipotence does nothing more than accomplish the will of the feelings. In prayer man turns to the Omnipotence of Goodness;—which simply means, that in prayer man adores his own heart, regards his own feelings as absolute.

---

* In the excellent work, *Theanthropos, eine Reihe von Aphorismen* (Zurich, 1838), the idea of the sense of dependence, of omnipotence, of prayer, and of love, is admirably developed.

CHAPTER XIII.

THE MYSTERY OF FAITH—THE MYSTERY OF MIRACLE.

FAITH in the power of prayer—and only where a power, an objective power, is ascribed to it, is prayer still a religious truth—is identical with faith in miraculous power; and faith in miracles is identical with the essence of faith in general. Faith alone prays; the prayer of faith is alone effectual. But faith is nothing else than confidence in the reality of the subjective in opposition to the limitations or laws of Nature and reason,—that is, of natural reason. The specific object of faith, therefore, is miracle; faith is the belief in miracle; faith and miracle are absolutely inseparable. That which is objectively miracle or miraculous power is subjectively faith; miracle is the outward aspect of faith, faith the inward soul of miracle; faith is the miracle of mind, the miracle of feeling, which merely becomes objective in external miracles. To faith nothing is impossible, and miracle only gives actuality to this omnipotence of faith: miracles are but a visible example of what faith can effect. Unlimitedness, supernaturalness, exaltation of feeling,—transcendence is therefore the essence of faith. Faith has reference only to things which, in contradiction with the limits or laws of Nature and reason, give objective reality to human feelings and human desires. Faith unfetters the wishes of subjectivity from the bonds of natural reason; it confers what Nature and reason deny; hence it makes man happy, for it satisfies his most personal wishes. And true faith is discomposed by no doubt. Doubt arises only where I go out of myself, overstep the bounds of my personality, concede reality and a right of suffrage to that which is distinct from myself;—where I know myself to be a subjective, *i.e.*, a limited being, and seek to widen my limits by admitting things external to myself. But in faith the very principle of doubt is annulled; for to faith the subjective is in and by itself the objective—nay, the absolute. Faith is nothing else than belief in the absolute reality of subjectivity.

"Faith is that courage in the heart which trusts for all good to God. Such a faith, in which the heart places its reliance on God alone, is enjoined by God in the first commandment, where he says, I am the Lord thy God. . . . That is, I alone will be thy God; thou shalt seek no other God; I will help thee out of all trouble. Thou shalt not think that I am an enemy to thee, and will not help thee. When thou thinkest so, thou makest me in thine heart into another God than I am. Wherefore hold it for certain that I am willing to be merciful to thee."—"As thou behavest thyself, so does God behave. If thou thinkest that he is angry with thee, he is angry; if thou thinkest that he is unmerciful and will cast thee into hell, he is so. As thou believest of God, so is he to thee."—"If thou believest it, thou hast it; but if thou believest not, thou hast none of it."—"Therefore, as we believe so does it happen to us. If we regard him as our God, he will not be our devil. But if we regard him not as our God, then truly he is not our God, but must be a consuming fire."—"By unbelief we make God a devil." * Thus, if I believe in a God, I have a God, *i.e.*, faith in God is the God of man. If God is such, whatever it may be, as I believe him, what else is the nature of God than the nature of faith? Is it possible for thee to believe in a God who regards thee favourably, if thou dost not regard thyself favourably, if thou despairest of man, if he is nothing to thee? What else then is the being of God but the being of man, the absolute self-love of man? If thou believest that God is for thee, thou believest that nothing is or can be against thee, that nothing contradicts thee. But if thou believest that nothing is or can be against thee, thou believest —what?—nothing less than that thou art God.† That God is another being is only illusion, only imagination. In declaring that God is for thee, thou declarest that he is thy own being. What then is faith but the infinite self-certainty of man, the undoubting certainty that his own subjective being is the objective, absolute being, the being of beings?

* Luther (Th. xv. p. 282 ; Th. xvi. pp. 491–493).
† "God is Almighty; but he who believes is a God." Luther (in Chr. Kapps *Christus u. die Weltgeschichte*, s. |11). In another place Luther calls faith the "Creator of the Godhead;" it is true that he immediately adds, as he must necessarily do on his standpoint, the following limitation :— "Not that it creates anything in the Divine Eternal Being, but that it creates that Being in us" (Th. xi. p. 161).

Faith does not limit itself by the idea of a world, a universe, a necessity. For faith there is nothing but God, *i.e.*, limitless subjectivity. Where faith rises the world sinks, nay, has already sunk into nothing. Faith in the real annihilation of the world—in an immediately approaching, a mentally present annihilation of this world, a world antagonistic to the wishes of the Christian, is therefore a phenomenon belonging to the inmost essence of Christianity; a faith which is not properly separable from the other elements of Christian belief, and with the renunciation of which, true, positive Christianity is renounced and denied.* The essence of faith, as may be confirmed by an examination of its objects down to the minutest speciality, is the idea that that which man wishes actually is : he wishes to be immortal, therefore he is immortal; he wishes for the existence of a being who can do everything which is impossible to Nature and reason, therefore such a being exists; he wishes for a world which corresponds to the desires of the heart, a world of unlimited subjectivity, *i.e.*, of unperturbed feeling, of uninterrupted bliss, while nevertheless there exists a world the opposite of that subjective one, and hence this world must pass away,—as necessarily pass away as God, or absolute subjectivity, must remain. Faith, love, hope, are the Christian Trinity. Hope has relation to the fulfilment of the promises, the wishes which are not yet fulfilled, but which are to be fulfilled; love has relation to the Being who gives and fulfils these promises ; faith to the promises, the wishes, which are already fulfilled, which are historical facts.

Miracle is an essential object of Christianity, an essential article of faith. But what is miracle ? A supranaturalistic

* This belief is so essential to the Bible, that without it the biblical writers can scarcely be understood. The passage 2 Pet. iii. 8, as is evident from the tenor of the whole chapter, says nothing in opposition to an immediate destruction of the world ; for though with the Lord a thousand years are as one day, yet at the same time one day is as a thousand years, and therefore the world may, even by to-morrow, no longer exist. That in the Bible a very near end of the world is expected and prophesied, although the day and hour are not determined, only falsehood or blindness can deny. (See on this subject *Lützelberger.*) Hence religious Christians, in almost all times, have believed that the destruction of the world is near at hand—Luther, for example, often says that " The last day is not far off " (*e.g.*, Th. xvi. p. 26) ;—or at least their souls have longed for the end of the world, though they have prudently left it undecided whether it be near or distant. See Augustin (de Fine Sæculi ad Hesychium, c. 13).

wish realised—nothing more. The Apostle Paul illustrates the nature of Christian faith by the example of Abraham. Abraham could not, in a natural way, ever hope for posterity; Jehovah nevertheless promised it to him out of special favour, and Abraham believed in spite of Nature. Hence this faith was reckoned to him as righteousness, as merit; for it implies great force of subjectivity to accept as certain something in contradiction with experience, at least with rational, normal experience. But what was the object of this divine promise? Posterity, the object of a human wish. And in what did Abraham believe when he believed in Jehovah? In a Being who can do everything, and can fulfil all wishes. "Is anything too hard for the Lord?"*

But why do we go so far back as to Abraham? We have the most striking examples much nearer to us. Miracle feeds the hungry, cures men born blind, deaf, and lame, rescues from fatal diseases, and even raises the dead at the prayer of relatives. Thus it satisfies human wishes, and wishes which, though not always intrinsically like the wish for the restoration of the dead, yet in so far as they appeal to miraculous power, to miraculous aid, are transcendental, supranaturalistic. But miracle is distinguished from that mode of satisfying human wishes and needs which is in accordance with Nature and reason, in this respect, that it satisfies the wishes of men in a way corresponding to the nature of wishes—in the most desirable way. Wishes own no restraint, no law, no time; they would be fulfilled without delay on the instant. And behold! miracle is as rapid as a wish is impatient. Miraculous power realises human wishes in a moment, at one stroke, without any hindrance. That the sick should become well is no miracle; but that they should become so immediately, at a mere word of command,—that is the mystery of miracle. Thus it is not in its product or object that miraculous agency is distinguished from the agency of Nature and reason, but only in its mode and process; for if miraculous power were to effect something absolutely new, never before beheld, never conceived, or not even conceivable, it would be practically proved to be an essentially different, and at the same time objective, agency. But the agency which in essence, in substance, is natural and accordant with the

* Gen. xviii. 14.

forms of the senses, and which is supernatural, supersensual, only in the mode or process, is the agency of the imagination. The power of miracle is therefore nothing else than the power of the imagination.

Miraculous agency is agency directed to an end. The yearning after the departed Lazarus, the desire of his relatives to possess him again, was the motive of the miraculous resuscitation; the satisfaction of this wish, the end. It is true that the miracle happened " for the glory of God, that the Son of God might be glorified thereby ; " but the message sent to the Master by the sisters of Lazarus, " Behold, he whom thou lovest is sick," and the tears which Jesus shed, vindicate for the miracle a human origin and end. The meaning is : to that power which can awaken the dead no human wish is impossible to accomplish.* And the glory of the Son consists in this : that he is acknowledged and reverenced as the being who is able to do what man is unable but wishes to do. Activity towards an end is well known to describe a circle : in the end it returns upon its beginning. But miraculous agency is distinguished from the ordinary realisation of an object in that it realises the end without means, that it effects an immediate identity of the wish and its fulfilment ; that consequently it describes a circle, not in a curved, but in a straight line, that is, the shortest line. A circle in a straight line is the mathematical symbol of miracle. The attempt to construct a circle with a straight line would not be more ridiculous than the attempt to deduce miracle philosophically. To reason, miracle is absurd, inconceivable ; as inconceivable as wooden iron or a circle without a periphery. Before it is discussed whether a miracle can happen, let it be shown that miracle, *i.e.*, the inconceivable, is conceivable.

What suggests to man the notion that miracle is conceiv-

---

* " To the whole world it is impossible to raise the dead, but to the Lord Christ, not only is it not impossible, but it is no trouble or labour to him. . . . This Christ did as a witness and a sign that he can and will raise from death. He does it not at all times and to every one. . . . It is enough that he has done it a few times ; the rest he leaves to the last day." —Luther (Th. xvi. p. 518). The positive, essential significance of miracle is therefore that the divine nature is the human nature. Miracles confirm, authenticate doctrine. What doctrine ? Simply this, that God is a Saviour of men, their Redeemer out of all trouble, *i.e.*, a being corresponding to the wants and wishes of man, and therefore a human being. What the God-man declares in words, miracle demonstrates *ad oculos* by deeds.

able is that miracle is represented as an event perceptible by the senses, and hence man cheats his reason by material images which screen the contradiction. The miracle of the turning of water into wine, for example, implies in fact nothing else than that water is wine,—nothing else than that two absolutely contradictory predicates or subjects are identical; for in the hand of the miracle-worker there is no distinction between the two substances; the transformation is only the visible appearance of this identity of two contradictories. But the transformation conceals the contradiction, because the natural conception of change is interposed. Here, however, is no gradual, no natural, or, so to speak, organic change; but an absolute, immaterial one; a pure *creatio ex nihilo*. In the mysterious and momentous act of miraculous power, in the act which constitutes the miracle, water is suddenly and imperceptibly wine : which is equivalent to saying that iron is wood, or wooden iron.

The miraculous act—and miracle is only a transient act—is therefore not an object of thought, for it nullifies the very principle of thought; but it is just as little an object of sense, an object of real or even possible experience. Water is indeed an object of sense, and wine also; I first see water and then wine; but the miracle itself, that which makes this water suddenly wine,—this, not being a natural process, but a pure perfect without any antecedent imperfect, without any *modus*, without way or means, is no object of real, or even of possible experience. Miracle is a thing of the imagination ; and on that very account is it so agreeable : for the imagination is the faculty which alone corresponds to personal feeling, because it sets aside all limits, all laws which are painful to the feelings, and thus makes objective to man the immediate, absolutely unlimited satisfaction of his subjective wishes." * Accordance with subjective inclination is the essential characteristic of miracle. It is true that miracle produces also an awful, agitating impression, so far as it expresses a power which nothing can resist, —the power of the imagination. But this impression lies only in the transient miraculous act ; the abiding, essential

---

* This satisfaction is certainly so far limited, that it is united to religion, to faith in God : a remark which however is so obvious as to be superfluous. But this limitation is in fact *no* limitation, for God himself is unlimited, absolutely satisfied, self-contented human feeling.

impression is the agreeable one. At the moment in which
the beloved Lazarus is raised up, the surrounding relatives
and friends are awestruck at the extraordinary, almighty
power which transforms the dead into the living; but soon
the relatives fall into the arms of the risen one, and lead
him with tears of joy to his home, there to celebrate a festival of rejoicing. Miracle springs out of feeling, and has its
end in feeling. Even in the traditional representation it
does not deny its origin; the representation which gratifies
the feelings is alone the adequate one. Who can fail to
recognise in the narrative of the resurrection of Lazarus the
tender, pleasing, legendary tone?* Miracle is agreeable,
because, as has been said, it satisfies the wishes of man
without labour, without effort. Labour is unimpassioned,
unbelieving, rationalistic; for man here makes his existence
dependent on activity directed to an end, which activity
again is itself determined solely by the idea of the objective
world. But feeling does not at all trouble itself about the
objective world; it does not go out of or beyond itself; it
is happy in itself. The element of culture, the Northern
principle of self-renunciation, is wanting to the emotional
nature. The Apostles and Evangelists were no scientifically
cultivated men. Culture, in general, is nothing else than
the exaltation of the individual above his subjectivity to
objective universal ideas, to the contemplation of the world.
The Apostles were men of the people; the people live only
in themselves, in their feelings; therefore Christianity took
possession of the people. *Vox populi vox Dei.* Did Christianity conquer a single philosopher, historian, or poet of
the classical period? The philosophers who went over to
Christianity were feeble, contemptible philosophers. All
who had yet the classic spirit in them were hostile, or at
least indifferent to Christianity. The decline of culture
was identical with the victory of Christianity. The classic
spirit, the spirit of culture, limits itself by laws,—not indeed
by arbitrary, finite laws, but by inherently true and valid
ones; it is determined by the necessity, the truth of the

* The legends of Catholicism—of course only the best, the really pleasing
ones—are, as it were, only the echo of the keynote which predominates in
this New Testament narrative. Miracle might be fitly defined as religious
humour. Catholicism especially has developed miracle on this its humorous
side.

nature of things; in a word, it is the objective spirit. In place of this, there entered with Christianity the principle of unlimited, extravagant, fanatical, supranaturalistic subjectivity; a principle intrinsically opposed to that of science, of culture.* With Christianity man lost the capability of conceiving himself as a part of Nature, of the universe. As long as true, unfeigned, unfalsified, uncompromising Christianity existed, as long as Christianity was a living, practical truth, so long did real miracles happen; and they necessarily happened, for faith in dead, historical, past miracles is itself a dead faith, the first step towards unbelief, or rather the first and therefore the timid, uncandid, servile mode in which unbelief in miracle finds vent. But where miracles happen, all definite forms melt in the golden haze of imagination and feeling; there the world, reality, is no truth; there the miracle-working, emotional, *i.e.*, subjective being, is held to be alone the objective, real being.

To the merely emotional man the imagination is immediately, without his willing or knowing it, the highest, the dominant activity; and being the highest, it is the activity of God, the creative activity. To him feeling is an immediate truth and reality; he cannot abstract himself from his feelings, he cannot get beyond them: and equally real is his imagination. The imagination is not to him what it is to us men of active understanding, who distinguish it as subjective from objective cognition; it is immediately identical with himself, with his feelings; and since it is identical with his being, it is his essential, objective, necessary view of things. For us, indeed, imagination is an arbitrary activity; but where man has not imbibed the principle of culture, of theory, where he lives and moves only in his feelings, the imagination is an immediate, involuntary activity.

The explanation of miracles by feeling and imagination is regarded by many in the present day as superficial. But let any one transport himself to the time when living, present miracles were believed in; when the reality of

---

* Culture in the sense in which it is here taken. It is highly characteristic of Christianity, and a popular proof of our positions, that the only language in which the Divine Spirit was and is held to reveal himself in Christianity is not the language of a Sophocles or a Plato, of art and philosophy, but the vague, unformed, crudely emotional language of the Bible.

things without us was as yet no sacred article of faith; when men were so void of any theoretic interest in the world, that they from day to day looked forward to its destruction; when they lived only in the rapturous prospect and hope of heaven, that is, in the imagination of it (for whatever heaven may be, for them, so long as they were on earth, it existed only in the imagination); when this imagination was not a fiction but a truth, nay, the eternal, alone abiding truth, not an inert, idle source of consolation, but a practical moral principle determining actions, a principle to which men joyfully sacrificed real life, the real world with all its glories;—let him transport himself to those times and he must himself be very superficial to pronounce the psychological genesis of miracles superficial. It is no valid objection that miracles have happened, or are supposed to have happened, in the presence of whole assemblies: no man was independent, all were filled with exalted supranaturalistic ideas and feelings; all were animated by the same faith, the same hope, the same hallucinations. And who does not know that there are common or similar dreams, common or similar visions, especially among impassioned individuals who are closely united and restricted to their own circle? But be that as it may. If the explanation of miracles by feeling and imagination is superficial, the charge of superficiality falls not on the explainer, but on that which he explains, namely, on miracle; for, seen in clear daylight, miracle presents absolutely nothing else than the sorcery of the imagination, which satisfies without contradiction all the wishes of the heart.*

* Many miracles may really have had originally a physical or physiological phenomenon as their foundation. But we are here considering only the religious significance and genesis of miracle.

CHAPTER XIV.

THE MYSTERY OF THE RESURRECTION AND OF THE MIRACULOUS CONCEPTION.

THE quality of being agreeable to subjective inclination belongs not only to practical miracles, in which it is conspicuous, as they have immediate reference to the interest or wish of the human individual; it belongs also to theoretical, or more properly dogmatic miracles, and hence to the Resurrection and the Miraculous Conception.

Man, at least in a state of ordinary well-being, has the wish not to die. This wish is originally identical with the instinct of self-preservation. Whatever lives seeks to maintain itself, to continue alive, and consequently not to die. Subsequently, when reflection and feeling are developed under the urgency of life, especially of social and political life, this primary negative wish becomes the positive wish for a life, and that a better life, after death. But this wish involves the further wish for the certainty of its fulfilment. Reason can afford no such certainty. It has therefore been said that all proofs of immortality are insufficient, and even that unassisted reason is not capable of apprehending it, still less of proving it. And with justice; for reason furnishes only general proofs; it cannot give the certainty of any personal immortality, and it is precisely this certainty which is desired. Such a certainty requires an immediate personal assurance, a practical demonstration. This can only be given to me by the fact of a dead person, whose death has been previously certified, rising again from the grave; and he must be no indifferent person, but, on the contrary, the type and representative of all others, so that his resurrection also may be the type, the guarantee of theirs. The resurrection of Christ is therefore the satisfied desire of man for an immediate certainty of his personal existence after death,—personal immortality as a sensible, indubitable fact.

Immortality was with the heathen philosophers a question in which the personal interest was only a collateral point.

They concerned themselves chiefly with the nature of the soul, of mind, of the vital principle. The immortality of the vital principle by no means involves the idea, not to mention the certainty, of personal immortality. Hence the vagueness, discrepancy, and dubiousness with which the ancients express themselves on this subject. The Christians, on the contrary, in the undoubting certainty that their personal, self-flattering wishes will be fulfilled, *i.e.*, in the certainty of the divine nature of their emotions, the truth and unassailableness of their subjective feelings, converted that which to the ancients was a theoretic problem into an immediate fact, —converted a theoretic, and in itself open question, into a matter of conscience, the denial of which was equivalent to the high treason of atheism. He who denies the resurrection denies the resurrection of Christ, but he who denies the resurrection of Christ denies Christ himself, and he who denies Christ denies God. Thus did "spiritual" Christianity unspiritualise what was spiritual! To the Christians the immortality of the reason, of the soul, was far too abstract and negative; they had at heart only a personal immortality, such as would gratify their feelings, and the guarantee of this lies in a bodily resurrection alone. The resurrection of the body is the highest triumph of Christianity over the sublime but certainly abstract spirituality and objectivity of the ancients. For this reason the idea of the resurrection could never be assimilated by the pagan mind.

As the Resurrection, which terminates the sacred history (to the Christian not a mere history, but the truth itself), is a realised wish, so also is that which commences it, namely, the Miraculous Conception, though this has relation not so much to an immediately personal interest as to a particular subjective feeling.

The more man alienates himself from Nature, the more subjective, *i.e.*, supranatural or antinatural, is his view of things, the greater the horror he has of Nature, or at least of those natural objects and processes which displease his imagination, which affect him disagreeably.* The free, objec-

---

* "If Adam had not fallen into sin, nothing would have been known of the cruelty of wolves, lions, bears, &c., and there would not have been in all creation anything vexatious and dangerous to man . . . ; no thorns, or thistles, or diseases . . .; his brow would not have been wrinkled ; no foot, or hand, or other member of the body would have been feeble or infirm."— "But now, since the Fall, we all know and feel what a fury lurks in our

tive man doubtless finds things repugnant and distasteful in
Nature, but he regards them as natural, inevitable results,
and under this conviction he subdues his feeling as a merely
subjective and untrue one. On the contrary, the subjective
man, who lives only in the feelings and imagination, regards
these things with a quite peculiar aversion. He has the eye
of that unhappy foundling, who even in looking at the love-
liest flower could pay attention only to the little " black
beetle " which crawled over it, and who by this perversity of
perception had his enjoyment in the sight of flowers always
embittered. Moreover, the subjective man makes his feelings
the measure, the standard of what ought to be. That which
does not please him, which offends his transcendental, supranatural, or antinatural feelings, ought not to be. Even if
that which pleases him cannot exist without being associated
with that which displeases him, the subjective man is not
guided by the wearisome laws of logic and physics, but by
the self-will of the imagination; hence he drops what is disagreeable in a fact, and holds fast alone what is agreeable.
Thus the idea of the pure, holy Virgin pleases him ; still he
is also pleased with the idea of the Mother, but only of the
Mother who already carries the infant on her arms.

Virginity in itself is to him the highest moral idea, the
cornu copiæ of his supranaturalistic feelings and ideas, his
personified sense of honour and of shame before common
nature.* Nevertheless, there stirs in his bosom a natural
feeling also, the compassionate feeling which makes the
Mother beloved. What then is to be done in this difficulty
of the heart, in this conflict between a natural and a supra-

flesh, which not only burns and rages with lust and desire, but also loathes,
when once obtained, the very thing it has desired. But this is the fault of
original sin, which has polluted all creatures ; wherefore I believe that
before the Fall the sun was much brighter, water much clearer, and the
land much richer, and fuller of all sorts of plants."—Luther (Th. i. s. 322,
323, 329, 337).
* "Tantum denique abest incesti cupido, ut nonnullis rubori sit etiam
pudica conjunctio."—M. Felicis, Oct. c. 31. One Father was so extraordinarily chaste that he had never seen a woman's face, nay, he dreaded even
touching himself, " se quoque ipsum attingere quodammodo horrebat."
Another Father had so fine an olfactory sense in this matter, that on the
approach of an unchaste person he perceived an insupportable odour."—
Bayle (Dict. Art. Mariana Rem. C.). But the supreme, the divine principle of this hyperphysical delicacy is the Virgin Mary ; hence the Catholics name her Virginum Gloria, Virginitatis corona, Virginitatis typus et
forma puritatis, Virginum vexillifera, Virginitatis magistra, Virginum
prima, Virginitatis primiceria.

natural feeling? The supranaturalist must unite the two, must comprise in one and the same subject two predicates which exclude each other.* Oh, what a plenitude of agreeable, sweet, supersensual, sensual emotions lies in this combination!

Here we have the key to the contradiction in Catholicism, that at the same time marriage is holy and celibacy is holy. This simply realises, as a practical contradiction, the dogmatic contradiction of the Virgin Mother. But this wondrous union of virginity and maternity, contradicting Nature and reason, but in the highest degree accordant with the feelings and imagination, is no product of Catholicism; it lies already in the twofold part which marriage plays in the Bible, especially in the view of the Apostle Paul. The supernatural conception of Christ is a fundamental doctrine of Christianity, a doctrine which expresses its inmost dogmatic essence, and which rests on the same foundation as all other miracles and articles of faith. As death, which the philosopher, the man of science, the free objective thinker in general, accepts as a natural necessity, and as indeed all the limits of nature, which are impediments to feeling, but to reason are rational laws, were repugnant to the Christians, and were set aside by them through the supposed agency of miraculous power; so, necessarily, they had an equal repugnance to the natural process of generation, and superseded it by miracle. The Miraculous Conception is not less welcome than the Resurrection to all believers; for it was the first step towards the purification of mankind, polluted by sin and Nature. Only because the God-man was not infected with original sin, could he, the pure one, purify mankind in the eyes of God, to whom the natural process of generation was an object of aversion, because he himself is nothing else but supranatural feeling.

Even the arid Protestant orthodoxy, so arbitrary in its criticism, regarded the conception of the God-producing Virgin as a great, adorable, amazing, holy mystery of faith, transcending reason.† But with the Protestants, who con-

---

* " Salve sancta parens, enixa puerpera Regem,
    Gaudia matris habens cum virginitatis honore."
                                    Theol. Schol. Mezger. t. iv. p. 132.
† See *e.g.* J. D. Winckler, Philolog. Lactant. s. Brunsvigæ, 1754, pp. 247-254.

fined the speciality of the Christian to the domain of faith, and with whom, in life, it was allowable to be a man, even this mystery had only a dogmatic, and no longer a practical significance; they did not allow it to interfere with their desire of marriage. With the Catholics, and with all the old, uncompromising, uncritical Christians, that which was a mystery of faith was a mystery of life, of morality. * Catholic morality is Christian, mystical; Protestant morality was, in its very beginning, rationalistic. Protestant morality is and was a carnal mingling of the Christian with the man, the natural, political, civil, social man, or whatever else he may be called in distinction from the Christian; Catholic morality cherished in its heart the mystery of the unspotted virginity. Catholic morality was the *Mater dolorosa;* Protestant morality a comely, fruitful matron. Protestantism is from beginning to end the contradiction between faith and love; for which very reason it has been the source, or at least the condition, of freedom. Just because the mystery of the *Virgo Deipara* had with the Protestants a place only in theory, or rather in dogma, and no longer in practice, they declared that it was impossible to express oneself with sufficient care and reserve concerning it, and that it ought not to be made an object of speculation. That which is denied in practice has no true basis and durability in man, is a mere spectre of the mind; and hence it is withdrawn from the investigation of the understanding. Ghosts do not brook daylight.

Even the later doctrine (which, however, had been already enunciated in a letter to St. Bernard, who rejects it), that Mary herself was conceived without taint of original sin, is by no means a "strange school-bred doctrine," as it is called by a modern historian. That which gives birth to a miracle, which brings forth God, must itself be of miraculous divine origin or nature. How could Mary have had the honour of being overshadowed by the Holy Ghost if she had not been from the first pure? Could the Holy Ghost take up his abode in a body polluted by original sin? If the principle of Christianity, the miraculous birth of the Saviour, does not appear strange to you, why think strange the naïve, well-meaning inferences of Catholicism?

---

* See on this subject *Philos. und Christenthum*, by L. Feuerbach.

CHAPTER XV.

THE fundamental dogmas of Christianity are realised wishes of the heart;—the essence of Christianity is the essence of human feeling. It is pleasanter to be passive than to act, to be redeemed and made free by another than to free oneself; pleasanter to make one's salvation dependent on a person than on the force of one's own spontaneity; pleasanter to set before oneself an object of love than an object of effort; pleasanter to know oneself beloved by God than merely to have that simple, natural self-love which is innate in all beings; pleasanter to see oneself imaged in the love-beaming eyes of another personal being, than to look into the concave mirror of self or into the cold depths of the ocean of Nature; pleasanter, in short, to allow oneself to be acted on by one's own feeling, as by another, but yet fundamentally identical being, than to regulate oneself by reason. Feeling is the oblique case of the *ego*, the *ego* in the accusative. The *ego* of Fichte is destitute of feeling, because the accusative is the same as the nominative, because it is indeclinable. But feeling or sentiment is the *ego* acted on by itself, and by itself as another being,—the passive *ego*. Feeling changes the active in man into the passive, and the passive into the active. To feeling, that which thinks is the thing thought, and the thing thought is that which thinks. Feeling is the dream of Nature; and there is nothing more blissful, nothing more profound than dreaming. But what is dreaming? The reversing of the waking consciousness. In dreaming, the active is the passive, the passive the active; in dreaming, I take the spontaneous action of my own mind for an action upon me from without, my emotions for events, my conceptions and sensations for true existences apart from myself. I suffer what I also perform. Dreaming is a double refraction of the rays of light; hence its indescribable charm. It is the same *ego*, the same being in dreaming as in waking;

the only distinction is, that in waking, the *ego* acts on itself; whereas in dreaming it is acted on by itself as by another being. *I think myself*—is a passionless, rationalistic position; *I am thought by God*, and think myself only as thought by God—is a position pregnant with feeling, religious. Feeling is a dream with the eyes open; religion the dream of waking consciousness : dreaming is the key to the mysteries of religion.

The highest law of feeling is the immediate unity of will and deed, of wishing and reality. This law is fulfilled by the Redeemer. As external miracles, in opposition to natural activity, realise immediately the physical wants and wishes of man; so the Redeemer, the Mediator, the God-man, in opposition to the moral spontaneity of the natural or rationalistic man, satisfies immediately the inward moral wants and wishes, since he dispenses man on his own side from any intermediate activity. What thou wishest is already effected. Thou desirest to win, to deserve happiness. Morality is the condition, the means of happiness. But thou canst not fulfil this condition; that is, in truth, thou needest not. That which thou seekest to do has already been done. Thou hast only to be passive, thou needest only believe, only enjoy. Thou desirest to make God favourable to thee, to appease his anger, to be at peace with thy conscience. But this peace exists already; this peace is the Mediator, the God-man. He is thy appeased conscience; he is the fulfilment of the law, and therewith the fulfilment of thy own wish and effort.

Therefore it is no longer the law, but the fulfiller of the law, who is the model, the guiding thread, the rule of thy life. He who fulfils the law annuls the law. The law has authority, has validity, only in relation to him who violates it. But he who perfectly fulfils the law says to it : What thou willest I spontaneously will, and what thou commandest I enforce by deeds; my life is the true, the living law. The fulfiller of the law, therefore, necessarily steps into the place of the law; moreover he becomes a new law, one whose yoke is light and easy. For in place of the merely imperative law, he presents himself as an example, as an object of love, of admiration and emulation, and thus becomes the Saviour from sin. The law does not give me the power to fulfil the law; no! it is hard and merciless; it only commands, without troubling itself whether I can fulfil it, or how I am to fulfil it; it leaves me to myself, without counsel or aid. But he who presents himself to me as an example lights up my path, takes me by the hand, and imparts to me his own strength. The law lends no power of resisting sin, but example works miracles. The law is dead; but example animates, inspires, carries men involuntarily along with it. The law speaks only to the understanding, and sets itself directly in opposition to the instincts; example, on the contrary, appeals to a powerful instinct immediately connected with the activity of the senses, that of involuntary imitation. Example operates on the feelings and imagination. In short, example has magical, *i.e.*, sense-affecting powers; for the magical or involuntary force of attraction is an essential property, as of matter in general, so in particular of that which affects the senses.

The ancients said that if virtue could become visible, its beauty would win and inspire all hearts. The Christians were so happy as to see even this wish fulfilled. The heathens had an unwritten, the Jews a written law; the Christians had a model—a visible, personal, living law, a law made flesh. Hence the joyfulness especially of the primitive Christians, hence the glory of Christianity that it alone contains and bestows the power to resist sin. And this glory is not to be denied it. Only, it is to be observed that the power of the exemplar of virtue is not so much the power of virtue as the power of example in general; just as the power of religious music is not the power of religion, but the power of music; * and that therefore, though the image of virtue has virtuous actions as its consequences, these actions are destitute of the dispositions and motives of virtue. But this simple and true sense of the redeeming and reconciling power of example in distinction from the power of law, to which we have reduced the antithesis of the law and Christ, by no means expresses the full religious significance of the Christian redemption and reconciliation. In this everything reduces itself to the personal power of

---

* In relation to this, the confession of Augustine is interesting: " Ita fluctuo inter periculum voluptatis et experimentum salubritatis : magisque adducor . . . cantandi consuetudinem approbare in ecclesia, ut per oblectamenta aurium infirmior animus in affectum pietatis assurgat. Tamen cum mihi accidit, ut nos amplius cantus, quam res quæ canitur moveat, pœnaliter me peccare confiteor."—Confess. l. x. c. 33.

that miraculous intermediate being who is neither God alone nor man alone, but a man who is also God, and a God who is also man, and who can therefore only be comprehended in connection with the significance of miracle. In this, the miraculous Redeemer is nothing else than the realised wish of feeling to be free from the laws of morality, *i.e.*, from the conditions to which virtue is united in the natural course of things; the realised wish to be freed from moral evils instantaneously, immediately, by a stroke of magic, that is, in an absolutely subjective, agreeable way. " The word of God," says Luther, for example, " accomplishes all things swiftly, brings forgiveness of sins, and gives thee eternal life, and costs nothing more than that thou shouldst hear the word, and when thou hast heard it shouldst believe. If thou believest, thou hast it without pains, cost, delay, or difficulty." * But that hearing of the word of God which is followed by faith is itself a " gift of God." Thus faith is nothing else than a psychological miracle, a supernatural operation of God in man, as Luther likewise says. But man becomes free from sin and from the consciousness of guilt only through faith,—morality is dependent on faith, the virtues of the heathens are only splendid sins ; thus he becomes morally free and good only through miracle.

That the idea of miraculous power is one with the idea of the intermediate being, at once divine and human, has historical proof in the fact that the miracles of the Old Testament, the delivery of the law, providence—all the elements which constitute the essence of religion, were in the later Judaism attributed to the Logos. In Philo, however, this Logos still hovers in the air between heaven and earth, now as abstract, now as concrete ; that is, Philo vacillates between himself as a philosopher and himself as a religious Israelite—between the positive element of religion and the metaphysical idea of deity ; but in such a way that even the abstract element is with him more or less invested with imaginative forms. In Christianity this Logos first attained perfect consistence, *i.e.*, religion now concentrated itself exclusively on that element, that object, which is the basis of its essential difference. The Logos is the personified essence of religion. Hence the definition of God as the essence of feeling has its complete truth only in the Logos.

* Th. xvi. p. 490.

God as God is feeling as yet shut up, hidden; only Christ is the unclosed, open feeling or heart. In Christ feeling is first perfectly certain of itself, and assured beyond doubt of the truth and divinity of its own nature; for Christ denies nothing to feeling; he fulfils all its prayers. In God the soul is still silent as to what affects it most closely,—it only sighs; but in Christ it speaks out fully; here it has no longer any reserves. To him who only sighs, wishes are still attended with disquietude; he rather complains that what he wishes is not, than openly, positively declares what he wishes; he is still in doubt whether his wishes have the force of law. But in Christ all anxiety of the soul vanishes; he is the sighing soul passed into a song of triumph over its complete satisfaction; he is the joyful certainty of feeling that its wishes hidden in God have truth and reality, the actual victory over death, over all the powers of the world and Nature, the resurrection no longer merely hoped for, but already accomplished; he is the heart released from all oppressive limits, from all sufferings,—the soul in perfect blessedness, the Godhead made visible.*

To see God is the highest wish, the highest triumph of the heart. Christ is this wish, this triumph, fulfilled. God, as an object of thought only, i.e., God as God, is always a remote being; the relation to him is an abstract one, like that relation of friendship in which we stand to a man who is distant from us, and personally unknown to us. However his works, the proofs of love which he gives us, may make his nature present to us, there always remains an unfilled void,—the heart is unsatisfied, we long to see him. So long as we have not met a being face to face, we are always in doubt whether he be really such as we imagine him; actual presence alone gives final confidence, perfect repose. Christ

---

* "Because God has given us his Son, he has with him given us everything, whether it be called devil, sin, hell, heaven, righteousness, life; all, all must be ours, because the Son is ours as a gift, in whom all else is included."—Luther (Th. xv. p. 311). "The best part of the resurrection has already happened; Christ, the head of all Christendom, has passed through death and risen from the dead. Moreover, the most excellent part of me, my soul, has likewise passed through death, and is with Christ in the heavenly being. What harm, then, can death and the grave do me?"—Luther (Th. xvi. p. 235). "A Christian man has equal power with Christ, has fellowship with him and a common tenure." (Th. xiii. p. 648.) "Whoever cleaves to Christ has as much as he." (Th. xvi. p. 574.)

is God known personally; Christ, therefore, is the blessed certainty that God is what the soul desires and needs him to be. God, as the object of prayer, is indeed already a human being, since he sympathises with human misery, grants human wishes; but still he is not yet an object to the religious consciousness as a real man. Hence, only in Christ is the last wish of religion realised, the mystery of religious feeling solved:—solved however in the language of imagery proper to religion, for what God is in essence, that Christ is in actual appearance. So far the Christian religion may justly be called the absolute religion. That God, who in himself is nothing else than the nature of man, should also have a real existence as such, should be as man an object to the consciousness—this is the goal of religion; and this the Christian religion has attained in the incarnation of God, which is by no means a transitory act, for Christ remains man even after his ascension,—man in heart and man in form, only that his body is no longer an earthly one, liable to suffering.

The incarnations of the Deity with the Orientals—the Hindoos, for example—have no such intense meaning as the Christian incarnation; just because they happen often they become indifferent, they lose their value. The manhood of God is his personality; the proposition, God is a personal being, means: God is a human being, God is a man. Personality is an abstraction, which has reality only in an actual man.* The idea which lies at the foundation of the incarnations of God is therefore infinitely better conveyed by one incarnation, one personality. Where God appears in several persons successively, these personalities are evanescent. What is required is a permanent, an exclusive personality. Where there are many incarnations, room is given for innumerable others; the imagination is not restrained; and even those incarnations which are already real pass into the category of the merely possible and conceivable, into the category of fancies or of mere appearances. But where one personality is exclusively believed in and contemplated, this at once

---

* This exhibits clearly the untruthfulness and vanity of the modern speculations concerning the personality of God. If you are not ashamed of a personal God, do not be ashamed of a corporeal God. An abstract colourless personality, a personality without flesh and blood, is an empty shade.

impresses with the power of an historical personality;
imagination is done away with, the freedom to imagine
others is renounced. This one personality presses on me
the belief in its reality. The characteristic of real personality is precisely exclusiveness,—the Leibnitzian principle
of distinction, namely, that no one existence is exactly like
another. The tone, the emphasis, with which the one
personality is expressed, produces such an effect on the
feelings, that it presents itself immediately as a real one,
and is converted from an object of the imagination into an
object of historical knowledge.

Longing is the *necessity* of feeling, and feeling longs for
a personal God. But this longing after the personality of
God is true, earnest, and profound only when it is the
longing for one personality, when it is satisfied with one.
With the plurality of persons the truth of the want
vanishes, and personality becomes a mere luxury of the
imagination. But that which operates with the force of necessity, operates with the force of reality on man. That which
to the feelings is a necessary being, is to them immediately
a real being. Longing says : There must be a personal God,
i.e., it cannot be that there is not; satisfied feeling says : He is.
The guarantee of his existence lies for feeling in its sense
of the necessity of his existence the necessity of the satisfaction in the force of the want. Necessity knows no law
besides itself ; necessity breaks iron. Feeling knows no
other necessity than its own, than the necessity of feeling,
than longing; it holds in extreme horror the necessity of
Nature, the necessity of reason. Thus to feeling, a subjective, sympathetic, personal God is necessary ; but it demands
one personality alone, and this an historical, real one. Only
when it is satisfied in the unity of personality has feeling
any concentration ; plurality dissipates it.

But as the truth of personality is unity, and as the truth
of unity is reality, so the truth of real personality is—*blood.*
The last proof, announced with peculiar emphasis by the
author of the fourth Gospel, that the visible person of God
was no phantasm, no illusion, but a real man, is that blood
flowed from his side on the cross. If the personal God has
a true sympathy with distress, he must himself suffer distress. Only in his suffering lies the assurance of his reality ;
only on this depends the impressiveness of the incarnation.

To see God does not satisfy feeling; the eyes give no sufficient guarantee. The truth of vision is confirmed only by touch. But as subjectively touch, so objectively the capability of being touched, palpability, passibility, is the last criterion of reality; hence the passion of Christ is the highest confidence, the highest self-enjoyment, the highest consolation of feeling; for only in the blood of Christ is the thirst for a personal, that is, a human, sympathising, tender God allayed.

"Wherefore we hold it to be a pernicious error when such (namely, divine) majesty is taken away from Christ according to his manhood, thereby depriving Christians of their highest consolation, which they have in . . . the promise of the presence of their Head, King and High Priest, who has promised them that not his mere Godhead, which to us poor sinners is as a consuming fire to dry stubble, but he—he the Man—who has spoken with us, who has proved all sorrows in the human form which he took upon him, who therefore can have fellow-feeling with us as his brethren,—that he will be with us in all our need, according to the nature whereby he is our brother and we are flesh of his flesh." *

It is superficial to say that Christianity is not the religion of one personal God, but of three personalities. These three personalities have certainly an existence in dogma; but even there the personality of the Holy Spirit is only an arbitrary decision which is contradicted by impersonal definitions; as, for example, that the Holy Spirit is the gift of the Father and Son.† Already the very "procession" of the Holy Ghost presents an evil prognostic for his personality, for a personal being is produced only by generation, not by an indefinite emanation or by *spiratio*. And even the Father, as the representative of the rigorous idea of the Godhead, is a personal being only according to opinion and assertion, not according to his definitions; he is an abstract idea, a purely rationalistic being. Only Christ is the plastic personality. To personality belongs form; form is the reality

---

* Concordienb. Erklär. Art. 8.
† This was excellently shown by Faustus Socinus. See his Defens. Animadv. in Assert. Theol. Coll. Posnan. de trino et uno Deo. Irenopoli, 1656, c. 11.

of personality. Christ alone is the personal God; he is the real God of Christians, a truth which cannot be too often repeated.* In him alone is concentrated the Christian religion, the essence of religion in general. He alone meets the longing for a personal God; he alone is an existence identical with the nature of feeling; on him alone are heaped all the joys of the imagination, and all the sufferings of the heart; in him alone are feeling and imagination exhausted. Christ is the blending in one of feeling and imagination.

Christianity is distinguished from other religions by this, that in other religions the heart and imagination are divided, in Christianity they coincide. Here the imagination does not wander, left to itself; it follows the leadings of the heart; it describes a circle, whose centre is feeling. Imagination is here limited by the wants of the heart, it only realises the wishes of feeling, it has reference only to the one thing needful; in brief, it has, at least generally, a practical, concentric tendency, not a vagrant, merely poetic one. The miracles of Christianity—no product of free, spontaneous activity, but conceived in the bosom of yearning, necessitous feeling—place us immediately on the ground of common, real life; they act on the emotional man with irresistible force, because they have the necessity of feeling on their side. The power of imagination is here at the same time the power of the heart,—imagination is only the victorious, triumphant heart. With the Orientals, with the Greeks, imagination, untroubled by the wants of the heart, revelled

---

* Let the reader examine, with reference to this, the writings of the Christian orthodox theologians against the heterodox; for example, against the Socinians. Modern theologians, indeed, agree with the latter, as is well known, in pronouncing the divinity of Christ as accepted by the Church to be unbiblical; but it is undeniably the characteristic principle of Christianity, and even if it does not stand in the Bible in the form which is given to it by dogma, it is nevertheless a necessary consequence of what is found in the Bible. A being who is the fulness of the Godhead bodily, who is omniscient (John xvi. 30) and almighty (raises the dead, works miracles), who is before all things, both in time and rank, who has life in himself (though an imparted life) like as the Father has life in himself,—what, if we follow out the consequences, can such a being be, but God? "Christ is one with the Father in will;"—but unity of will presupposes unity of nature. "Christ is the ambassador, the representative of God;"— but God can only be represented by a divine being. I can only choose as my representative one in whom I find the same or similar qualities as in myself; otherwise I belie myself.

in the enjoyment of earthly splendour and glory ; in Christianity, it descended from the palace of the gods into the
abode of poverty, where only want rules,—it humbled itself
under the sway of the heart. But the more it limited itself
in extent, the more intense became its strength. The wan-
tonness of the Olympian gods could not maintain itself
before the rigorous necessity of the heart ; but imagination
is omnipotent when it has a bond of union with the heart.
And this bond between the freedom of the imagination and
the necessity of the heart is Christ. All things are subject
to Christ ; he is the Lord of the world, who does with it
what he will ; but this unlimited power over Nature is
itself again subject to the power of the heart ;—Christ commands raging Nature to be still, but only that he may hear
the sighs of the needy.

CHAPTER XVI.

CHRIST is the omnipotence of subjectivity, the heart released from all the bonds and laws of Nature, the soul excluding the world, and concentrated only on itself, the reality of all the heart's wishes, the Easter festival of the heart, the ascent to heaven of the imagination:—Christ therefore is the distinction of Christianity from heathenism.

In Christianity, man was concentrated only on himself, he unlinked himself from the chain of sequences in the system of the universe, he made himself a self-sufficing whole, an absolute, extra- and supra-mundane being. Because he no longer regarded himself as a being immanent in the world, because he severed himself from connection with it, he felt himself an unlimited being—(for the sole limit of subjectivity is the world, is objectivity),—he had no longer any reason to doubt the truth and validity of his subjective wishes and feelings.

The heathens, on the contrary, not shutting out Nature by retreating within themselves, limited their subjectivity by the contemplation of the world. Highly as the ancients estimated the intelligence, the reason, they were yet liberal and objective enough, theoretically as well as practically, to allow that which they distinguished from mind, namely, matter, to live, and even to live eternally; the Christians evinced their theoretical as well as practical intolerance in their belief that they secured the eternity of their subjective life only by annihilating, as in the doctrine of the destruction of the world, the opposite of subjectivity—Nature. The ancients were free from themselves, but their freedom was that of indifference towards themselves; the Christians were free from Nature, but their freedom was not that of reason, not true freedom, which limits itself by the contemplation of the world, by Nature,—it was the freedom of feeling and imagination, the freedom of miracle. The ancients were so enraptured by the cosmos, that they lost sight of themselves, suffered themselves to be merged in the whole; the Christians despised the world ;—what is the creature compared with the Creator ?'what are sun, moon, and earth compared with the human soul ?* The world passes away, but man, nay, the individual, personal man, is eternal. If the Christians severed man from all community with Nature, and hence fell into the extreme of an arrogant fastidiousness, which stigmatised the remotest comparison of man with the brutes as an impious violation of human dignity ; the heathens, on the other hand, fell into the opposite extreme, into that spirit of depreciation which abolishes the distinction between man and the brute, or even, as was the case, for example, with Celsus, the opponent of Christianity, degrades man beneath the brute.

But the heathens considered man not only in connection with the universe ; they considered the individual man, in connection with other men, as member of a commonwealth. They rigorously distinguished the individual from the species, the individual as a part from the race as a whole, and they subordinated the part to the whole. Men pass away, but mankind remains, says a heathen philosopher. "Why wilt thou grieve over the loss of thy daughter ?" writes Sulpicius to Cicero. "Great, renowned cities and empires have passed away, and thou behavest thus at the death of an *homunculus*, a little human being! Where is thy philosophy ?" The idea of man as an individual was to the ancients a secondary one, attained through the idea of the species. Though they thought highly of the race, highly of the excellences of mankind, highly and sublimely of the intelligence, they nevertheless thought slightly of the individual. Christianity, on the contrary, cared nothing for the species, and had only the individual in its eye and mind. Christianity—not, certainly, the Christianity of the present day, which has incorporated with itself the culture of heathenism, and has preserved only the name and some general positions of Christianity—is the direct opposite of heathenism, and only when it is regarded as such is it truly com-

---

* "How much better is it that I should lose the whole world than that I should lose God, who created the world, and can create innumerable worlds, who is better than a hundred thousand, than innumerable worlds? For what sort of a comparison is that of the temporal with the eternal? . . . One soul is better than the whole world."—Luther (Th. xix. p. 21).

prehended, and untravestied by arbitrary speculative interpretation; it is true so far as its opposite is false, and false
so far as its opposite is true. The ancients sacrificed the
individual to the species; the Christians sacrificed the
species to the individual. Or, heathenism conceived the
individual only as a part in distinction from the whole of
the species; Christianity, on the contrary, conceived the
individual only in immediate, undistinguishable unity with
the species.

To Christianity the individual was the object of an immediate providence, that is, an immediate object of the Divine
Being. The heathens believed in a providence for the individual only through his relation to the race, through law,
through the order of the world, and thus only in a mediate,
natural, and not miraculous providence; * but the Christians
left out the intermediate process, and placed themselves in
immediate connection with the prescient, all-embracing, universal Being; i.e., they immediately identified the individual
with the universal Being.

But the idea of deity coincides with the idea of humanity.
All divine attributes, all the attributes which make God God,
are attributes of the species—attributes which in the individual are limited, but the limits of which are abolished in
the essence of the species, and even in its existence, in so
far as it has its complete existence only in all men taken
together. My knowledge, my will, is limited; but my limit
is not the limit of another man, to say nothing of mankind;
what is difficult to me is easy to another; what is impossible,
inconceivable, to one age, is to the coming age conceivable
and possible. My life is bound to a limited time; not so the
life of humanity. The history of mankind consists of nothing
else than a continuous and progressive conquest of limits,
which at a given time pass for the limits of humanity, and

* It is true that the heathen philosophers also, as Plato, Socrates, the
Stoics (see e.g. J. Lipsius, Physiol. Stoic. l. i. diss. xi.), believed that the
divine providence extended not merely to the general, but also to the particular, the individual ; but they identified providence with Nature, law,
necessity. The Stoics, who were the orthodox speculatists of heathenism,
did indeed believe in miracles wrought by providence (Cic. de Nat. Deor. l.
ii. and De Divinat. l. i.) ; but their miracles had no such supranaturalistic
significance as those of Christianity, though they also appealed to the supranaturalistic axiom : " Nihil est quod Deus efficere non possit."

therefore for absolute insurmountable limits. But the future always unveils the fact that the alleged limits of the species were only limits of individuals. The most striking proofs of this are presented by the history of philosophy and of physical science. It would be highly interesting and instructive to write a history of the sciences entirely from this point of view, in order to exhibit in all its vanity the presumptuous notion of the individual than he can set limits to his race. Thus the species is unlimited; the individual alone limited.

But the sense of limitation is painful, and hence the individual frees himself from it by the contemplation of the perfect Being; in this contemplation he possesses what otherwise is wanting to him. With the Christians God is nothing else than the immediate unity of species and individuality, of the universal and individual being. God is the idea of the species as an individual—the idea or essence of the species, which as a species, as universal being, as the totality of all perfections, of all attributes or realities, freed from all the limits which exist in the consciousness and feeling of the individual, is at the same time again an individual, personal being. *Ipse suum esse est.* Essence and existence are in God identical; which means nothing else than that he is the idea, the essence of the species, conceived immediately as an existence, an individual. The highest idea on the standpoint of religion is: God does not love, he is himself love; he does not live, he is life; he is not just, but justice itself; not a person, but personality itself,— the species, the idea, as immediately a concrete existence.*

Because of this immediate unity of the species with individuality, this concentration of all that is universal and real in one personal being, God is a deeply moving object, enrapturing to the imagination; whereas, the idea of humanity has little power over the feelings, because humanity is only an abstraction; and the reality which presents itself to us in distinction from this abstraction is the multitude of separate, limited individuals. In God, on the contrary, feeling has immediate satisfaction, because here all is embraced in one, *i.e.,* because here the species has an immediate existence,—

---

* "Dicimur amare et Deus ; dicimur nosse et Deus. Et multa in hunc modum. Sed Deus amat ut charitas, novit ut veritas, etc."—Bernard. (de Consider. l. v.).

is an individuality. God is love, is justice, as itself a subject; he is the perfect universal being as one being, the infinite extension of the species as an all-comprehending unity. But God is only man's intuition of his own nature; thus the Christians are distinguished from the heathens in this, that they immediately identify the individual with the species— that with them the individual has the significance of the species, the individual by himself is held to be the perfect representative of the species—that they deify the human individual, make him the absolute being.

Especially characteristic is the difference between Christianity and heathenism concerning the relation of the individual to the intelligence, to the understanding, to the νοῦς. The Christians individualised the understanding, the heathens made it a universal essence. To the heathens, the understanding, the intelligence, was the essence of man; to the Christians, it was only a part of themselves. To the heathens therefore only the intelligence, the species, to the Christians, the individual, was immortal, *i.e.*, divine. Hence follows the further difference between heathen and Christian philosophy.

The most unequivocal expression, the characteristic symbol of this immediate identity of the species and individuality in Christianity is Christ, the real God of the Christians. Christ is the ideal of humanity become existent, the compendium of all moral and divine perfections to the exclusion of all that is negative ; pure, heavenly, sinless man, the typical man, the Adam Kadmon ; not regarded as the totality of the species, of mankind, but immediately as one individual, one person. Christ, *i.e.*, the Christian, religious Christ, is therefore not the central, but the terminal point of history. The Christians expected the end of the world, the close of history. In the Bible, Christ himself, in spite of all the falsities and sophisms of our exegetists, clearly prophesies the speedy end of the world. History rests only on the distinction of the individual from the race. Where this distinction ceases, history ceases; the very soul of history is extinct. Nothing remains to man but the contemplation and appropriation of this realised Ideal, and the spirit of proselytism, which seeks to extend the prevalence of a fixed belief,—the preaching that God has appeared, and that the end of the world is at hand.

Since the immediate identity of the species and the individual oversteps the limits of reason and Nature, it followed of course that this universal, ideal individual was declared to be a transcendent, supernatural, heavenly being. It is therefore a perversity to attempt to deduce from reason the immediate identity of the species and individual, for it is only the imagination which effects this identity, the imagination to which nothing is impossible, and which is also the creator of miracles; for the greatest of miracles is the being who, while he is an individual, is at the same time the ideal, the species, humanity in the fulness of its perfection and infinity, *i.e.*, the Godhead. Hence it is also a perversity to adhere to the biblical or dogmatic Christ, and yet to thrust aside miracles. If the principle be retained, wherefore deny its necessary consequences ?

The total absence of the idea of the species in Christianity is especially observable in its characteristic doctrine of the universal sinfulness of men. For there lies at the foundation of this doctrine the demand that the individual shall not be an individual, a demand which again is based on the presupposition that the individual by himself is a perfect being, is by himself the adequate presentation or existence of the species.* Here is entirely wanting the objective perception, the consciousness, that the *thou* belongs to the perfection of the *I*, that *men* are required to constitute humanity, that only men taken together are what man should and can be. All men are sinners. Granted; but they are not all sinners in the same way ; on the contrary, there exists a great and essential difference between them. One man is inclined to falsehood, another is not; he would rather give up his life than break his word or tell a lie ; the third has a propensity to intoxication, the fourth to licentiousness; while the fifth, whether by favour of Nature, or from the energy of his character, exhibits none of these vices. Thus, in the moral as well as the physical and intellectual elements, men compensate for each other, so that,

---

* It is true that in one sense the individual is the absolute—in the phraseology of Leibnitz, the mirror of the universe, of the infinite. But in so far as there are many individuals, each is only a single, and, as such, a finite mirror of the infinite. It is true also, in opposition to the abstraction of a sinless man, that each individual regarded in himself is perfect, and only by comparison imperfect, for each is what alone he can be.

taken as a whole, they are as they should be, they present the perfect man.

Hence intercourse ameliorates and elevates; involuntarily and without disguise, man is different in intercourse from what he is when alone. Love especially works wonders, and the love of the sexes most of all. Man and woman are the complement of each other, and thus united they first present the species, the perfect man.* Without species, love is inconceivable. Love is nothing else than the self-consciousness of the species as evolved within the difference of sex. In love, the reality of the species, which otherwise is only a thing of reason, an object of mere thought, becomes a matter of feeling, a truth of feeling; for in love, man declares himself unsatisfied in his individuality taken by itself, he postulates the existence of another as a need of the heart; he reckons another as part of his own being; he declares the life which he has through love to be the truly human life, corresponding to the idea of man, *i.e.*, of the species. The individual is defective, imperfect, weak, needy; but love is strong, perfect, contented, free from wants, self-sufficing, infinite; because in it the self-consciousness of the individuality is the mysterious self-consciousness of the perfection of the race. But this result of love is produced by friendship also, at least where it is intense, 'where it is a religion,† as it was with the ancients. Friends compensate for each other; friendship is a means of virtue, and more: it is itself virtue, dependent however on participation. Friendship can only exist between the virtuous, as the ancients said. But it cannot be based on perfect similarity; on the contrary, it requires diversity, for friendship rests on a desire for self-completion. One friend obtains through the other what he does not himself possess. The virtues of the one atone for the failings of the other.

* With the Hindoos (Inst. of Menu) he alone is "a perfect man who consists of three united persons, his wife, himself, and his son. For man and wife, and father and son, are one." The Adam of the Old Testament also is incomplete without woman ; he feels his need of her. But the Adam of the New Testament, the Christian, heavenly Adam, the Adam who is constituted with a view to the destruction of this world, has no longer any sexual impulses or functions.

† "Hæ sane vires amicitiæ mortis contemptum ingenerare . . . potuerunt : quibus pene tantum venerationis, quantum Deorum immortalium ceremoniis debetur. Illis enim publica salus, his privata continetur."—Valerius Max. l. iv. c. 7.

Friend justifies friend before God. However faulty a man may be, it is a proof that there is a germ of good in him if he has worthy men for his friends. If I cannot be myself perfect, I yet at least love virtue, perfection in others. If therefore I am called to account for any sins, weaknesses, and faults, I interpose as advocates, as mediators, the virtues of my friend. How barbarous, how unreasonable would it be to condemn me for sins which I doubtless have committed, but which I have myself condemned in loving my friends, who are free from these sins!

But if friendship and love, which themselves are only subjective realisations of the species, make out of singly imperfect beings an at least relatively perfect whole, how much more do the sins and failings of individuals vanish in the species itself, which has its adequate existence only in the sum total of mankind, and is therefore only an object of reason! Hence the lamentation over sin is found only where the human individual regards himself in his individuality as a perfect, complete being, not needing others for the realisation of the species, of the perfect man; where instead of the consciousness of the species has been substituted the exclusive self-consciousness of the individual; where the individual does not recognise himself as a part of mankind, but identifies himself with the species, and for this reason makes his own sins, limits and weaknesses, the sins, limits, and weaknesses of mankind in general. Nevertheless man cannot lose the consciousness of the species, for his self-consciousness is essentially united to his consciousness of another than himself. Where therefore the species is not an object to him as a species, it will be an object to him as God. He supplies the absence of the idea of the species by the idea of God, as the being who is free from the limits and wants which oppress the individual, and, in his opinion (since he identifies the species with the individual), the species itself. But this perfect being, free from the limits of the individual, is nothing else than the species, which reveals the infinitude of its nature in this, that it is realised in infinitely numerous and various individuals. If all men were absolutely alike, there would then certainly be no distinction between the race and the individual. But in that case the existence of many men would be a pure superfluity; a single man would have achieved the ends of the species.

In the one who enjoyed the happiness of existence all would have had their complete substitute.

Doubtless the essence of man is *one*, but this essence is infinite; its real existence is therefore an infinite, reciprocally compensating variety, which reveals the riches of this essence. Unity in essence is multiplicity in existence. Between me and another human being—and this other is the representative of the species, even though he is only one, for he supplies to me the want of many others, has for me a universal significance, is the deputy of mankind, in whose name he speaks to me, an isolated individual, so that, when united only with one, I have a participated, a human life;—between me and another human being there is an essential, qualitative distinction. The other is my *thou*,— the relation being reciprocal,—my *alter ego*, man objective to me, the revelation of my own nature, the eye seeing itself. In another I first have the consciousness of humanity; through him I first learn, I first feel, that I am a man : in my love for him it is first clear to me that he belongs to me and I to him, that we two cannot be without each other, that only community constitutes humanity. But morally, also, there is a qualitative, critical distinction between the *I* and *thou*. My fellow-man is my objective conscience; he makes my failings a reproach to me; even when he does not expressly mention them, he is my personified feeling of shame. The consciousness of the moral law, of right, of propriety, of truth itself, is indissolubly united with my consciousness of another than myself. That is true in which another agrees with me,—agreement is the first criterion of truth; but only because the species is the ultimate measure of truth. That which I think only according to the standard of my individuality is not binding on another; it can be conceived otherwise ; it is an accidental, merely subjective view. But that which I think according to the standard of the species, I think as man in general only can think, and consequently as every individual must think if he thinks normally, in accordance with law, and therefore truly. That is true which agrees with the nature of the species, that is false which contradicts it. There is no other rule of truth. But my fellow-man is to me the representative of the species, the substitute of the rest, nay, his judgment may be of more authority with me than the judgment of the innumerable multitude. Let the fanatic make disciples as the sand on the sea-shore ; the sand is still sand ; mine be the pearl—a judicious friend. The agreement of others is therefore my criterion of the normalness, the universality, the truth of my thoughts. I cannot so abstract myself from myself as to judge myself with perfect freedom and disinterestedness ; but another has an impartial judgment ; through him I correct, complete, extend my own judgment, my own taste, my own knowledge. In short, there is a qualitative, critical difference between men. But Christianity extinguishes this qualitative distinction ; it sets the same stamp on all men alike, and regards them as one and the same individual, because it knows no distinction between the species and the individual : it has one and the same means of salvation for all men, it sees one and the same original sin in all.

Because Christianity thus, from exaggerated subjectivity, knows nothing of the species, in which alone lies the redemption, the justification, the reconciliation and cure of the sins and deficiencies of the individual, it needed a supernatural and peculiar, nay, a personal, subjective aid in order to overcome sin. If I alone am the species, if no other, that is, no qualitatively different men exist, or, which is the same thing, if there is no distinction between me and others, if we are all perfectly alike, if my sins are not neutralised by the opposite qualities of other men : then assuredly my sin is a blot of shame which cries up to heaven ; a revolting horror which can be exterminated only by extraordinary, superhuman, miraculous means. Happily, however, there *is* a natural reconciliation. My fellow-man is *per se* the mediator between me and the sacred idea of the species. *Homo homini Deus est.* My sin is made to shrink within its limits, is thrust back into its nothingness, by the fact that it is only mine, and not that of my fellows.

CHAPTER XVII.

THE CHRISTIAN SIGNIFICANCE OF VOLUNTARY CELIBACY AND MONACHISM.

THE idea of man as a species, and with it the significance of the life of the species, of humanity as a whole, vanished as Christianity became dominant. Herein we have a new confirmation of the position advanced, that Christianity does not contain within itself the principle of culture. Where man immediately identifies the species with the individual, and posits this identity as his highest being, as God, where the idea of humanity is thus an object to him only as the idea of Godhead, there the need of culture has vanished; man has all in himself, all in his God, consequently he has no need to supply his own deficiencies by others as the representatives of the species, or by the contemplation of the world generally; and this need is alone the spring of culture. The individual man attains his end by himself alone; he attains it in God,—God is himself the attained goal, the realised highest aim of humanity; but God is present to each individual separately. God only is the want of the Christian; others, the human race, the world, are not necessary to him; he is not the inward need of others. God fills to me the place of the species, of my fellow-men; yes, when I turn away from the world, when I am in isolation, I first truly feel my need of God, I first have a lively sense of his presence, I first feel what God is, and what he ought to be to me. It is true that the religious man has need also of fellowship, of edification in common; but this need of others is always in itself something extremely subordinate. The salvation of the soul is the fundamental idea, the main point in Christianity; and this salvation lies only in God, only in the concentration of the mind on him. Activity for others is required, is a condition of salvation; but the ground of salvation is God, immediate reference in all things to God. And even activity for others has only a religious significance, has reference only to God, as its motive and end, is essentially only an activity for God, —for the glorifying of his name, the spreading abroad of his praise. But God is absolute subjectivity,—subjectivity separated from the world, above the world, set free from matter, severed from the life of the species, and therefore from the distinction of sex. Separation from the world, from matter, from the life of the species, is therefore the essential aim of Christianity.* And this aim had its visible, practical realisation in Monachism.

It is a self-delusion to attempt to derive monachism from the East. At least, if this derivation is to be accepted, they who maintain it should be consistent enough to derive the opposite tendency of Christendom, not from Christianity, but from the spirit of the Western nations, the occidental nature in general. But how, in that case, shall we explain the monastic enthusiasm of the West? Monachism must rather be derived directly from Christianity itself: it was a necessary consequence of the belief in heaven promised to mankind by Christianity. Where the heavenly life is a truth, the earthly life is a lie; where imagination is all, reality is nothing. To him who believes in an eternal heavenly life, the present life loses its value,—or rather, it has already lost its value: belief in the heavenly life is belief in the worthlessness and nothingness of this life. I cannot represent to myself the future life without longing for it, without casting down a look of compassion or contempt on this pitiable earthly life, and the heavenly life can be no object, no law of faith, without, at the same time, being a law of morality: it must determine my actions,† at least if my life is to be in accordance with my faith: I ought not to cleave to the transitory things of this earth. I *ought* not;—but neither do I *wish ;* for what are all things here below compared with the glory of the heavenly life?‡

---

* "The life for God is not this natural life, which is subject to decay. . . . Ought we not then to sigh after future things, and be averse to all these temporal things? . . . Wherefore we should find consolation in heartily despising this life and this world, and from our hearts sigh for and desire the future honour and glory of eternal life."—Luther (Th. i. s. 466, 467).

† "Eo dirigendus est spiritus, quo aliquando est iturus."—Meditat. Sacræ Joh. Gerhardi. Med. 46.

‡ "Affectanti cœlestia, terrena non sapiunt. Æternis inhianti, fastidio sunt transitoria."—Bernard. (Epist. Ex Persona Heliæ Monachi ad Parentes).

It is true that the quality of that life depends on the quality, the moral condition of this; but morality is itself determined by the faith in eternal life. The morality corresponding to the super-terrestrial life is simply separation from the world, the negation of this life; and the practical attestation of this spiritual separation is the monastic life.* Everything must ultimately take an external form, must present itself to the senses. An inward disposition must become an outward practice. The life of the cloister, indeed ascetic life in general, is the heavenly life as it is realised and can be realised here below. If my soul belongs to heaven, ought I, nay, can I belong to the earth with my body? The soul animates the body. But if the soul is in heaven, the body is forsaken, dead, and thus the medium, the organ of connection between the world and the soul is annihilated. Death, the separation of the soul from the body, at least from this gross, material, sinful body, is the entrance into heaven. But if death is the condition of blessedness and moral perfection, then necessarily mortification is the one law of morality. Moral death is the necessary anticipation of natural death; I say necessary, for it would be the extreme of immorality to attribute the obtaining of heaven to physical death, which is no moral act, but a natural one common to man and the brute. Death must therefore be exalted into a moral, a spontaneous act. " I die daily," says the apostle, and this dictum Saint Anthony, the founder of monachism,† made the theme of his life.

But Christianity, it is contended, demanded only a spiritual freedom. True; but what is that spiritual freedom which does not pass into action, which does not attest itself in practice? Or dost thou believe that it only depends on thyself, on thy will, on thy intention, whether thou be free from anything? If so, thou art greatly in error, and hast

"Nihil nostra referti n hoc ævo, nisi de eo quam celeriter excedere."—Tertullian (Apol. adv. Gentes, c. 41). "Wherefore a Christian man should rather be advised to bear sickness with patience, yea, even to desire that death should come,—the sooner the better. For, as St. Cyprian says, nothing is more for the advantage of a Christian than soon to die. But we rather listen to the pagan Juvenal when he says : 'Orandum est ut sit mens sana in corpore sano.'"—Luther (Th. iv. s. 15).

* "Ille perfectus est qui mente et corpore a seculo est elongatus."—De Modo Bene Vivendi ad Sororem, s. vii. (Among the spurious writings of St. Bernard.)

† On this subject see " Hieronymus, de Vita Pauli Primi Eremitæ."

never experienced what it is to be truly made free. So long as thou art in a given rank, profession, or relation, so long art thou, willingly or not, determined by it. Thy will, thy determination, frees thee only from conscious limitations and impressions, not from the unconscious ones which lie in the nature of the case. Thus we do not feel at home, we are under constraint, so long as we are not locally, physically separated from one with whom we have inwardly broken. External freedom is alone the full truth of spiritual freedom. A man who has really lost spiritual interest in earthly treasures soon throws them out at window, that his heart may be thoroughly at liberty. What I no longer possess by inclination is a burden to me; so away with it! What affection has let go, the hand no longer holds fast. Only affection gives force to the grasp; only affection makes possession sacred. He who having a wife is as though he had her not, will do better to have no wife at all. To have as though one had not, is to have without the disposition to have, is in truth not to have. And therefore he who says that one ought to have a thing as though one had it not, merely says in a subtle, covert, cautious way, that one ought not to have it at all. That which I dismiss from my heart is no longer mine,—it is free as air. St. Anthony took the resolution to renounce the world when he had once heard the saying, "If thou wilt be perfect, go thy way, sell that thou hast and give to the poor, and thou shalt have treasure in heaven; and come and follow me." St. Anthony gave the only true interpretation of this text. He went his way, and sold his possessions, and gave the proceeds to the poor. Only thus did he prove his spiritual freedom from the treasures of this world.*

Such freedom, such truth, is certainly in contradiction with the Christianity of the present day, according to which the Lord has required only a spiritual freedom, *i.e.*, a freedom which demands no sacrifice, no energy,—an illusory, self-deceptive freedom;—a freedom from earthly good, which consists in its possession and enjoyment! For certainly the Lord said, "My yoke is easy." How harsh, how

---

* Naturally Christianity had only such power when, as Jerome writes to Demetrius, Domini nostri adhuc calebat cruor et fervebat recens in credentibus fides. See also on this subject G. Arnold.—*Von der ersten Christen Genügsamkeit u. Verschmähung alles Eigennutzes,* l. c. B. iv. c. 12, § 7-16.

unreasonable would Christianity be if it exacted from man the renunciation of earthly riches! Then assuredly Christianity would not be suited to this world. So far from this, Christianity is in the highest degree practical and judicious; it defers the freeing oneself from the wealth and pleasures of this world to the moment of natural death (monkish mortification is an unchristian suicide);—and allots to our spontaneous activity the acquisition and enjoyment of earthly possessions. Genuine Christians do not indeed doubt the truth of the heavenly life,—God forbid! Therein they still agree with the ancient monks; but they await that life patiently, submissive to the will of God, *i.e.*, to their own selfishness, to the agreeable pursuit of worldly enjoyment.* But I turn away with loathing and contempt from modern Christianity, in which the bride of Christ readily acquiesces in polygamy, at least in successive polygamy, and this in the eyes of the true Christian does not essentially differ from contemporaneous polygamy; but yet at the same time—oh! shameful hypocrisy!—swears by the eternal, universally binding, irrefragable sacred truth of God's Word. I turn back with reverence to the misconceived truth of the chaste monastic cell, where the soul betrothed to heaven did not allow itself to be wooed into faithlessness by a strange earthly body!

The unworldly, supernatural life is essentially also an unmarried life. The celibate lies already, though not in the form of a law, in the inmost nature of Christianity. This is sufficiently declared in the supernatural origin of the Saviour,—a doctrine in which unspotted virginity is hallowed as the saving principle, as the principle of the new, the Christian world. Let not such passages as, "Be fruitful and multiply," or, "What God has joined together let not man put asunder," be urged as a sanction of marriage. The first passage relates, as Tertullian and Jerome have already observed, only to the unpeopled earth, not to the earth when filled with men, only to the

---

* How far otherwise the ancient Christians! "Difficile, imo impossibile est, ut et præsentibus quis et futuris fruatur bonis."—Hieronymus (Epist. Juliano). "Delicatus es, frater, si et hic vis gaudere cum seculo et postea regnare cum Christo."—Ib. (Epist. ad Heliodorum). "Ye wish to have both God and the creature together, and that is impossible. Joy in God and joy in the creature cannot subsist together."—Tauler (ed. c. p. 334). But they were abstract Christians. And we live now in the age of conciliation. Yes, truly!

beginning, not to the end of the world, an end which was initiated by the immediate appearance of God upon earth. And the second also refers only to marriage as an institution of the Old Testament. Certain Jews proposed the question whether it were lawful for a man to separate from his wife; and the most appropriate way of dealing with this question was the answer above cited. He who has once concluded a marriage ought to hold it sacred. Marriage is intrinsically an indulgence to the weakness or rather the strength of the flesh, an evil which therefore must be restricted as much as possible. The indissolubleness of marriage is a *nimbus*, a sacred irradiance, which expresses precisely the opposite of what minds, dazzled and perturbed by its lustre, seek beneath it. Marriage in itself is, in the sense of perfected Christianity, a sin,* or rather a weakness which is permitted and forgiven thee only on condition that thou for ever limitest thyself to a single wife. In short, marriage is hallowed only in the Old Testament, but not in the New. The New Testament knows a higher, a supernatural principle, the mystery of unspotted virginity.† " He who can receive it let him receive it." " The children of this world marry, and are given in marriage : but they which shall be accounted worthy to obtain that world, and the resurrection from the dead, neither marry nor are given in marriage : neither can they die any more : for they are equal unto the angels; and are the children of God, being the children of the resurrection." Thus in heaven there is no marriage ; the principle of sexual love is excluded from heaven as an earthly, worldly principle. But the heavenly life is the true, perfected, eternal life of the Christian. Why then should I, who am destined for heaven, form a tie which is unloosed in my true destination ? Why should I, who am potentially a heavenly being, not realise this possibility even here?‡ Marriage is already proscribed from

* "Perfectum autem esse nolle delinquere est."—Hieronymus (Epist. ad Heliodorum de laude Vitæ solit.). Let me observe once for all that I interpret the biblical passages concerning marriage in the sense in which they have been interpreted by the history of Christianity.

† "The marriage state is nothing new or unwonted, and is lauded and held good even by heathens according to the judgment of reason."—Luther (Th. ii. p. 377a).

‡ "Præsumendum est hos qui intra paradisum recipi volunt debere cessare ab ea re, a qua paradisus intactus est."—Tertullian (de Exhort. cast. c. 13). "Cœlibatus angelorum est imitatio."—Jo. Damasceni (Orthod. Fidei, l. iv. c. 25).

my mind, my heart, since it is expelled from heaven, the essential object of my faith, hope, and life. How can an earthly wife have a place in my heaven-filled heart? How can I divide my heart between God and man?* The Christian's love to God is not an abstract or general love such as the love of truth, of justice, of science ; it is a love to a subjective, personal God, and is therefore a subjective, personal love. It is an essential attribute of this love that it is an exclusive, jealous love, for its object is a personal and at the same time the highest being, to whom no other can be compared. " Keep close to Jesus [Jesus Christ is the Christian's God], in life and in death ; trust his faithfulness: he alone can help thee, when all else leaves thee. Thy beloved has this quality, that he will suffer no rival ; he alone will have thy heart, will rule alone in thy soul as a king on his throne."—"What can the world profit thee without Jesus ? To be without Christ is the pain of hell ; to be with Christ, heavenly sweetness."—" Thou canst not live without a friend : but if the friendship of Christ is not more than all else to thee, thou wilt be beyond measure sad and disconsolate."—" Love everything for Jesus' sake, but Jesus for his own sake. Jesus Christ alone is worthy to be loved."—" My God, my love [my heart]: thou art wholly mine, and I am wholly thine."—" Love hopes and trusts ever in God, even when God is not gracious to it [or tastes bitter, *non sapit*] ; for we cannot live in love without sorrow. . . . . For the sake of the beloved, the loving one must accept all things, even the hard and bitter."—" My God and my all, ... in thy presence everything is sweet to me, in thy absence everything is distasteful . . . . Without thee nothing can please me."—" Oh, when at last will that blessed, longed-for hour appear, when thou wilt satisfy me wholly, and be all in all to me ? So long as this is not granted me, my joy is only fragmentary."—"When was it well with me without thee ? or when was it ill with me in thy presence ? I will rather be poor for thy sake, than rich without thee. I will rather be a pilgrim on earth with thee, than the possessor of heaven without thee. Where thou art is heaven ; death and hell where thou art

* " Quæ non nubit, soli Deo dat operam et ejus cura non dividitur ; pudica autem, quæ nupsit, vitam cum Deo et cum marito dividit."— Clemens Alex. (Pædag. l. ii.).

not. I long only for thee."—"Thou canst not serve God and at the same time have thy joys in earthly things: thou must wean thyself from all acquaintances and friends, and sever thy soul from all temporal consolation. Believers in Christ should regard themselves, according to the admonition of the Apostle Peter, only as strangers and pilgrims on the earth." * Thus love to God as a personal being is a literal, strict, personal, exclusive love. How then can I at once love God and a mortal wife? Do I not thereby place God on the same footing with my wife? No! to a soul which truly loves God, the love of woman is an impossibility is adultery. "He that is unmarried," says the Apostle Paul, "careth for the things that belong to the Lord, how he may please the Lord; but he that is married careth for the things that are of the world, how he may please his wife."

The true Christian not only feels no need of culture, because this is a worldly principle and opposed to feeling; he has also no need of (natural) love. God supplies to him the want of culture, and in like manner God supplies to him the want of love, of a wife, of a family. The Christian immediately identifies the species with the individual; hence he strips off the difference of sex as a burdensome, accidental adjunct.† Man and woman together first constitute the true man; man and woman together are the existence of the race, for their union is the source of multiplicity, the source of other men. Hence the man who does not deny his manhood, is conscious that he is only a part of a being, which needs another part for the making up of the whole of true humanity. The Christian, on the contrary, in his excessive, transcendental subjectivity, conceives that he is, by himself, a perfect being. But the sexual instinct runs counter to this view; it is in contradiction with his ideal: the Christian must therefore deny this instinct.

The Christian certainly experienced the need of sexual love, but only as a need in contradiction with his heavenly

* Thomas à Kempis de Imit. (l. ii. c. 7, c. 8, l. iii. c. 5, c. 34, c. 53, c. 59). "Felix illa conscientia et beata virginitas, in cujus corde præter amorem Christi . . . . . . nullus alius versatur amor."—Hieronymus (Demetriadi, Virgini Deo consecratæ).

† "Divisa est . . . . mulier et virgo. Vide quantæ felicitatis sit, quæ et nomen sexus amiserit. Virgo jam mulier non vocatur."—Hieronymus (adv. Helvidium de perpet. Virg. p. 14. Th. ii. Erasmus).

destination, and merely natural, in the depreciatory, contemptuous sense which this word had in Christianity,—not as a moral, inward need—not, if I may so express myself, as a metaphysical, *i.e.*, an essential need, which man can experience only where he does not separate difference of sex from himself, but, on the contrary, regards it as belonging to his inmost nature. Hence marriage is not holy in Christianity; at least it is so only apparently, illusively; for the natural principle of marriage, which is the love of the sexes,—however civil marriage may in endless instances contradict this, —is in Christianity an unholy thing, and excluded from heaven.* But that which man excludes from heaven he excludes from his true nature. Heaven is his treasure-casket. Believe not in what he establishes on earth, what he permits and sanctions here: here he must accommodate himself; here many things come athwart him which do not fit into his system; here he shuns thy glance, for he finds himself among strangers who intimidate him. But watch for him when he throws off his incognito, and shows himself in his true dignity, his heavenly state. In heaven he speaks as he thinks; there thou hearest his true opinion. Where his heaven is, there is his heart,—heaven is his heart laid open. Heaven is nothing but the idea of the true, the good, the valid,—of that which ought to be; earth, nothing but the idea of the untrue, the unlawful, of that which ought not to be. The Christian excludes from heaven the life of the species: there the species ceases, there dwell only pure sexless individuals, "spirits;" there absolute subjectivity reigns:—thus the Christian excludes the life of the species

---

* This may be expressed as follows : Marriage has in Christianity only a moral, no religious significance, no religious principle and exemplar. It is otherwise with the Greeks, where, for example, "Zeus and Here are the great archetype of every marriage" (Creuzer, Symbol.); with the ancient Parsees, where procreation, as "the multiplication of the human race, is the diminution of the empire of Ahriman," and thus a religious act and duty (Zend-Avesta); with the Hindoos, where the son is the regenerated father. Among the Hindoos no regenerate man could assume the rank of a Sanyassi, that is, of an anchorite absorbed in God, if he had not previously paid three debts, one of which was that he had had a legitimate son. Amongst the Christians, on the contrary, at least the Catholics, it was a true festival of religious rejoicing when betrothed or even married persons—supposing that it happened with mutual consent—renounced the married state and sacrificed conjugal to religious love.

from his conception of the true life; he pronounces the principle of marriage sinful, negative ; for the sinless, positive life is the heavenly one.*

* Inasmuch as the religious consciousness restores everything which it begins by abolishing, and the future life is ultimately nothing else than the present life re-established, it follows that sex must be re-established. "Erunt . . . similes angelorum. Ergo homines non desinent . . . ut apostolus apostolus sit et Maria Maria."—Hieronymus (ad Theodoram Viduam). But as the body in the other world is an incorporeal body, so necessarily the sex there is one without difference, *i.e.*, a sexless sex.

CHAPTER XVIII.

THE unwedded and ascetic life is the direct way to the heavenly, immortal life, for heaven is nothing else than life liberated from the conditions of the species, supernatural, sexless, absolutely subjective life. The belief in personal immortality has at its foundation the belief that difference of sex is only an external adjunct of individuality, that in himself the individual is a sexless, independently complete, absolute being. But he who belongs to no sex belongs to no species; sex is the cord which connects the individuality with the species, and he who belongs to no species, belongs only to himself, is an altogether independent, divine, absolute being. Hence only when the species vanishes from the consciousness is the heavenly life a certainty. He who lives in the consciousness of the species, and consequently of its reality, lives also in the consciousness of the reality of sex. He does not regard it as a mechanically inserted, adventitious stone of stumbling, but as an inherent quality, a chemical constituent of his being. He indeed recognises himself as a man in the broader sense, but he is at the same time conscious of being rigorously determined by the sexual distinction, which penetrates not only bones and marrow, but also his inmost self, the essential mode of his thought, will, and sensation. He therefore who lives in the consciousness of the species, who limits and determines his feelings and imagination by the contemplation of real life, of real man, can conceive no life in which the life of the species, and therewith the distinction of sex, is abolished; he regards the sexless individual, the heavenly spirit, as an agreeable figment of the imagination.

But just as little as the real man can abstract himself from the distinction of sex, so little can he abstract himself from his moral or spiritual constitution, which indeed is profoundly connected with his natural constitution. Precisely because he lives in the contemplation of the whole, he also lives in the consciousness that he is himself no more than a part, and that he is what he is only by virtue of the conditions which constitute him a member of the whole, or a relative whole. Every one, therefore, justifiably regards his occupation, his profession, his art or science, as the highest; for the mind of man is nothing but the essential mode of his activity. He who is skilful in his profession, in his art, he who fills his post well, and is entirely devoted to his calling, thinks that calling the highest and best. How can he deny in thought what he emphatically declares in act by the joyful devotion of all his powers? If I despise a thing, how can I dedicate to it my time and faculties? If I am compelled to do so in spite of my aversion, my activity is an unhappy one, for I am at war with myself. Work is worship. But how can I worship or serve an object, how can I subject myself to it, if it does not hold a high place in my. mind? In brief, the occupations of men determine their judgment, their mode of thought, their sentiments. And the higher the occupation, the more completely does a man identify himself with it. In general, whatever a man makes the essential aim of his life, he proclaims to be his soul; for it is the principle of motion in him. But through his aim, through the activity in which he realises this aim, man is not only something for himself, but also something for others, for the general life, the species. He therefore who lives in the consciousness of the species as a reality, regards his existence for others, his relation to society, his utility to the public, as that existence which is one with the existence of his own essence—as his immortal existence. He lives with his whole soul, with his whole heart, for humanity. How can he hold in reserve a special existence for himself, how can he separate himself from mankind? How shall he deny in death what he has enforced in life? And in life his faith is this: *Nec sibi sed toti genitum se credere mundo.*

The heavenly life, or what we do not here distinguish from it—personal immortality, is a characteristic doctrine of Christianity. It is certainly in part to be found among the heathen philosophers; but with them it had only the significance of a subjective conception, because it was not connected with their fundamental view of things. How contradictory, for example, are the expressions of the Stoics on this subject! It was among the Christians that personal immortality first found that principle, whence it follows as a necessary and obvious consequence. The contemplation of the world, of Nature, of the race, was always coming athwart the ancients; they distinguished between the principle of life and the living subject, between the soul, the mind, and self: whereas the Christian abolished the distinction between soul and person, species and individual, and therefore placed immediately in self what belongs only to the totality of the species. But the immediate unity of the species and individuality is the highest principle, the God of Christianity,—in it the individual has the significance of the absolute being,—and the necessary, immanent consequence of this principle is personal immortality.

Or rather: the belief in personal immortality is perfectly identical with the belief in a personal God;—*i.e.*, that which expresses the belief in the heavenly, immortal life of the person, expresses God also, as he is an object to Christians, namely, as absolute, unlimited personality. Unlimited personality is God; but heavenly personality, or the perpetuation of human personality in heaven, is nothing else than personality released from all earthly encumbrances and limitations; the only distinction is, that God is heaven spiritualised, while heaven is God materialised, or reduced to the forms of the senses: that what in God is posited only *in abstracto* is in heaven more an object of the imagination. God is the implicit heaven; heaven is the explicit God. In the present, God is the kingdom of heaven; in the future, heaven is God. God is the pledge, the as yet abstract presence and existence of heaven; the anticipation, the epitome of heaven. Our own future existence, which, while we are in this world, in this body, is a separate, objective existence, —is God: God is the idea of the species, which will be first realised, individualised in the other world. God is the heavenly, pure, free essence, which exists there as heavenly pure beings, the bliss which there unfolds itself in a plenitude of blissful individuals. Thus God is nothing else than the idea or the essence of the absolute, blessed, heavenly life, here comprised in an ideal personality. This is clearly enough expressed in the belief that the blessed life is unity with God. Here we are distinguished and separated from God, there the partition falls; here we are men, there gods;

here the Godhead is a monopoly, there it is a common possession; here it is an abstract unity, there a concrete multiplicity.* The only difficulty in the recognition of this is created by the imagination, which, on the one hand by the conception of the personality of God, on the other by the conception of the many personalities which it places in a realm ordinarily depicted in the hues of the senses, hides the real unity of the idea. But in truth there is no distinction between the absolute life which is conceived as God and the absolute life which is conceived as heaven, save that in heaven we have stretched into length and breadth what in God is concentrated in one point. The belief in the immortality of man is the belief in the divinity of man, and the belief in God is the belief in pure personality, released from all limits, and consequently *eo ipso* immortal. The distinctions made between the immortal soul and God are either sophistical or imaginative; as when, for example, the bliss of the inhabitants of heaven is again circumscribed by limits, and distributed into degrees, in order to establish a distinction between God and the dwellers in heaven.

The identity of the divine and heavenly personality is apparent even in the popular proofs of immortality. If there is not another and a better life, God is not just and good. The justice and goodness of God are thus made dependent on the perpetuity of individuals; but without justice and goodness God is not God;—the Godhead, the existence of God, is therefore made dependent on the existence of individuals. If I am not immortal, I believe in no God; he who denies immortality denies God. But that is impossible to me: as surely as there is a God, so surely is there an immortality. God is the certainty of my future felicity. The interest I have in knowing that *God is*, is one with the interest I have

---

* " Bene dicitur, quod tunc plene videbimus eum sicuti est, cum similes ei erimus, h. e. erimus quod ipse est. Quibus enim potestas data est filios Dei fieri, data est potestas, non quidem ut sint Deus, sed sint tamen quod Deus est : sint sancti, futuri plene beati, quod Deus est. Nec aliunde hic sancti, nec ibi futuri beati, quam ex Deo qui eorum et sanctitas et beatitudo est."—De Vita solitaria (among the spurious writings of St. Bernard). " Finis autem bonæ voluntatis beatitudo est : vita æterna ipse Deus."— Augustin. (ap. Petrus Lomb. l. ii. dist. 38, c. 1). " The other man will be renovated in the spiritual life, *i.e.*, will become a.spiritual man, when he shall be restored into the image of God. For he will be like God, in life, in righteousness, glory, and wisdom."—Luther (Th. i. p. 324).

in knowing that *I am*, that I am immortal. God is my
hidden, my assured existence ; he is the subjectivity of subjects, the personality of persons. How then should that not
belong to persons which belongs to personality ? In God I
make my future into a present, or rather a verb into a sub-
stantive ; how should I separate the one from the other ?
God is the existence corresponding to my wishes and feelings : he is the just one, the good, who fulfils my wishes.
Nature, this world, is an existence which contradicts my
wishes, my feelings. Here it is not as it ought to be ; this
world passes away ; but God is existence as it ought to be.
God fulfils my wishes ;—this is only a popular personification of the position : God is the fulfiller, *i.e.*, the reality, the
fulfilment of my wishes.*   But heaven is the existence
adequate to my wishes, my longing ; † thus there is no
distinction between God and heaven.   God is the power by
which man realises his eternal happiness ; God is the absolute personality in which all individual persons have the
certainty of their blessedness and immortality ; God is to
subjectivity the highest, last certainty of its absolute truth
and essentiality.

The doctrine of immortality is the final doctrine of religion ; its testament, in which it declares its last wishes.
Here therefore it speaks out undisguisedly what it has
hitherto suppressed.   If elsewhere the religious soul concerns itself with the existence of another being, here it openly
considers only its own existence ; if elsewhere in religion
man makes his existence dependent on the existence of God,
he here makes the reality of God dependent on his own
reality ; and thus what elsewhere is a primitive, immediate
truth to him, is here a derivative, secondary truth : if I am
not immortal, God is not God ; if there is no immortality,
there is no God ;—a conclusion already drawn by the Apostle
Paul.   If we do not rise again, then Christ is not risen, and
all is vain.   Let us eat and drink.   It is certainly possible

* " Si bonum est habere corpus incorruptibile, quare hoc facturum Deum
volumus dasperere ? "—Augustinus (Opp. Antwerp, 1700, Th. v. p. 698).
† " Quare dicitur spiritale corpus, nisi quia ad nutum spiritus serviet ?
Nihil tibi contradicet ex te, nihil in te rebellabit adversus te. . . . . Ubi
volueris, eris. . . . . Credere enim debemus talia corpora nos habituros, ut
ubi velimus, quando voluerimus, ibi simus."—Augustinus (l. c. pp. 703, 705).
" Nihil indecorum ibi erit, summa pax erit, nihil discordans, nihil mons-
truosum, nihil quod offendat adspectum " (l. c. 707).   " Nisi beatus, non
vivit ut vult."   (De Civ. Dei, l. 14, c. 25.)

to do away with what is apparently or really objectionable in the popular argumentation, by avoiding the inferential form; but this can only be done by making immortality an analytic instead of a synthetic truth, so as to show that the very idea of God as absolute personality or subjectivity is *per se* the idea of immortality. God is the guarantee of my future existence, because he is already the certainty and reality of my present existence, my salvation, my trust, my shield from the forces of the external world; hence I need not expressly deduce immortality, or prove it as a separate truth, for if I have God, I have immortality also. Thus it was with the more profound Christian mystics; to them the idea of immortality was involved in the idea of God; God was their immortal life,—God himself their subjective blessedness : he was for them, for their consciousness, what he is in himself, that is, in the essence of religion.

Thus it is shown that God is heaven; that the two are identical. It would have been easier to prove the converse, namely, that heaven is the true God of men. As man conceives his heaven, so he conceives his God; the content of his idea of heaven is the content of his idea of God, only that what in God is a mere sketch, a concept, is in heaven depicted and developed in the colours and forms of the senses. Heaven is therefore the key to the deepest mysteries of religion. As heaven is objectively the displayed nature of God, so subjectively it is the most candid declaration of the inmost thoughts and dispositions of religion. For this reason, religions are as various as are the kingdoms of heaven, and there are as many different kingdoms of heaven as there are characteristic differences among men. The Christians themselves have very heterogeneous conceptions of heaven.*

The more judicious among them, however, think and say nothing definite about heaven or the future world in general, on the ground that it is inconceivable, that it can only be thought of by us according to the standard of this world, a standard not applicable to the other. All conceptions of heaven here below are, they allege, mere images, whereby

---

* And their conceptions of God are just as heterogeneous. The pious Germans have a German God, the pious Spaniards a Spanish God, the French a French God. The French actually have the proverb : "*Le bon Dieu est Français.*" In fact, polytheism must exist so long as there are various nations. The real God of a people is the *point d'honneur* of its nationality.

man represents to himself that future, the nature of which
is unknown to him, but the existence of which is certain.
It is just so with God. The existence of God, it is said, is
certain; but what he is, or how he exists, is inscrutable.
But he who speaks thus has already driven the future world
out of his head; he still holds it fast, either because he does
not think at all about such matters, or because it is still a
want of his heart; but, preoccupied with real things, he
thrusts it as far as possible out of his sight; he denies with
his head what he affirms with his heart; for it is to deny
the future life, to deprive it of the qualities by which alone
it is a real and effective object for man. Quality is not
distinct from existence; quality is nothing but real existence. Existence without quality is a chimera, a spectre.
Existence is first made known to me by quality; not existence first, and after that quality. The doctrines that God
is not to be known or defined, and that the nature of the
future life is inscrutable, are therefore not originally religious doctrines; on the contrary, they are the products
of irreligion while still in bondage to religion, or rather
hiding itself behind religion; and they are so for this reason,
that originally the existence of God is posited only with a
definite conception of God, the existence of a future life
only with a definite conception of that life. Thus to the
Christian, only his own paradise, the paradise which has
Christian qualities, is a certainty, not the paradise of the
Mahometan or the Elysium of the Greeks. The primary
certainty is everywhere quality; existence follows of course
when once quality is certain. In the New Testament we
find no proofs or general propositions such as: there is a
God, there is a heavenly life; we find only qualities of the
heavenly life adduced;—"in heaven they marry not."
Naturally;—it may be answered,—because the existence of
God and of heaven is presupposed. But here reflection introduces a distinction of which the religious sentiment
knows nothing. Doubtless the existence is presupposed,
but only because the quality is itself existence, because the
inviolate religious feeling lives only in the quality, just as
to the natural man the real existence, the thing in itself, lies
only in the quality which he perceives. Thus in the passage above cited from the New Testament, the virgin or
rather sexless life is presupposed as the true life, which,

however, necessarily becomes a future one, because the actual life contradicts the ideal of the true life. But the certainty of this future life lies only in the certainty of its qualities, as those of the true, highest life, adequate to the ideal. Where the future life is really believed in, where it is a certain life, there, precisely because it is certain, it is also definite. If I know not now what and how I shall be; if there is an essential, absolute difference between my future and my present; neither shall I then know what and how I was before, the unity of consciousness is at an end, personal identity is abolished, another being will appear in my place; and thus my future existence is not in fact distinguished from non-existence. If, on the other hand, there is no essential difference, the future is to me an object that may be defined and known. And so it is in reality. I am the abiding subject under changing conditions; I am the substance which connects the present and the future into a unity. How then can the future be obscure to me? On the contrary, the life of this world is the dark, incomprehensible life, which only becomes clear through the future life; here I am in disguise; there the mask will fall; there I shall be as I am in truth. Hence the position that there indeed is another, a heavenly life, but that *what* and *how* it is must here remain inscrutable, is only an invention of religious scepticism, which, being entirely alien to the religious sentiment, proceeds upon a total misconception of religion. That which irreligious-religious reflection converts into a known image of an unknown yet certain thing, is originally, in the primitive, true sense of religion, not an image, but the thing itself. Unbelief, in the garb of belief, doubts the existence of the thing, but it is too shallow or cowardly directly to call it in question; it only expresses doubt of the image or conception, *i.e.*, declares the image to be only an image. But the untruth and hollowness of this scepticism has been already made evident historically. Where it is once doubted that the images of immortality are real, that it is possible to exist as faith conceives, for example, without a material, real body, and without difference of sex; there the future existence in general is soon a matter of doubt. With the image falls the thing, simply because the image is the thing itself.

The belief in heaven, or in a future life in general, rests

on a mental judgment. It expresses praise and blame; it selects a wreath from the flora of this world, and this critical florilegium is heaven. That which man thinks beautiful, good, agreeable, is for him what alone ought to be; that which he thinks bad, odious, disagreeable, is what ought not to be; and hence, since it nevertheless exists, it is condemned to destruction, it is regarded as a negation. Where life is not in contradiction with a feeling, an imagination, an idea, and where this feeling, this idea, is not held authoritative and absolute, the belief in another and a heavenly life does not arise. The future life is nothing else than life in unison with the feeling, with the idea, which the present life contradicts. The whole import of the future life is the abolition of this discordance, and the realisation of a state which corresponds to the feelings, in which man is in unison with himself. An unknown, unimagined future is a ridiculous chimera: the other world is nothing more than the reality of a known idea, the satisfaction of a conscious desire, the fulfilment of a wish; * it is only the removal of limits which here oppose themselves to the realisation of the idea. Where would be the consolation, where the significance of a future life, if it were midnight darkness to me? No! from yonder world there streams upon me with the splendour of virgin gold what here shines only with the dimness of unrefined ore. The future world has no other significance, no other basis of its existence, than the separation of the metal from the admixture of foreign elements, the separation of the good from the bad, of the pleasant from the unpleasant, of the praiseworthy from the blamable. The future world is the *bridal* in which man concludes his union with his beloved. Long has he loved his bride, long has he yearned after her; but external relations, hard reality, have stood in the way of his union to her. When the wedding takes place, his beloved one does not become a different being; else how could he so ardently long for her? She only becomes his own; from an object of yearning and affectionate desire she becomes an object of actual possession. It is true that here below, the other world is

---

* "Ibi nostra spes erit res."—Augustin. "Therefore we have the first fruits of immortal life in hope, until perfection comes at the last day, wherein we shall see and feel the life we have believed in and hoped for."— Luther (Th. i. s. 459).

only an image, a conception; still it is not the image of a remote, unknown thing, but a portrait of that which man loves and prefers before all else. What man loves is his soul. The heathens enclosed the ashes of the beloved dead in an urn; with the Christian the heavenly future is the mausoleum in which he enshrines his soul.

In order to comprehend a particular faith, or religion in general, it is necessary to consider religion in its rudimentary stages, in its lowest, rudest condition. Religion must not only be traced in an ascending line, but surveyed in the entire course of its existence. It is requisite to regard the various earlier religions as present in the absolute religion, and not as left behind it in the past, in order correctly to appreciate and comprehend the absolute religion as well as the others. The most frightful "aberrations," the wildest excesses of the religious consciousness, often afford the profoundest insight into the mysteries of the absolute religion. Ideas, seemingly the rudest, are often only the most childlike, innocent, and true. This observation applies to the conceptions of a future life. The "savage," whose consciousness does not extend beyond his own country, whose entire being is a growth of its soil, takes his country with him into the other world, either leaving Nature as it is, or improving it, and so overcoming in the idea of the other life the difficulties he experiences in this.* In this limitation of uncultivated tribes there is a striking trait. With them the future expresses nothing else than home-sickness. Death separates man from his kindred, from his people, from his country. But the man who has not extended his consciousness, cannot endure this separation; he must come back again to his native land. The negroes in the West Indies killed themselves that they might come to life again in their fatherland. And, according to Ossian's conception, "the spirits of those who die in a strange land float back towards their birthplace."† This limitation is the direct opposite of imaginative spiritualism, which makes

* According to old books of travel, however, there are many tribes which do not believe that the future is identical with the present, or that it is better, but that it is even worse. Parny (Œuv. Chois. t. i. Melang.) tells of a dying negro-slave who refused the inauguration to immortality by baptism in these words: "Je ne veux point d'une autre vie, car peut-être y serais-je encore votre esclave."
† Ahlwardt (Ossian Anm. zu Carthonn.).

man a vagabond, who, indifferent even to the earth, roams from star to star; and certainly there lies a real truth at its foundation. Man is what he is through Nature, however much may belong to his spontaneity; for even his spontaneity has its foundation in Nature, of which his particular character is only an expression. Be thankful to Nature! Man cannot be separated from it. The German, whose God is spontaneity, owes his character to Nature just as much as the Oriental. To find fault with Indian art, with Indian religion and philosophy, is to find fault with Indian Nature. You complain of the reviewer who tears a passage in your works from the context that he may hand it over to ridicule. Why are you yourself guilty of that which you blame in others? Why do you tear the Indian religion from its connection, in which it is just as reasonable as your absolute religion?

Faith in a future world, in a life after death, is therefore with "savage" tribes essentially nothing more than direct faith in the present life—immediate unbroken faith in this life. For them, their actual life, even with its local limitations, has all, has absolute value; they cannot abstract from it, they cannot conceive its being broken off; *i.e.*, they believe directly in the infinitude, the perpetuity of this life. Only when the belief in immortality becomes a critical belief, when a distinction is made between what is to be left behind here, and what is in reserve there, between what here passes away, and what there is to abide, does the belief in life after death form itself into the belief in another life; but this criticism, this distinction, is applied to the present life also. Thus the Christians distinguish between the natural and the Christian life, the sensual or worldly and the spiritual or holy life. The heavenly life is no other than that which is, already here below, distinguished from the merely natural life, though still tainted with it. That which the Christian excludes from himself now—for example, the sexual life— is excluded from the future: the only distinction is, that he is there free from that which he here wishes to be free from, and seeks to rid himself of by the will, by devotion, and by bodily mortification. Hence this life is, for the Christian, a life of torment and pain, because he is here still beset by a hostile power, and has to struggle with the lusts of the flesh and the assaults of the devil.

The faith of cultured nations is therefore distinguished
from that of the uncultured in the same way that culture in
general is distinguished from inculture: namely, that the
faith of culture is a discriminating, critical, abstract faith.
A distinction implies a judgment; but where there is a
judgment there arises the distinction between positive and
negative. The faith of savage tribes is a faith without a
judgment. Culture, on the contrary, judges: to the cultured
man only cultured life is the true life; to the Christian only
the Christian life. The rude child of Nature steps into the
other life just as he is, without ceremony : the other world
is his natural nakedness. The cultivated man, on the contrary, objects to the idea of such an unbridled life after
death, because even here he objects to the unrestricted life
of Nature. Faith in a future life is therefore only faith in
the *true* life of the present; the essential elements of this
life are also the essential elements of the other: accordingly,
faith in a future life is not faith in another unknown life;
but in the truth and infinitude, and consequently in the perpetuity, of that life which already here below is regarded as
the authentic life.

As God is nothing else than the nature of man purified
from that which to the human individual appears, whether
in feeling or thought, a limitation, an evil; so the future life
is nothing else than the present life freed from that which
appears a limitation or an evil. The more definitely and
profoundly the individual is conscious of the limit as a limit,
of the evil as an evil, the more definite and profound is his
conviction of the future life, where these limits disappear.
The future life is the feeling, the conception of freedom from
those limits which here circumscribe the feeling of self, the
existence of the individual. The only difference between the
course of religion and that of the natural or rational man is,
that the end which the latter arrives at by a straight line,
the former only attains by describing a curved line—a circle.
The natural man remains at home because he finds it agreeable, because he is perfectly satisfied; religion which commences with a discontent, a disunion, forsakes its home and
travels far, but only to feel the more vividly in the distance
the happiness of home. In religion man separates himself
from himself, but only to return always to the same point

from which he set out. Man negatives himself, but only to posit himself again, and that in a glorified form: he negatives this life, but only, in the end, to posit it again in the future life.* The future life is this life once lost, but found again, and radiant with all the more brightness for the joy of recovery. The religious man renounces the joys of this world, but only that he may win in return the joys of heaven; or rather he renounces them because he is already in the ideal possession of heavenly joys; and the joys of heaven are the same as those of earth, only that they are freed from the limits and contrarieties of this life. Religion thus arrives, though by a circuit, at the very goal, the goal of joy, towards which the natural man hastens in a direct line. To live in images or symbols is the essence of religion. Religion sacrifices the thing itself to the image. The future life is the present in the mirror of the imagination: the enrapturing image is in the sense of religion the true type of earthly life,—real life only a glimmer of that ideal, imaginary life. The future life is the present embellished, contemplated through the imagination, purified from all gross matter; or, positively expressed, it is the beauteous present intensified.

Embellishment, emendation, presupposes blame, dissatisfaction. But the dissatisfaction is only superficial. I do not deny the thing to be of value; just as it is, however, it does not please me; I deny only the modification, not the substance, otherwise I should urge annihilation. A house which absolutely displeases me I cause to be pulled down, not to be embellished. To the believer in a future life joy is agreeable—who can fail to be conscious that joy is something positive?—but it is disagreeable to him that here joy is followed by opposite sensations, that it is transitory. Hence he places joy in the future life also, but as eternal, uninterrupted, divine joy (and the future life is therefore called the world of joy), such as he here conceives it in God; for God is nothing but eternal, uninterrupted joy, posited as a subject. Individuality or per-

* There everything will be restored. "Qui modo vivit, erit, nec me vel dente, vel ungue fraudatum revomet patefacti fossa sepulchri."—Aurelius Prud. (Apotheos. de Resurr. Carnis Hum.). And this faith, which you consider rude and carnal, and which you therefore disavow, is the only consistent, honest, and true faith. To the identity of the person belongs the identity of the body.

sonality is agreeable to him, but only as unencumbered by objective forces; hence, he includes individuality also, but pure, absolutely subjective individuality. Light pleases him; but not gravitation, because this appears a limitation of the individual; not night, because in it man is subjected to Nature: in the other world, there is light, but no weight, no night,—pure, unobstructed light.*

As man in his utmost remoteness from himself, in God, always returns upon himself, always revolves round himself; so in his utmost remoteness from the world, he always at last comes back to it. The more extra- and supra-human God appears at the commencement, the more human does he show himself to be in the subsequent course of things, or at the close: and just so, the more supernatural the heavenly life looks in the beginning or at a distance, the more clearly does it, in the end or when viewed closely, exhibit its identity with the natural life,—an identity which at last extends even to the flesh, even to the body. In the first instance the mind is occupied with the separation of the soul from the body, as in the conception of God the mind is first occupied with the separation of the essence from the individual;—the individual dies a spiritual death, the dead body which remains behind is the human individual; the soul which has departed from it is God. But the separation of the soul from the body, of the essence from the individual, of God from man, must be abolished again. Every separation of beings essentially allied is painful. The soul yearns after its lost half, after its body; as God, the departed soul yearns after the real man. As, therefore, God becomes a man again, so the soul returns to its body, and the perfect identity of this world and the other is now restored. It is true that this new body is a bright, glorified, miraculous body, but—and this is the main point—it is another and yet the same body,† as God is another being than man, and yet the same. Here we come again to the idea of miracle, which unites contradictories. The supernatural body is a body constructed by

---

* "Neque enim post resurrectionem tempus diebus ac noctibus numerabitur. Erit magis una dies sine vespere."—Joh. Damascen. (Orth. Fidei l. ii. c. 1).

† "Ipsum (corpus) erit et non ipsum erit."—Augustinus (v. J. Ch. Doederlein, Inst. Theol. Christ. Altorf, 1781, § 280).

the imagination, for which very reason it is adequate to the feelings of man : an unburdensome, purely subjective body. Faith in the future life is nothing else than faith in the truth of the imagination, as faith in God is faith in the truth and infinity of human feeling. Or : as faith in God is only faith in the abstract nature of man, so faith in the heavenly life is only faith in the abstract earthly life.

But the sum of the future life is happiness, the everlasting bliss of personality, which is here limited and circumscribed by Nature. Faith in the future life is therefore faith in the freedom of subjectivity from the limits of Nature ; it is faith in the eternity and infinitude of personality, and not of personality viewed in relation to the idea of the species, in which it for ever unfolds itself in new individuals, but of personality as belonging to already existing individuals : consequently, it is the faith of man in himself. But faith in the kingdom of heaven is one with faith in God—the content of both ideas is the same ; God is pure absolute subjectivity released from all natural limits ; he is what individuals ought to be and will be : faith in God is therefore the faith of man in the infinitude and truth of his own nature ; the Divine Being is the subjective human being in his absolute freedom and unlimitedness.

Our most essential task is now fulfilled. We have reduced the supermundane, supernatural, and superhuman nature of God to the elements of human nature as its fundamental elements. Our process of analysis has brought us again to the position with which we set out. The beginning, middle and end of religion is MAN.

PART II.

THE FALSE OR THEOLOGICAL ESSENCE OF RELIGION.

CHAPTER XIX.

THE ESSENTIAL STANDPOINT OF RELIGION.

THE essential standpoint of religion is the practical or subjective. The end of religion is the welfare, the salvation, the ultimate felicity of man; the relation of man to God is nothing else than his relation to his own spiritual good; God is the realised salvation of the soul, or the unlimited power of effecting the salvation, the bliss of man.* The Christian religion is specially distinguished from other religions in this,—that no other has given equal prominence to the salvation of man. But this salvation is not temporal earthly prosperity and well-being. On the contrary, the most genuine Christians have declared that earthly good draws man away from God, whereas adversity, suffering, afflictions lead him back to God, and hence are alone suited to Christians. Why? Because in trouble man is only practically or subjectively disposed; in trouble he has resource only to the one thing needful; in trouble God is felt to be a want of man. Pleasure, joy, expands man; trouble, suffering, contracts and concentrates him; in suffering man denies the reality of the world; the things that

* "Præter salutem tuam nihil cogites; solum quæ Dei sunt cures."— Thomas à K. (de Imit. l. i. c. 23). "Contra salutem proprium cogites nihil. Minus dixi: contra, præter dixisse debuéram."—Bernhardus (de Consid. ad Eugenium Pontif. Max. l. ii.). "Qui Deum quærit, de propria salute sollicitus est."—Clemens Alex. (Cohort. ad Gent.).

charm the imagination of the artist and the intellect of the thinker lose their attraction for him, their power over him; he is absorbed in himself, in his own soul. The soul thus self-absorbed, self-concentrated, seeking satisfaction in itself alone, denying the world, idealistic in relation to the world, to Nature in general, but realistic in relation to man, caring only for its inherent need of salvation,—this soul is God. God, as the object of religion,—and only as such is he God,—God in the sense of a *nomen proprium*, not of a vague, metaphysical entity, is essentially an object only of religion, not of philosophy,—of feeling, not of the intellect, —of the heart's necessity, not of the mind's freedom: in short, an object which is the reflex not of the theoretical but of the practical tendency in man.

Religion annexes to its doctrines a curse and a blessing, damnation and salvation. Blessed is he that believeth, cursed is he that believeth not. Thus it appeals not to reason, but to feeling, to the desire of happiness, to the passions of hope and fear. It does not take the theoretic point of view; otherwise it must have been free to enunciate its doctrines without attaching to them practical consequences, without to a certain extent compelling belief in them; for when the case stands thus : I am lost if I do not believe,—the conscience is under a subtle kind of constraint; the fear of hell urges me to believe. Even supposing my belief to be in its origin free, fear inevitably intermingles itself; my conscience is always under constraint; doubt, the principle of theoretic freedom, appears to me a crime. And as in religion the highest idea, the highest existence is God, so the highest crime is doubt in God, or the doubt that God exists. But that which I do not trust myself to doubt, which I cannot doubt without feeling disturbed in my soul, without incurring guilt; that is no matter of theory, but a matter of conscience, no being of the intellect, but of the heart.

Now as the sole standpoint of religion is the practical or subjective standpoint, as therefore to religion the whole, the essential man is that part of his nature which is practical, which forms resolutions, which acts in accordance with conscious aims, whether physical or moral, and which considers the world not in itself, but only in relation to those aims or wants: the consequence is that everything which lies behind the practical consciousness, but which is the essential object of theory—theory in its most original and general sense, namely, that of objective contemplation and experience, of the intellect, of science *—is regarded by religion as lying outside man and Nature, in a special, personal being. All good, but especially such as takes possession of man apart from his volition, such as does not correspond with any resolution or purpose, such as transcends the limits of the practical consciousness, comes from God; all wickedness, evil, but especially such as overtakes him against his will in the midst of his best moral resolutions, or hurries him along with terrible violence, comes from the devil. The scientific knowledge of the essence of religion includes the knowledge of the devil, of Satan, of demons.† These things cannot be omitted without a violent mutilation of religion. Grace and its works are the antitheses of the devil and his works. As the involuntary, sensual impulses which flash out from the depths of the nature, and, in general, all those phenomena of moral and physical evil which are inexplicable to religion, appear to it as the work of the Evil Being; so the involuntary movements of inspiration and ecstasy appear to it as the work of the Good Being, God, of the Holy Spirit or of grace. Hence the arbitrariness of grace—the complaint of the pious that grace at one time visits and blesses them, at another forsakes and rejects them. The life, the agency of grace, is the life, the agency of emotion. Emotion is the Paraclete of Christians. The moments which are forsaken by divine grace are the moments destitute of emotion and inspiration.

In relation to the inner life, grace may be defined as *religious genius;* in relation to the outer life as *religious chance.* Man is good or wicked by no means through himself, his own power, his will; but through that complete synthesis of hidden and evident determinations of things

---

* Here and in other parts of this work, theory is taken in the sense in which it is the source of true objective activity,—the science which gives birth to art,—for man can do only so much as he knows: "tantum potest quantum scit."

† Concerning the biblical conceptions of Satan, his power and works, see Lützelberger's "Grundzüge der Paulinischen Glaubenslehre," and G. Ch. Knapp's "Vorles. über d. Christl. Glaubensl.," § 62-65. To this subject belongs demoniacal possession, which also has its attestation in the Biblo. See Knapp (§ 65, iii. 2, 3).

which, because they rest on no evident necessity, we ascribe to the power of "chance." Divine grace is the power of chance beclouded with additional mystery. Here we have again the confirmation of that which we have seen to be the essential law of religion. Religion denies, repudiates chance, making everything dependent on God, explaining everything by means of him; but this denial is only apparent; it merely gives chance the name of the divine sovereignty. For the divine will, which, on incomprehensible grounds, for incomprehensible reasons, that is, speaking plainly, out of groundless, absolute arbitrariness, out of divine caprice, as it were, determines or predestines some to evil and misery, others to good and happiness, has not a single positive characteristic to distinguish it from the power of chance. The mystery of the election of grace is thus the mystery of chance. I say the *mystery* of chance ; for in reality chance is a mystery, although slurred over and ignored by our speculative religious philosophy, which, as in its occupation with the illusory mysteries of the Absolute Being, *i.e.*, of theology, it has overlooked the true mysteries of thought and life, so also in the mystery of divine grace or freedom of election, has forgotten the profane mystery of chance.*

But to return. The devil is the negative, the evil, that springs from the nature, but not from the will; God is the positive, the good, which comes from the nature, but not from the conscious action of the will; the devil is involuntary, inexplicable wickedness; God involuntary, inexplicable goodness. The source of both is the same, the quality only is different or opposite. For this reason, the belief in a devil was, until the most recent times, intimately connected with the belief in God, so that the denial of the devil was held to be virtually as atheistic as the denial of God. Nor without reason ; for when men once begin to derive the phenomena of evil from natural causes, they at the same time begin to derive the phenomena of good, of the divine, from the nature of things, and come at length either to abolish the idea of God altogether, or at least to believe in another God than the God of religion. In this case it most commonly happens

---

* Doubtless, this unveiling of the mystery of predestination will be pronounced atrocious, impious, diabolical. I have nothing to allege against this ; I would rather be a devil in alliance with truth, than an angel in alliance with falsehood.

that they make the Deity an idle inactive being, whose existence is equivalent to non-existence, since he no longer actively interposes in life, but is merely placed at the summit of things, at the beginning of the world, as the First Cause. God created the world : this is all that is here retained of God. The past tense is necessary; for since that epoch the world pursues its course like a machine. The addition: He still creates, he is creating at this moment, is only the result of external reflection; the past tense adequately expresses the religious idea in this stage; for the spirit of religion is gone when the operation of God is reduced to a *fecit* or *creavit*. It is otherwise when the genuine religious consciousness says : The *fecit* is still to-day a *facit*. This, though here also it is a product of reflection, has nevertheless a legitimate meaning, because by the religious spirit God is really thought of as active.

Religion is abolished where the idea of the world, of so-called second causes, intrudes itself between God and man. Here a foreign element, the principle of intellectual culture, has insinuated itself, peace is broken, the harmony of religion, which lies only in the immediate connection of man with God, is destroyed. Second causes are a capitulation of the unbelieving intellect with the still believing heart. It is true that, according to religion also, God works on man by means of other things and beings. But God alone is the cause, he alone is the active and efficient being. What a fellow-creature does is in the view of religion done not by him, but by God. The other is only an appearance, a medium, a vehicle, not a cause. But the " second cause " is a miserable anomaly, neither an independent nor a dependent being: God, it is true, gives the first impulse, but then ensues the spontaneous activity of the second·cause.*

Religion of itself, unadulterated by foreign elements, knows nothing of the existence of second causes; on the contrary, they are a stone of stumbling to it; for the realm of second causes, the sensible world, Nature, is precisely

---

* A kindred doctrine is that of the *Concursus Dei,* according to which, God not only gives the first impulse, but also co-operates in the agency of the second cause. For the rest, this doctrine is only a particular form of the contradictory dualism between God and Nature, which runs through the history of Christianity. On the subject of this remark, as of the whole paragraph, see Strauss : *Die Christliche Glaubenslehre,* B. ii. § 75, 76.

what separates man from God, although God as a real God, *i.e.*, an external being, is supposed himself to become in the other world a sensible existence.* Hence religion believes that one day this wall of separation will fall away. One day there will be no Nature, no matter, no body, at least none such as to separate man from God: then there will be only God and the pious soul. Religion derives the idea of the existence of second causes, that is, of things which are interposed between God and man, only from the physical, natural, and hence the irreligious or at least non-religious theory of the universe: a theory which it nevertheless immediately subverts by making the operations of Nature operations of God. But this religious idea is in contradiction with the natural sense and understanding, which concedes a real, spontaneous activity to natural things. And this contradiction of the physical view with the religious theory, religion resolves by converting the undeniable activity of things into an activity of God. Thus, on this view, the positive idea is God; the negative, the world.

On the contrary, where second causes, having been set in motion, are, so to speak, emancipated, the converse occurs; Nature is the positive, God a negative idea. The world is independent in its existence, its persistence; only as to its commencement is it dependent. God is here only a hypothetical Being, an inference, arising from the necessity of a limited understanding, to which the existence of a world viewed by it as a machine is inexplicable without a self-moving principle;—he is no longer an original, absolutely necessary Being. God exists not for his own sake, but for

---

* "Dum sumus in hoc corpore, peregrinamur ab eo qui summe est."— Bernard. Epist. 18 (ed. Basle, 1552). "As long as we live, we are in the midst of death."—Luther (Th. i. p. 331). The idea of the future life is therefore nothing else than the idea of true, perfected religion, freed from the limits and obstructions of this life,—the future life, as has been already said, nothing but the true opinion and disposition, the open heart, of religion. Here we believe—there we behold; *i.e.*, *there* there is nothing besides God, and thus nothing between God and the soul; but only for this reason, that there ought to be nothing between them, because the immediate union of God and the soul is the true opinion and desire of religion. "We have as yet so to do with God as with one hidden from us, and it is not possible that in this life we should hold communion with him face to face. All creatures are now nothing else than vain masks, under which God conceals himself, and by which he deals with us."—Luther (Th. xi. p. 70). "If thou wert only free from the images of created things, thou mightest have God without intermission."—Tauler (l. c. p. 313).

the sake of the world,—merely that he may, as a First Cause, explain the existence of the world. The narrow rationalising man takes objection to the original self-subsistence of the world, because he looks at it only from the subjective, practical point of view, only in its commoner aspect, only as a piece of mechanism, not in its majesty and glory, not as the Cosmos. He conceives the world as having been launched into existence by an original impetus, as, according to mathematical theory, is the case with matter once set in motion and thenceforth going on for ever: that is, he postulates a mechanical origin. A machine must have a beginning; this is involved in its very idea; for it has not the source of motion in itself.

All religious speculative cosmogony is tautology, as is apparent from this example. In cosmogony man declares or realises the idea he has of the world; he merely repeats what he has already said in another form. Thus here, if the world is a machine, it is self-evident that it did not make itself, that, on the contrary, it was created, i.e., had a mechanical origin. Herein, it is true, the religious consciousness agrees with the mechanical theory, that to it also the world is a mere fabric, a product of Will. But they agree only for an instant, only in the moment of creation; that moment past, the harmony ceases. The holder of the mechanical theory needs God only as the creator of the world; once made, the world turns its back on the Creator, and rejoices in its godless self-subsistence. But religion creates the world only to maintain it in the perpetual consciousness of its nothingness, its dependence on God.* To the mechanical theorist, the creation is the last thin thread which yet ties him to religion; the religion to which the nothingness of the world is a present truth (for all power and activity is to it the power and activity of God), is with him only a surviving reminiscence of youth; hence he removes the creation of the world, the act of religion, the non-existence of the world (for in the beginning, before the creation, there was no world, only God),

* "Voluntate igitur Dei immobilis manet et stat in seculum terra . . . et voluntate Dei movetur et nutat. Non ergo fundamentis suis nixa subsistit, nec fulcris suis stabilis perseverat, sed Dominus statuit eam et firmamento voluntatis suæ continet, quia in manu ejus omnes fines terræ."— Ambrosius (Hexæmeron. l. i. c. 61).

into the far distance, into the past, while the self-subsistence of the world, which absorbs all his senses and endeavours, acts on him with the force of the present. The mechanical theorist interrupts and cuts short the activity of God by the activity of the world. With him God has indeed still an historical right, but this is in contradiction with the right he awards to Nature; hence he limits as much as possible the right yet remaining to God, in order to gain wider and freer play for his natural causes, and thereby for his understanding.

With this class of thinkers the creation holds the same position as miracles, which also they can and actually do acquiesce in, because miracles exist, at least according to religious opinion. But not to say that he explains miracles naturally, that is, mechanically, he can only digest them when he relegates them to the past; for the present he begs to be excused from believing in them, and explains every-thing to himself charmingly on natural principles. When a belief has departed from the reason, the intelligence, when it is no longer held spontaneously, but merely because it is a common belief, or because on some ground or other it must be held; in short, when a belief is inwardly a past one; then externally also the object of the belief is referred to the past. Unbelief thus gets breathing space, but at the same time concedes to belief at least an historical validity. The past is here the fortunate means of compromise between belief and unbelief: I certainly believe in miracles, but, *nota bene*, in no miracles which happen now—only in those which once happened, which, thank God! are already *plus quam perfecta.* So also with the creation. The creation is an immediate act of God, a miracle, for there was once nothing but God. In the idea of the creation man transcends the world, he rises into abstraction from it; he conceives it as non-existent in the moment of creation; thus he dispels from his sight what stands between himself and God, the sensible world; he places himself in immediate contact with God. But the mechanical thinker shrinks from this im-mediate contact with God; hence he at once makes the *præsens,* if indeed he soars so high, into a *perfectum;* he interposes millenniums between his natural or materialistic view and the thought of an immediate operation of God.

To the religious spirit, on the contrary, God alone is the

cause of all positive effects, God alone the ultimate and also
the sole ground wherewith it answers, or rather repels, all
questions which theory puts forward; for the affirmative of
religion is virtually a negative; its answer amounts to
nothing, since it solves the most various questions always
with the same answer, making all the operations of Nature
immediate operations of God, of a designing, personal, extra-
natural or supranatural Being. God is the idea which supplies the lack of theory. The idea of God is the explanation
of the inexplicable,—which explains nothing because it is
supposed to explain everything without distinction; he is
the night of theory, a night, however, in which everything
is clear to religious feeling, because in it the measure of
darkness, the discriminating light of the understanding,
is extinct; he is the ignorance which solves all doubt by
repressing it, which knows everything because it knows
nothing definite, because all things which impress the intellect disappear before religion, lose their individuality, in the
eyes of divine power are nothing. Darkness is the mother
of religion.

The essential act of religion, that in which religion puts
into action what we have designated as its essence, is prayer.
Prayer is all-powerful. What the pious soul entreats for
in prayer God fulfils. But he prays not for spiritual gifts*
alone, which lie in some sort in the power of man; he
prays also for things which lie out of him, which are in the
power of Nature, a power which it is the very object of
prayer to overcome; in prayer he lays hold on a supernatural means, in order to attain ends in themselves natural.
God is to him not the *causa remota* but the *causa proxima*,
the immediate, efficient cause of all natural effects. All
so-called secondary forces and second causes are nothing
to him when he prays; if they were anything to him, the
might, the fervour of prayer would be annihilated. But in
fact they have no existence for him; otherwise he would
assuredly seek to attain his end only by some intermediate
process. But he desires immediate help. He has recourse
to prayer in the certainty that he can do more, infinitely
more, by prayer, than by all the efforts of reason and all
the agencies of Nature,—in the conviction that prayer pos-

* It is only unbelief in the efficacy of prayer which has subtly limited
prayer to spiritual matters.

sesses superhuman and supernatural powers.* But in
prayer he applies immediately to God. Thus God is to
him the *immediate* cause, the fulfilment of prayer, the
power which realises prayer. But an immediate act of God
is a miracle; hence miracle is essential to the religious
view. Religion explains everything miraculously. That
miracles do not always happen is indeed obvious, as that
man does not always pray. But the consideration that
miracles do not always happen lies outside the nature of
religion, in the empirical or physical mode of view only.
Where religion begins, there also begins miracle. Every true
prayer is a miracle, an act of the wonder-working power.
External miracles themselves only make visible internal
miracles, that is, they are only a manifestation in time and
space, and therefore as a special fact, of what in and by
itself is a fundamental position of religion, namely, that God
is, in general, the supernatural, immediate cause of all things.
The miracle of fact is only an impassioned expression of
religion, a moment of inspiration. Miracles happen only
in extraordinary crises, in which there is an exaltation of the
feelings: hence there are miracles of anger. No miracle is
wrought in cold blood. But it is precisely in moments of
passion that the latent nature reveals itself. Man does not
always pray with equal warmth and power. Such prayers
are therefore ineffective. Only ardent prayer reveals the
nature of prayer. Man truly prays when he regards prayer
as in itself a sacred power, a divine force. So it is with
miracles. Miracles happen—no matter whether few or
many—wherever there is, as a basis for them, a belief in
the miraculous. But the belief in miracle is no theoretic
or objective mode of viewing the world and Nature; miracle
realises practical wants, and that in contradiction with the
laws which are imperative to the reason; in miracle man
subjugates Nature, as in itself a nullity, to his own ends,
which he regards as a reality; miracle is the superlative
expression of spiritual or religious utilitarianism; in miracle
all things are at the service of necessitous man. It is clear

* According to the notion of barbarians, therefore, prayer is a coercive
power, a charm. But this conception is an unchristian one (although even
among many Christians the idea is accepted that prayer constrains God);
for in Christianity God is essentially feeling satisfied in itself, Almighty
goodness, which denies nothing to (religious) feeling. The idea of coercion
presupposes an unfeeling God.

from this, that the conception of the world which is essential to religion is that of the practical or subjective standpoint, that God—for the miracle-working power is identical with God—is a purely practical or subjective Being, serving, however, as a substitute for a theoretic view, and is thus no object of thought, of the knowing faculty, any more than miracle, which owes its origin to the negation of thought. If I place myself in the point of view of thought, of investigation, of theory, in which I consider things in themselves, in their mutual relations, the miracle-working being vanishes into nothing, miracle disappears ; *i.e.,* the religious miracle, which is absolutely different from the natural miracle, though they are continually interchanged, in order to stultify reason, and, under the appearance of natural science, to introduce religious miracle into the sphere of rationality and reality.

But for this very reason—namely, that religion is removed from the standpoint, from the nature of theory—the true, universal essence of Nature and humanity, which as such is hidden from religion and is only visible to the theoretic eye, is conceived as another, a miraculous and supernatural essence ; the idea of the species becomes the idea of God, who again is himself an individual being, but is distinguished from human individuals in this, that he possesses their qualities according to the measure of the species. Hence, in religion man necessarily places his nature out of himself, regards his nature as a separate nature ; necessarily, because the nature which is the object of theory lies outside of him, because all his conscious existence spends itself in his practical subjectivity. God is his *alter ego,* his other lost half ; God is the complement of himself ; in God he is first a perfect man. God is a need to him ; something is wanting to him without his knowing what it is—God is this something wanting, indispensable to him ; God belongs to his nature. The world is nothing to religion,*—the world, which is in truth the sum of all reality, is revealed in its glory only by theory. The joys of

* "Natura enim remota providentia et potestate divina prorsus nihil est." —Lactantius (Div. Inst. lib. 3, c. 28). "Omnia quæ creata sunt, quamvis ea Deus fecerit valde bona, Creatori tamen comparata, nec bona sunt, cui comparata nec sunt ; altissime quippe et proprio modo quodam de se ipso dixit : Ego sum, qui sum."—Augustinus (de Perfectione Just. Hom. c. 14).

theory are the sweetest intellectual pleasures of life; but religion knows nothing of the joys of the thinker, of the investigator of Nature, of the artist. The idea of the universe is wanting to it, the consciousness of the really infinite, the consciousness of the species. God only is its compensation for the poverty of life, for the want of a substantial import, which the true life of rational contemplation presents in unending fulness. God is to religion the substitute for the lost world,—God is to it in the stead of pure contemplation, the life of theory.

That which we have designated as the practical or subjective view is not pure, it is tainted with egoism, for therein I have relation to a thing only for my own sake; neither is it self-sufficing, for it places me in relation to an object above my own level. On the contrary, the theoretic view is joyful, self-sufficing, happy; for here the object calls forth love and admiration; in the light of the free intelligence it is radiant as a diamond, transparent as a rock-crystal. The theoretic view is æsthetic, whereas the practical is unæsthetic. Religion therefore finds in God a compensation for the want of an æsthetic view. To the religious spirit the world is nothing in itself; the admiration, the contemplation of it is idolatry; for the world is a mere piece of mechanism.* Hence in religion it is God that serves as the object of pure, untainted, *i.e.*, theoretic or æsthetic contemplation. God is the existence to which the religious man has an objective relation; in God the object is contemplated by him for its own sake. God is an end in himself; therefore in religion he has the significance which in the theoretic view belongs to the object in general. The general being of theory is to religion a special being. It is true that in religion man, in his relation to God, has relation to his own wants as well as in a higher as in the lower sense: "Give us this day our daily bread;" but God can satisfy all wants of man only because he in himself has no wants,—because he is perfect blessedness.

* "Pulchras formas et varias, nitidos et amœnos colores amant oculi. Non teneant hæc animam meam ; teneat eam Deus qui hæc fecit, bona quidem valde, sed ipse est bonum meum, non hæc."—Augustinus (Confess. l. x. c. 34). "Vetiti autem sumus (2 Cor. iv. 18.) converti ad ea quæ videntur. . . . Amandus igitur solus Deus est : omnis vero iste mundus, *i.e.* omnia sensibilia contemnenda, utendum autem his ad hujus vitæ necessitatem."— Ib. de Moribus Eccl. Cathol. l. i. c. 20.

CHAPTER XX.

RELIGION is the relation of man to his own nature,—therein lies its truth and its power of moral amelioration;—but to his nature not recognised as his own, but regarded as another nature, separate, nay, contradistinguished from his own: herein lies its untruth, its limitation, its contradiction to reason and morality; herein lies the noxious source of religious fanaticism, the chief metaphysical principle of human sacrifices, in a word, the *prima materia* of all the atrocities, all the horrible scenes, in the tragedy of religious history.

The contemplation of the human nature as another, a separately existent nature, is, however, in the original conception of religion an involuntary, childlike, simple act of the mind, that is, one which separates God and man just as immediately as it again identifies them. But when religion advances in years, and, with years, in understanding; when, within the bosom of religion, reflection on religion is awakened, and the consciousness of the identity of the divine being with the human begins to dawn,—in a word, when religion becomes theology, the originally involuntary and harmless separation of God from man becomes an intentional, excogitated separation, which has no other object than to banish again from the consciousness this identity which has already entered there.

Hence the nearer religion stands to its origin, the truer, the more genuine it is, the less is its true nature disguised; that is to say, in the origin of religion there is no qualitative or essential distinction whatever between God and man. And the religious man is not shocked at this identification; for his understanding is still in harmony with his religion. Thus in ancient Judaism, Jehovah was a being differing from the human individual in nothing but in duration of existence; in his qualities, his inherent nature, he was entirely similar to man,—had the same passions, the same human, nay, even corporeal properties. Only in the later

Judaism was Jehovah separated in the strictest manner from man, and recourse was had to allegory in order to give to the old anthropomorphisms another sense than that which they originally had. So again in Christianity: in its earliest records the divinity of Christ is not so decidedly stamped as it afterwards became. With Paul especially, Christ is still an undefined being, hovering between heaven and earth, between God and man, or in general, one amongst the existences subordinate to the highest,—the first of the angels, the first created, but still created; begotten indeed for our sake; but then neither are angels and men created, but begotten, for God is their·Father also. The Church first identified him with God, made him the exclusive Son of God, defined his distinction from men and angels, and thus gave him the monopoly of an eternal, uncreated existence.

In the genesis of ideas, the first mode in which reflection on religion, or theology, makes the divine being a distinct being, and places him outside of man, is by making the existence of God the object of a formal proof.

The proofs of the existence of God have been pronounced contradictory to the essential nature of religion. They are so, but only in their form as proofs. Religion immediately represents the inner nature of man as an objective, external being. And the proof aims at nothing more than to prove that religion is right. The most perfect being is that than which no higher can be conceived : God is the highest that man conceives or can conceive. This premiss of the onto-logical proof—the most interesting proof, because it proceeds from within—expresses the inmost nature of religion. That which is the highest for man, from which he can make no further abstraction, which is the positive limit of his intellect, of his feeling, of his sentiment, that is to him God— *id quo nihil majus cogitari potest.* But this highest being would not be the highest if he did not exist; we could then conceive a higher being who would be superior to him in the fact of existence ; the idea of the highest being directly precludes this fiction. Not to exist is a deficiency ; to exist is perfection, happiness, bliss. From a being to whom man gives all, offers up all that is precious to him, he cannot withhold the bliss of existence. The contradiction to the religious spirit in the proof of the existence of God lies only in this, that the existence is thought of separately, and thence arises the appearance that God is a mere conception, a being existing in idea only,—an appearance, however, which is immediately dissipated; for the very result of the proof is, that to God belongs an existence distinct from an ideal one, an existence apart from man, apart from thought, —a real self-existence.

The proof therefore is only thus far discordant with the spirit of religion, that it presents as a formal deduction the implicit enthymeme or immediate conclusion of religion, exhibits in logical relation, and therefore distinguishes, what religion immediately unites; for to religion God is not a matter of abstract thought,—he is a present truth and reality. But that every religion in its idea of God makes a latent, unconscious inference, is confessed in its polemic against other religions. " Ye heathens," says the Jew or the Christian, " were able to conceive nothing higher as your deities because ye were sunk in sinful desires. Your God rests on a conclusion, the premisses of which are your sensual impulses, your passions. You thought thus : the most excellent life is to live out one's impulses without restraint ; and because this life was the most excellent, the truest, you made it your God. Your God was your carnal nature, your heaven only a free theatre for the passions which, in society and in the conditions of actual life generally, had to suffer restraint." But, naturally, in relation to itself no religion is conscious of such an inference, for the highest of which it is capable is its limit, has the force of necessity, is not a thought, not a conception, but immediate reality.

The proofs of the existence of God have for their aim to make the internal external, to separate it from man.* His existence being proved, God is no longer a merely relative, but a noumenal being (*Ding an sich*) : he is not only a being for us, a being in our faith, our feeling, our nature, he is a being in himself, a being external to us,—in a word, not merely a belief, a feeling, a thought, but also a real existence apart from belief, feeling, and thought. But such an existence is no other than a sensational existence ;

* At the same time, however, their result is to prove the nature of man. The various proofs of the existence of God are nothing else than various highly interesting forms in which the human nature affirms itself. Thus, for example, the physico-theological proof (or proof from design) is the self-affirmation of the calculated activity of the understanding. Every philosophic system is, in this sense, a proof of the existence of God.

i.e., an existence conceived according to the forms of our senses.

The idea of sensational existence is indeed already involved in the characteristic expression " external to us." It is true that a sophistical theology refuses to interpret the word " external " in its proper, natural sense, and substitutes the indefinite expression of independent, separate existence. But if the externality is only figurative, the existence also is figurative. And yet we are here only concerned with existence in the proper sense, and external existence is alone the definite, real, unshrinking expression for separate existence.

Real, sensational existence is that which is not dependent on my own mental spontaneity or activity, but by which I am involuntarily affected, which is when I am not, when I do not think of it or feel it. The existence of God must therefore be in space—in general, a qualitative, sensational existence. But God is not seen, not heard, not perceived by the senses. He does not exist for me, if I do not exist for him ; if I do not believe in a God, there is no God for me. If I am not devoutly disposed, if I do not raise myself above the life of the senses, he has no place in my consciousness. Thus he exists only in so far as he is felt, thought, believed in ;—the addition " for me " is unnecessary. His existence therefore is a real one, yet at the same time not a real one ;—a spiritual existence, says the theologian. But spiritual existence is only an existence in thought, in feeling, in belief ; so that his existence is a medium between sensational existence and conceptional existence, a medium full of contradiction. Or: he is a sensational existence, to which however all the conditions of sensational existence are wanting :—consequently an existence at once sensational and not sensational, an existence which contradicts the idea of the sensational, or only a vague existence in general, which is fundamentally a sensational one, but which, in order that this may not become evident, is divested of all the predicates of a real, sensational existence. But such an " existence in general " is self-contradictory. To existence belongs full, definite reality.

A necessary consequence of this contradiction is Atheism. The existence of God is essentially an empirical existence, without having its distinctive marks ; it is in itself a matter of experience, and yet in reality no object of experience. It calls upon man to seek it in Reality: it impregnates his mind with sensational conceptions and pretensions; hence, when these are not fulfilled—when, on the contrary, he finds experience in contradiction with these conceptions, he is perfectly justified in denying that existence.

Kant is well known to have maintained, in his critique of the proofs of the existence of God, that that existence is not susceptible of proof from reason. He did not merit, on this account, the blame which was cast on him by Hegel. The idea of the existence of God in those proofs is a thoroughly empirical one; but I cannot deduce empirical existence from an *à priori* idea. The only real ground of blame against Kant is, that in laying down this position he supposed it to be something remarkable, whereas it is self-evident. Reason cannot constitute itself an object of sense. I cannot, in thinking, at the same time represent what I think as a sensible object, external to me. The proof of the existence of God transcends the limits of the reason; true; but in the same sense in which sight, hearing, smelling transcend the limits of the reason. It is absurd to reproach reason that it does not satisfy a demand which can only address itself to the senses. Existence, empirical existence, is proved to me by the senses alone; and in the question as to the being of God, the existence implied has not the significance of inward reality, of truth, but the significance of a formal, external existence. Hence there is perfect truth in the allegation that the belief that God is or is not has no consequence with respect to inward moral dispositions. It is true that the thought: There is a God, is inspiring; but here the *is* means inward reality; here the existence is a movement of inspiration, an act of aspiration. Just in proportion as this existence becomes a prosaic, an empirical truth, the inspiration is extinguished.

Religion, therefore, in so far as it is founded on the existence of God as an empirical truth, is a matter of indifference to the inward disposition. As, necessarily, in the religious cultus, ceremonies, observances, sacraments, apart from the moral spirit or disposition, become in themselves an important fact: so also, at last, belief in the existence of God becomes, apart from the inherent quality, the spiritual import of the idea of God, a chief point in religion. If thou only believest in God—believest that God is, thou art already saved. Whether under this God thou conceivest a really divine being or a monster, a Nero or a Caligula, an image of thy passions, thy revenge, or ambition, it is all one,—the main point is that thou be not an atheist. The history of religion has amply confirmed this consequence which we here draw from the idea of the divine existence. If the existence of God, taken by itself, had not rooted itself as a religious truth in minds, there would never have been those infamous, senseless, horrible ideas of God which stigmatise the history of religion and theology. The existence of God was a common, external, and yet at the same time a holy thing :—what wonder, then, if on this ground the commonest, rudest, most unholy conceptions and opinions sprang up !

Atheism was supposed, and is even now supposed, to be the negation of all moral principle, of all moral foundations and bonds : if God is not, all distinction between good and bad, virtue and vice, is abolished. Thus the distinction lies only in the existence of God ; the reality of virtue lies not in itself, but out of it. And assuredly it is not from an attachment to virtue, from a conviction of its intrinsic worth and importance, that the reality of it is thus bound up with the existence of God. On the contrary, the belief that God is the necessary condition of virtue is the belief in the nothingness of virtue in itself.

It is indeed worthy of remark that the idea of the empirical existence of God has been perfectly developed in modern times, in which empiricism and materialism in general have arrived at their full blow. It is true that even in the original, simple religious mind, God is an empirical existence to be found in a place, though above the earth. But here this conception has not so naked, so prosaic a significance ; the imagination identifies again the external God with the soul of man. The imagination is, in general, the true place of an existence which is absent, not present to the senses, though nevertheless sensational in its essence.*

* "Christ is ascended on high, . . . that is, he not only sits there above, but he is also here below. And he is gone thither to the very end that he might be here below, and fill all things, and be in all places, which he could not do while on earth, for here he could not be seen by all bodily eyes. Therefore he sits above, where every man can see him, and he has to do with every man."—Luther (Th. xiii. p. 643). That is to say : Christ or God is an object, an existence, of the imagination ; in the imagination he is

Only the imagination solves the contradiction in an existence which is at once sensational and not sensational;
only the imagination is the preservative from atheism. In
the imagination existence has sensational effects,—existence
affirms itself as a power; with the essence of sensational
existence the imagination associates also the phenomena of
sensational existence. Where the existence of God is a
living truth, an object on which the imagination exercises
itself, there also appearances of God are believed in.* Where,
on the contrary, the fire of the religious imagination is
extinct, where the sensational effects or appearances necessarily connected with an essentially sensational existence
cease, there the existence becomes a dead, self-contradictory
existence, which falls irrecoverably into the negation of
atheism.

The belief in the existence of God is the belief in a
special existence, separate from the existence of man and
Nature. A special existence can only be proved in a special
manner. This faith is therefore only *then* a true and living
one when special effects, immediate appearances of God,
miracles, are believed in. Where, on the other hand, the
belief in God is identified with the belief in the world,
where the belief in God is no longer a special faith, where
the general being of the world takes possession of the
whole man, there also vanishes the belief in special effects
and appearances of God. Belief in God is wrecked, is
stranded on the belief in the world, in natural effects as the
only true ones. As here the belief in miracles is no longer
anything more than the belief in historical, past miracles, so
the existence of God is also only an historical, in itself
atheistic conception.

limited to no place,—he is present and objective to every one. God exists
in heaven, but is for that reason omnipresent; for this heaven is the imagination.

* "Thou hast not to complain that thou art less experienced than was
Abraham or Isaac. Thou also hast appearances. . . . Thou hast holy
baptism, the supper of the Lord, the bread and wine, which are figures and
forms, under and in which the present God speaks to thee, and acts upon
thee, in thy ears, eyes, and heart. . . . He appears to thee in baptism,
and it is he himself who baptizes thee, and speaks to thee. . . . Everything is full of divine appearances and utterances, if he is on thy side."—
Luther (Th. ii. p. 466. See also on this subject, Th. xix. p. 407).

CHAPTER XXI.

WITH the idea of the existence of God is connected the idea of revelation. God's attestation of his existence, the authentic testimony that God exists, is revelation. Proofs drawn from reason are merely subjective; the objective, the only true proof of the existence of God, is his revelation. God speaks to man; revelation is the word of God; he sends forth a voice which thrills the soul, and gives it the joyful certainty that God really is. The word is the gospel of life, —the criterion of existence and non-existence. Belief in revelation is the culminating point of religious objectivism. The subjective conviction of the existence of God here becomes an indubitable, external, historical fact. The existence of God, in itself, considered simply as existence, is already an external, empirical existence; still, it is as yet only thought, conceived, and therefore doubtful; hence the assertion that all proofs produce no satisfactory certainty. This conceptional existence converted into a real existence, a fact, is revelation. God has revealed himself, has demonstrated himself: who then can have any further doubt? The certainty of the existence of God is involved for me in the certainty of the revelation. A God who only exists without revealing himself, who exists for me only through my own mental act, such a God is a merely abstract, imaginary, subjective God; a God who gives me a knowledge of himself through his own act is alone a God who truly exists, who proves himself to exist,—an objective God. Faith in revelation is the immediate certainty of the religious mind, that what it believes, wishes, conceives, really is. Religion is a dream, in which our own conceptions and emotions appear to us as separate existences, beings out of ourselves. The religious mind does not distinguish between subjective and objective,—it has no doubts; it has the faculty, not of discerning other things than itself, but of seeing its own conceptions out of itself as distinct beings. What is in itself a mere theory is to the religious mind a practical belief, a matter of conscience,—a fact. A fact is that which from being an object of the intellect becomes a matter of conscience; a fact is that which one cannot criticise or attack without being guilty of a crime;* a fact is that which one must believe *nolens volens;* a fact is a physical force, not an argument,—it makes no appeal to the reason. O ye shortsighted religious philosophers of Germany, who fling at our heads the facts of the religious consciousness, to stun our reason and make us the slaves of your childish superstition,—do you not see that facts are just as relative, as various, as subjective, as the ideas of the different religions? Were not the gods of Olympus also facts, self-attesting existences? † Were not the ludicrous miracles of paganism regarded as facts? Were not angels and demons historical persons? Did they not really appear to men? Did not Balaam's ass really speak? Was not the story of Balaam's ass just as much believed even by enlightened scholars of the last century, as the Incarnation or any other miracle? A fact, I repeat, is a conception about the truth of which there is no doubt, because it is no object of theory, but of feeling, which desires that what it wishes, what it believes, should be true. A fact is that, the denial of which is forbidden, if not by an external law, yet by an internal one. A fact is every possibility which passes for a reality, every conception which, for the age wherein it is held to be a fact, expresses a want, and is for that reason an impassable limit of the mind. A fact is every wish that projects itself on

* The denial of a fact is not a matter of indifference; it is something morally evil,—a disowning of what is known to be true. Christianity made its articles of faith objective, *i.e.*, undeniable, unassailable facts, thus overpowering the reason, and taking the mind prisoner by the force of external reality : herein we have the true explanation why and how Christianity, Protestant as well as Catholic, enunciated and enforced with all solemnity the principle, that heresy—the denial of an idea or a fact which forms an article of faith—is an object of punishment by the temporal power, *i.e.*, a crime. What in theory is an external fact becomes in practice an external force. In this respect Christianity is far below Mohammedanism, to which the crime of heresy is unknown.

† "Præsentiam sæpe divi suam declarant."—Cicero (de Nat. D. l. ii.). Cicero's works (de Nat. D. and de Divinatione) are especially interesting, because the arguments there used for the reality of the objects of pagan faith are virtually the same as those urged in the present day by theologians and the adherents of positive religion generally for the reality of the objects of Christian faith.

reality : in short, it is everything that is not doubted simply because it is not—must not be—doubted.

The religious mind, according to its nature as hitherto unfolded, has the immediate certainty that all its involuntary, spontaneous affections are impressions from without, manifestations of another being. The religious mind makes itself the passive, God the active being. God is activity ; but that which determines him to activity, which causes his activity (originally only omnipotence, *potentia*) to become real activity, is not himself,—he needs nothing,—but man, the religious subject. At the same time, however, man is reciprocally determined by God ; he views himself as passive ; he receives from God determinate revelations, determinate proofs of his existence. Thus in revelation man determines himself as that which determines God, *i.e.*, revelation is simply the self-determination of man, only that between himself the determined, and himself the determining, he interposes an object—God, a distinct being. God is the medium by which man brings about the reconciliation of himself with his own nature : God is the bond, the *vinculum substantiale*, between the essential nature—the species—and the individual.

The belief in revelation exhibits in the clearest manner the characteristic illusion of the religious consciousness. The general premiss of this belief is : man can of himself know nothing of God ; all his knowledge is merely vain, earthly, human. But God is a superhuman being ; God is known only by himself. Thus we know nothing of God beyond what he reveals to us. The knowledge imparted by God is alone divine, superhuman, supernatural knowledge. By means of revelation, therefore, we know God through himself ; for revelation is the word of God—God declaring himself. Hence, in the belief in revelation man makes himself a negation, he goes out of and above himself ; he places revelation in opposition to human knowledge and opinion ; in it is contained a hidden knowledge, the fulness of all supersensuous mysteries ; here reason must hold its peace. But nevertheless the divine revelation is determined by the human nature. God speaks not to brutes or angels, but to men ; hence he uses human speech and human conceptions. Man is an object to God, before God perceptibly imparts himself to man ; he thinks of man ; he determines his action in accordance with the nature of man and his needs. God is indeed free in will; he can reveal himself or not; but he is not free as to the understanding; he cannot reveal to man whatever he will, but only what is adapted to man, what is commensurate with his nature such as it actually is; he reveals what he must reveal, if his revelation is to be a revelation for man, and not for some other kind of being. Now what God thinks in relation to man is determined by the idea of man—it has arisen out of reflection on human nature. God puts himself in the place of man, and thinks of himself as this other being can and should think of him; he thinks of himself, not with his own thinking power, but with man's. In the scheme of his revelation God must have reference not to himself, but to man's power of comprehension. That which comes from God to man, comes to man only from *man in God*, that is, only from the ideal nature of man to the phenomenal man, from the species to the individual. Thus, between the divine revelation and the so-called human reason or nature, there is no other than an illusory distinction;—the contents of the divine revelation are of human origin, for they have proceeded not from God as God, but from God as determined by human reason, human wants, that is, directly from human reason and human wants. And so in revelation man goes out of himself, in order, by a circuitous path, to return to himself! Here we have a striking confirmation of the position that the secret of theology is nothing else than anthropology—the knowledge of God nothing else than a knowledge of man!

Indeed, the religious consciousness itself admits, in relation to past times, the essentially human quality of revelation. The religious consciousness of a later age is no longer satisfied with a Jehovah who is from head to foot a man, and does not shrink from becoming visible as such. It recognises that those were merely images in which God accommodated himself to the comprehension of men in that age, that is, merely human images. But it does not apply this mode of interpretation to ideas accepted as revelation in the present age, because it is yet itself steeped in those ideas. Nevertheless, every revelation is simply a revelation of the nature of man to existing men. In revelation man's latent nature is disclosed to him, because an object to him. He is determined, affected by his own nature as by another being; he receives from the hands of God what his own unrecognised nature entails upon him as a necessity, under certain conditions of time and circumstance. Reason, the mind of the species, operates on the subjective, uncultured man only under the image of a personal being. Moral laws have force for him only as the commandments of a Divine Will, which has at once the power to punish and the glance which nothing escapes. That which his own nature, his reason, his conscience says to him, does not bind him, because the subjective, uncultured man sees in conscience, in reason, so far as he recognises it as his own, no universal objective power; hence he must separate from himself that which gives him moral laws, and place it in opposition to himself, as a distinct personal being.

Belief in revelation is a childlike belief, and is only respectable so long as it is childlike. But the child is determined from without, and revelation has for its object to effect by God's help what man cannot attain by himself. Hence revelation has been called the education of the human race. This is correct; only revelation must not be regarded as outside the nature of man. There is within him an inward necessity which impels him to present moral and philosophical doctrines in the form of narratives and fables, and an equal necessity to represent that impulse as a revelation. The mythical poet has an end in view—that of making men good and wise; he designedly adopts the form of fable as the most appropriate and vivid method of representation; but at the same time, he is himself urged to this mode of teaching by his love of fable, by his inward impulse. So it is with a revelation enunciated by an individual. This individual has an aim; but at the same time he himself lives in the conceptions by means of which he realises this aim. Man, by means of the imagination, involuntarily contemplates his inner nature; he represents it as out of himself. The nature of man, of the species— thus working on him through the irresistible power of the imagination, and contemplated as the law of his thought and action—is God.

Herein lie the beneficial moral effects of the belief in revelation.

But as Nature " unconsciously produces results which look as if they were produced consciously," so revelation generates moral actions, which do not, however, proceed from morality ;—moral actions, but no moral dispositions. Moral rules are indeed observed, but they are severed from the inward disposition, the heart, by being represented as the commandments of an external lawgiver, by being placed in the category of arbitrary laws, police regulations. What is done is done not because it is good and right, but because it is commanded by God. The inherent quality of the deed is indifferent ; whatever God commands is right.* If these commands are in accordance with reason, with ethics, it is well ; but so far as the idea of revelation is concerned, it is accidental. The ceremonial laws of the Jews were revealed, divine, though in themselves adventitious and arbitrary. The Jews received from Jehovah the command to steal ;—in a special case, it is true.

But the belief in revelation not only injures the moral sense and taste,—the æsthetics of virtue ; it poisons, nay it destroys, the divinest feeling in man—the sense of truth, the perception and sentiment of truth. The revelation of God is a determinate revelation, given at a particular epoch : God revealed himself once for all in the year so and so, and that, not to the universal man, to the man of all times and places, to the reason, to the species, but to certain limited individuals. A revelation in a given time and place must be fixed in writing, that its blessings may be transmitted uninjured. Hence the belief in revelation is, at least for those of a subsequent age, belief in a written revelation ; but the necessary consequence of a faith in which an historical book, necessarily subject to all the conditions of a temporal, finite production, is regarded as an eternal, absolute, universally authoritative word, is—superstition and sophistry.

Faith in a written revelation is a real, unfeigned, and so far respectable faith, only where it is believed that all in the sacred writings is significant, true, holy, divine. Where, on

---

* " Quod crudeliter ab hominibus sine Dei jussu fieret aut factum est, id debuit ab Hebrais fieri, quia a deo vitæ et necis summo arbitrio, jussi bellum ita gerebant."—J. Clericus (Comm. in Mos. Num. c. 31, 7). " Multa gessit Samson, quæ vix possent defendi, nisi Dei, a quo homines pendent, instrumentum fuisse censeatur."—Ib. (Comm. in Judicum, c. 14, 19). See also Luther, *e.g.* (Th. i. p. 339, Th. xvi. p. 495).

the contrary, the distinction is made between the human and divine, the relatively true and the absolutely true, the historical and the permanent,—where it is not held that all without distinction is unconditionally true; there the verdict of unbelief, that the Bible is no divine book, is already introduced into the interpretation of the Bible,— there, at least indirectly, that is, in a crafty, dishonest way, its title to the character of a divine revelation is denied. Unity, unconditionality, freedom from exceptions, immediate certitude, is alone the character of divinity. A book that imposes on me the necessity of discrimination, the necessity of criticism, in order to separate the divine from the human, the permanent from the temporary, is no longer a divine, certain, infallible book,—it is degraded to the rank of profane books; for every profane book has the same quality, that together with or in the human it contains the divine, that is, together with or in the individual it contains the universal and eternal. But that only is a truly divine book in which there is not merely something good and something bad, something permanent and something temporary, but in which all comes as it were from one crucible, all is eternal, true and good. What sort of a revelation is that in which I must first listen to the apostle Paul, then to Peter, then to James, then to John, then to Matthew, then to Mark, then to Luke, until at last I come to a passage where my soul, athirst for God, can cry out: EUREKA! here speaks the Holy Spirit himself! here is something for me, something for all times and men. How true, on the contrary, was the conception of the old faith, when it extended inspiration to the very words, to the very letters of Scripture! The word is not a matter of indifference in relation to the thought; a definite thought can only be rendered by a definite word. Another word, another letter— another sense. It is true that such faith is superstition; but this superstition is alone the true, undisguised, open faith, which is not ashamed of its consequences. If God numbers the hairs on the head of a man, if no sparrow falls to the ground without his will, how could he leave to the stupidity and caprice of scribes his Word—that Word on which depends the everlasting salvation of man? Why should he not dictate his thoughts to their pen in order to guard them from the possibility of disfiguration? " But if man were a mere organ of the Holy Spirit, human freedom would be abolished!"* Oh, what a pitiable argument! Is human freedom, then, of more value than divine truth? Or does human freedom consist only in the distortion of divine truth?

And just as necessarily as the belief in a determinate historical revelation is associated with superstition, so necessarily is it associated with sophistry. The Bible contradicts morality, contradicts reason, contradicts itself, innumerable times; and yet it is the Word of God, eternal truth, and "truth cannot contradict itself."† How does the believer in revelation elude this contradiction between the idea in his own mind of revelation as divine, harmonious truth, and this supposed actual revelation? Only by self-deception, only by the silliest subterfuges, only by the most miserable, transparent sophisms. Christian sophistry is the necessary product of Christian faith, especially of faith in the Bible as a divine revelation.

Truth, absolute truth, is given objectively in the Bible, subjectively in faith; for towards that which God himself speaks I can only be believing, resigned, receptive. Nothing is left to the understanding, the reason, but a formal, subordinate office; it has a false position, a position essentially contradictory to its nature. The understanding in itself is here indifferent to truth, indifferent to the distinction between the true and the false; it has no criterion in itself; whatever is found in revelation is true, even when it is in direct contradiction with reason. The understanding is helplessly given over to the haphazard of the most ignoble empiricism;—whatever I find in divine revelation I must believe, and if necessary, my understanding must defend it; the understanding is the watchdog of revelation; it must let everything without distinction be imposed on it as truth, —discrimination would be doubt, would be a crime: consequently, nothing remains to it but an adventitious, indif-

---

* It was very justly remarked by the Jansenists against the Jesuits: "Vouloir reconnoître dans l'Ecriture quelque chose de la foiblesse et de l'esprit naturel de l'homme, c'est donner la liberté à chacun d'en faire le discernment et de rejetter ce qui lui plaira de l'Ecriture, comme venant plûtot de la foiblesse de l'homme que de l'esprit de Dieu."—Bâyle (Dict. art. Adam (Jean) Rem. E.).

† "Nec in scriptura divina fas sit sentire aliquid contrarietatis."—Petrus L. (l. ii. dist. ii. c. i.). Similar thoughts are found in the Fathers.

ferent, *i.e.*, disingenuous, sophistical, tortuous mode of thought, which is occupied only with groundless distinctions and subterfuges, with ignominious tricks and evasions. But the more man, by the progress of time, becomes estranged from revelation, the more the understanding ripens into independence,—the more glaring, necessarily, appears the contradiction between the understanding and belief in revelation. The believer can then prove revelation only by incurring contradiction with himself, with truth, with the understanding, only by the most impudent assumptions, only by shameless falsehoods, only by the sin against the Holy Ghost.

CHAPTER XXII.

THE grand principle, the central point of Christian sophistry, is the idea of God. God is the human being, and yet he must be regarded as another, a superhuman being. God is universal, abstract Being, simply the idea of Being; and yet he must be conceived as a personal, individual being;—or God is a person, and yet he must be regarded as God, as universal, *i.e.*, not as a personal being. God is; his existence is certain, more certain than ours; he has an existence distinct from us and from things in general, *i.e.*, an individual existence; and yet his existence must be held a spiritual one, *i.e.*, an existence not perceptible as a special one. One half of the definition is always in contradiction with the other half: the statement of what must be held always annihilates the statement of what is. The fundamental idea is a contradiction which can be concealed only by sophisms. A God who does not trouble himself about us, who does not hear our prayers, who does not see us and love us, is no God; thus humanity is made an essential predicate of God;—but at the same time it is said: A God who does not exist in and by himself, out of men, above men, as another being, is a phantom; and thus it is made an essential predicate of God that he is non-human and extra-human. A God who is not as we are, who has not consciousness, not intelligence, *i.e.*, not a personal understanding, a personal consciousness (as, for example, the "substance" of Spinoza), is no God. Essential identity with us is the chief condition of deity; the idea of deity is made dependent on the idea of personality, of consciousness, *quo nihil majus cogitari potest*. But it is said in the same breath, a God who is not essentially distinguished from us is no God.

The essence of religion is the immediate, involuntary, unconscious contemplation of the human nature as another, a distinct nature. But when this projected image of human nature is made an object of reflection, of theology, it becomes an inexhaustible mine of falsehoods, illusions, contradictions, and sophisms.

A peculiarly characteristic artifice and pretext of Christian sophistry is the doctrine of the unsearchableness, the incomprehensibility of the divine nature. But, as will be shown, the secret of this incomprehensibility is nothing further than that a known quality is made into an unknown one, a natural quality into a supernatural, *i.e.*, an unnatural one, so as to produce the appearance, the illusion, that the divine nature is different from the human, and is *eo ipso* an incomprehensible one.

In the original sense of religion, the incomprehensibility of God has only the significance of an impassioned expression. Thus, when we are affected by a surprising phenomenon, we exclaim : It is incredible, it is beyond conception ! though afterwards, when we recover our self-possession, we find the object of our astonishment nothing less than incomprehensible. In the truly religious sense, incomprehensibility is not the dead full stop which reflection places wherever understanding deserts it, but a pathetic note of exclamation marking the impression which the imagination makes on the feelings. The imagination is the original organ of religion. Between God and man, in the primitive sense of religion, there is on the one hand only a distinction in relation to existence, according to which God, as a self-subsistent being, is the antithesis of man as a dependent being; on the other hand, there is only a *quantitative* distinction, *i.e.*, a distinction derived from the imagination, for the distinctions of the imagination are only quantitative. The infinity of God in religion is quantitative infinity; God is and has all that man has, but in an infinitely greater measure. The nature of God is the nature of the imagination unfolded, made objective.* God is a being conceived under the forms of the senses, but freed from the limits of sense,—a being at once unlimited and sensational. But what is the imagination ?—limitless activity of the senses. God is eternal, *i.e.*, he exists at all times; God is omni-

---

* This is especially apparent in the superlative, and the preposition *super*, ὑπερ, which distinguish the divine predicates, and which very early—as, for example, with the Neo-Platonists, the Christians among heathen philosophers—played a chief part in theology.

present, *i.e.*, he exists in all places; God is the omniscient being, *i.e.*, the being to whom every individual thing, every sensible existence, is an object without distinction, without limitation of time and place.

Eternity and omnipresence are sensational qualities, for in them there is no negation of existence in time and space, but only of exclusive limitation to a particular time, to a particular place. In like manner omniscience is a sensational quality, a sensational knowledge. Religion has no hesitation in attributing to God himself the nobler senses: God sees and hears all things. But the divine omniscience is a power of knowing through the senses while yet the necessary quality, the essential determination of actual knowledge through the senses is denied to it. My senses present sensible objects to me only separately and in succession; but God sees all sensible things at once, all locality in an unlocal manner, all temporal things in an untemporal manner, all objects of sense in an unsensational manner.* That is to say: I extend the horizon of my senses by the imagination; I form to myself a confused conception of the whole of things; and this conception, which exalts me above the limited standpoint of the senses, and therefore affects me agreeably, I posit as a divine reality. I feel the fact that my knowledge is tied to a local standpoint, to sensational experience, as a limitation; what I feel as a limitation I do away with in my imagination, which furnishes free space for the play of my feelings. This negativing of limits by the imagination is the positing of omniscience as a divine power and reality. But at the same time there is only a *quantitative* distinction between omniscience and my knowledge; the *quality* of the knowledge is the same. In fact, it would be impossible for me to predicate omniscience of an object or being external to myself, if this omniscience were essentially different from my own knowledge, if it were not a mode of perception of my own, if it had nothing in common with my own power of cognition. That which is recognised by the senses is as much the object and content of the divine omniscience as of my knowledge. Imagination does away only with the

* "Scit itaque Deus, quanta sit multitudo pulicum, culicum, muscarum et piscium et quot nascantur, quotve moriantur, sed non scit hoc per momenta singula, imo simul et semel omnia."—Petrus L. (l. i. dist. 39, c. 3).

limit of quantity, not of quality. The proposition that
our knowledge is limited, means: we know only some
things, a few things, not all.

The beneficial influence of religion rests on this extension
of the sensational consciousness. In religion man is in the
open air, *sub deo;* in the sensational consciousness he is in
his narrow confined dwelling-house. Religion has relation
essentially, originally—and only in its origin is it something holy, true, pure, and good—to the immediate sensational consciousness alone; it is the setting aside of the limits
of sense. Isolated, uninstructed men and nations preserve
religion in its original sense, because they themselves remain in that mental state which is the source of religion.
The more limited a man's sphere of vision, the less he
knows of history, Nature, philosophy—the more ardently
does he cling to his religion.

For this reason the religious man feels no need of culture.
Why had the Hebrews no art, no science, as the Greeks
had? Because they felt no need of it. To them this need
was supplied by Jehovah. In the divine omniscience man
raises himself above the limits of his own knowledge;* in
the divine omnipresence, above the limits of his local standpoint; in the divine eternity, above the limits of his time.
The religious man is happy in his imagination; he has all
things *in nuce;* his possessions are always portable. Jehovah accompanies me everywhere; I need not travel out
of myself; I have in my God the sum of all treasures and
precious things, of all that is worth knowledge and remembrance. But culture is dependent on external things; it
has many and various wants, for it overcomes the limits of
sensational consciousness and life by real activity, not by
the magical power of the religious imagination. Hence the
Christian religion also, as has been often mentioned already,
has in its essence no principle of culture, for it triumphs
over the limitations and difficulties of earthly life only
through the imagination, only in God, in heaven. God is
all that the heart needs and desires—all good things, all
blessings. "Dost thou desire love, or faithfulness, or truth,
or consolation, or perpetual presence?—this is always in him

* "Qui scientem cuncta sciunt, quid nescire nequeunt?"—Liber Meditat.
c. 26 (among the spurious writings of Augustine).

without measure. Dost thou desire beauty?—he is the supremely beautiful. Dost thou desire riches?—all riches are in him. Dost thou desire power?—he is supremely powerful. Or whatever thy heart desires, it is found a thousandfold in Him, in the best, the single good, which is God." * But how can he who has all in God, who already enjoys heavenly bliss in the imagination, experience that want, that sense of poverty, which is the impulse to all culture? Culture has no other object than to realise an earthly heaven; and the religious heaven is only realised or won by religious activity.

The difference, however, between God and man, which is originally only quantitative, is by reflection developed into a qualitative difference; and thus what was originally only an emotional impression, an immediate expression of admiration, of rapture, an influence of the imagination on the feelings, has fixity given to it as an objective quality, as real incomprehensibility. The favourite expression of reflection in relation to this subject is, that we can indeed know concerning God that he has such and such attributes, but not *how* he has them. For example, that the predicate of the Creator essentially belongs to God, that he created the world, and not out of matter already existing, but out of nothing, by an act of almighty power,—this is clear, certain—yes, indubitable; but how this is possible naturally passes our understanding. That is to say: the generic idea is clear, certain, but the specific idea is unclear, uncertain.

The idea of activity, of making, of creation, is in itself a divine idea; it is therefore unhesitatingly applied to God. In activity, man feels himself free, unlimited, happy; in passivity, limited, oppressed, unhappy. Activity is the positive sense of one's personality. That is positive which in man is accompanied with joy; hence God is, as we have already said, the idea of pure, unlimited joy. We succeed only in what we do willingly; joyful effort conquers all things. But that is joyful activity which is in accordance with our nature, which we do not feel as a limitation, and consequently not as a constraint. And the happiest, the most blissful activity is that which is productive. To read is delightful, reading is passive activity; but to produce what is worthy to be read is more delightful still. It is

* Tauler, l. c. p. 312.

more blessed to give than to receive. Hence this attribute of the species—productive activity—is assigned to God ; that is, realised and made objective as divine activity. But every special determination, every *mode* of activity is abstracted, and only the fundamental determination, which, however, is essentially human, namely, production of what is external to self, is retained. God has not, like man, produced something in particular, this or that, but all things; his activity is absolutely universal, unlimited. Hence it is self-evident, it is a necessary consequence, that the mode in which God has produced the All is incomprehensible, because this activity is no *mode* of activity, because the question concerning the *how* is here an absurdity, a question which is excluded by the fundamental idea of unlimited activity. Every special activity produces its effects in a special manner, because there the activity itself is a determinate mode of activity; and thence necessarily arises the question: How did it produce this ?   But the answer to the question: How did God make the world ? has necessarily a negative issue, because the world-creating activity in itself negatives every determinate activity, such as would alone warrant the question, every mode of activity connected with a determinate medium, *i.e.*, with matter.   This question illegitimately foists in between the subject or producing activity, and the object or thing produced, an irrelevant, nay, an excluded intermediate idea, namely, the idea of particular, individual existence.   The activity in question has relation only to the collective—the All, the world ; God created all things, not some particular thing; the indefinite whole, the All, as it is embraced by the imagination,—not the determinate, the particular, as, in its particularity, it presents itself to the senses, and as, in its totality as the universe, it presents itself to the reason.   Every particular thing arises in a natural way; it is something determinate, and as such it has—what it is only tautology to state—a determinate cause.   It was not God, but carbon that produced the diamond; a given salt owes its origin, not to God, but to the combination of a particular acid with a particular base.   God only created all things together without distinction.

It is true that according to the religious conception, God has created every individual thing, as included in the whole;

—but only indirectly; for he has not produced the individual in an individual manner, the determinate in a determinate manner; otherwise he would be a determinate or conditioned being. It is certainly incomprehensible how out of this general, indeterminate, or unconditioned activity the particular, the determinate, can have proceeded; but it is so only because I here intrude the object of sensational, natural experience, because I assign to the divine activity another object than that which is proper to it. Religion has no physical conception of the world; it has no interest in a natural explanation, which can never be given but with a mode of origin. Origin is a theoretical, natural-philosophical idea. The heathen philosophers busied themselves with the origin of things. But the Christian religious consciousness abhorred this idea as heathen, irreligious, and substituted the practical or subjective idea of creation, which is nothing else than a prohibition to conceive things as having arisen in a natural way, an interdict on all physical science. The religious consciousness connects the world immediately with God; it derives all from God, because nothing is an object to him in its particularity and reality, nothing is to him as it presents itself to our reason. All proceeds from God:—that is enough, that perfectly satisfies the religious consciousness. The question, *how* did God create? is an indirect doubt that he *did* create the world. It was this question which brought man to atheism, materialism, naturalism. To him who asks it, the world is already an object of theory, of physical science, *i.e.*, it is an object to him in its reality, in its determinate constituents. It is this mode of viewing the world which contradicts the idea of unconditioned, immaterial activity : and this contradiction leads to the negation of the fundamental idea—the creation.

The creation by omnipotence is in its place, is a truth, only when all the phenomena of the world are derived from God. It becomes, as has been already observed, a myth of past ages where physical science introduces itself, where man makes the determinate causes, the *how* of phenomena, the object of investigation. To the religious consciousness, therefore, the creation is nothing incomprehensible, *i.e.*, unsatisfying; at least it is so only in moments of irreligiousness, of doubt, when the mind turns away from God to actual things; but it is highly unsatisfactory to reflection, to theology, which looks with one eye at heaven and with the other at earth. As the cause, so is the effect. A flute sends forth the tones of a flute, not those of a bassoon or a trumpet. If thou hearest the tones of a bassoon, but hast never before seen or heard any wind-instrument but the flute, it will certainly be inconceivable to thee how such tones can come out of a flute. Thus it is here:—the comparison is only so far inappropriate as the flute itself is a particular instrument. But imagine, if it be possible, an absolutely universal instrument, which united in itself all instruments, without being in itself a particular one; thou wilt then see that it is an absurd contradiction to desire a particular tone which only belongs to a particular instrument, from an instrument which thou hast divested precisely of that which is characteristic in all particular instruments.

But there also lies at the foundation of this dogma of incomprehensibility the design of keeping the divine activity apart from the human, of doing away with their similarity, or rather their essential identity, so as to make the divine activity essentially different from the human. This distinction between the divine and human activity is "nothing." God makes,—he makes something external to himself, as man does. Making is a genuine human idea. Nature gives birth to, brings forth; man makes. Making is an act which I can omit, a designed, premeditated, external act;—an act in which my inmost being is not immediately concerned, in which, while active, I am not at the same time passive, carried away by an internal impulse. On the contrary, an activity which is identical with my being is not indifferent, is necessary to me, as, for example, intellectual production, which is an inward necessity to me, and for that reason lays a deep hold on me, affects me pathologically. Intellectual works are not made,—making is only the external activity applied to them;—they arise in us. *To make* is an indifferent, therefore a free, *i.e.*, optional activity. Thus far then—that he makes—God is entirely at one with man, not at all distinguished from him; but an especial emphasis is laid on this, that his making is free, arbitrary, at his pleasure. "It has pleased God" to create a world. Thus man here deifies satisfaction in self-pleasing, in caprice and groundless arbitrariness. The fundamentally human character of the divine activity is by the idea of arbitrariness degraded into a human manifestation of a low kind; God, from a mirror of human nature, is converted into a mirror of human vanity and self-complacency.

And now all at once the harmony is changed into discord; man, hitherto at one with himself, becomes divided :—God makes *out of nothing;* he creates,—to make out of nothing is to create,—this is the distinction. The positive condition —the act of making—is a human one; but inasmuch as all that is determinate in this conception is immediately denied, reflection steps in and makes the divine activity not human. But with this negation, comprehension, understanding comes to a stand; there remains only a negative, empty notion, because conceivability is already exhausted, *i.e.,* the distinction between the divine and human determination is in truth a nothing, a *nihil negativum* of the understanding. The naïve confession of this is made in the supposition of "nothing" as an object.

God is Love, but not human love; Understanding, but not human understanding,—no! an essentially different understanding. But wherein consists this difference? I cannot conceive an understanding which acts under other forms than those of our own understanding; I cannot halve or quarter understanding so as to have several understandings; I can only conceive one and the same understanding. It is true that I can and even must conceive understanding in itself, *i.e.,* free from the limits of my individuality; but in so doing I only release it from limitations essentially foreign to it; I do not set aside its essential determinations or forms. Religious reflection, on the contrary, denies precisely that determination or quality which makes a thing what it is. Only that in which the divine understanding is identical with the human is something, is understanding, is a real idea; while that which is supposed to make it another—yes, essentially another than the human—is objectively nothing, subjectively a mere chimera.

In all other definitions of the Divine Being the "nothing" which constitutes the distinction is hidden; in the creation, on the contrary, it is an evident, declared, objective nothing; —and is therefore the official, notorious nothing of theology in distinction from anthropology.

But the fundamental determination by which man makes

his own nature a foreign, incomprehensible nature is the idea of individuality or—what is only a more abstract expression—personality. The idea of the existence of God first realises itself in the idea of revelation, and the idea of revelation first realises itself in the idea of personality. God is a personal being:—this is the spell which charms the ideal into the real, the subjective into the objective. All predicates, all attributes of the Divine Being are fundamentally human; but as attributes of a personal being, and therefore of a being distinct from man and existing independently, they appear immediately to be really other than human, yet so as that at the same time the essential identity always remains at the foundation. Hence reflection gives rise to the idea of so-called anthropomorphisms. Anthropomorphisms are resemblances between God and man. The attributes of the divine and of the human being are not indeed the same, but they are analogous.

Thus personality is the antidote to pantheism; i.e., by the idea of personality religious reflection expels from its thought the identity of the divine and human nature. The rude but characteristic expression of pantheism is: Man is an effluence or a portion of the Divine Being; the religious expression is: Man is the image of God, or a being akin to God;—for according to religion man does not spring from Nature, but is of divine race, of divine origin. But kinship is a vague, evasive expression. There are degrees of kinship, near and distant. What sort of kinship is intended? For the relation of man to God there is but one form of kinship which is appropriate,—the nearest, profoundest, most sacred that can be conceived,—the relation of the child to the father. According to this, God is the father of man, man the son, the child of God. Here is posited at once the self-subsistence of God and the dependence of man, and posited as an immediate object of feeling; whereas in pantheism the part appears just as self-subsistent as the whole, since this is represented as made up of its parts. Nevertheless this distinction is only an appearance. The father is not a father without the child; both together form a correlated being. In love man renounces his independence, and reduces himself to a part; a self-humiliation which is only compensated by the fact that the one whom he loves at the same time voluntarily becomes a part also;

that they both submit to a higher power, the power of the
spirit of family, the power of love. Thus there is here the
same relation between God and man as in pantheism, save
that in the one it is represented as a personal, patriarchal
relation, in the other as an impersonal, general one,—save
that pantheism expresses logically and therefore definitely,
directly, what religion invests with the imagination. The
correlation, or rather the identity of God and man is veiled
in religion by representing both as persons or individuals,
and God as a self-subsistent, independent being apart from
his paternity:—an independence which, however, is only
apparent, for he who, like the God of religion, is a father
from the depths of the heart, has his very life and being in
his child.

The reciprocal and profound relation of dependence between God as father and man as child cannot be shaken by
the distinction that only Christ is the true, natural son of
God, and that men are but his adopted sons; so that it is
only to Christ as the only-begotten Son, and by no means
to men, that God stands in an essential relation of dependence. For this distinction is only a theological, *i.e.*, an
illusory one. God adopts only men, not brutes. The ground
of adoption lies in the *human* nature. The man adopted
by divine grace is only the man conscious of his divine
nature and dignity. Moreover, the only-begotten Son himself is nothing else than the idea of humanity, than man
preoccupied with himself, man hiding from himself and the
world in God,—the heavenly man. The Logos is latent,
tacit man; man is the revealed, expressed Logos. The
Logos is only the prelude of man. That which applies to
the Logos applies also to the nature of man.* But between
God and the only-begotten Son there is no real distinction,
—he who knows the Son knows the Father also,—and thus
there is none between God and man.

It is the same with the idea that man is the image of
God. The image is here no dead, inanimate thing, but a
living being. "Man is the image of God," means nothing
more than that man is a being who resembles God. Simi-

* "The closest union which Christ possessed with the Father, it is possible for me to win. . . . All that God gave to his only-begotten Son, he has
given to me as perfectly as to him."—Predigten etzlicher Lehrer vor und zu
Tauleri Zeiten. Hamburg, 1621, p. 14. "Between the only-begotten Son
and the soul there is no distinction."—Ib. p. 68.

larity between living beings rests on natural relationship. The idea of man being the image of God reduces itself therefore to kinship; man is like God, because he is the child of God. Resemblance is only kinship presented to the senses; from the former we infer the latter.

But resemblance is just as deceptive, illusory, evasive an idea as kinship. It is only the idea of personality which does away with the identity of nature. Resemblance is identity which will not admit itself to be identity, which hides itself behind a dim medium, behind the vapour of the imagination. If I disperse this vapour, I come to naked identity. The more similar beings are, the less are they to to be distinguished; if I know the one, I know the other. It is true that resemblance has its degrees. But also the resemblance between God and man has its degrees. The good, pious man is more like God than the man whose resemblance to Him is founded only on the nature of man in general. And even with the pious man there is a highest degree of resemblance to be supposed, though this may not be obtained here below, but only in the future life. But that which man is to become belongs already to him, at least so far as possibility is concerned. The highest degree of resemblance is that where there is no further distinction between two individuals or beings than that they are two. The essential qualities, those by which we distinguish things from each other, are the same in both. Hence I cannot distinguish them in thought, by the reason,—for this all data are wanting;—I can only distinguish them by figuring them as visible in my imagination or by actually seeing them. If my eyes do not say, There are really two separately existent beings, my reason will take both for one and the same being. Nay, even my eyes may confound the one with the other. Things are capable of being confounded with each other which are distinguishable by the sense and not by the reason, or rather which are different only as to existence, not as to essence. Persons altogether alike have an extraordinary attraction not only for each other, but for the imagination. Resemblance gives occasion to all kinds of mystifications and illusions, because it is itself only an illusion; my eyes mock my reason, for which the idea of an independent existence is always allied to the idea of a determinate difference.

Religion is the mind's light, the rays of which are broken by the medium of the imagination and the feelings, so as to make the same being appear a double one. Resemblance is to the Reason identity, which in the realm of reality is divided or broken up by immediate sensational impressions, in the sphere of religion by the illusions of the imagination ; in short, that which is identical to the reason is made separate by the idea of individuality or personality. I can discover no distinction between father and child, archetype and image, God and man, if I do not introduce the idea of personality. Resemblance is here the external guise of identity ;—the identity which reason, the sense of truth, affirms, but which the imagination denies ; the identity which allows an appearance of distinction to remain,—a mere phantasm, which says neither directly yes, nor directly no.

CHAPTER XXIII.

THE personality of God is thus the means by which man converts the qualities of his own nature into the qualities of another being,—of a being external to himself. The personality of God is nothing else than the projected personality of man.

On this process of projecting self outwards rests also the Hegelian speculative doctrine, according to which *man's* consciousness of God is the *self*-consciousness of God. God is thought, cognised by us. According to speculation, God, in being thought by us, thinks himself or is conscious of himself; speculation identifies the two sides which religion separates. In this it is far deeper than religion, for the fact of God being thought is not like the fact of an external object being thought. God is an inward, spiritual being; thinking, consciousness, is an inward, spiritual act; to think God is therefore to affirm what God is, to establish the being of God as an act. That God is thought, cognised, is essential; that this tree is thought, is to the tree accidental, unessential. God is an indispensable thought, a necessity of thought. But how is it possible that this necessity should simply express the subjective, and not the objective also?—how is it possible that God—if he is to exist for us, to be an object to us—must necessarily be thought, if he is in himself like a block, indifferent whether he be thought, cognised or not? No! it is not possible. We are necessitated to regard the fact of God being thought by us, as his thinking himself, or his self-consciousness.

Religious objectivism has two passives, two modes in which God is thought. On the one hand, God is thought by us, on the other, he is thought by himself. God thinks himself, independently of his being thought by us: he has a self-consciousness distinct from, independent of, our conscious-

ness. This is certainly consistent when once God is conceived as a real personality; for the real human person
thinks himself, and is thought by another; my thinking of
him is to him an indifferent, external fact. This is the
last degree of anthropopathism. In order to make God free
and independent of all that is human, he is regarded as a
formal, real person, his thinking is confined within himself,
and the fact of his being thought is excluded from him,
and is represented as occurring in another being. This
indifference or independence with respect to us, to our
thought, is the attestation of a self-subsistent, *i.e.*, external,
personal existence. It is true that religion also makes the
fact of God being thought into the self-thinking of God;
but because this process goes forward *behind* its consciousness, since God is immediately presupposed as a self-existent
personal being, the religious consciousness only embraces
the indifference of the two facts.

Even religion, however, does not abide by this indifference
of the two sides. God creates in order to reveal himself :
creation is the revelation of God. But for stones, plants,
and animals there is no God, but only for man; so that
Nature exists for the sake of man, and man purely for the
sake of God. God glorifies himself in man: man is the
pride of God. God indeed knows himself even without
man; but so long as there is no other *me*, so long is he only
a possible, conceptional person. First when a difference
from God, a non-divine is posited, is God conscious of himself; first when he knows what is not God, does he know
what it is to be God, does he know the bliss of his Godhead.
First in the positing of what is other than himself, of the
world, does God posit himself as God. Is God almighty
without creation ? No ! Omnipotence first realises, proves
itself in creation. What is a power, a property, which does
not exhibit, attest itself ? What is a force which affects
nothing ? a light that does not illuminate ? a wisdom which
knows nothing, *i.e.*, nothing real ? And what is omnipotence, what all other divine attributes, if man does not exist?
Man is nothing without God; but also, God is nothing
without man; * for only in man is God an object as God;

---

* "God can as little do without us as we without him."—Predigten
etzlicher Lehrer, &c., p. 16. See also on this subject—Strauss, *Christl.
Glaubensl.* B. i. § 47, and the author's work entitled, *P. Bayle*, pp. 104, 107.

only in man is he God. The various qualities of man first give difference, which is the ground of reality in God. The physical qualities of man make God a physical being—God the Father, who is the creator of Nature, *i.e.*, the personified, anthropomorphised essence of Nature;* the intellectual qualities of man make God an intellectual being, the moral, a moral being. Human misery is the triumph of divine compassion; sorrow for sin is the delight of the divine holiness. Life, fire, emotion comes into God only through man. With the stubborn sinner God is angry; over the repentant sinner he rejoices. Man is the revealed God: in man the divine essence first realises and unfolds itself. In the creation of Nature God goes out of himself, he has relation to what is other than himself, but in man he returns into himself:—man knows God, because in him God finds and knows himself, feels himself as God. Where there is no pressure, no want, there is no feeling;—and feeling is alone real knowledge. Who can know compassion without having felt the want of it? justice without the experience of injustice? happiness without the experience of distress? Thou must feel what a thing is; otherwise thou wilt never learn to know it. It is in man that the divine properties first become feelings, *i.e.*, man is the self-feeling of God;—and the feeling of God is the real God; for the qualities of God are indeed only real qualities, realities, as felt by man,—as feelings. If the experience of human misery were outside of God, in a being personally separate from him, compassion also would not be in God, and we should hence have again the Being destitute of qualities, or more correctly the *nothing*, which God was before man or without man. For example:—Whether I be a good or sympathetic being—for that alone is good which gives, imparts itself, *bonum est communicativum sui*, —is unknown to me before the opportunity presents itself of showing goodness to another being. Only in the act of imparting do I experience the happiness of beneficence, the joy of generosity, of liberality. But is this joy apart

---

* "This temporal, transitory life in this world (*i.e.*, natural life) we have through God, who is the almighty Creator of heaven and earth. But the eternal untransitory life we have through the Passion and Resurrection of our Lord Jesus Christ. . . . Jesus Christ a Lord over that life."—Luther (Th. xvi. s. 459).

from the joy of the recipient? No; I rejoice because he rejoices. I feel the wretchedness of another, I suffer with him; in alleviating his wretchedness, I alleviate my own; —sympathy with suffering is itself suffering. The joyful feeling of the giver is only the reflex, the self-consciousness of the joy in the receiver. Their joy is a common feeling, which accordingly makes itself visible in the union of hands, of lips. So it is here. Just as the feeling of human misery is human, so the feeling of divine compassion is human. It is only a sense of the poverty of finiteness that gives a sense of the bliss of infiniteness. Where the one is not, the other is not. The two are inseparable,—inseparable the feeling of God as God, and the feeling of man as man, inseparable the knowledge of man and the self-knowledge of God. God is a Self only in the human self,—only in the human power of discrimination, in the principle of difference that lies in the human being. Thus compassion is only felt as a *me*, a self, a force, *i.e.*, as something special, through its opposite. The opposite of God gives qualities to God, realises him, makes him a Self. God is God, only through that which is not God. Herein we have also the mystery of Jacob Böhme's doctrine. It must only be borne in mind that Jacob Böhme, as a mystic and theologian, places outside of man the feelings in which the divine being first realises himself, passes from nothing to something, to a qualitative being apart from the feelings of man (at least in imagination),—and that he makes them objective in the form of natural qualities, but in such a way that these qualities still only represent the impressions made on his feelings. It will then be obvious that what the empirical religious consciousness first posits with the real creation of Nature and of man, the mystical consciousness places before the creation in the premundane God, in doing which, however, it does away with the reality of the creation. For if God has what is not-God, already in himself, he has no need first to create what is not-God in order to be God. The creation of the world is here a pure superfluity, or rather an impossibility; this God for very reality does not come to reality; he is already in himself the full and restless world. This is especially true of Schelling's doctrine of God, who though made up of innumerable "potences" is yet thoroughly impotent. Far more reasonable, therefore, is the empirical religious consciousness, which makes God reveal, *i.e.*, realise himself in real man, real nature, and according to which man is created purely for the praise and glory of God. That is to say, man is the mouth of God, which articulates and accentuates the divine qualities as human feelings. God wills that he be honoured, praised. Why? because the passion of man for God is the self-consciousness of God. Nevertheless, the religious consciousness separates these two properly inseparable sides, since by means of the idea of personality it makes God and man independent existences. Now the Hegelian speculation identifies the two sides, but so as to leave the old contradiction still at the foundation;—it is therefore only the consistent carrying out, the completion of a religious truth. The learned mob was so blind in its hatred towards Hegel as not to perceive that his doctrine, at least in this relation, does not in fact contradict religion;—that it contradicts it only in the same way as, in general, a developed, consequent process of thought contradicts an undeveloped, inconsequent, but nevertheless radically identical conception.

But if it is only in human feelings and wants that the divine "nothing" becomes something, obtains qualities, then the being of man is alone the real being of God,—man is the real God. And if in the consciousness which man has of God first arises the self-consciousness of God, then the human consciousness is, *per se*, the divine consciousness. Why then dost thou alienate man's consciousness from him, and make it the self-consciousness of a being distinct from man, of that which is an object to him? Why dost thou vindicate existence to God, to man only the consciousness of that existence? God has his consciousness in man, and man his being in God? Man's knowledge of God is God's knowledge of himself? What a divorcing and contradiction! The true statement is this: man's knowledge of God is man's knowledge of himself, of his own nature. Only the unity of being and consciousness is truth. Where the consciousness of God is, there is the being of God, —in man, therefore; in the being of God it is only thy own being which is an object to thee, and what presents itself *before* thy consciousness is simply what lies *behind* it. If the divine qualities are human, the human qualities are divine.

Only when we abandon a philosophy of religion, or a

theology, which is distinct from psychology and anthropology, and recognise anthropology as itself theology, do we attain to a true, self-satisfying identity of the divine and human being, the identity of the human being with itself. In every theory of the identity of the divine and human which is not true identity, unity of the human nature with itself, there still lies at the foundation a division, a separation into two, since the identity is immediately abolished, or rather is supposed to be abolished. Every theory of this kind is in contradiction with itself and with the understanding,—is a half measure—a thing of the imagination—a perversion, a distortion; which, however, the more perverted and false it is, all the more *appears* to be profound.

CHAPTER XXIV.

THE CONTRADICTION IN THE TRINITY.

RELIGION gives reality or objectivity not only to the human or divine nature in general as a personal being; it further gives reality to the fundamental determinations or fundamental distinctions of that nature as persons. The Trinity is therefore originally nothing else than the sum of the essential fundamental distinctions which man perceives in the human nature. According as the mode of conceiving this nature varies, so also the fundamental determinations on which the Trinity is founded vary. But these distinctions, perceived in one and the same human nature, are hypostasised as substances, as divine persons. And herein, namely, that these different determinations are in God, hypostases, subjects, is supposed to lie the distinction between these determinations as they are in God, and as they exist in man, —in accordance with the law already enunciated, that only in the idea of personality does the human personality transfer and make objective its own qualities. But the personality exists only in the imagination; the fundamental determinations are therefore only for the imagination hypostases, persons; for reason, for thought, they are mere relations or determinations. The idea of the Trinity contains in itself the contradiction of polytheism and monotheism, of imagination and reason, of fiction and reality. Imagination gives the Trinity, reason the Unity of the persons. According to reason, the things distinguished are only distinctions; according to imagination, the distinctions are things distinguished, which therefore do away with the unity of the divine being. To the reason, the divine persons are phantoms, to the imagination realities. The idea of the Trinity demands that man should think the opposite of what he imagines, and imagine the opposite of what he thinks,—that he should think phantoms realities.*

* It is curious to observe how the speculative religious philosophy undertakes the defence of the Trinity against the godless understanding, and yet, by doing away with the personal substances, and explaining the relation of

There are three Persons, but they are not essentially distinguished. *Tres personæ,* but *una essentia.* So far the conception is a natural one. We can conceive three and even more persons, identical in essence. Thus we men are distinguished from one another by personal differences, but in the main, in essence, in humanity we are one. And this identification is made not only by the speculative understanding, but even by feeling. A given individual is a man as we are; *punctum satis;* in this feeling all distinctions vanish,—whether he be rich or poor, clever or stupid, culpable or innocent. The feeling of compassion, sympathy, is therefore a substantial, essential, speculative feeling. But the three or more human persons exist apart from each other, have a separate existence, even when they verify and confirm the unity of their nature by fervent love. They together constitute, through love, a single moral personality, but each has a physical existence for himself. Though they may be reciprocally absorbed in each other, may be unable to dispense with each other, they have yet always a formally independent existence. Independent existence, existence apart from others, is the essential characteristic of a person, of a substance. It is otherwise in God, and necessarily so; for while his personality is the same as that of man, it is held to be the same with a difference, on the ground simply of this postulate: there *must* be a difference. The three Persons in God have no existence out of each other; else there would meet us in the heaven of Christian dogmatics, not indeed many gods, as in Olympus, but at least three divine Persons in an individual form, three Gods. The gods of Olympus were real persons, for they existed apart from each other, they had the criterion of real personality in their individuality, though they were one in essence, in divinity; they had different personal attributes, but were each singly a god, alike in divinity, different as existing subjects or persons; they were genuine divine personalities.

Father and Son as merely an inadequate image borrowed from organic life, robs the Trinity of its very heart and soul. Truly, if the cabalistic artifices which the speculative religious philosophy applies in the service of the absolute religion were admissible in favour of finite religions, it would not be difficult to squeeze the Pandora's box of Christian dogmatics out of the horns of the Egyptian Apis. Nothing further would be needed for this purpose than the ominous distinction of the understanding from the speculative reason,—a distinction which is adapted to the justification of every absurdity.

The three Persons of the Christian Godhead, on the contrary, are only imaginary, pretended persons, assuredly different from real persons, just because they are only phantasms, shadows of personalities, while, notwithstanding, they are assumed to be real persons. The essential characteristic of personal reality, the polytheistic element, is excluded, denied as non-divine. But by this negation their personality becomes a mere phantasm. Only in the truth of the plural lies the truth of the Persons. The three persons of the Christian Godhead are not *tres Dii*, three Gods;—at least they are not meant to be such;—but *unus Deus*, one God. The three Persons end, not, as might have been expected, in a plural, but in a singular; they are not only *Unum*—the gods of Olympus are that—but *Unus*. Unity has here the significance not of essence only, but also of existence; unity is the existential form of God. Three are one: the plural is a singular. God is a personal being consisting of three persons.*

The three persons are thus only phantoms in the eyes of reason, for the conditions or modes under which alone their personality could be realised, are done away with by the command of monotheism. The unity gives the lie to the personality; the self-subsistence of the persons is annihilated in the self-subsistence of the unity—they are mere relations. The Son is not without the Father, the Father not without the Son: the Holy Spirit, who indeed spoils the symmetry, expresses nothing but the relation of the two to each other. But the divine persons are distinguished from each other only by that which constitutes their relation to each other. The essential in the Father as a person is that he is a Father, of the Son that he is a Son. What the Father is over and above his fatherhood, does not belong to his personality; therein he is God, and as God identical with the Son as God. Therefore it is said: God the Father, God the Son, and God the Holy Ghost:—God is in all three alike. "There is one person of the Father, another of the Son, and another of the Holy Ghost. But

---

* The unity has not the significance of *genus*, not of *unum* but of *unus*. (See Augustine and Petrus Lomb. l. i. dist. 19, c. 7, 8, 9.) "*Hi ergo tres, qui unum sunt propter ineffabilem conjunctionem deitatis qua ineffabiliter copulantur, unus Deus est.*" (Petrus L. l. c. c. 6.) "How can reason bring itself into accord with this, or believe, that three is one and one is three?"—Luther (Th. x. iv. p. 13).

the Godhead of the Father, of the Son, and of the Holy Ghost, is all one;" *i.e.*, they are distinct persons, but without distinction of substance. The personality, therefore, arises purely in the relation of the Fatherhood; *i.e.*, the idea of the person is here only a relative idea, the idea of a relation. Man as a father is dependent, he is essentially the correlative of the son; he is not a father without the son; by fatherhood man reduces himself to a relative, dependent, impersonal being. It is before all things necessary not to allow oneself to be deceived by these relations as they exist in reality, in men. The human father is, over and above his paternity, an independent personal being; he has at least a formal existence for himself, an existence apart from his son; he is not merely a father, with the exclusion of all the other predicates of a real personal being. Fatherhood is a relation which the oad man can make quite an external one, not touching his personal being. But in God the Father, there is no distinction between God the Father and God the Son *as God;* the abstract fatherhood alone constitutes his personality, his distinction from the Son, whose personality likewise is founded only on the abstract sonship.

But at the same time these relations, as has been said, are maintained to be not mere relations, but real persons, beings, substances. Thus the truth of the plural, the truth of polytheism is again affirmed,* and the truth of monotheism is denied. To require the reality of the persons is to require the unreality of the unity, and conversely, to require the reality of the unity is to require the unreality of the persons. Thus in the holy mystery of the Trinity,—that is to say, so far as it is supposed to represent a truth distinct from human nature,—all resolves itself into delusions, phantasms, contradictions, and sophisms.†

---

* "Quia ergo pater Deus et filius Deus et spiritus s. Deus cur non dicuntur tres Dii? Ecce proposuit hanc propositionem (Augustinus) attende quid respondeat . . . Si autem dicerem : tres Deos, contradiceret scriptura dicens : Audi Israel : Deus tuus unus est. Ecce absolutio quæstionis : quare potius dicamus tres personas quam tres Deos, quia scil. illud non contradicit scriptura."—Petrus L. (l. i. dist. 23, c. 3). How much did even Catholicism repose upon Holy Writ !

† A truly masterly presentation of the overwhelming contradictions in which the mystery of the Trinity involves the genuine religious sentiment, is to be found in the work already cited—*Theanthropos. Eine Reihe von Aphorismen*—which expresses in the form of the religious sentiment what in the present work is expressed in the form of the reason ; and which is therefore especially to be recommended to women.

CHAPTER XXV.

THE CONTRADICTION IN THE SACRAMENTS.

As the objective essence of religion, the idea of God, resolves itself into mere contradictions, so also, on grounds easily understood, does its subjective essence.

The subjective elements of religion are on the one hand Faith and Love; on the other hand, so far as it presents itself externally in a cultus, the sacraments of Baptism and the Lord's Supper. The sacrament of Faith is Baptism, the sacrament of Love is the Lord's Supper. In strictness there are only two sacraments, as there are two subjective elements in religion, Faith and Love: for Hope is only faith in relation to the future; so that there is the same logical impropriety in making it a distinct mental act as in making the Holy Ghost a distinct being.

The identity of the sacraments with the specific essence of religion as hitherto developed is at once made evident, apart from other relations, by the fact that they have for their basis natural materials or things, to which, however, is attributed a significance and effect in contradiction with their nature. Thus the material of baptism is water, common, natural water, just as the material of religion in general is common, natural humanity. But as religion alienates our own nature from us, and represents it as not ours, so the water of baptism is regarded as quite other than common water; for it has not a physical but a hyperphysical power and significance; it is the *Lavacrum regenerationis,* it purifies man from the stains of original sin, expels the inborn devil, and reconciles with God. Thus it is natural water only in appearance; in *truth* it is supernatural. In other words: the baptismal water has supernatural effects (and that which operates supernaturally is itself supernatural) only in idea, only in the imagination.

And yet the material of Baptism is said to be natural water. Baptism has no validity and efficacy if it is not performed with water. Thus the natural quality of water has in itself value and significance, since the supernatural effect of baptism is associated in a supernatural manner with water only, and not with any other material. God, by means of his omnipotence, could have united the same effect to anything whatever. But he does not; he accommodates himself to natural qualities; he chooses an element corresponding, analogous to his operation. Thus the natural is not altogether set aside; on the contrary, there always remains a certain analogy with the natural, an appearance of naturalness. In like manner wine represents blood; bread, flesh.[*] Even miracle is guided by analogies; water is changed into wine or blood, one species into another, with the retention of the indeterminate generic idea of liquidity. So it is here. Water is the purest, clearest of liquids; in virtue of this its natural character it is the image of the spotless nature of the Divine Spirit. In short, water has a significance in itself, as water; it is on account of its natural quality that it is consecrated and selected as the vehicle of the Holy Spirit. So far there lies at the foundation of Baptism a beautiful, profound natural significance. But, at the very same time, this beautiful meaning is lost again because water has a transcendental effect,—an effect which it has only through the supernatural power of the Holy Spirit, and not through itself. The natural quality becomes indifferent: he who makes wine out of water, can at will unite the effects of baptismal water with any material whatsoever.

Baptism cannot be understood without the idea of miracle. Baptism is itself a miracle. The same power which works miracles, and by means of them, as a proof of the divinity of Christ, turns Jews and Pagans into Christians,—this same power has instituted baptism and operates in it. Christianity began with miracles, and it carries itself forward with miracles. If the miraculous power of baptism is denied, miracles in general must be denied. The miracle-working water of baptism springs from the same source as the water which at the wedding at Cana in Galilee was turned into wine.

The faith which is produced by miracle is not dependent

---

[*] "Sacramentum ejus rei similitudinem gerit, cujus signum est."—Petrus Lomb. (l. iv. dist. 1, c. 1).

on me, on my spontaneity, on freedom of judgment and conviction. A miracle which happens before my eyes I must believe, if I am not utterly obdurate. Miracle compels me to believe in the divinity of the miracle-worker.[*] It is true that in some cases it presupposes faith, namely, where it appears in the light of a reward; but with that exception it presupposes not so much actual faith as a believing disposition, willingness, submission, in opposition to an unbelieving, obdurate, and malignant disposition, like that of the Pharisees. The end of miracle is to prove that the miracle-worker is really that which he assumes to be. Faith based on miracle is the only thoroughly warranted, well-grounded, objective faith. The faith which is presupposed by miracle is only faith in a Messiah, a Christ in general; but the faith that this very man is Christ—and this is the main point—is first wrought by miracle as its consequence. This presupposition even of an indeterminate faith is, however, by no means necessary. Multitudes first became believers through miracles; thus miracle was the cause of their faith. If then miracles do not contradict Christianity,—and how should they contradict it?—neither does the miraculous efficacy of baptism contradict it. On the contrary, if baptism is to have a Christian significance it must of necessity have a supernaturalistic one. Paul was converted by a sudden miraculous appearance, when he was still full of hatred to the Christians. Christianity took him by violence. It is in vain to allege that with another than Paul this appearance would not have had the same consequences, and that therefore the effect of it must still be attributed to Paul. For if the same appearance had been vouchsafed to others, they would assuredly have become as thoroughly Christian as Paul. Is not divine grace omnipotent? The unbelief and non-convertibility of the Pharisees is no counter-argument; for from them grace was expressly withdrawn. The Messiah must necessarily, according to a divine decree, be betrayed, maltreated and crucified. For this purpose there must be individuals who should maltreat and crucify him: and hence it was a

---

[*] In relation to the miracle-worker faith (confidence in God's aid) is certainly the *causa efficiens* of the miracle. (See Matt. xvii. 20; Acts vi. 8.) But in relation to the spectators of the miracle—and it is they who are in question here—miracle is the *causa efficiens* of faith.

prior necessity that the divine grace should be withdrawn from those individuals. It was not indeed totally withdrawn from them, but this was only in order to aggravate their guilt, and by no means with the earnest will to convert them. How would it be possible to resist the will of God, supposing of course that it was his real will, not a mere velleity? Paul himself represents his conversion as a work of divine grace thoroughly unmerited on his part; * and quite correctly. Not to resist divine grace, *i.e.*, to accept divine grace, to allow it to work upon one, is already something good, and consequently is an effect of the Holy Spirit. Nothing is more perverse than the attempt to reconcile miracle with freedom of inquiry and thought, or grace with freedom of will. In religion the nature of man is regarded as separate from man. The activity, the grace of God is the projected spontaneity of man, Free Will made objective. †

It is the most flagrant inconsequence to adduce the experience that men are not sanctified, not converted by baptism, as an argument against its miraculous efficacy, as is done by rationalistic orthodox theologians; ‡ for all kinds of miracles, the objective power of prayer, and in general all the supernatural truths of religion, also contradict experience. He who appeals to experience renounces faith. Where experience is a datum, there religious faith and feeling have already vanished. The unbeliever denies the objective efficacy of prayer only because it contradicts experience; the atheist goes yet further,—he denies even the existence of God, because he does not find it in experience. Inward experience creates no difficulty to him; for what thou experiencest in thyself of another existence, proves only that there is something in thee which thou thyself art not,

---

* "Here we see a miracle surpassing all miracles, that Christ should have so mercifully converted his greatest enemy."—Luther (Th. xvi. p. 560).

† Hence it is greatly to the honour of Luther's understanding and sense of truth that, particularly when writing against Erasmus, he unconditionally denied the free will of man as opposed to divine grace. "The name Free Will," says Luther, quite correctly from the standpoint of religion, "is a divine title and name, which none ought to bear but the Divine Majesty alone" (Th. xix. p. 28).

‡ Experience indeed extorted even from the old theologians, whose faith was an uncompromising one, the admission that the effects of baptism are, at least in this life, very limited. "Baptismus non aufert omnes pœnalitates hujus vitæ."—Mezger. Theol. Schol. Th. iv. p. 251. See also Petrus L. l. iv. dist. 4, c. 4; l. ii. dist. 32, c. 1.

which works upon thee independently of thy personal will and consciousness, without thy knowing what this mysterious something is. But faith is stronger than experience. The facts which contradict faith do not disturb it; it is happy in itself; it has eyes only for itself, to all else it is blind.

It is true that religion, even on the standpoint of its mystical materialism, always requires the co-operation of subjectivity, and therefore requires it in the sacraments; but herein is exhibited its contradiction with itself. And this contradiction is particularly glaring in the sacrament of the Lord's Supper; for baptism is given to infants,—though even in them, as a condition of its efficacy, the co-operation of subjectivity is insisted on, but, singularly enough, is supplied in the faith of others, in the faith of the parents, or of their representatives, or of the church in general.*

The object in the sacrament of the Lord's Supper is the body of Christ,—a real body; but the necessary predicates of reality are wanting to it. Here we have again, in an example presented to the senses, what we have found in the nature of religion in general. The object or subject in the religious syntax is always a real human or natural subject or predicate; but the closer definition, the essential predicate of this predicate is denied. The subject is sensuous, but the predicate is not sensuous, *i.e.*, is contradictory to the subject. I distinguish a real body from an imaginary one only by this, that the former produces corporeal effects, involuntary effects, upon me. If therefore the bread be the real body of God, the partaking of it must produce in me immediate, involuntary sanctifying effects; I need to make no special preparation, to bring with me no holy disposition. If I eat an apple, the apple of itself gives rise to the taste of apple. At the utmost I need nothing more than a healthy stomach to perceive that the apple is an apple. The Catholics require a state of fasting as a condition of partaking the Lord's Supper. This is enough. I take hold of the body with my lips, I crush it with my

---

* Even in the absurd fiction of the Lutherans, that "infants believe in baptism," the action of subjectivity reduces itself to the faith of others, since the faith of infants is "wrought by God through the intercession of the god-parents and their bringing np of the children in the faith of the Christian Church."—Luther (Th. xiii. pp. 360, 361). "Thus the faith of another helps me to obtain a faith of my own."—Ib. (T. xiv. p. 347*a*).

teeth, by my œsophagus it is carried into my stomach; I assimilate it corporeally, not spiritually.* Why are its effects not held to be corporeal? Why should not this body, which is a corporeal, but at the same time heavenly, supernatural substance, also bring forth in me corporeal and yet at the same time holy, supernatural effects? If it is my disposition, my faith, which alone makes the divine body a means of sanctification to me, which transubstantiates the dry bread into pneumatic animal substance, why do I still need an external object? It is I myself who give rise to the effect of the body on me, and therefore to the reality of the body; I am acted on by myself. Where is the objective truth and power? He who partakes the Lord's Supper unworthily has nothing further than the physical enjoyment of bread and wine. He who brings nothing, takes nothing away. The specific difference of this bread from common natural bread rests therefore only on the difference between the state of mind at the table of the Lord, and the state of mind at any other table. "He that eateth and drinketh unworthily, eateth and drinketh damnation to himself, not discerning the Lord's body." † But this mental state itself is dependent only on the significance which I give to this bread. If it has for me the significance not of bread, but of the body of Christ, then it has not the effect of common bread. In the significance attached to it lies its effect. I do not eat to satisfy hunger; hence I consume only a small quantity. Thus to go no further than the quantity taken, which in every other act of taking food plays an essential part, the significance of common bread is externally set aside.

But this supernatural significance exists only in the imagination; to the senses, the wine remains wine, the bread,

---

* "This," says Luther, "is *in summa* our opinion, that in and with the bread, the body of Christ is truly eaten; thus, that all which the bread undergoes and effects, the body of Christ undergoes and effects; that it is divided, eaten and chewed with the teeth *propter unionem sacramentalem.*" (Plank's Gesch. der Entst des protest. Lehrbeg. B. viii. s. 369). Elsewhere, it is true, Luther denies that the body of Christ, although it is partaken of corporeally, "is chewed and digested like a piece of beef." (Th. xix. p. 429.) No wonder; for that which is partaken of is an object without objectivity, a body without corporeality, flesh without the qualities of flesh; "spiritual flesh," as Luther says, *i.e.*, imaginary flesh. Be it observed further, that the Protestants also take the Lord's Supper fasting, but this is merely a custom with them, not a law. (See Luther, Th. xviii. p. 200, 201.)
† 1 Cor. xi. 29.

bread. The Schoolmen therefore had recourse to the precious distinction of substance and accidents. All the accidents which constitute the nature of wine and bread are still there; only that which is made up by these accidents, the subject, the substance, is wanting, is changed into flesh and blood. But all the properties together, whose combination forms this unity, are the substance itself. What are wine and bread if I take from them the properties which make them what they are? Nothing. Flesh and blood have therefore no objective existence; otherwise they must be an object to the unbelieving senses. On the contrary: the only valid witnesses of an objective existence—taste, smell, touch, sight—testify unanimously to the reality of the wine and bread, and nothing else. The wine and bread are in reality natural, but in imagination divine substances.

Faith is the power of the imagination, which makes the real unreal, and the unreal real: in direct contradiction with the truth of the senses, with the truth of reason. Faith denies what objective reason affirms, and affirms what it denies.* The mystery of the Lord's Supper is the mystery of faith : †—hence the partaking of it is the highest, the most rapturous, blissful act of the believing soul. The negation of objective truth which is not gratifying to feeling, the truth of reality, of the objective world and reason,—a negation which constitutes the essence of faith,—reaches its highest point in the Lord's Supper; for faith here denies an immediately present, evident, indubitable object, maintaining that it is not what the reason and senses declare it to be, that it is only in appearance bread, but in

* "Videtur enim species vini et panis, et substantia panis et vini non creditur. Creditur autem substantia corporis et sanguinis Christi et tamen species non cernitur."—Bernardus (ed. Bas. 1552, pp. 189-191).

† It is so in another relation not developed here, but which may be mentioned in a note : namely, the following. In religion, in faith, man is an object to himself as the object, *i.e.*, the end or determining motive, of God. Man is occupied with himself in and through God. God is the means of human existence and happiness. This religious truth, embodied in a cultus, in a sensuous form, is the Lord's Supper. In this sacrament man feeds upon God—the Creator of heaven and earth—as on material food ; by the act of eating and drinking he declares God to be a mere means of life to man. Here man is virtually supposed to be the *God* of God : hence the Lord's Supper is the highest self-enjoyment of human subjectivity. Even the Protestant—not indeed in words, but in truth—transforms God into an external thing, since he subjects Him to himself as an object of sensational enjoyment.

reality flesh. The position of the Schoolmen, that according to the accidents it is bread, and according to the substance flesh, is merely the abstract, explanatory, intellectual expression of what faith accepts and declares, and has therefore no other meaning than this : to the senses or to common perception it is bread, but in truth, flesh. Where therefore the imaginative tendency of faith has assumed such power over the senses and reason as to deny the most evident sensible truths, it is no wonder if believers can raise themselves to such a degree of exaltation as actually to see blood instead of wine. Such examples Catholicism has to show. Little is wanting in order to perceive externally what faith and imagination hold to be real.

So long as faith in the mystery of the Lord's Supper as a holy, nay the holiest, highest truth, governed man, so long was his governing principle the imagination. All criteria of reality and unreality, of unreason and reason, had disappeared : anything whatever that could be imagined passed for real possibility. Religion hallowed every contradiction of reason, of the nature of things. Do not ridicule the absurd questions of the Schoolmen ! They were necessary consequences of faith. That which is only a matter of feeling had to be made a matter of reason, that which contradicts the understanding had to be made not to contradict it. This was the fundamental contradiction of Scholasticism, whence all other contradictions followed of course.

And it is of no particular importance whether I believe the Protestant or the Catholic doctrine of the Lord's Supper. The sole distinction is, that in Protestantism it is only on the tongue, in the act of partaking, that flesh and blood are united in a thoroughly miraculous manner with bread and wine;* while in Catholicism, it is before the act of partaking, by the power of the priest,—who however here acts only in the name of the Almighty,—that bread and wine are really transmuted into flesh and blood. The Protestant prudently avoids a definite explanation ; he does not lay himself open, like the pious, uncritical simplicity of Catho-

---

* "Nostrates, præsentiam realem consecrationis effectum esse, adfirmant ; idque ita, ut tum se exserat, cum usus legitimus accedit. Nec est quod regeras, Christum hæc verba : hoc est corpus meum, protulisse, antequam discipuli ejus comederent, adeoque panem jam ante usum corpus Christi fuisse."—Buddeus (l. c. l. v. c. 1, §§ 13, 17). See, on the other hand, Concil. Trident. Sessio 13, cc. 3, 8, Can. 4.

licism, whose God, as an external object, can be devoured
by a mouse : he shuts up his God within himself, where he
can no more be torn from him, and thus secures him as well
from the power of accident as from that of ridicule ; yet,
notwithstanding this, he just as much as the Catholic con-
sumes real flesh and blood in the bread and wine. Slight
indeed was the difference at first between Protestants and
Catholics in the doctrine of the Lord's Supper! Thus at
Anspach there arose a controversy on the question—
"whether the body of Christ enters the stomach, and is
digested like other food ?" *

But although the imaginative activity of faith makes the
objective existence the mere appearance, and the emotional,
imaginary existence the truth and reality ; still, in itself or
in truth, that which is really objective is only the natural
elements. Even the host in the pyx of the Catholic priest
is in itself only to faith a divine body,—this external thing,
into which he transubstantiates the divine being, is only a
thing of faith ; for even here the body is not visible, tangible, tasteable as a body. That is : the bread is only in its
significance flesh. It is true that to faith this significance
has the sense of actual existence ;—as, in general, in the
ecstasy of fervid feeling that which signifies becomes the
thing signified ;—it is held not to signify, but to *be* flesh.
But this state of being flesh is not that of real flesh ; it is
a state of being which is only believed in, imagined, *i.e.*, it
has only the value, the quality, of a significance, a truth
conveyed in a symbol.† A thing which has a special significance for me, is another thing in my imagination than
in reality. The thing signifying is not itself that which is
signified. What it *is*, is evident to the senses ; what it
signifies, is only in my feelings, conception, imagination,—
is only for me, not for others, is not objectively present.
So here. When therefore Zwinglius said that the Lord's
Supper has only a subjective significance, he said the same
thing as his opponents ; only he disturbed the illusion of

* Apologie Melancthon. Strobel. Nürnb. 1783, p. 127.
† "The fanatics, however, believe that it is mere bread and wine, and it is
assuredly so as they believe ; they have it so, and eat mere bread and wine."
—Luther (Th. xix. p. 432). That is to say, if thou believest, representest to
thyself, conceivest, that the bread is not bread, but the body of Christ, it
is not bread ; but if thou dost not believe so, it is not so. What it is in
thy belief that it actually is.

the religious imagination ; for that which " is " in the Lord's Supper, is only an illusion of the imagination, but with the further illusion that it is not an illusion. Zwinglius only expressed simply, nakedly, prosaically, rationalistically, and therefore offensively, what the others declared mystically, indirectly,—inasmuch as they confessed * that the effect of the Lord's Supper depends only on a worthy disposition or on faith ; *i.e.*, that the bread and wine are the flesh and blood of the Lord, are the Lord himself, only for him for whom they have the supernatural significance of the divine body, for on this alone depends the worthy disposition, the religious emotion.†

But if the Lord's Supper effects nothing, consequently is nothing,—for only that which produces effects, *is*,—without a certain state of mind, without faith, then in faith alone lies its reality ; the entire event goes forward in the feelings alone. If the idea that I here receive the real body of the Saviour acts on the religious feelings, this idea itself arises from the feelings ; it produces devout sentiments, because it is itself a devout idea. Thus here also the religious subject is acted on by himself as if by another being, through the conception of an imaginary object. Therefore the process of the Lord's Supper can quite well, even without the intermediation of bread and wine, without any church ceremony, be accomplished in the imagination. There are innumerable devout poems, the sole theme of which is the blood of Christ. In these we have a genuinely poetical celebration of the Lord's Supper. In the lively representation of the suffering, bleeding Saviour, the soul identifies itself with him ; here the saint in poetic exaltation drinks the pure blood, unmixed with any contradictory, material elements ; here there is no disturbing object between the idea of the blood and the blood itself.

But though the Lord's Supper, or a sacrament in general, is nothing without a certain state of mind, without faith,

---

* " Even the Catholics also. " Hujus sacramenti effectus, quem in anima operatur digne sumentis, est adunatio hominis ad Christum."—Concil. Florent. de S. Euchar.

† " If the body of Christ is in the bread and is eaten with faith, it strengthens the soul, in that the soul believes that it is the body of Christ which the mouth eats."—Luther (Th. xix. p. 433 ; see also p. 205). " For what we believe that we receive, that we receive in truth."—Ib. (Th. xvii. p. 557).

nevertheless religion presents the sacrament at the same time as something in itself real, external, distinct from the human being, so that in the religious consciousness the true thing, which is faith, is made only a collateral thing, a condition, and the imaginary thing becomes the principal thing. And the necessary, immanent consequences and effects of this religious materialism, of this subordination of the human to the supposed divine, of the subjective to the supposed objective, of truth to imagination, of morality to religion,— the necessary consequences are superstition and immorality : superstition, because a thing has attributed to it an effect which does not lie in its nature, because a thing is held up as *not* being what it in truth *is*, because a mere conception passes for objective reality; immorality, because necessarily, in feeling, the holiness of the action as such is separated from morality, the partaking of the sacrament, even apart from the state of mind, becomes a holy and saving act. Such, at least, is the result in practice, which knows nothing of the sophistical distinctions of theology. In general : *wherever religion places itself in contradiction with reason, it places itself also in contradiction with the moral sense.* Only with the sense of truth coexists the sense of the right and good. Depravity of understanding is always depravity of heart. He who deludes and cheats his understanding has not a veracious, honourable heart; sophistry corrupts the whole man. And the doctrine of the Lord's Supper is sophistry.

The Truth of the disposition, or of faith as a requisite to communion, involves the Untruth of the bodily presence of God ; and again the Truth of the objective existence of the divine body involves the Untruth of the disposition.

CHAPTER XXVI.

THE CONTRADICTION OF FAITH AND LOVE.

THE Sacraments are a sensible presentation of that contradiction of idealism and materialism, of subjectivism and objectivism, which belongs to the inmost nature of religion. But the sacraments are nothing without Faith and Love. Hence the contradiction in the sacraments carries us back to the primary contradiction of Faith and Love.

The essence of religion, its latent nature, is the *identity* of the divine being with the human; but the form of religion, or its apparent, conscious nature, is the *distinction* between them. God is the human being; but he presents himself to the religious consciousness as a distinct being. Now, that which reveals the basis, the hidden essence of religion, is Love; that which constitutes its conscious form is Faith. Love identifies man with God and God with man, consequently it identifies man with man; faith separates God from man, consequently it separates man from man, for God is nothing else than the idea of the species invested with a mystical form,—the separation of God from man is therefore the separation of man from man, the unloosening of the social bond. By faith religion places itself in contradiction with morality, with reason, with the unsophisticated sense of truth in man; by love, it opposes itself again to this contradiction. Faith isolates God, it makes him a particular, distinct being: love universalises; it makes God a common being, the love of whom is one with the love of man. Faith produces in man an inward disunion, a disunion with himself, and by consequence an outward disunion also; but love heals the wounds which are made by faith in the heart of man. Faith makes belief in its God a law: love is freedom,—it condemns not even the atheist, because it is itself atheistic, itself denies, if not theoretically, at least practically, the existence of a particular, individual God, opposed to man. Love has God in

247

itself : faith has God out of itself ; it estranges God from man, it makes him an external object.

Faith, being inherently external, proceeds even to the adoption of outward fact as its object, and becomes historical faith.   It is therefore of the nature of faith that it can become a totally external confession ; and that with mere faith, as such, superstitious, magical effects are associated.* The devils believe that God is, without ceasing to be devils. Hence a distinction has been made between faith in God, and belief that there is a God.†   But even with this bare belief in the existence of God, the assimilating power of love is intermingled ;—a power which by no means lies in the idea of faith as such, and in so far as it relates to external things.

The only distinctions or judgments which are immanent to faith, which spring out of itself, are the distinctions of right or genuine, and wrong or false faith ; or in general, of belief and unbelief.   Faith discriminates thus : This is true, that is false.   And it claims truth to itself alone.   Faith has for its object a definite, specific truth, which is necessarily united with negation.   Faith is in its nature exclusive. One thing alone is truth, one alone is God, one alone has the monopoly of being the Son of God ; all else is nothing, error, delusion.   Jehovah alone is the true God ; all other gods are vain idols.

Faith has in its mind something peculiar to itself ; it rests on a peculiar revelation of God ; it has not come to its possessions in an ordinary way, that way which stands open to all men alike.   What stands open to all is common, and for that reason cannot form a special object of faith. That God is the creator, all men could know from Nature ; but what this God is in person, can be known only by special grace, is the object of a special faith.   And because he is only revealed in a peculiar manner, the object of this faith is himself a peculiar being.   The God of the Christians is indeed the God of the heathens, but with a wide difference :—just such a difference as there is between me as I am to a friend, and me as I am to a stranger, who only knows me at a distance.   God as he is an object to the Christians, is quite another than as he is an object to the heathens.

---

* Hence the mere name of Christ has miraculous powers.
† " *Gott glauben und an Gott glauben.*"

The Christians know God personally, face to face. The heathens know only—and even this is too large an admission—"what," and not "who," God is; for which reason they fell into idolatry. The identity of the heathens and Christians before God is therefore altogether vague; what the heathens have in common with the Christians—if indeed we consent to be so liberal as to admit anything in common between them—is not that which is specifically Christian, not that which constitutes faith. In whatsoever the Christians are Christians, therein they are distinguished from the heathens; * and they are Christians in virtue of their special knowledge of God; thus their mark of distinction is God. Speciality is the salt which first gives a flavour to the common being. What a being is in special, is the being itself; he alone knows me, who knows me *in specie*. Thus the special God, God as he is an object to the Christians, the personal God, is alone God. And this God is unknown to heathens, and to unbelievers in general; he does not exist for them. He is, indeed, said to exist for the heathens; but mediately, on condition that they cease to be heathens, and become Christians. Faith makes man partial and narrow; it deprives him of the freedom and ability to estimate duly what is different from himself. Faith is imprisoned within itself. It is true that the philosophical, or, in general, any scientific theorist, also limits himself by a definite system. But theoretic limitation, however fettered, short-sighted and narrow-hearted it may be, has still a freer character than faith, because the domain of theory is in itself a free one, because here the ground of decision is the nature of things, argument, reason. But faith refers the decision to conscience and interest, to the instinctive desire of happiness; for its object is a special, personal Being, urging himself on recognition, and making salvation dependent on that recognition.

Faith gives man a peculiar sense of his own dignity and importance. The believer finds himself distinguished above other men, exalted above the natural man; he knows himself to be a person of distinction, in the possession of peculiar privileges; believers are aristocrats, unbelievers plebeians. God is this distinction and pre-eminence of

* " If I wish to be a Christian, I must believe and do what other people do not believe or do."—Luther (Th. xvi. p. 569).

believers above unbelievers, personified.* Because faith represents man's own nature as that of another being, the believer does not contemplate his dignity immediately in himself, but in this supposed distinct person. The consciousness of his own pre-eminence presents itself as a consciousness of this person; he has the sense of his own dignity in this divine personality.† As the servant feels himself honoured in the dignity of his master, nay, fancies himself greater than a free, independent man of lower rank than his master, so it is with the believer.‡ He denies all merit in himself, merely that he may leave all merit to his Lord, because his own desire of honour is satisfied in the honour of his Lord. Faith is arrogant, but it is distinguished from natural arrogance in this, that it clothes its feeling of superiority, its pride, in the idea of another person, for whom the believer is an object of peculiar favour. This distinct person, however, is simply his own hidden self, his personified, contented desire of happiness: for he has no other qualities than these, that he is the benefactor, the Redeemer, the Saviour—qualities in which the believer has reference only to himself, to his own eternal salvation. In fact, we have here the characteristic principle of religion, that it changes that which is naturally active into the passive. The heathen elevates himself, the Christian feels himself elevated. The Christian converts into a matter of feeling, of receptivity, what to the heathen is a matter of spontaneity. The humility of the believer is an inverted arrogance,—an arrogance none the less because it has not the appearance, the external characteristics of arrogance. He feels himself pre-eminent: this pre-eminence, however, is not a result of his activity, but a matter of grace; he has been made pre-eminent; he can do nothing towards it himself. He does not make himself the end of his own activity, but the end, the object of God.

---

* Celsus makes it a reproach to the Christians that they boast: "Est Deus et post illum nos." (Origenes adv. Cels. ed. Hœschelius. Aug. Vind. 1605, p. 182).

† "I am proud and exulting on account of my blessedness and the forgiveness of my sins, but through what? Through the glory and pride of another, namely, the Lord Christ."—Luther (Th. ii. p. 344). "He that glorieth let him glory in the Lord."—1 Cor. i. 31.

‡ A military officer who had been adjutant of the Russian general Münnich said: "When I was his adjutant I felt myself greater than now that I command."

Faith is essentially determinate, specific. God according to the specific view taken of him by faith, is alone the true God. This Jesus, such as I conceive him, is the Christ, the true, sole prophet, the only-begotten Son of God, And this particular conception thou must believe, if thou wouldst not forfeit thy salvation. Faith is imperative. It is therefore necessary—it lies in the nature of faith—that it be fixed as dogma. Dogma only gives a formula to what faith had already on its tongue or in its mind. That when once a fundamental dogma is established, it gives rise to more special questions, which must also be thrown into a dogmatic form, that hence there results a burdensome multiplicity of dogmas,—this is certainly a fatal consequence, but does not do away with the necessity that faith should fix itself in dogmas, in order that every one may know definitely what he must believe and how he can win salvation.

That which in the present day, even from the standpoint of believing Christianity, is rejected, is compassionated as an aberration, as a misinterpretation, or is even ridiculed, is purely a consequence of the inmost nature of faith. Faith is essentially illiberal, prejudiced; for it is concerned not only with individual salvation, but with the honour of God. And just as we are solicitous as to whether we show due honour to a superior in rank, so it is with faith. The apostle Paul is absorbed in the glory, the honour, the merits of Christ. Dogmatic, exclusive, scrupulous particularity, lies in the nature of faith. In food and other matters, indifferent to faith, it is certainly liberal; but by no means in relation to objects of faith. He who is not for Christ is against him; that which is not christian is antichristian. But what is christian? This must be absolutely determined, this cannot be free. If the articles of faith are set down in books which proceed from various authors, handed down in the form of incidental, mutually contradictory, occasional dicta,—then dogmatic demarcation and definition are even an external necessity. Christianity owes its perpetuation to the dogmatic formulas of the Church.

It is only the believing unbelief of modern times which hides itself behind the Bible, and opposes the biblical dicta to dogmatic definitions, in order that it may set itself free from the limits of dogma by arbitrary exegesis. But faith has already disappeared, is become indifferent, when the

252 THE ESSENCE OF CHRISTIANITY.

determinate tenets of faith are felt as limitations. It is only religious indifference under the appearance of religion that makes the Bible, which in its nature and origin is indefinite, a standard of faith, and under the pretext of believing only the essential, retains nothing which deserves the name of faith ;—for example, substituting for the distinctly characterised Son of God, held up by the Church, the vague negative definition of a Sinless Man, who can claim to be the Son of God in a sense applicable to no other being,—in a word, of a man, whom one may not trust oneself to call either a man or a God. But that it is merely indifference which makes a hiding-place for itself behind the Bible, is evident from the fact that even what stands in the Bible, if it contradicts the standpoint of the present day, is regarded as not obligatory, or is even denied ; nay, actions which are essentially christian, which are the logical consequences of faith, such as the separation of believers from unbelievers, are now designated as unchristian.

The Church was perfectly justified in adjudging damnation to heretics and unbelievers,* for this condemnation is involved in the nature of faith. Faith at first appears to be only an unprejudiced separation of believers from unbelievers ; but this separation is a highly critical distinction. The believer has God for him, the unbeliever, against him ; —it is only as a possible believer that the unbeliever has God not against him ;—and therein precisely lies the ground of the requirement that he should leave the ranks of unbelief. But that which has God against it is worthless, rejected, reprobate ; for that which has God against it is itself against God. To believe, is synonymous with goodness ; not to believe, with wickedness. Faith, narrow and prejudiced refers all unbelief to the moral disposition. In its view the unbeliever is an enemy to Christ out of obduracy, out of wickedness.† Hence faith has fellowship with believers only ; unbelievers it rejects. It is well-disposed towards believers, but ill-disposed towards unbelievers. *In faith there lies a malignant principle.*

* To faith, so long as it has any vital heat, any character, the heretic is always on a level with the unbeliever, with the atheist.

† Already in the New Testament the idea of disobedience is associated with unbelief. "The cardinal wickedness is unbelief."—Luther (xiii. p. 647).

It is owing to the egoism, the vanity, the self-complacency of Christians, that they can see the motes in the faith of non-christian nations, but cannot perceive the beam in their own. It is only in the mode in which faith embodies itself that Christians differ from the followers of other religions. The distinction is founded only on climate or on natural temperament. A warlike or ardently sensuous people will naturally attest its distinctive religious character by deeds, by force of arms. But the nature of faith as such is everywhere the same. It is essential to faith to condemn, to anathematise. All blessings, all good it accumulates on itself, on its God, as the lover on his beloved; all curses, all hardship and evil it casts on unbelief. The believer is blessed, well-pleasing to God, a partaker of everlasting felicity; the unbeliever is accursed, rejected of God and abjured by men : for what God rejects man must not receive, must not indulge ;—that would be a criticism of the divine judgment. The Turks exterminate unbelievers with fire and sword, the Christians with the flames of hell. But the fires of the other world blaze forth into this, to glare through the night of unbelief. As the believer already here below anticipates the joys of heaven, so the flames of the abyss must be seen to flash here as a foretaste of the awaiting hell,—at least in the moments when faith attains its highest enthusiasm.* It is true that Christianity ordains no persecution of heretics, still less conversion by force of arms. But so far as faith anathematises, it necessarily generates hostile dispositions,—the dispositions out of which the persecution of heretics arises. To love the man who does not believe in Christ, is a sin against Christ, is to love the enemy of Christ.† That which God, which Christ does not love, man must not love; his love would be a contradiction of the divine will, consequently a sin. God, it is true, loves all men; but only when and because they are Christians, or at least may be and desire to be such.

* God himself by no means entirely reserves the punishment of blasphemers, of unbelievers, of heretics, for the future; he often punishes them in this life also, " for the benefit of Christendom and the strengthening of faith :" as, for example, the heretics Cerinthus and Arius. See Luther (Th. xiv. p. 13).

† " Si quis spiritum Dei habet, illius versiculi recordetur : Nonne qui oderunt te, Domine, oderam ?" (Psal. cxxxix. 21); Bernhardus, Epist. (193) ad magist. Yvonem Cardin.

254 THE ESSENCE OF CHRISTIANITY.

To be a Christian is to be beloved by God; not to be a Christian is to be hated by God, an object of the divine anger.* The Christian must therefore love only Christians —others only as possible Christians; he must only love what faith hallows and blesses. Faith is the baptism of love. Love to man as man is only natural love. Christian love is supernatural, glorified, sanctified love; therefore it loves only what is Christian. The maxim, "Love your enemies," has reference only to personal enemies, not to public enemies, the enemies of God, the enemies of faith, unbelievers. He who loves the men whom Christ denies, does not believe Christ, denies his Lord and God. Faith abolishes the natural ties of humanity; to universal, natural unity, it substitutes a particular unity.

Let it not be objected to this, that it is said in the Bible, "Judge not, that ye be not judged;" and that thus, as faith leaves to God the judgment, so it leaves to him the sentence of condemnation. This and other similar sayings have authority only as the private law of Christians, not as their public law; belong only to ethics, not to dogmatics. It is an indication of indifference to faith, to introduce such sayings into the region of dogma. The distinction between the unbeliever and the man is a fruit of modern philanthropy. To faith, the man is merged in the believer; to it, the essential difference between man and the brute rests only on religious belief. Faith alone comprehends in itself all virtues which can make man pleasing to God; and God is the absolute measure, his pleasure the highest law: the believer is thus alone the legitimate, normal man, man as he ought to be, man as he is recognised by God. Wherever we find Christians making a distinction between the man and the believer, there the human mind has already severed itself from faith; there man has value in himself, independently of faith. Hence faith is true, unfeigned, only where the specific difference of faith operates in all its severity. If the edge of this difference is blunted, faith itself naturally becomes indifferent, effete. Faith is liberal only in things intrinsically indifferent. The liberalism of the apostle Paul presupposes the acceptance of the fundamental articles of faith. Where everything is made to depend on the funda-

* "Qui Christum negat, negatur a Christo."—Cyprian (Epist. E. 73, § 18, edit. Gersdorf.).

mental articles of faith, there arises the distinction between essential and non-essential belief. In the sphere of the non-essential there is no law,—there you are free. But obviously it is only on condition of your leaving the rights of faith intact, that faith allows you freedom.

It is therefore an altogether false defence to say, that faith leaves judgment to God. It leaves to him only the moral judgment with respect to faith, only the judgment as to its moral character, as to whether the faith of Christians be feigned or genuine. So far as classes are concerned, faith knows already whom God will place on the right hand, and whom on the left; in relation to the persons who compose the classes faith is uncertain; but that believers are heirs of the Eternal Kingdom is beyond all doubt Apart from this, however, the God who distinguishes between believers and unbelievers, the condemning and rewarding God, is nothing else than faith itself. What God condemns, faith condemns, and *vice versâ*. Faith is a consuming fire to its opposite.* This fire of faith regarded objectively, is the anger of God, or what is the same thing, hell; for hell evidently has its foundation in the anger of God. But this hell lies in faith itself, in its sentence of damnation. The flames of hell are only the flashings of the exterminating, vindictive glance which faith casts on unbelievers.

Thus faith is essentially a spirit of partisanship. He who is not for Christ is against him.† Faith knows only friends or enemies, it understands no neutrality; it is preoccupied only with itself. Faith is essentially intolerant; essentially, because with faith is always associated the illusion that its cause is the cause of God, its honour his honour. The God of faith is nothing else than the objective nature of faith— faith become an object to itself. Hence in the religious consciousness also the cause of faith and the cause of God are identified. God himself is interested: the interest of faith is the nearest interest of God. "He who toucheth you," says the prophet Zachariah, "toucheth the apple of

---

* Thus the apostle Paul cursed "Elymas the sorcerer" with blindness, because he withstood the faith.—Acts xiii. 8–11.

† Historically considered, this saying, as well as the others cited pp. 384, 385, may be perfectly justified. But the Bible is not to be regarded as an historical or temporal, but as an eternal book.

His eye."* That which wounds faith, wounds God, that
which denies faith, denies God himself.

Faith knows no other distinction than that between the
service of God and the service of idols. Faith alone gives
honour to God; unbelief withdraws from God that which is
due to him. Unbelief is an injury to God, religious high
treason. The heathens worship demons; their gods are
devils. " I say that the things which the Gentiles sacrifice,
they sacrifice to devils, and not to God: and I would not
that ye should have fellowship with devils."† But the
devil is the negation of God; he hates God, wills that there
should be no God. Thus faith is blind to what there is of
goodness and truth lying at the foundation of heathen worship; it sees in everything which does not do homage to its
God, *i.e.*, to itself, a worship of idols, and in the worship of
idols only the work of the devil. Faith must therefore,
even in feeling, be only negative towards this negation of
God: it is by inherent necessity intolerant towards its opposite, and in general towards whatever does not thoroughly
accord with itself. Tolerance on its part would be intolerance towards God, who has the right to unconditional, undivided sovereignty. Nothing ought to subsist, nothing
to exist, which does not acknowledge God, which does
not acknowledge faith :—" That at the name of Jesus
every knee should bow, of things in heaven and things
on earth, and things under the earth; and that every
tongue should confess that Jesus Christ is Lord, to the
glory of the Father." ‡ Therefore faith postulates a future,
a world where faith has no longer an opposite, or where
at least this opposite exists only in order to enhance
the self-complacency of triumphant faith. Hell sweetens
the joys of happy believers. " The elect will come forth to
behold the torments of the ungodly, and at this spectacle
they will not be smitten with sorrow; on the contrary,

* "Tenerrimam partem humani corporis nominavit, ut apertissime in-
telligeremus, eum (Deum) tam parva Sanctorum suorum contumelia lædi,
quam parvi verberis tactu humani visus acies læditur."—Salvianus, l. 8, de
Gubern. Dei.

† 1 Cor. x. 20.

‡ Phil. ii. 10, 11. "When the name of Jesus Christ is heard, all that is
unbelieving and ungodly in heaven or on earth shall be terrified."—Luther
(Th. xvi. p. 322). "In morte pagani Christianus gloriatur, quia Christus
glorificatur."—Divus Bernardus. Sermo exhort. ad Milites Templi.

while they see the unspeakable sufferings of the ungodly, they, intoxicated with joy, will thank God for their own salvation."*

Faith is the opposite of love. Love recognises virtue even in sin, truth in error. It is only since the power of faith has been supplanted by the power of the natural unity of mankind, the power of reason, of humanity, that truth has been seen even in polytheism, in idolatry generally,—or at least that there has been any attempt to explain on positive grounds what faith, in its bigotry, derives only from the devil. Hence love is reconcilable with reason alone, not with faith; for as reason, so also love is free, universal, in its nature; whereas faith is narrow-hearted, limited. Only where reason rules, does universal love rule; reason is itself nothing else than universal love. It was faith, not love, not reason, which invented Hell. To love, Hell is a horror; to reason, an absurdity. It would be a pitiable mistake to regard Hell as a mere aberration of faith, a false faith. Hell stands already in the Bible. Faith is everywhere like itself; at least positive religious faith, faith in the sense in which it is here taken, and must be taken unless we would mix with it the elements of reason, of culture,—a mixture which indeed renders the character of faith unrecognisable.

Thus if faith does not contradict Christianity, neither do those dispositions which result from faith, neither do the actions which result from those dispositions. Faith condemns, anathematises; all the actions, all the dispositions, which contradict love, humanity, reason, accord with faith. All the horrors of Christian religious history, which our believers aver not to be due to Christianity, have truly arisen out of

* Petrus L. l. iv. dist. 50, c. 4. But this passage is by no means a declaration of Peter Lombard himself. He is far too modest, timid, and dependent on the authorities of Christianity to have ventured to advance such a tenet on his own account. No! This position is a universal declaration, a characteristic expression of Christian, of believing love. The doctrine of some Fathers of the Church, *e.g.*, of Origen and Gregory of Nyssa, that the punishment of the damned would have an end, sprung not out of Christian or Church doctrine, but out of Platonism. Hence the doctrine that the punishment of hell is finite, was rejected not only by the Catholic but also by the Protestant church. (Augsb. Confess. art. 17). A precious example of the exclusive, misanthropical narrowness of Christian love, is the passage cited from Buddeus by Strauss (Christl. Glaubensl. B. ii. s. 547), according to which not infants in general, but those of Christians exclusively, would have a share in the divine grace and blessings if they died unbaptized.

Christianity, because they have arisen out of faith. This repudiation of them is indeed a necessary consequence of faith; for faith claims for itself only what is good, every thing bad it casts on the shoulders of unbelief, or of misbelief, or of men in general. But this very denial of faith that it is itself to blame for the evil in Christianity, is a striking proof that it is really the originator of that evil, because it is a proof of the narrowness, partiality, and intolerance which render it well-disposed only to itself, to its own adherents, but ill-disposed, unjust towards others. According to faith, the good which Christians do, is not done by the man, but by the Christian, by faith; but the evil which Christians do, is not done by the Christian, but by the man. The evil which faith has wrought in Christendom thus corresponds to the nature of faith,—of faith as it is described in the oldest and most sacred records of Christianity, of the Bible. "If any man preach any other gospel unto you than that ye have received, let him be accursed,"* ἀνάθεμα ἔστω, Gal. i. 9. "Be ye not unequally yoked together with unbelievers: for what fellowship hath righteousness with unrighteousness? and what communion hath light with darkness? And what concord hath Christ with Belial? or what part hath he that believeth with an infidel? And what agreement hath the temple of God with idols? for ye are the temple of the living God; as God hath said, I will dwell in them and walk in them; and I will be their God, and they shall be my people. Wherefore come out from among them, and be ye separate, saith the Lord, and touch not the unclean thing; and I will receive you," 2 Cor. iv. 14–17. "When the Lord Jesus shall be revealed from heaven with his mighty angels, in flaming fire taking vengeance on them that know not God, and that obey not the Gospel of our Lord Jesus Christ: who shall be punished with everlasting destruction from the presence of the Lord, and from the glory of his power; when he shall come to be glorified in his saints, and admired in all them that believe," 2 Thess. i. 7–10. "Without faith it is impossible to please God," Heb. xi. 6. "God so loved the world, that he gave his only begotten Son, that whosoever believeth in him, should not perish, but have everlasting life," John iii. 16. "Every

---

* "Fugite, abhorrete hunc doctorem." But why should I flee from him? because the anger, *i.e.*, the curse of God rests on his head.

spirit that confesseth that Jesus Christ is come in the flesh
is of God: and every spirit that confesseth not that Jesus
Christ is come in the flesh is not of God: and this is the
spirit of antichrist," 1 John iv. 2, 3. "Who is a liar, but
he that denieth that Jesus is the Christ? He is antichrist
that denieth the Father and the Son," 1 John ii. 22. "Whosoever transgresseth, and abideth not in the doctrine of Christ,
hath not God: he that abideth in the doctrine of Christ, he
hath both the Father and the Son. If there come any unto
you, and bring not this doctrine, receive him not into your
house, neither bid him God speed: for he that biddeth him
God speed, is partaker of his evil deeds," 2 John ix. 11.
Thus speaks the apostle of love. But the love which he
celebrates is only the brotherly love of Christians. "God
is the Saviour of all men, specially of those that believe,"
1 Tim. iv. 10. A fatal "specially!" "Let us do good unto
all men, especially unto them who are of the household of
faith," Gal. vi. 10. An equally pregnant "especially!" "A
man that is a heretic, after the first and second admonition
reject; knowing that he that is such is subverted, and sinneth,
being condemned of himself,"* Titus iii. 10, 11. "He that
believeth on the Son hath everlasting life : and he that
believeth not the Son shall not see life; but the wrath of
God abideth on him,"† John iii. 36. "And whosoever shall
offend one of these little ones that believe in me, it were
better for him that a millstone were hanged about his neck,
and that he were cast into the sea," Mark ix. 42; Matt. xviii.
6. "He that believeth and is baptized shall be saved; but
he that believeth not shall be damned," Mark xvi. 16. The
distinction between faith as it is expressed in the Bible and
faith as it has exhibited itself in later times, is only the
distinction between the bud and the plant. In the bud I
cannot so plainly see what is obvious in the matured plant;
and yet the plant lay already in the bud. But that which

---

* There necessarily results from this-a sentiment which, *e.g.*, Cyprian
expresses : "Si vero ubique hæretici nihil aliud quam adversarii et anti-
christi nominantur, si vitandi et perversi et a semet ipsis damnati pro-
nuntiantur; quale est ut videantur damnandi a nobis non esse, quos constat
apostolica contestatione a semet ipsis damnatos esse." Epistol. 74. (Edit. cit.)

† The passage Luke ix. 56, as the parallel of which is cited John iii. 17,
receives its completion and rectification in the immediately following v. 18:
"He that believeth in him is not condemned ; but he that believeth not is
condemned already, because he hath not believed in the name of the only
begotten Son of God."

is obvious, sophists of course will not condescend to recognise; they confine themselves to the distinction between explicit and implicit existence,—wilfully overlooking their essential identity.

Faith necessarily passes into hatred, hatred into persecution, where the power of faith meets with no contradiction, where it does not find itself in collision with a power foreign to faith, the power of love, of humanity, of the sense of justice. Faith left to itself necessarily exalts itself above the laws of natural morality. The doctrine of faith is the doctrine of duty towards God,—the highest duty of faith. By how much God is higher than man, by so much higher are duties to God than duties towards man; and duties towards God necessarily come into collision with common human duties. God is not only believed in, conceived as the universal being, the Father of men, as Love:—such faith is the faith of love;—he is also represented as a personal being, a being by himself. And so far as God is regarded as separate from man, as an individual being, so far are duties to God separated from duties to man :—faith is, in the religious sentiment, separated from morality, from love.* Let it not be replied that faith in God is faith in love, in goodness itself; and that thus faith is itself an expression of a morally good disposition. In the idea of personality, ethical definitions vanish; they are only collateral things, mere accidents. The chief thing is the subject, the divine *Ego*. Love to God himself, since it is love to a personal being, is not a moral but a personal love. Innumerable devout hymns breathe nothing but love to the Lord; but in this love there appears no spark of an exalted moral idea or disposition.

Faith is the highest to itself, because its object is a divine

---

* "Faith, it is true, is not "without good works," nay, according to Luther's declaration, it is as impossible to separate faith from works as to separate heat and light from fire. Nevertheless, and this is the main point, good works do not belong to the article of justification before God, *i.e.*, men are justified and "saved without works, through faith alone." Faith is thus expressly distinguished from good works; faith alone avails before God, not good works; faith alone is the cause of salvation, not virtue; thus faith alone has substantial significance, virtue only accidental; *i.e.*, faith alone has religious significance, divine authority—and not morality. It is well known that many have gone so far as to maintain that good works are not necessary, but are even "injurious, obstructive to salvation." Quite correctly.

personality. Hence it makes salvation dependent on itself, not on the fulfilment of common human duties. But that which has eternal salvation as its consequence, necessarily becomes in the mind of man the chief thing. As therefore inwardly morality is subordinate to faith, so it must also be outwardly, practically subordinate, nay, sacrificed, to faith. It is inevitable that there should be actions in which faith exhibits itself in distinction from morality, or rather in contradiction with it;—actions which are morally bad, but which according to faith are laudable, because they have in view the advantage of faith. All salvation depends on faith: it follows that all again depends on the salvation of faith. If faith is endangered, eternal salvation and the honour of God are endangered. Hence faith absolves from everything; for, strictly considered, it is the sole subjective good in man, as God is the sole good and positive being:— the highest commandment therefore is : Believe ! *

For the very reason that there is no natural, inherent connection between faith and the moral disposition, that, on the contrary, it lies in the nature of faith that it is indifferent to moral duties,† that it sacrifices the love of man to the honour of God,—for this reason it is required that faith should have good works as its consequence, that it should prove itself by love. Faith destitute of love, or indifferent to love, contradicts the reason, the natural sense of right in man, moral feeling, on which love immediately urges itself as a law. Hence faith, in contradiction with its intrinsic character, has limits imposed on it by morality : a faith which effects nothing good, which does not attest itself

---

* "Causa fidei . . . . exorbitantem et irregularem prorsus favorem habet et ab omni jure deviare, omnem captivare rationem, nec judiciis laicorum ratione corrupta utentium subjecta creditur. Etenim Causa fidei ad multa obligat, quæ alias sunt voluntaria, multa, imo infinita remittit, quæ alias præcepta ; quæ alius valide gesta annullat, et contra quæ alias nulla et irrita, fiunt valida . . . ex jure canonico."—J. H. Boehmeri (Jus Eccles. lib. v. tit. vii. § 32. See also § 44 et seq.).

† "Placetta de Fide, ii. Il ne faut pas chercher dans la nature des choses mêmes la veritable cause de l'inseparabilité de la foi et de la piété. Il faut, si je ne me trompe, la chercher uniquement dans la volonté de Dieu . . . Bene facit et nobiscum sentit, cum illam conjunctionem (*i.e.*, of sanctity or virtue with faith) a benifica Dei voluntate et dispositione repetit ; nec id novum est ejus inventum, sed cum antiquioribus Theologis nostris commune."—J. A. Ernesti. (Vindiciæ arbitrii divini. Opusc. theol. p. 297.) "Si quis dixerit . . . qui fidem sine charitate habet, Christianum non esse, anathema sit."—Concil. Trid. (Sess. vi. de Justif. can. 28).

by love, comes to be held as not a true and living faith. But this limitation does not arise out of faith itself. It is the power of love, a power independent of faith, which gives laws to it; for moral character is here made the criterion of the genuineness of faith, the truth of faith is made dependent on the truth of ethics:—a relation which, however, is subversive of faith.

Faith does indeed make man happy; but thus much is certain: it infuses into him no really moral dispositions. If it ameliorate man, if it have moral dispositions as its consequence, this proceeds solely from the inward conviction of the irreversible reality of morals:—a conviction independent of religious faith. It is morality alone, and by no means faith, that cries out in the conscience of the believer: thy faith is nothing, if it does not make thee good. It is not to be denied that the assurance of eternal salvation, the forgiveness of sins, the sense of favour and release from all punishment, inclines man to do good. The man who has this confidence possesses all things; he is happy;* he becomes indifferent to the good things of this world; no envy, no avarice, no ambition, no sensual desire, can enslave him; everything earthly vanishes in the prospect of heavenly grace and eternal bliss. But in him good works do not proceed from essentially virtuous dispositions. It is not love, not the object of love, man, the basis of all morality, which is the motive of his good works. No! he does good not for the sake of goodness itself, not for the sake of man, but for the sake of God;—out of gratitude to God, who has done all for him, and for whom therefore he must on his side do all that lies in his power. He forsakes sin, because it wounds God, his Saviour, his Benefactor.† The idea of virtue is here the idea of compensatory sacrifice. God has sacrificed himself for man; therefore man must sacrifice himself to God. The greater the sacrifice the better the deed. The more anything contradicts man and Nature,

---

* See on this subject Luther, *e.g.*, T. xiv. p. 286.

† "Therefore good works must follow faith, as an expression of thankfulness to God."—Apol. der Augs. Conf. art. 3. "How can I make a return to thee for thy deeds of love in works? yet it is something acceptable to thee, if I quench and tame the lusts of the flesh, that they may not anew inflame my heart with fresh sins." "If sin bestirs itself, I am not overcome; a glance at the cross of Jesus destroys its charms."—Gesangbuch der Evangel. Brüdergemeinen (Moravian Hymn-book).

the greater the abnegation, the greater is the virtue. This merely negative idea of goodness has been especially realised and developed by Catholicism. Its highest moral idea is that of sacrifice; hence the high significance attached to the denial of sexual love,—to virginity. Chastity, or rather virginity, is the characteristic virtue of the Catholic faith,— for this reason, that it has no basis in Nature. It is the most fanatical, transcendental, fantastical virtue, the virtue of supranaturalistic faith;—to faith, the highest virtue, but in itself no virtue at all. Thus faith makes that a virtue which intrinsically, substantially, is no virtue; it has there-fore no sense of virtue; it must necessarily depreciate true virtue because it so exalts a merely apparent virtue, because it is guided by no idea but that of the negation, the contra-diction of human nature.

But although the deeds opposed to love which mark Chris-tian religious history, are in accordance with Christianity, and its antagonists are therefore right in imputing to it the horrible actions resulting from dogmatic creeds; those deeds nevertheless at the same time contradict Christianity, because Christianity is not only a religion of faith, but of love also,— pledges us not only to faith, but to love. Uncharitable actions, hatred of heretics, at once accord and clash with Christianity? how is that possible? Perfectly. Christianity sanctions both the actions that spring out of love, and the actions that spring from faith without love. If Christianity had made love only its law, its adherents would be right,— the horrors of Christian religious history could not be im-puted to it; if it had made faith only its law, the reproaches of its antagonists would be unconditionally, unrestrictedly true. But Christianity has not made love free; it has not raised itself to the height of accepting love as absolute. And it has not given this freedom, nay, cannot give it, because it is a religion,—and hence subjects love to the dominion of faith. Love is only the exoteric, faith the esoteric doctrine of Christianity; love is only the *morality*, faith the *religion* of the Christian religion.

God is love. This is the sublimest dictum of Christianity. But the contradiction of faith and love is contained in the very proposition. Love is only a predicate, God the subject. What, then, is this subject in distinction from love? And I must necessarily ask this question, make this distinction.

The necessity of the distinction would be done away with only if it were said conversely: Love is God, love is the absolute being. Thus love would take the position of the substance. In the proposition " God is love," the subject is the darkness in which faith shrouds itself; the predicate is the light, which first illuminates the intrinsically dark subject. In the predicate I affirm love, in the subject faith. Love does not alone fill my soul: I leave a place open for my uncharitableness by thinking of God as a subject in distinction from the predicate. It is therefore inevitable that at one moment I lose the thought of love, at another the thought of God, that at one moment I sacrifice the personality of God to the divinity of love, at another the divinity of love to the personality of God. The history of Christianity has given sufficient proof of this contradiction. Catholicism, especially, has celebrated Love as the essential deity with so much enthusiasm, that to it the personality of God has been entirely lost in this love. But at the same time it has sacrificed love to the majesty of faith. Faith clings to the self-subsistence of God; love does away with it. " God is love," means, God is nothing by himself: he who loves, gives up his egoistical independence; he makes what he loves indispensable, essential to his existence. But while Self is being sunk in the depths of love, the idea of the Person rises up again and disturbs the harmony of the divine and human nature which had been established by love. Faith advances with its pretensions, and allows only just so much to Love as belongs to a predicate in the ordinary sense. It does not permit love freely to unfold itself; it makes love the abstract, and itself the concrete, the fact, the basis. The love of faith is only a rhetorical figure, a poetical fiction of faith,—faith in ecstasy. If faith comes to itself, Love is fled.

This theoretic contradiction must necessarily manifest itself practically. Necessarily; for in Christianity love is tainted by faith, it is not free, it is not apprehended truly. A love which is limited by faith is an untrue love.* Love knows no law but itself; it is divine through itself; it needs

---

* The only limitation which is not contradictory to the nature of love is the self-limitation of love by reason, intelligence. The love which despises the stringency, the law of the intelligence, is theoretically false and practically noxious.

not the sanction of faith; it is its own basis. The love which is bound by faith is a narrow-hearted, false love, contradicting the idea of love, *i.e.*, self-contradictory,—a love which has only a semblance of holiness, for it hides in itself the hatred that belongs to faith; it is only benevolent so long as faith is not injured. Hence, in this contradiction with itself, in order to retain the semblance of love, it falls into the most diabolical sophisms, as we see in Augustine's apology for the persecution of heretics. Love is limited by faith; hence it does not regard even the uncharitable actions which faith suggests as in contradiction with itself; it interprets the deeds of hatred which are committed for the sake of faith as deeds of love. And it necessarily falls into such contradictions, because the limitation of love by faith is itself a contradiction. If it once is subjected to this limitation, it has given up its own judgment, its inherent measure and criterion, its self-subsistence; it is delivered up without power of resistance to the promptings of faith.

Here we have again an example, that much which is not found in the letter of the Bible, is nevertheless there in principle. We find the same contradictions in the Bible as in Augustine, as in Catholicism generally; only that in the latter they are definitely declared, they are developed into a conspicuous, and therefore revolting existence. The Bible curses through faith, blesses through love. But the only love it knows is a love founded on faith. Thus here already it is a love which curses, an unreliable love, a love which gives me no guarantee that it will not turn into hatred; for if I do not acknowledge the articles of faith, I am out of the sphere of love, a child of hell, an object of anathema, of the anger of God, to whom the existence of unbelievers is a vexation, a thorn in the eye. Christian love has not overcome hell, because it has not overcome faith. Love is in itself unbelieving, faith unloving. And love is unbelieving because it knows nothing more divine than itself, because it believes only in itself as absolute truth.

Christian love is already signalised as a particular, limited love, by the very epithet, Christian. But love is in its nature universal. So long as Christian love does not renounce its qualification of Christian, does not make love, simply, its highest law, so long is it a love which is injurious to the sense of truth, for the very office of love is to abolish the distinction between Christianity and so-called heathenism;—so long is it a love which by its particularity is in contradiction with the nature of love, an abnormal, loveless love, which has therefore long been justly an object of sarcasm. True love is sufficient to itself; it needs no special title, no authority. Love is the universal law of intelligence and Nature;—it is nothing else than the realisation of the unity of the species through the medium of moral sentiment. To found this love on the name of a person, is only possible by the association of superstitious ideas, either of a religious or speculative character. For with superstition is always associated particularism, and with particularism, fanaticism. Love can only be founded on the unity of the species, the unity of intelligence—on the nature of mankind; then only is it a well-grounded love, safe in its principle, guaranteed, free, for it is fed by the original source of love, out of which the love of Christ himself arose. The love of Christ was itself a derived love. He loved us not out of himself, by virtue of his own authority, but by virtue of our common human nature. A love which is based on his person is a particular, exclusive love, which extends only so far as the acknowledgment of this person extends, a love which does not rest on the proper ground of love. Are we to love each other because Christ loved us? Such love would be an affected, imitative love. Can we truly love each other only if we love Christ? Is Christ the cause of love? Is he not rather the apostle of love? Is not the ground of his love the unity of human nature? Shall I love Christ more than mankind? Is not such love a chimerical love? Can I step beyond the idea of the species? Can I love anything higher than humanity? What ennobled Christ was love; whatever qualities he had, he held in fealty to love; he was not the proprietor of love, as he is represented to be in all superstitious conceptions. The idea of love is an independent idea; I do not first deduce it from the life of Christ; on the contrary, I revere that life only because I find it accordant with the law, the idea of love.

This is already proved historically by the fact that the idea of love was by no means first introduced into the consciousness of mankind with and by Christianity,—is by no means peculiarly Christian. The horrors of the Roman Empire present themselves with striking significance in company with the appearance of this idea. The empire of policy which united men after a manner corresponding with its own idea, was coming to its necessary end. Political unity is a unity of force. The despotism of Rome must turn in upon itself, destroy itself. But it was precisely through this catastrophe of political existence that man released himself entirely from the heart-stifling toils of politics. In the place of Rome appeared the idea of humanity ; to the idea of dominion succeeded the idea of love. Even the Jews, by imbibing the principle of humanity contained in Greek culture, had by this time mollified their malignant religious separatism. Philo celebrates love as the highest virtue. The extinction of national differences lay in the idea of humanity itself. Thinking minds had very early overstepped the civil and political separation of man from man. Aristotle distinguishes the man from the slave, and places the slave, as a man, on a level with his master, uniting them in friendship. Epictetus, the slave, was a Stoic ; Antoninus, the emperor, was a Stoic also : thus did philosophy unite men. The Stoics taught * that man was not born for his own sake, but for the sake of others, *i.e.*, for love : a principle which implies infinitely more than the celebrated dictum of the Emperor Antoninus, which enjoined the love of enemies. The practical principle of the Stoics is so far the principle of love. The world is to them one city, men its citizens. Seneca, in the sublimest sayings, extols love, clemency, humanity, especially towards slaves. Thus political rigour and patriotic narrowness were on the wane.

Christianity was a peculiar manifestation of these human tendencies ;—a popular, consequently a religious, and certainly a most intense manifestation of this new principle of love. That which elsewhere made itself apparent in the process of culture, expressed itself here as religious feeling, as a matter of faith. Christianity thus reduced a general unity to a particular one, it made love collateral to faith ; and by this means it placed itself in contradiction with

* The Peripatetics also ; who founded love, even that towards all men, not on a particular, religious, but a natural principle.

universal love. The unity was not referred to its true origin. National differences indeed disappeared; but in their place difference of faith, the opposition of Christian and un-Christian, more vehement than a national antagonism, and also more malignant, made its appearance in history.

All love founded on a special historical phenomenon contradicts, as has been said, the nature of love, which endures no limits, which triumphs over all particularity. Man is to be loved for man's sake. Man is an object of love because he is an end in himself, because he is a rational and loving being. This is the law of the species, the law of the intelligence. Love should be immediate, undetermined by anything else than its object;—nay, only as such is it love. But if I interpose between my fellow-man and myself the idea of an individuality, in whom the idea of the species is supposed to be already realised, I annihilate the very soul of love, I disturb the unity by the idea of a third external to us; for in that case my fellow-man is an object of love to me only on account of his resemblance or relation to this model, not for his own sake. Here all the contradictions reappear which we have in the personality of God, where the idea of the personality by itself, without regard to the qualities which render it worthy of love and reverence, fixes itself in the consciousness and feelings. Love is the subjective reality of the species, as reason is its objective reality. In love, in reason, the need of an intermediate person disappears. Christ is nothing but an image, under which the unity of the species has impressed itself on the popular consciousness. Christ loved men: he wished to bless and unite them all without distinction of sex, age, rank, or nationality. Christ is the love of mankind to itself embodied in an image—in accordance with the nature of religion as we have developed it —or contemplated as a person, but a person who (we mean, of course, as a religious object) has only the significance of an image, who is only ideal. For this reason love is pronounced to be the characteristic mark of the disciples. But love, as has been said, is nothing else than the active proof, the realisation of the unity of the race, through the medium of the moral disposition. The species is not an abstraction; it exists in feeling, in the moral sentiment, in the energy of love. It is the species which infuses love into me. A loving heart is the heart of the species throbbing in the individual. Thus Christ, as the consciousness of love, is the consciousness of the species. We are all one in Christ. Christ is the consciousness of our identity. He therefore who loves man for the sake of man, who rises to the love of the species, to universal love, adequate to the nature of the species,* he is a Christian, is Christ himself. He does what Christ did, what made Christ Christ. Thus, where there arises the consciousness of the species as a species, the idea of humanity as a whole, Christ disappears, without, however, his true nature disappearing; for he was the substitute for the consciousness of the species, the image under which it was made present to the people, and became the law of the popular life.

* Active love is and must of course always be particular and limited, *i.e.,* directed to one's neighbour. But it is yet in its nature universal, since it loves man for man's sake, in the name of the race. Christian love, on the contrary, is in its nature exclusive.

CHAPTER XXVII.

CONCLUDING APPLICATION.

In the contradiction between Faith and Love which has just been exhibited, we see the practical, palpable ground of necessity that we should raise ourselves above Christianity, above the peculiar stand-point of all religion. We have shown that the substance and object of religion is altogether human; we have shown that divine wisdom is human wisdom; that the secret of theology is anthropology; that the absolute mind is the so-called finite subjective mind. But religion is not conscious that its elements are human; on the contrary, it places itself in opposition to the human, or at least it does not admit that its elements are human. The necessary turning-point of history is therefore the open confession, that the consciousness of God is nothing else than the consciousness of the species; that man can and should raise himself only above the limits of his individuality, and not above the laws, the positive essential conditions of his species; that there is no other essence which man can think, dream of, imagine, feel, believe in, wish for, love and adore as the *absolute*, than the essence of human nature itself.*

Our relation to religion is therefore not a merely negative, but a critical one; we only separate the true from the false; —though we grant that the truth thus separated from falsehood is a new truth, essentially different from the old. Religion is the first form of self-consciousness. Religions are sacred because they are the traditions of the primitive self-consciousness. But that which in religion holds the first place—namely, God—is, as we have shown, in itself and according to truth, the second, for it is only the nature of man regarded objectively; and that which to religion is the second—namely, man—must therefore be constituted

---

* Including external nature; for as man belongs to the essence of Nature, —in opposition to common materialism; so Nature belongs to the essence of man,—in opposition to subjective idealism; which is also the secret of our "absolute" philosophy, at least in relation to Nature. Only by uniting man with Nature can we conquer the supranaturalistic egoism of Christianity.

and declared the first. Love to man must be no derivative love; it must be original. If human nature is the highest nature to man, then practically also the highest and first law must be the love of man to man. *Homo homini Deus est:*—this is the great practical principle:—this is the axis on which revolves the history of the world. The relations of child and parent, of husband and wife, of brother and friend—in general, of man to man—in short, all the moral relations are *per se* religious. Life as a whole is, in its essential, substantial relations, throughout of a divine nature. Its religious consecration is not first conferred by the blessing of the priest. But the pretension of religion is that it can hallow an object by its essentially external co-operation; it thereby assumes to be itself the only holy power; besides itself it knows only earthly, ungodly relations; hence it comes forward in order to consecrate them and make them holy.

But marriage—we mean, of course, marriage as the free bond of love *—is sacred in itself, by the very nature of the union which is therein effected. That alone is a religious marriage, which is a true marriage, which corresponds to the essence of marriage—of love. And so it is with all moral relations. Then only are they moral,—then only are they enjoyed in a moral spirit, when they are regarded as sacred in themselves. True friendship exists only when the boundaries of friendship are preserved with religious conscientiousness, with the same conscientiousness with which the believer watches over the dignity of his God. Let friendship be sacred to thee, property sacred, marriage sacred, —sacred the well-being of every man; but let them be sacred *in and by themselves.*

In Christianity the moral laws are regarded as the commandments of God; morality is even made the criterion of piety; but ethics have nevertheless a subordinate rank, they have not in themselves a religious significance. This belongs only to faith. Above morality hovers God, as a being distinct from man, a being to whom the best is due,

---

* Yes, only as the free bond of love; for a marriage the bond of which is merely an external restriction, not the voluntary, contented self-restriction of love, in short, a marriage which is not spontaneously concluded, spontaneously willed, self-sufficing, is not a true marriage, and therefore not a truly moral marriage.

while the remnants only fall to the share of man. All those dispositions which ought to be devoted to life, to man—all the best powers of humanity, are lavished on the being who wants nothing. The real cause is converted into an impersonal means, a merely conceptional, imaginary cause usurps the place of the true one. Man thanks God for those benefits which have been rendered to him even at the cost of sacrifice by his fellow-man. The gratitude which he expresses to his benefactor is only ostensible; it is paid, not to him, but to God. He is thankful, grateful to God, but unthankful to man.* Thus is the moral sentiment subverted into religion! Thus does man sacrifice man to God! The bloody human sacrifice is in fact only a rude, material expression of the inmost secret of religion. Where bloody human sacrifices are offered to God, such sacrifices are regarded as the highest thing, physical existence as the chief good. For this reason life is sacrificed to God, and it is so on extraordinary occasions; the supposition being that this is the way to show him the greatest honour. If Christianity no longer, at least in our day, offers bloody sacrifices to its God, this arises, to say nothing of other reasons, from the fact that physical existence is no longer regarded as the highest good. Hence the soul, the emotions are now offered to God, because these are held to be something higher. But the common case is, that in religion man sacrifices some duty towards man—such as that of respecting the life of his fellow, of being grateful to him— to a religious obligation,—sacrifices his relation to man to his relation to God. The Christians, by the idea that God is without wants, and that he is only an object of pure adoration, have certainly done away with many pernicious conceptions. But this freedom from wants is only a metaphysical idea, which is by no means part of the peculiar nature of religion. When the need for worship is supposed to exist only on one side, the subjective side, this has the invariable effect of one-sidedness, and leaves the religious

* " Because God does good through government, great men and creatures in general, people rush into error, lean on creatures and not on the Creator; —they do not look from the creature to the Creator. Hence it came that the heathens made gods of kings . . . For they cannot and will not perceive that the work or the benefit comes from God, and not merely from the creature, though the latter is a means, through which God works, helps us and gives to us."—Luther (T. iv. p. 237).

emotions cold; hence, if not in express words, yet in fact, there must be attributed to God a condition corresponding to the subjective need, the need of the worshipper, in order to establish reciprocity.* All the positive definitions of religion are based on reciprocity. The religious man thinks of God because God thinks of him; he loves God because God has first loved him. God is jealous of man; religion is jealous of morality; † it sucks away the best forces of morality; it renders to man only the things that are man's, but to God the things that are God's; and to him is rendered true, living emotion,—the heart.

When in times in which peculiar sanctity was attached to religion, we find marriage, property, and civil law respected, this has not its foundation in religion, but in the original, natural sense of morality and right, to which the true social relations are sacred *as such.* He to whom the Right is not holy for its own sake will never be made to feel it sacred by religion. Property did not become sacred because it was regarded as a divine institution, but it was regarded as a divine institution because it was felt to be in itself sacred. Love is not holy because it is a predicate of God, but it is a predicate of God because it is in itself divine. The heathens do not worship the light or the fountain because it is a gift of God, but because it has of

---

* "They who honour me, I will honour, and they who despise me shall be lightly esteemed."—1 Sam. ii. 30. "Jam se, o bone pater, vermis vilissimus et odio dignissimus sempiterno, tamen confidit amari, quoniam se sentit amare, imo quia se amari præsentit, non redamare confunditur. . . . Nemo itaque se amari diffidat, qui jam amat."—Bernardus ad Thomam (Epist. 107). A very fine and pregnant sentence. If I exist not for God, God exists not for me; if I do not love, I am not loved. The *passive* is the *active* certain of itself, the object is the subject certain of itself. To love is to be man, to be loved is to be God. I am loved, says God; I love, says man. It is not until later that this is reversed, that the passive transforms itself into the active, and conversely.

† "The Lord spake to Gideon: The people are too many that are with thee, that I should give Midian into their hands; Israel might glorify itself against me and say: My hand has delivered me,"—*i.e.,* "Ne Israel sibi tribuat, quæ mihi debentur." Judges vii. 2. "Thus saith the Lord: Cursed is the man that trusteth in man. But blessed is the man that trusteth in the Lord and whose hope is in the Lord."—Jer. xvii. 5. "God desires not our gold, body and possessions, but has given these to the emperor (that is, to the representative of the world, of the state), and to us through the emperor. But the heart, which is the greatest and best in man, he has reserved for himself;—this must be our offering to God—that we believe in him."—Luther (xvi. p. 505).

itself a beneficial influence on man, because it refreshes the sufferer; on account of this excellent quality they pay it divine honours.

Wherever morality is based on theology, wherever the right is made dependent on divine authority, the most immoral, unjust, infamous things can be justified and established. I can found morality on theology only when I myself have already defined the Divine Being by means of morality. In the contrary case, I have no criterion of the moral and immoral, but merely an *un*moral, arbitrary basis, from which I may deduce anything I please. Thus, if I would found morality on God, I must first of all place it in God: for Morality, Right, in short, all substantial relations, have their only basis in themselves, can only have a real foundation—such as truth demands—when they are thus based. To place anything in God, or to derive anything from God, is nothing more than to withdraw it from the test of reason, to institute it as indubitable, unassailable, sacred, without rendering an account *why*. Hence self-delusion, if not wicked, insidious design, is at the root of all efforts to establish morality, right, on theology. Where we are in earnest about the right we need no incitement or support from above. We need no Christian rule of political right: we need only one which is rational, just, human. The right, the true, the good, has always its ground of sacredness in itself, in its quality. Where man is in earnest about ethics, they have in themselves the validity of a divine power. If morality has no foundation in itself, there is no inherent necessity for morality; morality is then surrendered to the groundless arbitrariness of religion.

Thus the work of the self-conscious reason in relation to religion is simply to destroy an illusion:—an illusion, however, which is by no means indifferent, but which, on the contrary, is profoundly injurious in its effect on mankind; which deprives man as well of the power of real life as of the genuine sense of truth and virtue; for even love, in itself the deepest, truest emotion, becomes by means of religiousness merely ostensible, illusory, since religious love gives itself to man only for God's sake, so that it is given only in appearance to man, but in reality to God.

And we need only, as we have shown, invert the religious

relations—regard that as an end which religion supposes to be a means—exalt that into the primary which in religion is subordinate, the accessory, the condition,—at once we have destroyed the illusion, and the unclouded light of truth streams in upon us. The sacraments of Baptism and the Lord's Supper, which are the characteristic symbols of the Christian religion, may serve to confirm and exhibit this truth.

The Water of Baptism is to religion only the means by which the Holy Spirit imparts itself to man. But by this conception it is placed in contradiction with reason, with the truth of things. On the one hand, there is virtu : in the objective, natural quality of water; on the other, there is none, but it is a merely arbitrary medium of divine grace and omnipotence. We free ourselves from these and other irreconcilable contradictions, we give a true significance to Baptism, only by regarding it as a symbol of the value of water itself. Baptism should represent to us the wonderful but natural effect of water on man. Water has, in fact, not merely physical effects, but also, and as a result of these, moral and intellectual effects on man. Water not only cleanses man from bodily impurities, but in water the scales fall from his eyes: he sees, he thinks more clearly; he feels himself freer; water extinguishes the fire of appetite. How many saints have had recourse to the natural qualities of water in order to overcome the assaults of the devil! What was denied by Grace has been granted by Nature. Water plays a part not only in dietetics, but also in moral and mental discipline. To purify oneself, to bathe, is the first, though the lowest of virtues.* In the stream of water the

---

* Christian baptism also is obviously only a relic of the ancient Nature-worship, in which, as in the Persian, water was a means of religious purification. (S. Rhode: Die heilige Sage, &c., pp. 305, 426.) Here, however, water baptism had a much truer, and consequently a deeper meaning, than with the Christians, because it rested on the natural power and value of water. But indeed for these simple views of Nature which characterised the old religions, our speculative as well as theological supranaturalism has neither sense nor understanding. When therefore the Persians, the Hindoos, the Egyptians, the Hebrews, made physical purity a religious duty, they were herein far wiser than the Christian saints, who attested the supra-naturalistic principle of their religion by physical impurity. Supranaturalism in theory becomes anti-naturalism in practice. Supranaturalism is only a euphemism for anti-naturalism.

fever of selfishness is allayed.   Water is the readiest means
of making friends with Nature.   The bath is a sort of
chemical process, in which our individuality is resolved
into the objective life of Nature.   The man rising from the
water is a new, a regenerate man.   The doctrine that
morality can do nothing without means of grace has a valid
meaning if, in place of imaginary, supernatural means of
grace, we substitute natural means.   Moral feeling can
effect nothing without Nature; it must ally itself with the
simplest natural means.   The profoundest secrets lie in
common everyday things, such as supranaturalistic religion
and speculation ignore, thus sacrificing real mysteries to
imaginary, illusory ones; as here, for example, the real
power of water is sacrificed to an imaginary one.   Water
is the simplest means of grace or healing for the maladies
of the soul as well as of the body.   But water is effectual
only where its use is constant and regular.   Baptism, as a
single act, is either an altogether useless and unmeaning
institution, or, if real effects are attributed to it, a superstitious one.   But it is a rational, a venerable institution,
if it is understood to typify and celebrate the moral and
physical curative virtues of water.

But the sacrament of water required a supplement.
Water, as a universal element of life, reminds us of our
origin from Nature, an origin which we have in common
with plants and animals.   In Baptism we bow to the power
of a pure Nature-force; water is the element of natural
equality and freedom, the mirror of the golden age.   But
we men are distinguished from the plants and animals,
which together with the inorganic kingdom we comprehend
under the common name of Nature;—we are distinguished
from Nature.   Hence we must celebrate our distinction,
our specific difference.   The symbols of this our difference
are bread and wine.   Bread and wine are, as to their
materials, products of Nature; as to their form, products of
man.   If in water we declare: Man can do nothing without
Nature; by bread and wine we declare: Nature needs man,
as man needs Nature.   In water, human mental activity is
nullified; in bread and wine it attains self-satisfaction.
Bread and wine are supernatural products,—in the only
valid and true sense, the sense which is not in contradiction

with reason and Nature. If in water we adore the pure force of Nature, in bread and wine we adore the supernatural power of mind, of consciousness, of man. Hence this sacrament is only for man matured into consciousness; while baptism is imparted to infants. But we at the same time celebrate here the true relation of mind to Nature: Nature gives the material, mind gives the form. The sacrament of Baptism inspires us with thankfulness towards Nature, the sacrament of bread and wine with thankfulness towards man. Bread and wine typify to us the truth that Man is the true God and Saviour of man.

Eating and drinking is the mystery of the Lord's Supper; —eating and drinking is, in fact, in itself a religious act; at least, ought to be so.* Think, therefore, with every morsel of bread which relieves thee from the pain of hunger, with every draught of wine which cheers thy heart, of the God who confers these beneficent gifts upon thee,—think of man! But in thy gratitude towards man forget not gratitude towards holy Nature! Forget not that wine is the blood of plants, and flour the flesh of plants, which are sacrificed for thy well-being! Forget not that the plant typifies to thee the essence of Nature, which lovingly surrenders itself for thy enjoyment! Therefore forget not the gratitude which thou owest to the natural qualities of bread and wine! And if thou art inclined to smile that I call eating and drinking religious acts, because they are common everyday acts, and are therefore performed by multitudes without thought, without emotion; reflect, that the Lord's Supper is to multitudes a thoughtless, emotionless act, because it takes place often; and, for the sake of comprehending the religious significance of bread and wine, place thyself in a position where the daily act is unnaturally, violently interrupted. Hunger and thirst destroy not only the physical but also the mental and moral powers of man; they rob

---

* "Eating and drinking is the easiest of all work, for men like nothing better: yea, the most joyful work in the whole world is eating and drinking, as it is commonly said: Before eating no dancing, and, On a full stomach stands a merry head. In short, eating and drinking is a pleasant necessary work;—that is a doctrine soon learned and made popular. The same pleasant necessary work takes our blessed Lord Christ and says: 'I have prepared a joyful, sweat and pleasant meal, I will lay on you no hard heavy work . . . I institute a supper,' &c."—Luther (xvi. 222).

him of his humanity—of understanding, of consciousness.
Oh! if thou shouldst ever experience such want, how wouldst
thou bless and praise the natural qualities of bread and
wine, which restore to thee thy humanity, thy intellect!
It needs only that the ordinary course of things be interrupted in order to vindicate to common things an uncommon
significance, *to life, as such, a religious import.*   Therefore
let bread be sacred for us, let wine be sacred, and also let
water be sacred !   Amen.

APPENDIX.

APPENDIX.

—◆—

EXPLANATIONS—REMARKS—ILLUSTRATIVE CITATIONS.

---

§ 1.

Man has his highest being, his God, in himself; not in himself as an individual, but in his essential nature, his species. No individual is an adequate representation of his species, but only the human individual is conscious of the distinction between the species and the individual ; in the sense of this distinction lies the root of religion. The yearning of man after something above himself is nothing else than the longing after the perfect type of his nature, the yearning to be free from himself, *i.e.*, from the limits and defects of his individuality. Individuality is the self-conditionating, the self-limitation of the species. Thus man has cognisance of nothing above himself, of nothing beyond the nature of humanity ; but to the individual man this nature presents itself under the form of an individual man. Thus, for example, the child sees the nature of man *above itself* in the form of its parents, the pupil in the form of his tutor. But all feelings which man experiences towards a superior man, nay, in general, all moral feelings which man has towards man, are of a religious nature.* *Man feels nothing towards God which he does not also feel towards man. Homo homini deus est.* Want teaches prayer ; but in misfortune, in sorrow, man kneels to entreat help of man also. Feeling makes God a man, but for the same reason it makes man a God. How often in deep emotion, which alone speaks genuine truth, man exclaims to man : Thou art, thou hast been my redeemer, my saviour, my protecting spirit, my God! We feel awe, reverence, humility, devout admiration, in thinking of a truly great, noble man ; we feel ourselves worthless, we sink into nothing, even in

---

* "Manifestum igitur est tantum religionis sanguini et affinitati, quantum ipsis Diis immortalibus tributum : quia inter ista tam sancta vincula non magis, quam in aliquo loco sacrato nudare se, nefas esse credebatur."—Valer. Max. (L. ii. c. i.)

the presence of human greatness. The purely, truly human emotions are religious ; but for that reason the religious emotions are purely human : the only difference is, that the religious emotions are vague, indefinite; but even this is only the case when the object of them is indefinite. Where God is positively defined, is the object of positive religion, there God is also the object of positive, definite human feelings, the object of fear and love, and therefore he is a positively human being; for there is nothing more in God than what lies in feeling. If in the heart there is fear and terror, in God there is anger ; if in the heart there is joy, hope, confidence, in God there is love. Fear makes itself objective in anger ; joy in love, in mercy. "As it is with me in my heart, so is it with God." "As my heart is, so is God."—Luther (Th. i. p. 72). But a merciful and angry God—*Deus vere irascitur* (Melancthon)— is a God no longer distinguishable from the human feelings and nature. Thus even in religion man bows before the nature of man under the form of a personal human being ; religion itself expressly declares—and all anthropomorphisms declare this in opposition to Pantheism,—*quod supra nos nihil ad nos;* that is, a God who inspires us with no human emotions, who does not reflect our own emotions, in a word, who is not a man,—such a God is nothing to us, has no interest for us, does not concern us. (See the passages cited in this work from Luther.)

Religion has thus no dispositions and emotions which are peculiar to itself ; what it claims as belonging exclusively to its object, are simply the same dispositions and emotions that man experiences either in relation to himself (as, for example, to his conscience), or to his fellow-man, or to Nature. You must not fear men, but God; you must not love man,—*i.e.*, not truly, for his own sake,—but God; you must not humble yourselves before human greatness, but only before the Lord ; not believe and confide in man, but only in God. Hence comes the danger of worshipping false gods in distinction from the true God. Hence the "jealousy" of God. "Ego Jehova, Deus tuus, Deus sum zelotypus. Ut zelotypus vir dicitur, qui rivalem pati nequit : sic Deus socium in cultu, quem ab hominibus postulat, ferre non potest." (Clericus, Comment. in Exod. c. 20, v. 5.) Jealousy arises because a being preferred and loved by me directs to another the feelings and dispositions which I claim for myself. But how could I be jealous if the impressions and emotions which I excite in the beloved being were altogether peculiar and apart, were essentially different from the impressions which another can make on him ? If, therefore, the emotions of religion were objectively, essentially different from those which lie out of religion, there would be no possibility of idolatry in man or of jealousy in God. As the flute has another sound to me than the trumpet, and I cannot confound the impressions produced by the former with the impressions produced by the latter ; so I could not transfer to a natural or human being the emotions of religion, if the object of religion, God, were specifically different from the natural or human being, and consequently the impressions which he produced on me were specific, peculiar.

§ 2.

Feeling alone is the object of feeling. Feeling is sympathy; feeling arises only in the love of man to man. Sensations man has in isolation; feelings only in community. Only in sympathy does sensation rise into feeling. Feeling is æsthetic, human sensation; only what is human is the object of feeling. In feeling man is related to his fellow-man as to himself; he is alive to the sorrows, the joys of another as his own. Thus only by communication does man rise above merely egoistic sensation into feeling;—participated sensation is feeling. He who has no need of participating has no feeling. But what does the hand, the kiss, the glance, the voice, the tone, the word—as the expression of emotion—impart? Emotion. The very same thing which, pronounced or performed without the appropriate tone, without emotion, is only an object of indifferent perception, becomes, when uttered or performed with emotion, an object of feeling. To feel is to have a sense of sensations, to have emotion in the perception of emotion. Hence the brutes rise to feeling only in the sexual relation, and therefore only transiently; for here the being experiences sensation not in relation to itself taken alone, or to an object without sensation, but to a being having like emotions with itself,—not to another as a distinct object, but to an object which in species is identical. Hence Nature is an object of feeling to me only when I regard it as a being akin to me and in sympathy with me.

It is clear from what has been said, that only where in truth, if not according to the subjective conception, the distinction between the divine and human being is abolished, is the objective existence of God, the existence of God as an objective, distinct being, abolished:—only there, I say, is religion made a mere matter of feeling, or conversely, feeling the chief point in religion. The last refuge of theology therefore is feeling. God is renounced by the understanding; he has no longer the dignity of a real object, of a reality which imposes itself on the understanding; hence he is transferred to feeling; in feeling his existence is thought to be secure. And doubtless this is the safest refuge; for to make feeling the essence of religion is nothing else than to make feeling the essence of God. And as certainly as I exist, so certainly does my feeling exist; and as certainly as my feeling exists, so certainly does my God exist. The certainty of God is here nothing else than the self-certainty of human feeling, the yearning after God is the yearning after unlimited, uninterrupted, pure feeling. In life the feelings are interrupted; they collapse; they are followed by a state of void, of insensibility. The religious problem, therefore, is to give fixity to feeling in spite of the vicissitudes of life, and to separate it from repugnant disturbances and limitations: God himself is nothing else than undisturbed, uninterrupted feeling, feeling for which there exists no limits, no opposite. If God were a being distinct from thy feeling, he would be known to thee in some other way than simply in feeling; but just because thou perceivest him only by feeling, he exists only in feeling—he is himself only feeling.

§ 3.

God is man's highest feeling of self, freed from all contrarieties or disagreeables. God is the highest being ;. therefore, to feel God is the highest feeling. But is not the highest feeling also the highest feeling of self? So long as I have not had the feeling of the highest, so long I have not exhausted my capacity of feeling, so long I do not yet fully know the nature of feeling. What, then, is an object to me in my feeling of the highest being? Nothing else than the highest nature of my power of feeling. So much as a man can feel, so much is (his) God. But the highest degree of the power of feeling is also the highest degree of the feeling of self. In the feeling of the *low* I feel myself lowered, in the feeling of the *high* I feel myself exalted. The feeling of self and feeling are inseparable, otherwise feeling would not belong to myself. Thus God, as an object of feeling, or what is the same thing, the feeling of God, is nothing else than man's highest feeling of self. But God is the freest, or rather the absolutely only free being ; thus God is man's highest feeling of freedom. How couldst thou be conscious of the highest being as freedom, or freedom as the highest being, if thou didst not feel thyself free? But when dost thou feel thyself free? When thou feelest God. To feel God is to feel oneself free. For example, thou feelest desire, passion, the conditions of time and place, as limits. What thou feelest as a limit thou strugglest against, thou breakest loose from, thou deniest. The consciousness of a limit, as such, is already an anathema, a sentence of condemnation pronounced on this limit, for it is an oppressive, disagreeable, negative consciousness. Only the feeling of the good, of the positive, is itself good and positive—is joy. Joy alone is feeling in its element, its paradise, because it is unrestricted activity. The sense of pain in an organ is nothing else than the sense of a disturbed, obstructed, thwarted activity ; in a word, the sense of something abnormal, anomalous. Hence thou strivest to escape from the sense of limitation into unlimited feeling. By means of the will, or the imagination, thou negativest limits, and thus obtainest the feeling of freedom. This feeling of freedom is God. God is exalted above desire and passion, above the limits of space and time. But this exaltation is thy own exaltation above that which appears to thee as a limit. Does not this exaltation of the divine being exalt thee? How could it do so, if it were external to thee? No ; God is an exalted being only for him who himself has exalted thoughts and feelings. Hence the exaltation of the divine being varies according to that which different men or nations perceive as a limitation to the feeling of self, and which they consequently negative or eliminate from their ideal.

§ 4.

The distinction between the "heathen," or philosophic, and the Christian God—the non-human, or pantheistic, and the human, personal God—reduces itself only to the distinction between the understanding or reason and the heart or feelings. Reason is the self-consciousness of the species, as such ; feeling is the self-consciousness of individuality ; the reason has relation to existences, as things ; the heart to existences, as persons. *I am* is an expression of the heart ; *I think,* of the reason. *Cogito, ergo sum?* No! *Sentio, ergo sum.* Feeling only is my existence ; thinking is my non-existence, the negation of my individuality, the positing of the species ; reason is the annihilation of personality. To think is an act of spiritual marriage. Only beings of the same species understand each other ; the impulse to communicate thought is the intellectual impulse of sex. Reason is cold, because its maxim is, *audiatur et altera pars,* because it does not interest itself in man alone ; but the heart is a partisan of man. Reason loves all impartiality, but the heart only what is like itself. It is true that the heart has pity also on the brutes, but only because it sees in the brute something more than the brute. The heart loves only what it identifies with itself. It says : Whatsoever thou dost to this being, thou dost to me. The heart loves only itself ; does not get beyond itself, beyond man. The superhuman God is nothing else than the supernatural heart ; the heart does not give us the idea of *another,* of a being different from ourselves. "For the heart, Nature is an echo, in which it hears only itself. Emotion, in the excess of its happiness, transfers itself to external things. It is the love which can withhold itself from no existence, which gives itself forth to all ; but it only recognises as existing that which it knows to have emotion." * Reason, on the contrary, has pity on animals, not because it finds itself in them, or identifies them with man, but because it recognises them as beings distinct from man, not existing simply for the sake of man, but also as having rights of their own. The heart sacrifices the species to the individual, the reason sacrifices the individual to the species. The man without feeling has no home, no private hearth. Feeling, the heart, is the domestic life ; the reason is the *res publica* of man. Reason is the truth of Nature, the heart is the truth of man. To speak popularly, reason is the God of Nature, the heart the God of man ;—a distinction however which, drawn thus sharply, is, like the others, only admissible in antithesis. Everything which man wishes, but which reason, which Nature denies, the heart bestows. God, immortality, freedom, in the supranaturalistic sense, exist only in the heart. The heart is itself the existence of God, the existence of immortality. Satisfy yourselves with this existence ! You do not understand your heart ; therein lies the evil. You desire a real, external, objective immortality, a God out of yourselves. Here is the source of delusion.

* See the author's "Leibnitz."

But as the heart releases man from the limits, even the essential limits of Nature; reason, on the other hand, releases Nature from the limits of external finiteness. It is true that Nature is the light and measure of reason;—a truth which is opposed to abstract Idealism. Only what is *naturally* true is *logically* true; what has no basis in Nature has no basis at all. That which is not a physical law is not a metaphysical law. Every true law in metaphysics can and must be verified physically. But at the same time reason is also the light of Nature;—and this truth is the barrier against crude materialism. Reason is the nature of things come fully to itself, re-established in its entireness. Reason divests things of the disguises and transformations which they have undergone in the conflict and agitation of the external world, and reduces them to their true character. Most, indeed nearly all, crystals—to give an obvious illustration—appear in Nature under a form altogether different from their fundamental one; nay, many crystals never have appeared in their fundamental form. Nevertheless, the mineralogical reason has discovered that fundamental form. Hence nothing is more foolish than to place Nature in opposition to reason, as an essence in itself incomprehensible to reason. If reason reduces transformations and disguises to their fundamental forms, does it not effect that which lies in the idea of Nature itself, but which, prior to the operation of reason, could not be effected on account of external hindrances? What else then does reason do than remove external disturbances, influences, and obstructions, so as to present a thing as it ought to be, to make the existence correspond to the idea; for the fundamental form is the *idea* of the crystal. Another popular example. Granite consists of mica, quartz, and feldspar. But frequently other kinds of stone are mingled with it. If we had no other guide and tutor than the senses, we should without hesitation reckon as constituent parts of granite all the kinds of stone which we ever find in combination with it; we should say *yes* to everything the senses told us, and so never come to the true idea of granite. But reason says to the credulous senses: *Quod non.* It discriminates; it distinguishes the essential from the accidental elements. Reason is the midwife of Nature; it explains, enlightens, rectifies and completes Nature. Now that which separates the essential from the non-essential, the necessary from the accidental, what is proper to a thing from what is foreign, which restores what has been violently sundered to unity, and what has been forcibly united to freedom,—is not this divine? Is not such an agency as this the agency of the highest, of divine love? And how would it be possible that reason should exhibit the pure nature of things, the original text of the universe, if it were not itself the purest, most original essence? But reason has no partiality for this or that species of things. It embraces with equal interest the whole universe; it interests itself in all things and beings without distinction, without exception;—it bestows the same attention on the worm which human egoism tramples under its feet, as on man, as on the sun in the firmament. Reason is thus the all-embracing, all-compassionating being, the love of the universe to itself. To reason alone belongs the great work of the resurrection and restoration of all things and beings—universal redemption and reconciliation. Not even the unreasoning animal, the speechless plant, the unsentient stone, shall be excluded from this universal festival. But how would it be possible that reason should interest itself in all beings without exception, if reason were not itself universal and unlimited in its nature? Is a limited nature compatible with unlimited interest, or an unlimited interest with a limited nature? By what dost thou recognise the limitation of a being but by the limitation of his interest? As far as the interest extends, so far extends the nature. The desire of knowledge is infinite; reason then is infinite. Reason is the highest species of being;—hence it includes all species in the sphere of knowledge. Reason cannot content itself in the individual; it has its adequate existence only when it has the species for its object, and the species not as it has already developed itself in the past and present, but as it will develop itself in the unknown future. In the activity of reason I feel a distinction between myself and reason in me; this distinction is the limit of the individuality; in feeling I am conscious of no distinction between myself and feeling; and with this absence of distinction there is an absence also of the sense of limitation. Hence it arises that to so many men reason appears finite, and only feeling infinite. And, in fact, feeling, the heart of man as a rational being, is as infinite, as universal as reason; since man only truly perceives and understands that for which he has feeling.

Thus reason is the essence of Nature *and* Man, released from non-essential limits, in their identity; it is the universal being, the universal God. The heart, considered in its *difference* from the reason, is the private God of man; the personal God is the heart of man, emancipated from the limits or laws of Nature.*

§ 5.

Nature, the world, has no value, no interest for Christians. The Christian thinks only of himself and the salvation of his soul. " *A te* incipiat cogitatio tua et *in te* finiatur, nec frustra in alia distendaris, *te neglecto. Praeter salutem tuam nihil cogites. De inter. Domo.* (Among the spurious writings of St. Bernard.) Si te vigilanter homo attendas, mirum est, *si ad aliud unquam intendas.*—Divus Bernardus. (Tract. de XII grad. humil. et sup.)......Orbe sit sol major, an pedis unius latitudine metiatur? alieno ex lumine an propriis luceat fulgoribus luna? quae *neque scire compendium, neque ignorare detrimentum est ullum*......Res vestra in ancipiti sita est:

* [Here follows in the original a distinction between *Herz*, or feeling directed towards real objects, and therefore practically sympathetic; and *Gemüth*, or feeling directed towards imaginary objects, and therefore practically unsympathetic, self-absorbed. But the *verbal* distinction is not adhered to in the ordinary use of the language, or, indeed, by Feuerbach himself; and the *psychological* distinction is sufficiently indicated in other parts of the present work. The passage is therefore omitted, as likely to confuse the reader.—Tr.]

salus dico animarum vestrarum.—Arnobius (adv. gentes, l. ii. c. 61). Quaero igitur ad quam rem scientia referenda sit; si ad *causas rerum naturalium*, quae *beatitudo* erit mihi proposita, si sciero unde Nilus oriatur, vel quicquid de coelo Physici delirant?—Lactantius (Instit. div. l. iii. c. 8). Etiam curiosi esse prohibemur.......Sunt enim qui desertis virtutibus et nescientes quid sit Deus......magnum aliquid se agere putant, *si universam istam corporis molem*, quam *mundum* nuncupamus, curiosissime intentissimeque perquirant...... Reprimat igitur se anima ab hujusmodi vanae cognitionis cupiditate, si se castam Deo servare disposuit. Tali enim amore plerumque decipitur, ut (aut) *nihil putet esse nisi corpus.* — Augustinus (de Mor. Eccl. cath. l. i. c. 21). *De terrae* quoque vel qualitate vel positione tractare, nihil prosit ad *spem futuri*, cum *satis sit ad scientiam*, quod *scripturarum divinarum* series comprehendit, quod Deus suspendit terram *in nihilo.*—Ambrosius (Hexaemeron, l. i. c. 6). Longe utique praestantius est, nosse *resurrecturam* carnem ac *sine fine victuram*, quam quidquid in ea *medici* scrutando discere potuerunt.—Augustinus (de Anima et ejus orig. l. iv. c. 10)." " Let natural science alone......It is enough that thou knowest fire is hot, water cold and moist......Know how thou oughtest to treat thy field, thy cow, thy house and child—that is enough of natural science for thee. Think how thou mayest learn Christ, who will show thee thyself, who thou art, and what is thy capability. Thus wilt thou learn God and thyself, which no natural master or natural science ever taught."—Luther (Th. xiii. p. 264).

Such quotations as these, which might be multiplied indefinitely, show clearly enough that true, religious Christianity has within it no principle of scientific and material culture, no motive to it. The practical end and object of Christians is solely heaven, *i.e.*, the realised salvation of the soul. The theoretical end and object of Christians is solely God, as the being identical with the salvation of the soul. He who knows God knows all things ; and as God is infinitely more than the world, so theology is infinitely more than the knowledge of the world. Theology makes happy, for its object is personified happiness. *Infelix homo, qui scit illa omnia* (created things) *te autem nescit, Beatus autem qui te scit, etiam si illa nesciat.* —Augustin (Confess, l. v. c. 4). Who then would, who could exchange the blessed Divine Being for the unblessed worthless things of this world? It is true that God reveals himself in Nature, but only vaguely, dimly, only in his most general attributes; himself, his true personal nature, he reveals only in religion, in Christianity. The knowledge of God through Nature is heathenism ; the knowledge of God through himself, through Christ, in whom dwelt the fulness of the Godhead bodily, is Christianity. What interest, therefore, should Christians have in occupying themselves with material, natural things? Occupation with Nature, culture in general, presupposes, or, at least, infallibly produces, a heathenish, mundane, anti-theological, anti-supranaturalistic sentiment and belief. Hence the culture of modern Christian nations is so little to be derived from Christianity, that it is only to be explained by the negation of Christianity, a negation which certainly was, in the first instance, only practical. It is indeed necessary to distinguish between what the Christians were as Christians and what they were as heathens, as natural men, and thus between that which they have said and done in agreement, and that which they have said and done in contradiction with their faith. (See on this subject the author's *P. Bayle.*)

How frivolous, therefore, are modern Christians when they deck themselves in the arts and sciences of modern nations as products of Christianity! How striking is the contrast in this respect between these modern boasters and the Christians of older times! The latter knew of no other Christianity than that which is contained in the Christian faith, in faith in Christ; they did not reckon the treasures and riches, the arts and sciences of this world as part of Christianity. In all these points, they rather conceded the pre-eminence to the ancient heathens, the Greeks and Romans. "Why dost thou not also wonder, Erasmus, that from the beginning of the world there have always been among the heathens higher, rarer people, of greater, more exalted understanding, more excellent diligence and skill in all arts, than among Christians or the people of God? Christ himself says that the children of this world are wiser than the children of light. Yea, who among the Christians could we compare for understanding or application to Cicero (to say nothing of the Greeks, Demosthenes and others)?"—Luther (Th. xix. p. 37). *Quid igitur nos antecellimus? Num ingenio, doctrina, morum moderatione illos superamus? Nequaquam. Sed vera Dei agnitione, invocatione et celebratione præstamus.*—Melancthonis (et al. Declam. Th. iii. de vera invocat. Dei).

§ 6.

In religion man has in view himself alone, or, in regarding himself as the object of God, as the end of the divine activity, he is an object to himself, his own end and aim. The mystery of the incarnation is the mystery of the love of God to man, and the mystery of the love of God to man is the love of man to himself. God suffers—suffers for me—this is the highest self-enjoyment, the highest self-certainty of human feeling. "God so loved the world, that he gave his only-begotten Son."—John iii. 16. "If God be for us, who can be against us? He that spared not his own Son, but gave him up for us all, how shall he not with him also freely give us all things?"—Rom. viii. 31, 32. "God commendeth his love towards us, in that, while we were yet sinners, Christ died for us."—Rom. v. 8. "The life which I now live in the flesh I live by the faith of the Son of God, who loved me, and gave himself for me."—Gal. ii. 20. See also Titus iii. 4; Heb. ii. 11. "Credimus in unum Deum patrem......et in unum Dominum Jesum Christum filium Dei......Deum ex Deo......qui *propter nos homines et propter nostram salutem* descendit et incarnatus et homo factus est passus."—Fides Nicaenae Synodi. "Servator......ex *praeexcellenti in homines charitate* non despexit carnis humanae imbecillitatem, sed ea indutus ad communem venit hominum salutem."—Clemens Alex.

(Stromata, l. vii. ed. Wirceb. 1779). "Christianos autem haec universa docent, *providentiam* esse, *maxime vero divinissimum* et propter *excellentiam amoris erga homines incredibilissimum providentiae* opus, *dei incarnatio,* quae *propter nos* facta est."—Gregorii Nysseni (Philosophiae, l. viii. de Provid. c. i. 1512. B. Rhenanus. Jo. Cono interp.) "Venit siquidem *universitatis creator* et Dominus : venit *ad homines,* venit *propter homines,* venit *homo.*"—Divus Bernardus Clarev. (de Adventu Domini, Basil, 1552). "Videte, Fratres, quantum se humiliavit propter homines Deus......*Unde non se ipse homo despiciat, propter quem utique ista subire dignatus est Deus.*"— Augustinus (Sermones ad pop. S. 371, c. 3). " *O homo propter quem* Deus factus est homo, *aliquid magnum te credere debes.*" S. 380, c. 2). " Quis *de se desperet pro quo* tam humilis esse voluit Filius Dei ? " Id. (de Agone Chr. c. 11). " *Quis potest odire hominem cujus naturam* et *similitudinem* videt *in humanitate Dei?* Revera qui *odit illum, odit Deum.*"—(Manuale, c. 26. Among the spurious writings of Augustine.) " *Plus nos amat Deus quam filium pater......Propter nos filio non pepercit.* Et quid plus addo ? et hoc filio justo et hoc filio unigenito et hoc filio Deo. Et quid dici amplius potest ? et hoc *pro nobis,* i.e. pro malis, etc."—Salvianus (de gubernatione Dei. Rittershusius, 1611, pp. 126, 127). "Quid enim mentes nostras tantum erigit et ab *immortalitatis desperatione* liberat, quam quod *tanti nos fecit Deus,* ut Dei filius......dignatus nostrum inire consortium mala nostra moriendo perferret."—Petrus Lomb. (lib. iii. dist. 20, c. 1). " Attamen si illa quae miseriam nescit, *misericordia non praecessisset,* ad hanc cujus mater est miseria, non accessisset."—D. Bernardus (Tract. de XII. gradibus hum. et sup.). " Ecce omnia tua sunt, quae habeo et unde tibi servio. Verum tamen vice versa *tu magis mihi servis, quam ego tibi.* Ecce coelum et terra quae in ministerium hominis creasti, praesto sunt et faciunt quotidie quaecunque mandasti. Et hoc parum est : quin etiam Angelos in ministerium hominis ordinasti. Transcendit autem omnia, quia *tu ipse homini servire dignatus* es et te ipsum daturum ei promisisti."— Thomas à Kempis (de Imit. l. iii. c. 10). " Ego omnipotens et altissimus, qui *cuncta creavi ex nihilo me homini propter te humiliter subjeci......*Pepercit tibi oculus meus, quia *pretiosa* fuit anima tua in conspectu meo " (ibid. c. 13). " Fili ego descendi de coelo pro salute tua, suscepi tuas miserias, non necessitate, sed *charitate* trahente " (ibid. c. 18). "Si consilium rei tantae spectamus, quod totum pertinet, ut s. litterae demonstrant, ad salutem generis humani, quid potest esse dignius Deo, quam illa tanta hujus salutis cura, et ut ita dicamus, tantus in ea re sumptus ?......Itaque Jesus Christus ipse cum omnibus Apostolis......in hoc mysterio Filii Dei ἐν σαρκὶ φανερωθέντος angelis hominibusque patefactam esse dicunt magnitudinem sapientis *bonitatis divinae.*"—J. A. Ernesti (Dignit. et verit. inc. Filii Dei asserta. Opusc. Theol. Lipsiae, 1773, pp. 404, 405. How feeble, how spiritless compared with the expressions of the ancient faith !) " *Propter me* Christus suscepit meas infirmitates, mei corporis subiit passiones, pro me peccatum h. e. pro omni homine, pro me maledictum factus est, etc. Ille flevit, ne tu homo diu fleres. Ille injurias passus est, ne tu injuriam tuam dolere3."—Ambrosius (de fide ad Gratianum, l. ii. c. 4). "God is not against us men. For if God had been against us and hostile to us, he would not assuredly have taken the poor wretched human nature on himself." "How highly our Lord God has honoured us, that he has caused his own Son to become man ! How could he have made himself nearer to us?"—Luther (Th. xvi. pp. 533, 574). "It is to be remarked that he (Stephen) is said to have seen not God himself but the man Christ, whose nature is the dearest and likest and most consoling to man, for a man would rather see a man than an angel or any other creature, especially in trouble."—Id. (Th. xiii. p. 170). "It is not thy kingly rule which draws hearts to thee, O wonderful heart !—but thy having become a man in the fulness of time, and thy walk upon the earth, full of weariness." "Though thou guidest the sceptre of the starry realm, thou art still our brother ; flesh and blood never disowns itself." "The most powerful charm that melts my heart is that my Lord died on the cross *for me.*" "That it is which moves me ; I love thee for thy love, that thou, the creator, the supreme prince, be- camest the Lamb of God for me." "Thanks be to thee, dear Lamb of God, with thousands of sinners' tears ; thou didst die for me on the cross and didst seek me with yearning." "Thy blood it is which has made me give myself up to thee, else I had never thought of thee through my whole life." "If thou hadst not laid hold upon me, I should never have gone to seek thee." "O how sweetly the soul feeds on the passion of Jesus ! Shame and joy are stirred, O thou son of God and of man, when in spirit we see thee so willingly go to death on the cross for us, and each thinks : *for me.*" "The Father takes us under his care, the Son washes us with his blood, the Holy Spirit is always labouring that he may guide and teach us." "Ah ! King, great at all times, but never greater than in the blood-stained robe of the martyr." "My friend is to me and I to him as the Cherubim over the mercy-seat: we look at each other con- tinually. He seeks repose in my heart, and I ever hasten towards his : he wishes to be in my soul, and I in the wound in his side." These quotations are taken from the Moravian hymn-book (Gesang- buch der Evangelischen Brüdergemeine. Gnadau, 1824). We see clearly enough from the examples above given, that the deepest mystery of the Christian religion resolves itself into the mystery of human self-love, but that religious self-love is distinguished from natural in this, that it changes the active into the passive. It is true that the more profound, mystical religious sentiment abhors such naked, undisguised egoism as is exhibited in the Herrnhut hymns ; it does not in God expressly have reference to itself ; it rather forgets, denies itself, demands an unselfish, disinterested love of God, contemplates God in relation to God, not to itself. "Causa diligendi Deum, Deus est. Modus sine modo diligere......Qui Domino confitetur, non quoniam *sibi* bonus est, sed quoniam bonus est, hic vere diligit Deum *propter Deum et non propter seipsum.* Te enim quodammodo perdere, tanquam qui non sis et omnino non sentire te ipsum et a temetipso exinaniri et pene annullari, coelestis est conversationis, non humanae affectionis" (thus the ideal of love, which, however, is first realised in heaven).—Bernhardus, Tract. de dilig. Deo (ad Haymericum). But this free, unselfish love is only the culmination of religious enthusiasm, in which the subject is merged in the object. As soon as the distinction presents itself—and it necessarily does so—so soon does the subject have reference to itself as the object of God. And even apart from this : the religious subject denies its *ego*, its personality, only because it has the enjoyment of blissful personality in God—God *per se* the realised salvation of the soul, God the highest self-contentment, the highest rapture of human feeling. Hence the saying : "Qui Deum non diligit, seipsum non diligit."

§ 7.

Because God suffers man must suffer. The Christian religion is the religion of suffering. " Videlicet vestigia Salvatoris sequimur in theatris. Tale nobis scilicet Christus reliquit exemplum, quem *flevisse legimus, risisse non legimus.*"—Salvianus (l. c. l. vi. § 181). "Christianorum ergo est *pressuram pati* in hoc saeculo et *lugere,* quorum est *aeterna vita.*"—Origenes (Explan. in Ep. Pauli ad Rom. l. ii. c. ii. interp. Hieronymo). "Nemo vitam aeternam, incorruptibilem, immortalemque *desiderat,* nisi eum vitae hujus temporalis, corruptibilis, mortalisque *poeniteat......*Quid ergo *cupimus, nisi ita non esse ut nunc sumus?* Et quid *ingemiscimus, nisi poenitendo, quia ita sumus ?*"—Augustinus (Sermones ad pop. S. 351, c. 3). " Si quidem aliquid melius et utilius saluti hominum quam *pati* fuisset, *Christus* utique *verbo* et *exemplo* ostendisset.......Quoniam per multas tribulationes oportet nos intrare in regnum Dei."—Thomas à Kempis (de Imit. l. ii. c. 12). When, however, the Christian religion is designated as the religion of suffering, this of course applies only to the Christianity of the " mistaken " Christians of old times. Protestantism, in its very beginning, denied the sufferings of Christ as constituting a principle of morality. It is precisely the distinction between Catholicism and Protestantism, in relation to this subject, that the latter, out of self-regard, attached itself only to the merits of Christ, while the former, out of sympathy, attached itself to his sufferings. " Formerly in Popery the sufferings of the Lord were so preached, that it was only pointed out how his example should be imitated. After that, the time was filled up with the sufferings and sorrows of Mary, and the compassion with which Christ and his mother were bewailed ; and the only aim was how to make it piteous, and move the people to compassion and tears, and he who could do this well was held the best preacher for Passion-Week. But we preach the Lord's sufferings as the Holy Scripture teaches us......Christ suffered for the praise and glory of God......but to me, and thee, and all of us, he suffered in order to bring redemption and blessedness......The cause and end of the sufferings of Christ is comprised in this—he suffered for us. This honour is to be given to no other suffering."—Luther (Th. xvi. p. 182). " Lamb ! I weep only for joy over thy suffering ; the suffering was thine, but thy merit is mine ! " " I know of no joys but those which come from

thy sufferings." " It remains ever in my mind that it cost thee thy
blood to redeem me." " O my Immanuel! how sweet is it to my
soul when thou permittest me to enjoy the outpouring of thy blood."
" Sinners are glad at heart that they have a Saviour......it is won-
drously beautiful to them to see Jesus on the Cross" (Moravian
hymn-book). It is therefore not to be wondered at if Christians of
the present day decline to know anything more of the sufferings of
Christ. It is they, forsooth, who have first made out what true
Christianity is—they rely solely on the divine word of the Holy
Scriptures. And the Bible, as every one knows, has the valuable
quality that everything may be found in it which it is desired to find.
What once stood there, of course now stands there no longer. The
principle of stability has long vanished from the Bible. Divine
revelation is as changing as human opinion *Tempora mutantur.*

§ 8.

*The mystery of the Trinity is the mystery of participated, social
life—the mystery of I and thou.* " Unum Deum esse confitemur.
Non sic unum Deum, quasi *solitarium*, nec eundem, qui ipse sibi
pater, sit ipse filius, sed *patrem verum*, qui genuit *filium verum*,
i.e. Deum ex Deo......non creatum, sed *genitum.*"—Concil. Chalced.
(Carranza Summa, 1559. p. 139). "Si quis quod scriptum est :
Faciamus hominem, non patrem ad filium dicere, sed *ipsum ad
semetipsum* asserit dixisse Deum, anathema sit."—Concil. Syrmiense
(ibid. p. 68). " Jubet autem his verbis : *Faciamus hominem*, prodeat
herba. Ex quibus apparet, Deum cum *aliquo sibi proximo sermones* his de rebus *conserere.* Necesse est igitur *aliquem ei adfuisse,
cum quo* universa condens, *colloquium miscebat.*"—Athanasius (Contra Gentes Orat. Ath. Opp. Parisiis, 1627, Th. i. p. 51). " Professio
enim *consortii* sustulit intelligentiam singularitatis, quod consortium
aliquid nec potest esse *sibi ipsi solitario*, neque rursum solitudo
solitarii recipit : faciamus......Non solitario convenit dicere : *faciamus* et *nostram.*"—Petrus Lomb. (l. i. dist. 2, c. 3, e.). The Protestants explain the passage in the same way. " Quod profecto
aliter intelligi nequit, quam *inter ipsas trinitatis personas* quandam
de creando homine institutam fuisse *consultationem.*"—Buddeus
(comp. Inst. Theol. dog. cur. J. G. Walch. l. ii. c. i. § 45). " ' Let us
make' is the word of a deliberative council. And from these
words it necessarily follows again, that in the Godhead there must
be more than one person......For the little word ' us' indicates that
he who there speaks is not alone, though the Jews make the text
ridiculous by saying that there is a way of speaking thus, even where
there is only one person."—Luther (Th. i. p. 19). Not only consul-
tations, but compacts take place between the chief persons in the
Trinity, precisely as in human society. "Nihil aliud superest,
quam ut consensum quemdam patris ac filii adeoque quoddam
velut pactum (in relation, namely, to the redemption of men) inde
concludamus."—Buddeus (Comp. l. iv. c. i. § 4, note 2). And as
the essential bond of the Divine Persons is love, the Trinity is the
heavenly type of the closest bond of love—marriage. " Nunc

Filium Dei......precemur, ut spiritu sancto suo, qui nexus est et vinculum mutui amoris inter aeternum patrem ac filium, sponsi et sponsæ pectora conglutinet."—Or. de Conjugio (Declam. Melancth. Th. iii. p. 453).

The distinctions in the Divine essence of the Trinity are natural, physical distinctions. " Jam de proprietatibus personarum videamus ......Et est *proprium solius patris,* non quod non est natus ipse, sed quod *unum filium genuerit,* propriumque solius filii, non quod ipse non genuit, sed quod de *patris essentia natus est."*—Hylarius in l. iii. de Trinitate. " Nos filii Dei sumus, sed non talis hic filius. Hic enim *verus* et *proprius* est filius *origine,* non adoptione, veritate, non nuncupatione, nativitate, non creatione."—Petrus L. (l. i. dist. 26, cc. 2, 4). " Quodsi dum eum aeternum confitemur, profitemur ipsum Filium ex Patre, quomodo is, qui genitus est, genitoris *frater* esse poterit ?......Non enim ex aliquo principio praeexistente Pater et Filius procreati sunt, ut fratres existimari queant, sed Pater principium Filii et genitor est : et Pater Pater est neque ullius Filius fuit, et Filius *Filius est et non frater."*— Athanasius (Contra Arianos. Orat. II. Ed. c. T. i. p. 320). " Qui (Deus) cum in rebus quae nascuntur in tempore, sua bonitate effecerit, ut suae *substantiae prolem quaelibet res gignat, sicut homo gignit hominem,* non alterius naturae, sed ejus cujus ipse est, vide *quam impie dicatur ipse non genuisse id quod ipse est."*—Augustinus (Ep. 170, § 6. ed. Antwp. 1700. " Ut igitur in *natura hominum* filium dicimus genitum de substantia patris, similem patri : *ita* secunda persona Filius dicitur, quia de substantia Patris natus est et ejus est imago."—Melancthon (Loci praecipui Theol. Witebergae, 1595, p. 30). " As a corporeal son has his flesh and blood and nature from his father, so also the Son of God, born of the Father, has his divine nature from the Father of Eternity."— Luther (Th. ix. p. 408). H. A. Roel, a theologian of the school of Descartes and Coccejus, had advanced this thesis : " Filium Dei, Secundam Deitatis personam *improprie* dici genitam." This was immediately opposed by his colleague, Camp. Vitringa, who declared it an unheard-of thesis, and maintained : " Generationem Filii Dei ab aeterno *propriissime* enunciari." Other theologians also contended against Roel, and declared : " Generationem in Deo esse maxime veram et propriam."—(Acta Erudit. Supplem. T. i. S. vii. p. 377, etc.). That in the Bible also the *Filius Dei* signifies a real son is unequivocally implied in this passage : " God so loved the world that he gave his only-begotten Son." If the love of God, which this passage insists upon, is to be regarded as a truth, then the Son also must be a truth, and, in plain language, a physical truth. On this lies the emphasis that God gave his own Son for us—in this alone the proof of his great love. Hence the Herrnhut hymn-book correctly apprehends the sense of the Bible when it says of "the Father of our Lord Jesus Christ, who is also our Father : " " His Son is not too dear. No ! he gives him up for me, that he may save me from the eternal fire by his dear blood. Thou hast so loved the world that thy heart consents to give up the Son, thy joy and life, to suffering and death."

God is a threefold being, a trinity of persons, means : God is not only a metaphysical, abstract, spiritual, but a physical being. The central point of the Trinity is the Son, for the Father is Father only through the Son ; but' the mystery of the generation of the Son is the mystery of physical nature. The Son is the need of sensuousness, or of the heart, satisfied in God ; for all wishes of the heart, even the wish for a personal God and for heavenly felicity, are sensuous wishes ;—the heart is essentially materialistic, it contents itself only with an object which is seen and felt. This is especially evident in the conception that the Son, even in the midst of the Divine Trinity, has the human body as an essential, permanent attribute. Ambrosius : "Scriptum est Ephes. i. : Secundum carnem igitur omnia ipsi subjecta traduntur." Chrysostomus : " Christum secundum carnem pater jussit a cunctis angelis adorari." Theodoretus : "Corpus Dominicum surrexit quidem a mortuis, divina glorificata gloria......corpus tamen est et habet, quam prius habuit, circumscriptionem." (See Concordienbuchs-anhang. "Zeugnisse der h. Schrift und Altväter von Christo," and Petrus L. l. iii. dist. 10, cc. 1, 2. See also on this subject Luther, Th. xix. pp. 464-468.)' In accordance with this the United Brethren say : "I will ever embrace thee in love and faith, until, when at length my lips are pale in death, I shall see thee bodily." "Thy eyes, thy mouth, the body wounded for us, on which we so firmly rely,—all that I shall behold."

Hence the Son of God is the darling of the human heart, the bridegroom of the soul, the object of a formal, personal love. "O Domine Jesu, si adeo sunt *dulces istae lachrymae,* quae ex *memoria et desiderio* tui excitantur, quam dulce erit gaudium,. quod ex *manifesta tui visione* capietur ? Si adeo dulce est *flere pro te,* quam dulce erit *gaudere de te.* Sed quid hujusmodi secreta colloquia proferimus in publicum ? Cur ineffabiles et innarrabiles affectus communibus verbis conamur exprimere ? *Inexperti* talia non intelligunt. *Zelotypus* est sponsus iste......*Delicatus* est sponsus iste." —Scala Claustralium (sive de modo orandi. Among the spurious writings of St. Bernard). "Luge propter amorem Jesu Christi, sponsi tui, quosque eum *videre* possis."—(De modo bene vivendi. Sermo x. id.) "*Adspectum Christi,* qui adhuc inadspectabilis et absens amorem nostrum meruit et exercuit, frequentius scripturae commemorant. Joh. xiv. 3 ; 1 Joh. iii. 1 ; 1 Pet. i. 8 ; 1 Thess. iv. 17. Ac quis non jucundum credat videre *corpus illud,* cujus velut instrumento usus est filius Dei ad expianda peccata, et absentem tandem *amicum* salutare ?"—Doederlein (Inst. Theol. Chr. l. ii. P. ii. C. ii. Sect. ii. § 302. Obs. 3). "Quod *oculis corporis* Christum visuri simus, dubio caret."—J. Fr. Buddeus (Comp. Inst. Theol. Dogm. l. ii. c. iii. § 10).

The distinction between God *with* the Son, or the sensuous God, and God *without* the Son, or God divested of sensuousness, is nothing further than the distinction between the mystical and the rational man. The rational man *lives* and *thinks;* with him life is the complement of thought, and thought the complement of life, both theoretically, inasmuch as he convinces himself of the reality of sensuousness through the reason itself, and practically, inasmuch as he combines activity of life with activity of thought. That which I have in life, I do not need to posit beyond life, in spirit, in metaphysical existence, in God ; love, friendship, perception, the world in general, give me what thought does not, cannot give me, nor ought to give me. Therefore I dismiss the needs of the heart from the sphere of thought, that reason may not be clouded by desires ;—in the demarcation of activities consists the wisdom of life and thought ;—I do not need a God who supplies by a mystical, imaginary physicalness or sensuousness the absence of the real. My heart is satisfied before I enter into intellectual activity ; hence my thought is cold, indifferent, abstract, *i.e.*, free, in relation to the heart, which oversteps its limits, and improperly mixes itself with the affairs of the reason. Thus I do not think in order to satisfy my heart, but to satisfy my reason, which is not satisfied by the heart ; I think only in the interest of reason, from pure desire of knowledge, I seek in God only the contentment of the pure, unmixed intelligence. Necessarily, therefore, the God of the rational thinker is another than the God of the heart, which in thought, in reason, only seeks its own satisfaction. And this is the aim of the mystic, who cannot endure the luminous fire of discriminating and limiting criticism ; for his mind is always beclouded by the vapours which rise from the unextinguished ardour of his feelings. He never attains to abstract, *i.e.*, disinterested, free thought, and for that reason he never attains to the perception of things in their naturalness, truth, and reality.

One more remark concerning the Trinity.· The older theologians said that the essential attributes of God as God were made manifest by the light of natural reason. But how is it that reason can know the Divine Being, unless it be because the Divine Being is nothing else than the objective nature of the intelligence itself? Of the Trinity, on the other hand, they said that it could only be known through revelation, Why not through reason ; because it contradicts reason, *i.e.*, because it does not express a want of the reason, but a sensuous, emotional want. In general, the proposition that an idea springs from revelation means no more than that it has come to us by the way of tradition. The dogmas of religion have arisen at certain times out of definite wants, under definite relations and conceptions ; for this reason, to the men of a later time, in which these relations, wants, conceptions, have disappeared, they are something unintelligible, incomprehensible, only traditional, *i.e.*, revealed. The antithesis of revelation and reason reduces itself only to the antithesis of history and reason, only to this, that mankind at a given time is no longer capable of that which at another time it was quite capable of ; just as the individual man does not unfold his powers at all times indifferently, but only in moments of special appeal from without or incitement from within. Thus the works of genius arise only under altogether special inward and outward conditions which cannot thus coincide more than once ; they are ἅπαξ λεγόμενα. "Einmal ist alles wahre nur." The true is born but once. Hence a man's own works often appear to him in later years quite strange and incomprehensible. He no longer knows how he produced them or could produce them, *i.e.*, he can no longer explain them out of himself, still less reproduce them: And just as it would be folly if, in riper years, because the productions of our youth have become strange and inexplicable to us in their tenor and origin, we were to refer them to a special inspiration from above ; so it is folly, because the doctrines and ideas of a past age are no longer recognised by the reason of a subsequent age. to claim for them a supra- and extra-human, *i.e.*, an imaginary, illusory origin.

§ 9.

The creation out of nothing expresses the non-divineness, nonessentiality, i.e., *the nothingness of the world.*

That is *created* which once did not exist, which some time will exist no longer, to which, therefore, it is possible not to exist, which we can think of as not existing, in a word, which has not its existence in itself, is not necessary. " Cum enim res producantur ex suo non-esse, possunt ergo absolute non-esse, adeoque implicat, quod non sunt necessariæ."—Duns Scotus (ap. Rixner, B. ii. p. 78). But only necessary existence is existence. If I am not necessary, do not feel myself necessary, I feel that it is all one whether I exist or not, that thus my existence is worthless, nothing. " I am nothing," and " I am not necessary," is fundamentally the same thing. " Creatio non est motus, sed simplicis divinae voluntatis vocatio ad esse eorum, quae *antea nihil fuerunt et secundum se ipsa et nihil sunt et ex nihilo sunt.*"—Albertus M. (de. Mirab. Scient. Dei P. ii. Tr. i. Qu. 4, Art. 5, memb. ii.) But the position that the world is not necessary, has no other bearing than to prove that the extra- and supra-mundane being (*i.e.*, in fact, the human being) is the only necessary, only real being. Since the one is nonessential and temporal, the other is necessarily the essential, existent, eternal. The creation is the proof that God is, that he is exclusively true and real. "Sanctus Dominus Deus omnipotens in principio, quod est in te, in sapientia tua, quae nata est de substantia tua, fecisti aliquid et de nihilo. Fecisti enim coelum et terram *non de te*, nam *esset aequale* unigenito tuo, ac per hoc et tibi, et *nullo modo justum esset*, ut *aequale tibi esset, quod in te non esset.* Et aliud praeter te non erat, unde faceres ea Deus......Et ideo *de nihilo* fecisti coelum et terram."—Augustinus (Confessionum l. xii. c. 7). " *Vere enim ipse est*, quia *incommutabilis* est. Omnis enim mutatio facit non esse quod erat......Ei ergo qui summe est, non potest esse *contrarium nisi quod non est.*—Si solus ipse incommutabilis, omnia quae fecit, *quia ex nihilo* id est *ex eo quod omnino non est*—fecit, mutabilia sunt."—Augustin (de nat. boni adv. Manich. cc. 1, 19). " Creatura *in nullo debet parificari* Deo, si autem non habuisset *initium durationis* et *esse*, in hoc *parificaretur* Deo."— (Albertus M. l. c. Quaest. incidens 1). The positive, the essential in the world is not that which makes it a world, which distinguishes it from God—this is precisely its finiteness and nothingness—but rather that in it which is not itself, which is God. "All creatures are a pure nothing......they have no essential existence, for their existence hangs on the presence of God. If God turned himself away a moment, they would fall to nothing."—(Predigten vor. u. zu. Tauleri Zeiten, ed. c. p. 29. See also Augustine, *e.g.* Confess. l. vii. c. 11). This is quite correctly said from the standpoint of religion, for God is the principle of existence, the being of the world, though he is represented as a personal being distinct from the world. The world lasts so long as God wills. The world is transient, but man eternal. "*Quamdiu vult,* omnia ejus virtute manent atque consistunt, et *finis* eorum in *Dei voluntatem* recurrit, et *ejus arbitrio* resolvuntur."—Ambrosius (Hexaemeron. l. i. c. 5). "*Spiritus* enim a Deo creati *nunquam esse desinunt......Corpora coelestia* tam diu conservantur, quamdiu *Deus ea vult permanere.*" —Buddeus (Comp. l. ii. c. ii. § 47). "The dear God does not alone create, but what he creates he keeps with his own being, until he wills that it shall be no longer. For the time will come when the sun, moon, and stars shall be no more."—Luther (Th. ix. s. 418). "The end will come sooner than we think."—Id. (Th. xi. s. 536). By means of the creation out of nothing man gives himself the certainty that the world is nothing, is powerless against man. "We have a Lord who is greater than the whole world ; we have a Lord so powerful, that when he only speaks all things are born ......Wherefore should we fear, since he is favourable to us ?"—Id. (Th. vi. p. 293). Identical with the belief in the creation out of nothing is the belief in the eternal life of man, in the victory over death, the last constraint which nature imposes on man—in the resurrection of the dead. "Six thousand years ago the world was nothing ; and who has made the world ?......The same God and Creator can also awake thee from the dead ; he will do it, and can do it."—Id. (Th. xi. p. 426. See also 421, &c.) "We Christians are greater and more than all creatures, not in or by ourselves, but through the gift of God in Christ, against whom the world is nothing, and can do nothing."—Id. (Th. xi. p. 377).

§ 10.

The Creation in the Israelitish religion has only a particular, egoistic aim and purport. The Israelitish religion is the religion of the most narrow-hearted egoism. Even the later Israelites, scattered throughout the world, persecuted and oppressed, adhered with immovable firmness to the egoistic faith of their forefathers. "Every Israelitish soul by itself is, in the eyes of the blessed God, dearer and more precious than all the souls of a whole nation besides." "The Israelites are among the nations what the heart is among the members." "The end in the creation of the world was Israel alone. The world was created for the sake of the Israelites ; they are the fruit, other nations are their husks." "All the heathens are nothing for him (God) ; but for the Israelites God has a use......They adore and bless the name of the holy and blessed God every day, therefore they are numbered every hour, and made as (numerous as) the grains of corn." "If the Israelites were not, there would fall no rain on the world, and the sun would not rise but for their sakes." "He (God) is our kinsman, and we are his kindred......No power or angel is akin to us, for the Lord's portion is his people" (Deut. xxxii. 9). "He who rises up against an Israelite (to injure him), does the same thing as if he rose up against God." "If any one smite an Israelite on the cheek, it is the same as if he smote the cheek of the divine majesty."—Eisenmengers (Entdecktes Judenthum, T. i. Kap. 14). The Christians blamed the Jews for this arrogance, but only because the kingdom of God was taken from them and transferred to the Christians. Accordingly, we find the same thoughts and sentiments in the Christians as in the Israelites. "Know that God so takes thee unto himself that thy enemies are his enemies."—Luther (T. vi. p. 99). "It is the Christians for whose sake God spares the whole world......The Father makes his sun to rise on the evil and on the good, and sends rain on the just and on the unjust. Yet this happens only for the sake of the pious and thankful." (T. xvi. p. 506.) "He who despises me despises God." (T. xi. p. 538.) "God suffers, and is despised and persecuted, in us." (T. iv. p. 577.) Such declarations as these are, I should think, *argumenta ad hominem* for the identity of God and man.

§ 11.

The idea of Providence is the religious consciousness of man's distinction from the brutes, from Nature in general. "Doth God take care for oxen?" (1 Cor. ix. 9.) "Nunquid curae est Deo bobus? inquit Paulus. Ad *nos* ea cura dirigitur, *non ad boves, equos, asinos,* qui in *usum nostrum sunt conditi.*"—J. L. Vivis Val. (de Veritate Fidei Chr. Bas. 1544, p. 108). "Providentia Dei in omnibus aliis creaturis respicit *ad hominem* tanquam *ad metam suam.* Multis passeribus vos pluris estis. Matth. x. 31. Propter *peccatum hominis natura* subjecta est vanitati. Rom. viii. 20."—M. Chemnitii (Loci theol. Francof. 1608, P. i. p. 312). "Nunquid enim cura est Deo de bobus? Et sicut non est cura Deo de bobus, ita nec de aliis irrationalibus. Dicit *tamen scriptura* (Sapient. vi.) quia ipsi cura est de omnibus. Providentiam ergo et curam universaliter de cunctis, quae condidit, habet......Sed *specialem* providentiam atque curam habet de rationalibus."—Petrus L. (l. i. dist. 39, c. 3). Here we have again an example how Christian sophistry is a product of Christian faith, especially of faith in the Bible as the word of God. First we read that God cares not for oxen; then that God cares for everything, and therefore for oxen. That is a contradiction; but the word of God must not contradict itself. How does faith escape from this contradiction? By distinguishing between a general and a special providence. But *general* providence is illusory, is in truth no providence. Only special providence is providence in the sense of religion.

General providence—the providence which extends itself equally to irrational and rational beings, which makes no distinction between man and the lilies of the field or the fowls of the air, is nothing else than the idea of Nature—an idea which man may have without religion. The religious consciousness admits this when it says: he who denies providence abolishes religion, places man on a level with the brutes;—thus declaring that the providence in which the brutes have a share is in truth no providence. Providence partakes of the character of its object; hence the providence which has plants and animals for its object is in accordance with the qualities and relations of plants and animals. Providence is nothing else than the inward nature of a thing; this inward nature is its genius, its guardian spirit—the necessity of its existence. The higher, the more precious a being is,—the more ground of existence it has, the more necessary it is, the less is it open to annihilation. Every being is necessary only through that by which it is distinguished from other beings; its specific difference is the ground of its existence. So man is necessary only through that by which he is distinguished from the brutes; hence providence is nothing else than man's consciousness of the necessity of his existence, of the distinction between his nature and that of other beings; consequently that alone is the true providence in which this specific difference of man becomes an object to him. But this providence is special, *i.e.*, the providence of love, for only love interests itself in what is special to a being. Providence without love is a conception without basis, without reality. The truth of providence is love. God loves men, not brutes, not plants; for only for man's sake does he perform extraordinary deeds, deeds of love—miracles. Where there is no community there is no love. But what bond can be supposed to unite brutes, or natural things in general, with God? God does not recognise himself in them, for they do not recognise him;—where I find nothing of myself, how can I love? "God who thus promises, does not speak with asses and oxen, as Paul says: Doth God take care for oxen? but with rational creatures made in his likeness, that they may live for ever with him." Luther (Th. ii. s. 156). God is first with himself in man; in man first begins religion, providence; for the latter is not something different from the former, on the contrary, religion is itself the providence of man. He who loses religion, *i.e.*, faith in himself, faith in man, in the infinite significance of his being, in the necessity of his existence, loses providence. He alone is forsaken who forsakes himself; he alone is lost who despairs; he alone is without God who is without faith, *i.e.*, without courage. Wherein does religion place the true proof of providence? in the phenomena of Nature, as they are objects to us out of religion,—in astronomy, in physics, in natural history? No! In those appearances which are objects of religion, of faith only, which express only the faith of religion in itself, *i.e.*, in the truth and reality of man,—in the religious events, means, and institutions which God has ordained exclusively for the salvation of man, in a word, in miracles; for the means of grace, the sacraments, belong to the class of providential miracles. "Quamquam autem haec consideratio universae naturae nos admonet de Deo......tamen nos referamus initio mentem et oculos ad *omnia testimonia, in quibus se Deus ecclesiae patefecit ad eductionem ex Aegypto, ad vocem sonantem in Sinai, ad Christum resuscitantem mortuos et resuscitatum,* etc.......Ideo semper defixae sint mentes in *horum testimoniorum cogitationem* et his *confirmatae* articulum *de Creatione* meditentur, *deinde considerent* etiam vestigia Dei impressae *naturae.*"—Melancthon (Loci de Creat. p. 62, ed. cit.). "Mirentur alii creationem, *mihi magis libet mirari redemptionem.* Mirabile est, quod caro nostra et ossa nostra a Deo nobis sunt formata, *mirabilius* adhuc est, quod *ipse Deus caro de carne nostra* et os de ossibus nostris fieri voluit."—J. Gerhard (Med. s. M. 15). "The heathens know God no further than that he is a Creator."—Luther (T. ii. p. 327). That providence has only man for its essential object is evident from this, that to religious faith all things and beings are created for the sake of man. "We are lords not only of birds, but of all living creatures, and all things are given for our service, and are created only for our sake."—Luther (T. ix. p. 281). But if things are created only for the sake of man, they are also preserved only for the sake of man. And if things are mere instruments of man, they stand under the protection of no law, they are, in relation to man, *without rights.* This outlawing of things explains miracle.

The negation of providence is the negation of God. "Qui ergo providentiam tollit, totam Dei substantiam tollit et quid dicit nisi Deum non esse ?......Si non curat humana, sive nesciens, cessat omnis causa pietatis, cum sit *spes nulla salutis.*"—Joa. Trithemius (Tract. de Provid. Dei). "Nam qui nihil aspici a Deo affirmant prope est ut cui adspectum adimunt, etiam substantiam tollant." —Salvianus (l. c. l. iv.). "Aristotle almost falls into the opinion that God—though he does not expressly name him a fool—is such a one that he knows nothing of our affairs, nothing of our designs, understands, sees, regards nothing but himself.......But what is such a God or Lord to us ? of what use is he to us ?"—Luther (in Walch's Philos. Lexikon, art. Vorsehung). Providence is therefore the most undeniable, striking proof that in religion, in the nature of God himself, man is occupied only with himself, that the mystery of theology is anthropology, that the substance, the content of the infinite being, is the " finite " being. " God sees men," means : in God man sees only himself ; " God cares for man," means : a God who is not active is no real God. But there is no activity without an object: it is the object which first converts activity from a mere power into real activity. This object is man. If man did not exist, God would have no cause for activity. Thus man is the motive principle, the soul of God. A God who does not see and hear man, who has not man *in himself,* is blind and deaf, *i.e.,* inert, empty, unsubstantial. Thus the fulness of the divine nature is the fulness of the human; thus the *Godhead* of God is *humanity. I for myself,* is the comfortless mystery of epicureanism, stoicism, pantheism ; *God for me,* this is the consolatory mystery of religion, of Christianity. Is man for God's sake, or God for man's ? It is true that in religion man exists for God's sake, but only because God exists for man's sake. I am for God because God is for me.

Providence is identical with miraculous power, supernaturalistic freedom from Nature, the dominion of arbitrariness over law. "Etsi (sc. Deus) sustentat naturam, tamen *contra ordinem* jussit aliquando Solem regredi, etc.......Ut igitur invocatio vere fieri possit, cogitemus Deum sic adesse suo opificio, non, ut Stoici fingunt, *alligatum secundis causis,* sed sustentantem naturam et multa suo *liberrimo consilio* moderantem.......Multa facit prima causa *praeter secundas, quia est agens liberum.*"—Melancthon (Loci de Causâ Peccati, pp. 82, 83, ed. cit.) "Scriptura vero tradit, Deum in actione providentiae esse *agens liberum,* qui ut plurimum quidem ordinem sui operis servet, illi tamen *ordini non sit alligatus,* sed 1) quicquid facit per causas secundas, illud possit etiam *sine illis* per se solum facere 2) quod ex causis secundis possit *alium effectum* producere, quam ipsarum *dispositio* et *natura* ferat 3) quod positis ausis secundis in actu, Deus tamen *effectum* possit *impedire, mutare,* mitigare, exasperare.......Non igitur est *connexio causarum Stoica* in actionibus providentiae Dei."—M. Chemnitius (l. c. pp. 316, 317). "*Liberrime Deus imperat naturae*—Naturam saluti hominum attemperat propter Ecclesiam.......Omnino tribuendus est Deo hic honos, quod possit et velit opitulari nobis, etiam cum a tota natura destituimur, *contra seriem* omnium secundarum causarum. ......Et multa accidunt plurimis hominibus, in quibus mirandi eventus fateri eos cogunt, se a *Deo sine causis secundis* servatos esse."— C. Peucerus (de Praecip. Divinat. gen. Servestae, 1591, p. 44). "Ille tamen qui omnium est conditor, nullis instrumentis indiget. Nam si id continuo fit, quicquid ipse vult, velle illius erit author atque instrumentum ; nec magis ad haec regenda astris indiget, quam cum luto aperuit oculos coeci, sicut refert historia Evangelica. Lutum enim magis videbatur obturaturum oculos, quam aperturum. Sed ipse ostendere nobis voluit *omnem naturam esse sibi instrumentum ad quidvis, quantumcunque alienum.*"—J. L. Vives (l. c. 102). "How is this to be reconciled? The air gives food and nourishment, and here stones or rocks flow with water ; it is a marvellous gift. And it is also strange and marvellous that corn grows out of the earth. Who has this art and this power? God has it, who can do such *unnatural* things, that we may thence imagine what sort of a God he is and what sort of power he has, that we may not be terrified at him nor despair, but firmly believe and trust him, that he can make the leather in the pocket into gold, and can make dust into corn on the earth, and the air a cellar for me full of wine. He is to be trusted, as having such great power, and we may know that we have a God who can perform these deeds of skill, and that around him it rains and snows with miraculous works."—Luther (T. iii. p. 594).

The omnipotence of Providence is the omnipotence of human feeling releasing itself from all conditions and laws of Nature. This omnipotence is realised by prayer. Prayer is Almighty. "The prayer of faith shall save the sick.......The effectual fervent prayer of a righteous man availeth much. Elias was a man subject to like passions as we are, and he prayed earnestly that it might not rain ; and it rained not on the earth by the space of three years and six months. And he prayed again, and the heavens gave rain and the earth brought forth her fruit."—James v. 15–18. "If ye have faith and doubt not, ye shall not only do this which is done to the fig-tree, but also if ye shall say unto this mountain, Be thou removed and be thou cast into the sea, it shall be done, and all things whatsoever ye shall ask in prayer, believing, ye shall receive."—Matt. xxi. 21, 22. That under this mountain which the power of faith is to overcome are to be understood not only very difficult things— *res difficillimae,* as the exegetists say, who explain this passage as a proverbial, hyperbolical mode of speech among the Jews, but rather things which according to Nature and reason are impossible, is proved by the case of the instantaneously withered fig-tree, to which the passage in question refers. Here indubitably is declared the omnipotence of prayer, of faith, before which the power of Nature vanishes into nothing. "Mutantur quoque *ad preces* ea quae ex *naturae causis* erant sequutura, quemadmodum in Ezechia contigit, rege Juda, cui, quod naturales causarum progressus mortem minabantur, dictum est a propheta Dei : Morieris et non vives ; sed is *decursus naturae ad regis preces mutatus est* et mutaturum se Deus praeviderat."—J. L. Vives (l. c. p. 132). "Saepe fatorum saevitiam lenit Deus, placatus piorum votis."—Melancthon (Epist. Sim. Grynaeo). "*Cedit natura rerum precibus* Moysi, Eliae, Elisaei, Jesaiae et omnium piorum, sicut Christus inquit Matt. 21 : Omnia quae petetis, credentes accipietis."—Id. (Loci de Creat. p. 64, ed. cit.). Celsus calls on the Christians to aid the Emperor and not to decline military service. Whereupon Origen answers : "*Precibus nostris* profligantes omnes bellorum excitatores daemonas et perturbatores pacis ac foederum plus conferimus regibus, quam qui arma gestant pro Republica."—Origenes (adv. Celsum. S. Glenio int. l. viii.). Human need is the necessity of the Divine Will. In prayer man is the active, the determining, God the passive, the determined. God does the will of man. "God does the will of those that fear him, and he gives his will up to ours.......For the text says clearly enough, that Lot was not to stay in all the plain, but to escape to the mountain. But this his wish God changes, because Lot fears him and prays to him." "And we have other testimonies in the Scriptures which prove that God allows himself to be turned and subjects his will to our wish." "Thus it was according to the regular order of God's power that the sun should maintain its revolution and wonted course ; but when Joshua in his need called on the Lord and commanded the sun that it should stand still, it stood still at Joshua's word. How great a miracle this was, ask the astronomers."—Luther (T. ii. p. 226). "Lord, I am here and there in great need and danger of body and soul, and therefore want thy help and comfort. Item : I must have this and that ; therefore I entreat thee that thou give it me." "He who so prays and perseveres unabashed does right, and our Lord God is well pleased with him, for he is not so squeamish as we men."—Id. (T. xvi. p. 150).

§ 12.

*Faith is the freedom and blessedness which feeling finds in it-
self. Feeling objective to itself and active in this freedom, the
reaction of feeling against Nature, is the arbitrariness of the
imagination. The objects of faith therefore necessarily contradict
Nature, necessarily contradict Reason, as that which represents the
nature of things.* " Quid magis contra fidem, quam credere nolle,
quidquid non possit ratione attingere ?......Nam illam quae in
Deum est fides, beatus papa Gregorius negat plane habere meritum,
si ei humana ratio praebeat experimentum."—Bernardus (contr.
Abelard. Ep. ad. Dom. Papam Innocentium). " *Partus virginis* nec
ratione colligitur, nec exemplo monstratur. Quodsi *ratione colligitur*
non erit *mirabile.*"--Conc. Toletan. XI. Art. IV. (Summa. Carranza.)
" Quid autem incredibile, si *contra usum originis naturalis* peperit
Maria et virgo permanet : quando contra usum naturae mare vidit
et fugit atque in fontem suum Jordanis fluenta remearunt ?   Non
ergo excedit fidem, quod virgo peperit, quando legimus, quod petra
vomuit aquas et in montis speciem maris unda solidata est.   Non
ergo excedit fidem, quod homo exivit de virgine, quando petra pro-
fluit, scaturivit ferrum supra aquas, ambulavit homo supra aquas."
—Ambrosius (Epist. L. x. Ep. 81. edit. Basil. Amerbach. 1492 et
1516). " Mira sunt fratres, quae de isto sacramento dicuntur......
Haec sunt quae fidem necessario exigunt, rationem omnino non
admittunt."—Bernardus (de Coena Dom.).   " Quid ergo hic quaeris
naturae ordinem in Christi corpore, cum *praeter naturam* sit ipse
partus ex virgine."—Petrus Lomb. (l. iv. dist. 10, c. 2).   " Laus
fidei est credere quod est supra rationem, ubi homo *abnegat intel-
lectum* et *omnes sensus.*" (Addit. Henrici de Vurimaria. ibid. dist.
12, c. 5.)   " All the articles of our faith appear foolish and ridiculous
to reason.".......We Christians seem fools to the world for believing
that Mary was the true mother of this child, and was nevertheless a
pure virgin.   For this is not only against all reason. but also against
the creation of God, who said to Adam and Eve, " Be fruitful and
multiply."   " We ought not to inquire whether a thing be possible,
but we should say, God has said it, therefore it will happen, even if
it be impossible.   For although I cannot see or understand it, yet
the Lord can make the impossible possible, and out of nothing can
make all things."—Luther (T. xvi. pp. 148, 149, 570).   " What is
more miraculous than that God and man is one Person ? that he is
the Son of God and the Son of Mary, and yet only one Son ?   Who
will comprehend this mystery in all eternity, that God is man, that
a creature is the Creator, and the Creator a creature ?"—Id. (T. vii.
p. 128).   The essential object of. faith, therefore, is miracle ; but
not common, visible miracle, which is an object even to the bold
eye of curiosity and unbelief in general ; not the appearance, but
the essence of miracle ; not the *fact*, but the miraculous *power*, the
Being who works miracles, who attests and reveals himself in
miracle.   And this miraculous power is to faith always present ;
even Protestantism believes in the uninterrupted perpetuation of
miraculous power ; it only denies the necessity that it should still

manifest itself in special visible signs, for the furtherance of dogmatic ends. "Some have said that signs were the revelation of the
Spirit in the commencement of Christianity and have now ceased.
That is not correct ; for there is even now such a power, and though
it is not used, that is of no importance. For we have still the power
to perform such signs." "Now, however, that Christianity is spread
abroad and made known to all the world, there is no need to work
miracles, as in the times of the apostles. But if there were need for
it, if the Gospel were oppressed and persecuted, we must truly apply
ourselves to this, and must also work miracles."—Luther (Th. xiii.
pp. 642, 648). Miracle is so essential, so natural to faith, that
to it even natural phenomena are miracles, and not in the physical
sense, but in the theological, supranaturalistic sense. "God, in the
beginning, said : Let the earth bring forth grass and herbs, &c.
That same word which the Creator spoke brings the cherry out of
the dry bough and the cherry-tree out of the little kernel. It is the
omnipotence of God which makes young fowls and geese come out
of the eggs. Thus God preaches to us daily of the resurrection of
the dead, and has given us as many examples and experiences of
this article as there are creatures."—Luther (Th. x. p. 432. See also
Th. iii. pp. 586, 592, and Augustine, *e.g.*, Enarr. in Ps. 90, Sermo
ii. c. 6). If, therefore, faith desires and needs no special miracle,
this is only because to it everything is fundamentally miracle,
everything an effect of divine, miraculous power. Religious faith
has no sense, no perception for Nature. Nature, as it exists for us,
has no existence for faith. To it the will of God is alone the
ground, the bond, the necessity of things. "God......could indeed
have made us men, as he did Adam and Eve, by himself, without
father and mother, as he could reign without princes, as he could
give light without sun and stars, and bread without fields and
ploughs and labour. But it is not his will to do thus."—Luther
(Th. xvi. p. 614). It is true "God employs certain means, and so
conducts his miraculous works as to use the service of Nature and
instruments." Therefore we ought—truly on very natural grounds
—"not to despise the means and instruments of Nature." "Thus
it is allowable to use medicine, nay, it ought to be used, for it is a
means created in order to preserve health."—Luther (Th. i. p. 508)
But—and that alone is decisive—it is *not necessary* that I should
use natural means in order to be cured ; I can be cured immediately by God. What God ordinarily does by means of Nature,
he can also do without, nay, in opposition to Nature, and actually
does it thus, in extraordinary cases, when he will. "God," says
Luther in the same place, "could indeed easily have preserved
Noah and the animals through a whole year without food, as he
preserved Moses, Elijah, and Christ forty days without any food."
Whether he does it often or seldom is indifferent ; it is enough if
he only does it once ; what happens once can happen innumerable
times. A single miracle has universal significance—the significance of an example. "This deed, the passage through the Red
Sea, happened as a figure and example, to show us that it will be
so with us."—Luther (Th. iii. p. 596). "These miracles are written

for us, who are chosen."—Ib. (Th. ix. p. 142). The natural means which God employs when he does no miracle, have no more significance than those which he employs when he performs miracles. If the animals, God so willing it, can live as well without food as with it, food is in itself as unnecessary for the preservation of life, as indifferent, as non-essential, as arbitrary, as the clay with which Christ anointed the eyes of the blind man to whom he restored sight, as the staff with which Moses divided the sea ("God could have done it just as well without the staff"). "Faith is stronger than heaven and earth, or all creatures." "Faith turns water into stones; out of fire it can bring water, and out of water fire."— Luther (Th. iii. pp. 564, 565). That is to say, for faith there exists no limit, no law, no necessity, no Nature; there exists only the will of God, against which all things and powers are nothing. If therefore the believer, when in sickness and distress, has recourse notwithstanding to natural means, he only follows the voice of his natural reason. The one means of cure which is congruous with faith, which does not contradict faith, which is not thrust upon it, whether consciously and voluntarily or not, from without,—the one remedy for all evil and misery is prayer; for "prayer is almighty." —Luther (Th. iv. p. 27). Why then use a natural means also? For even in case of its application, the effect which follows is by no means its own, but the effect of the supernatural will of God, or rather the effect of faith, of prayer; for prayer, faith determines the will of God. "Thy faith hath saved thee." Thus the natural means which faith recognises in practice it nullifies in theory, since it makes the effect of such means an effect of God,—*i.e.*, an effect which could have taken place just as well without this means. The natural effect is therefore nothing else than a circumstantial, covert, concealed miracle; a miracle however which has not the appearance of a miracle, but can only be perceived as such by the eyes of faith. Only in expression, not in fact, is there any difference between an immediate and mediate, a miraculous and natural operation of God. When faith makes use of a natural means, *it speaks otherwise than it thinks;* when it supposes a miracle *it speaks as it thinks,* but in both cases it thinks the same. In the mediate agency of God faith is in disunion with itself, for the senses here deny what faith affirms; in miracle, on the contrary, it is at one with itself, for there the appearance coincides with the reality, the senses with faith, the expression with the fact. Miracle is the *terminus technicus* of faith.

§ 13.

The Resurrection of Christ is bodily, i.e., personal immortality, presented as a sensible indubitable fact.

"Resurrexit Christus, *absoluta res* est.—Ostendit se ipsum discipulis et fidelibus suis: *contrectata* est soliditas corporis...... *Confirmata* fides est non solum in cordibus, sed etiam in *oculis* hominum."—Augustinus (Sermones ad Pop. S. 242, c. 1, S. 361, c. 8. See also on this subject Melancthon, Loci: de Resurr. Mort.).

" The philosophers......held that by death the soul was released
from the body, and that after it was thus set free from the body, as
from a prison, it came into the assembly of the gods, and was
relieved from all corporeal burthens. Of such an immortality the
philosophers allowed men to dream, though they did not hold it
to be certain, nor could defend it. But the Holy Scriptures teach
of the resurrection and eternal life in another manner, and place
the hope of it so certainly before our eyes, that we cannot doubt
it."—Luther (Th. i. p. 549).

§ 14.

Christianity made man an extramundane, supernatural being.
" We have here no abiding city, but we seek one to come."—Heb.
xiii. 14. " Whilst we are at home in the body, we are absent from
the Lord."—2 Cor. v. 6. " If in this body, which is properly our
own, we are strangers, and our life in this body is nothing else
than a pilgrimage ; how much more then are the possessions which
we have for the sake of the body, such as fields, houses, gold, &c.,
nothing else than idle, strange things, to be used as if we were on a
pilgrimage ? " " Therefore we must in this life live like strangers
until we reach the true fatherland, and receive a better life which
is eternal."—Luther (Th. ii. pp. 240, 370 a). " Our conversation
(πολίτευμα, *civitas aut jus civitatis*) is in heaven, from whence also
we look for the Saviour, the Lord Jesus Christ, who shall change
our vile body that it may be like unto his glorious body, according
to the working whereby he is able even to subdue all things unto
himself."—Phil. iii. 20, 21. "*Neque mundus generat hominem, neque
mundi homo pars est.*"—Lactantius (Div. Inst. l. ii. c. 6). " Coelum
de mundo : *homo supra mundum.*"—Ambrosius (Epist. l. vi. Ep.
38, ed. cit.). " Agnosce o homo dignitatem tuam, agnosce gloriam
conditionis humanae. Est enim tibi *cum mundo corpus*......sed
est tibi etiam sublimius aliquid, *nec omnino comparandus es
caeteris creaturis.*"—Bernardus (Opp. Basil. 1552, p. 79). " At
Christianus......ita supra totum mundum ascendit, nec consistit
in coeli convexis, sed transcensis mente locis supercoelestibus ductu
divini spiritus velut jam *extra mundum raptus* offert Deo preces."
—Origenes (contra Celsum. ed. Hoeschelio, p. 370). "*Totus quidem
iste mundus ad unius animae pretium aestimari non potest.* Non
enim *pro toto mundo* Deus animam suam dare voluit, quam *pro
anima humana* dedit. Sublimius est ergo animae pretium, quae
non nisi *sanguine Christi* redimi potest."—Medit. devotiss. c. ii.
(Among the spurious writings of St. Bernard.) " Sapiens anima
......Deum tantummodo sapiens hominem in homine exuit, Deoque
plene et in omnibus affecta, *omnem infra Deum creaturam* non
aliter quam Deus attendit. Relicto ergo corpore et corporeis omnibus curis et impedimentis omnium quae sunt praeter Deum oblivis-
citur, nihilque praeter Deum attendens quasi *se solam, solumque
Deum* existimans," etc.—De Nat. et Dign. Amoris Divini, cc. 14, 15.
(Ib.) " Quid agis frater in saeculo, qui major es mundo ? "—Hieronymus (ad Heliod. de Laude Vitae solit.).

§ 15.

The celibate and monachism—of course only in their original, religious significance and form—are sensible manifestations, necessary consequences, of the supranaturalistic, extramundane character of Christianity. It is true that they also contradict Christianity; the reason of this is shown by implication in the present work, but only because Christianity is itself a contradiction. They contradict exoteric, practical, but not esoteric, theoretical Christianity; they contradict Christian love so far as this love relates to man, but not Christian faith, not Christian love so far as it loves man only for God's sake. There is certainly nothing concerning celibacy and monachism in the Bible; and that is very natural. In the beginning of Christianity the great matter was the recognition of Jesus as the Christ, the Messiah—the conversion of the heathens and Jews. And this conversion was the more pressing, the nearer the Christians supposed the day of judgment and the destruction of the world;—*periculum in mora.* There was not time or opportunity for a life of quietude, for the contemplation of monachism. Hence there necessarily reigned at that time a more practical and even liberal sentiment than at a later period, when Christianity had attained to worldly dominion, and thus the enthusiasm of proselytism was extinguished. "Apostoli (says the Church, quite correctly: Carranza, l. c. p. 256) cum *fides inciperet,* ad *fidelium imbecillitatem* se magis demittebant, cum autem evangelii praedicatio sit magis ampliata, oportet et Pontifices ad perfectam continentiam vitam suam dirigere." When once Christianity realised itself in a worldly form, it must also necessarily develop the supranaturalistic, supramundane tendency of Christianity into a literal separation from the world. And this disposition to separation from life, from the body, from the world,—this first hypercosmic then anti-cosmic tendency, is a genuinely biblical disposition and spirit. In addition to the passages already cited, and others universally known, the following may stand as examples: "He that hateth his life in this world shall keep it unto life eternal." "I know that in me, that is, in my flesh, dwelleth no good thing."—Rom. vii. 18. ("Veteres enim omnis vitiositatis in agendo origenes ad *corpus* referebant."—J. G. Rosenmüller Scholia.) "Forasmuch then as Christ hath suffered for us in the flesh, arm yourselves also with the same mind; for he that hath suffered in the flesh hath ceased from sin."—1 Pet. iv. 1. "I have a desire to depart, and to be with Christ."—Phil. i. 23. "We are confident and willing rather to be absent from the body and present with the Lord."—2 Cor. v. 8. Thus, according to these passages, the partition-wall between God and man is the body (at least the fleshly, actual body); thus the body as a hindrance to union with God is something worthless, to be denied. That by the world, which is denied in Christianity, is by no means to be understood a life of mere sensuality, but the real objective world, is to be inferred in a popular manner from the belief that at the advent of the Lord, *i.e.,*

the consummation of the Christian religion, heaven and earth will
pass away.

The difference between the belief of the Christians and that of
the heathen philosophers as to the destruction of the world is not
to be overlooked. The Christian destruction of the world is only a
crisis of faith,—the separation of the Christian from all that is antichristian, the triumph of faith over the world, a judgment of God,
an anti-cosmical, supernaturalistic act. "But the heavens and the
earth which are now, by the same word are kept in store, reserved
unto fire against the day of judgment and perdition of ungodly
men."—2 Pet. iii. 7. The heathen destruction of the world is a
crisis of the cosmos itself, a process which takes place according to
law, which is founded in the constitution of Nature. "Sic origo
mundi, non minus solem et lunam et vices siderum et animalium
ortus, quam quibus mutarentur terrena, continuit. In his fuit
inundatio, quae non secus quam hiems, quam aestas, *lege mundi*
venit."—Seneca (Nat. Qu. l. iii. c. 29). It is the principle of life
immanent in the world, the essence of the world itself, which evolves
this crisis out of itself. "*Aqua et ignis* terrenis dominantur. *Ex
his ortus* et *ex his interitus est.*"—(Ibid. c. 28.) "Quidquid est, non
erit; nec peribit, sed resolvetur."—(Idem. Epist. 71.) The Christians
excluded themselves from the destruction of the world. "And he
shall send his angels with a great sound of a trumpet ; and they
shall gather together his elect from the four winds, from one end of
heaven to the other."—Matt. xxiv. 31. "But there shall not a hair
of your head perish......And then shall they see the Son of Man
coming in a cloud with power and great glory. And when these
things begin to come to pass, then look up and lift up your heads ;
for your redemption draweth nigh."—Luke xxi. 18, 27, 28. "Watch
ye therefore and pray always, that ye may be accounted worthy to
escape all these things that shall come to pass, and to stand before
the Son of Man."—Ib. 36. The heathens, on the contrary, identified
their fate with the fate of the world. "Hoc universum, quod omnia
divina humanaque complectitur......dies aliquis dissipabit et in
confusionem veterem tenebrasque demerget. *Eat nunc aliquis et
singulas comploret animas.* Quis tam superbae impotentisque arro-
gantiae est, ut in hac naturae necessitate, omnia ad eundem finem
revocantis, *se unum ac suos seponi velit.*"—Seneca (Cons. ad Polyb.
cc. 20, 21). "Ergo quandoque erit terminus rebus humanis......
Non muri quenquam, non turres tuebuntur. *Non proderunt templa
supplicibus.*"—(Nat. Qu. L. iii. c. 29.) Thus here we have again
the characteristic distinction between heathenism and Christianity.
The heathen forgot himself in the world. the Christian forgot the
world in himself. And as the heathen identified his destruction
with the destruction of the world, so he identified his immortality
with the immortality of the world. To the heathen, man was a
common, to the Christian, a select being ; to the latter immortality
was a privilege of man, to the former a common good which he vindicated to himself only because, and in so far as, he assigned to other
beings a share in it also. The Christians expected the destruction of
the world immediately, because the Christian religion has in it no

cosmical principle of development :—all which developed itself in Christendom developed itself only in contradiction with the original nature of Christianity ;—because by the existence of God in the flesh, *i.e.*, by the immediate identity of the species with the individual, everything was attained, the thread of history was cut short, no other thought of the future remained than the thought of a repetition of the second coming of the Lord. The heathens, on the contrary, placed the destruction of the world in the distant future, because, living in the contemplation of the universe, they did not set heaven and earth in motion on their own account,—because they extended and freed their self-consciousness by the consciousness of the species, placed immortality only in the perpetuation of the species, and thus did not reserve the future to themselves, but left it to the coming generations. "Veniet tempus quo posteri nostri tam aperta nos nescisse mirentur."—Seneca (Nat. Qu. l. vii. c. 25). He who places immortality in himself abolishes the principle of historical development. The Christians did indeed, according to Peter, expect a new heaven and a new earth. But with this Christian, *i.e.*, superterrestrial earth, the theatre of history is for ever closed, the end of the actual world is come. The heathens, on the contrary, set no limits to the development of the cosmos ; they supposed the world to be destroyed only to arise again renovated as a real world ; they granted it eternal life. The Christian destruction of the world was a matter of feeling, an object of fear and longing ; the heathen, a matter of reason, an inference from the contemplation of nature.

Unspotted Virginity is the principle of Salvation, the principle of the regenerate Christian world. " *Virgo genuit mundi salutem ;* virgo peperit vitam universorum.......... *Virgo* portavit, quem *mundus iste capere aut sustinere non potest..........Per virum autem* et *mulierem caro ejecta de paradiso : per virginem juncta est Deo.*"— Ambrosius (Ep. L. x. Ep. 82). "Jure laudatur bona uxor, sed melius *pia virgo* praefertur, *dicente Apostolo* (1 Cor. vii.). Bonum conjugium, per quod est inventa posteritas successionis humanae ; sed *melius virginitas*, per quam regni coelestis haereditas acquisita et coelestium meritorum reperta successio. Per mulierem cura successit : *per virginem salus evenit.*"—(Id. Ep. 81.) "Castitas jungit hominem coelo.......Bona est castitas conjugalis, sed melior est continentia vidualis. *Optima vero integritas virginalis.*"—De modo bene vivendi, Sermo 22. (Among the spurious writings of Bernard.) "*Pulchritudinem* hominis non concupiscas."—(Ibid. S. 23.) "Fornicatio major est *omnibus peccatis*..........Audi *beati Isidori* verba : Fornicatione coinquinari deterius est omni peccato."—(Ibid.) "Virginitas cui gloriae merito non praefertur ? Angelicae ? Angelus habet virginitatem, sed non carnem, sane felicior, quam fortior in hac parte."—Bernardus (Ep. 113, ad Sophiam Virginem). "Memento semper, quod *paradisi colonum de possessione sua mulier ejecerit.*"—Hieronymus (Ep. Nepotiano). " In *paradiso virginitas* conversabatur.......Ipse Christus virginitatis gloria non modo ex patre sine initio et sine duorum concursu genitus, sed et homo secundum nos factus, super nos ex virgine sine alieno consortio incarnatus est. Et *ipse virginitatem veram et perfectam esse, in se ipso demonstravit.* Unde *hanc nobis legem non statuit* (non enim omnes capiunt verbum hoc, ut ipse dixit) sed *opere nos erudivit.*"—Joan. Damasc. (Orthod. Fidei, l. iv. c. 25).

Now if abstinence from the satisfaction of the sensual impulse, the negation of difference of sex and consequently of sexual love,—for what is this without the other?—is the principle of the Christian heaven and salvation ; then necessarily the satisfaction of the sexual impulse, sexual love, on which marriage is founded, is the source of sin and evil. And so it is held. The mystery of original sin is the mystery of sexual desire. All men are conceived in sin because they were conceived with sensual, *i.e.,* natural pleasure. The act of generation, as an act of sensual enjoyment, is sinful. Sin is propagated from Adam down to us, simply because its propagation is the natural act of generation. This is the mystery of Christian original sin. "Atque hic quam alienus a vero sit, etiam hic reprehenditur, quod *voluptatem* in homine *Deo authore* creatam asserit principaliter. Sed hoc divinae scriptura redarguit, quae serpentis insidiis atque illecebris infusam Adae atque Evae voluptatem docet, siquidem ipse *serpens voluptas* sit......Quomodo igitur voluptas ad paradisum revocare nos potest, quae *sola nos paradiso* exuit?"—Ambrosius (Ep. L. x. Ep. 82). " *Voluptas* ipsa *sine culpa* nullatenus esse potest."—Petrus L. (l. iv. dist. 31, c. 5). " Omnes in peccatis nati sumus, et ex *carnis delectatione* concepti culpam originalem nobiscum traximus."—Gregorius (Petrus L. l. ii. dist. 30, c. 2). " Firmissime tene et nullatenus dubites, omnem hominem, qui per *concubitum viri et mulieris* concipitur, cum originali peccato nasci......Ex his datur intelligi, *quid sit originale peccatum,* scl. *vitium concupiscentiae,* quod in omnes concupiscentialiter natos per Adam intravit."—(Ibid. c. 3, see also dist. 31, c. 1.) " Peccati causa *ex carne* est."—Ambrosius (ibid.) " Christus *peccatum* non habet, nec originale traxit, nec suum addidit : *extra voluptatem carnalis libidinis venit,* non ibi fuit *complexus maritalis.......*Omnis *generatus, damnatus.*"—Augustinus (Serm. ad Pop. S. 294, cc. 10, 16). " Homo *natus de muliere* et *ob hoc cum reatu.*"—Bernardus (de Consid. l. ii.). " Peccatum quomodo non fuit, ubi libido non defuit?......Quo pacto, inquam, aut sanctus asseretur conceptus, qui de spiritus non est, *ne dicam de peccato* est?" —Id. (Epist. 174, edit. cit.). " All that is born into the world of man and woman is sinful, under God's anger and curse, condemned to death." "All men born of a father and mother are children of wrath by nature, as St. Paul testifies, Ephes. ii." " We have by nature a tainted, sinful conception and birth."—Luther (Th. xvi. 246, 573). It is clear from these examples, that " carnal intercourse "—even a kiss is carnal intercourse—is the radical sin, the radical evil of mankind ; and consequently the basis of marriage, the sexual impulse, honestly outspoken, is a product of the devil. It is true that the creature as the work of God is good, but it has long ceased to exist as it was created. The devil has alienated the creature from God and corrupted it to the very foundation. "Cursed be the ground for thy sake." The fall of the creature, however, is only an hypothesis by which faith drives from its mind the burdensome, disquieting contradiction, that Nature is a product of God, and yet, as it actually is, does not harmonise with God, *i.e.*, with the Christian sentiment.

Christianity certainly did not pronounce the flesh as flesh, matter as matter, to be some thing sinful, impure ; on the contrary, it contended vehemently against the heretics who held this opinion and rejected marriage. (See for example Augustin. contra Faustum, l. 29, c. 4, l. 30, c. 6. Clemens Alex. Stromata, lib. iii. and Bernard. Super Cantica, Sermo 66.) But quite apart from the hatred to heretics which so inspired the holy Christian Church and made it so politic, this protest rested on grounds which by no means involved the recognition of Nature as such, and under limitations, *i.e.*, negations, which make the recognition of Nature merely apparent and illusory. The distinction between the heretics and the orthodox is only this, that the latter said indirectly, covertly, secretly, what the former declared plainly, directly, but for that very reason offensively. Pleasure is not separable from matter. Material pleasure is nothing further, so to speak, than the joy of matter in itself, matter proving itself by activity. Every joy is self-activity, every pleasure a manifestation of force, energy. Every organic function is, in a normal condition, united with enjoyment ; even breathing is a pleasurable act, which is not perceived as such only because it is an uninterrupted process. He therefore who declares generation, fleshly intercourse, as such, to be pure, but fleshly intercourse united with sensual pleasure to be a consequence of original sin and consequently itself a sin, acknowledges only the dead, not the living flesh—he raises a mist before us, he condemns, rejects the act of generation, and matter in general, though under the appearance of not rejecting it, of acknowledging it. The unhypocritical, honest acknowledgment of sensual life is the acknowledgment of sensual pleasure. In brief, he who, like the Bible, like the Church, does not acknowledge fleshly pleasure—that, be it understood, which is natural, normal, inseparable from life—does not acknowledge the flesh. That which is not recognised as an end in itself (it by no means follows that it should be the ultimate end) is in truth not recognised at all. Thus he who allows me wine only as medicine forbids me the *enjoyment* of wine. Let not the liberal supply of wine at the wedding at Cana be urged. For that scene transports us, by the metamorphosis of water into wine, beyond Nature into the region of supernaturalism. Where, as in Christianity, a supernatural, spiritual body is regarded as the true, eternal body, *i.e.*, a body from which all objective, sensual impulses, all flesh, all nature, is removed, there real, *i.e.*, sensual fleshly matter is denied, is regarded as worthless, nothing.

Certainly Christianity did not make celibacy a law (save at a later period for the priests). But for the very reason that chastity, or rather privation of marriage, of sex, is the highest, the most transcendent, supernaturalistic, heavenly virtue, it cannot and must not be lowered into a common object of duty ; it stands above the law, it is the virtue of Christian grace and freedom. "Christus hortatur *idoneos ad coelibatum*, ut donum recte tueantur ; idem Christus iis, qui *puritatem extra conjugium* non retinent, praecipit, ut pure in conjugio vivant."—Melancthon. (Responsio ad Colonienses. Declam. T. iii.). "*Virginitas non est jussa, sed admonita, quia nimis est excelsa.*"—De modo bene viv. (Sermo 21). "Et qui matrimonio jungit virginem suam, benefacit, et *qui non jungit, melius facit.* Quod igitur bonum est, non vitandum est, et quod *est melius eligendum* est. Itaque non imponitur, sed proponitur. Et ideo bene Apostolus dixit : De virginibus autem praeceptum non habeo, *consilium* autem do. Ubi praeceptum est, ibi *lex* est, ubi consilium, ibi *gratia* est.......Praeceptum enim castitatis est, *consilium* integritatis.......Sed *nec vidua* praeceptum accipit, sed consilium. Consilium autem non semel datum, sed *saepe repetitum.*"—Ambrosius (Liber. de viduis). That is to say : celibacy, abstinence from marriage, is no law in the common or Jewish sense, but a law in the Christian sense, or for the Christian sentiment, which takes Christian virtue and perfection as the rule of conscience, as the ideal of feeling,—no despotic but a friendly law, no public but a secret, esoteric law—a mere counsel, *i.e.*, a law which does not venture to express itself as a law, a law for those of finer feelings, not for the great mass. Thou mayst marry ; yes indeed ! without any fear of committing a sin, *i.e.*, a public, express, plebeian sin ; but thou dost all the better if thou dost not marry ; meanwhile this is only my undictatorial, friendly advice. *Omnia licent, sed omnia non expediunt.* What is allowed in the first member of the sentence is retracted in the second. *Licet,* says the man ; *non expedit,* says the Christian. But only that which is good for the Christian is for the man, so far as he desires to be a Christian, the standard of doing and abstaining. "*Quae non expediunt, nec licent,*" such is the conclusion arrived at by the sentiment of Christian nobility. Marriage is therefore only an indulgence to the weakness, or rather the strength of the flesh, a taint of nature in Christianity, a falling short of the genuine, perfect Christian sentiment ; being, however, nevertheless good, laudable, even holy, in so far as it is the best antidote to fornication. For its own sake, as the self-enjoyment of sexual love, it is not acknowledged, not consecrated ; thus the holiness of marriage in Christianity is only an ostensible holiness, only illusion, for that which is not acknowledged for its own sake is not acknowledged at all, while yet there is a deceitful show of acknowledgment. Marriage is sanctioned not in order to hallow and satisfy the flesh, but to restrict the flesh, to repress it, to kill it—to drive Beelzebub out by Beelzebub. "Quae res et viris et feminis omnibus adest ad matrimonium et stuprum ? Commixtio carnis scilicet, cujus concupiscentiam Dominus stupro adaequav:t.......Ideo virginis principalis sanctitas, quia caret stupri affinitati."—Tertullianus (de Exhort. Cast. c. 9). "Et de ipso conjugis melius aliquid, quam concessisti, monuisti."—Augustinus (Confess. x. c. 30). "It is better to marry than to burn."—1 Cor. vii. 9. But how much better is it, says Tertullian, developing this text, neither to marry nor to burn......"Possum dicere, quod permittitur *bonum non est.*"—(Ad Uxorem, l. i. c. 3.) "De minoribus bonis est conjugiam, quod non meretur palmam, sed est *in remedium*...... *Prima* institutio habuit *praeceptum,* secunda *indulgentiam.* Didi-

cimus enim ab Apostolo, humano generi propter vitandam fornica-
tionem indultum esse conjugium."—Petrus Lomb. (l. iv. dist. 26,
c. 2). "The Master of the Sentences says rightly, that in Paradise
marriage was ordained as service, but after sin as medicine."—Luther
(Th. i. p. 349). "Where marriage and virginity are compared, certainly chastity is a nobler gift than marriage."—Id. (Th. i. p. 319).
"Those whom the weakness of nature does not compel to marriage,
but who are such that they can dispense with marriage, these do
rightly to abstain from marriage."—Id. (Th. v. p. 538). Christian
sophistry will reply to this, that only marriage which is not Christian,
only that which is not consecrated by the spirit of Christianity, *i.e.*,
in which Nature is not veiled in pious images, is unholy. But if
marriage, if Nature is first made holy by relation to Christ, it is
not the holiness of marriage which is declared, but of Christianity;
and marriage, Nature, in and by itself, is unholy. And what is the
semblance of holiness with which Christianity invests marriage, in
order to becloud the understanding, but a pious illusion? Can the
Christian fulfil his marriage duties without surrendering himself,
willingly or not, to the passion of love? Yes indeed. The Christian
has for his object the replenishing of the Christian Church, not the
satisfaction of love. The end is holy, but the means in itself unholy. And the end sanctifies, exculpates the means. "Conjugalis
concubitus generandi gratia non habet culpam." Thus the Christian,
at least the true Christian, denies, or at least is bound to deny
Nature, while he satisfies it; he does not wish for, he rather con-
temns the means in itself; he seeks only the end *in abstracto;* he
does with religious, supranaturalistic horror what he does, though
against his will, with natural, sensual pleasure. The Christian does
not candidly confess his sensuality, he denies Nature before his
faith, and his faith before Nature, *i.e.*, he publicly disavows what he
privately does. Oh, how much better, truer, purer-hearted in this
respect were the heathens, who made no secret of their sensuality,
than the Christians, who, while gratifying the flesh, at the same
time deny that they gratify it! To this day the Christians adhere
theoretically to their heavenly origin and destination; to this day,
out of supranaturalistic affectation, they deny their sex, and turn
away with mock modesty from every sensuous picture, every naked
statue, as if they were angels; to this day they repress, even by
legal force, every open-hearted, ingenuous self-confession even of the
most uncorrupt sensuality, only stimulating by this public prohibition the secret enjoyment of sensuality. What then, speaking
briefly and plainly, is the distinction between Christians and
heathens in this matter? The heathens confirmed, the Christians
contradicted their faith by their lives. The heathens do what they
mean to do, the Christians what they do *not* mean: the former,
where they sin, sin with their conscience, the latter against their
conscience; the former sin simply, the latter doubly; the former
from hypertrophy, the latter from atrophy of the flesh. The specific
crime of the heathens is the ponderable, palpable crime of licentiousness, that of the Christians is the imponderable, theological
crime of hypocrisy,—that hypocrisy of which Jesuitism is indeed

APPENDIX.

315

the most striking, world-historical, but nevertheless only a particular manifestation. "Theology makes sinners," says Luther—
Luther, whose positive qualities, his heart and understanding, so
far as they applied themselves to natural things, were not perverted
by theology. And Montesquieu gives the best commentary on this
saying of Luther's when he says : "La dévotion trouve, pour faire
de mauvaises actions, des raisons, qu'un simple honnête homme ne
saurait trouver."—(Pensées Diverses.)

§ 16.

*The Christian heaven is Christian truth. That which is excluded
from heaven is excluded from true Christianity. In heaven the
Christian is free from that which he wishes to be free from here—
free from the sexual impulse, free from matter, free from Nature in
general.* "In the resurrection they neither marry nor are given in
marriage, but are as the angels of God in heaven."—Matt. xxii.
30. "Meats for the belly, and the belly for meats ; but God shall
destroy (καταργήσει, make useless) both it and them."—1 Cor. vi. 13.
"Now this I say, brethren, that flesh and blood cannot inherit the
kingdom of heaven, neither doth corruption inherit incorruption."
—Ib. xv. 50. "They shall hunger no more, neither thirst any
more ; neither shall the sun light on them, nor any heat."—Rev.
vii. 16. "And there shall be no night there ; and they need no
candle, neither light of the sun."—Ib. xxii. 5. "Comedere, bibere,
vigilare, dormire, quiescere, laborare et *caeteris necessitatibus
naturae* subjacere, vere magna miseria est et afflictio homini devoto,
qui libenter esset absolutus et liber ab omni peccato. Utinam non
essent *istae necessitates*, sed solum spirituales animae refectiones,
quas heu ! satis raro degustamus."—Thomas à K. (de Imit. l. i.
cc. 22, 25). See also on this subject S. Gregorii Nyss. de Anima
et Resurr., Lipsiae, 1837, pp. 98, 144, 153). It is true that the
Christian immortality, in distinction from the heathen, is not
the immortality of the soul, but that of the flesh, that is, of the
whole man. "Scientia immortalis visa est res illis (the heathen
philosophers) atque incorruptibilis. Nos autem, quibus divina
revelatio illuxit......novimus, non solum *mentem*, sed *affectus per-
purgatos*, neque animam tantum, sed etiam *corpus ad immortali-
tatem* assumptum iri suo tempore."—Baco de Verul. (de Augm.
Scien. l. i.). On this account Celsus reproached the Christians with
a *desiderium corporis*. But this immortal body is, as has been
already remarked, an immaterial, *i.e.*, a thoroughly fanciful, subjective body—a body which is the direct negation of the real,
natural body. The ideal on which this faith hinges is not the
recognition or glorification of nature, of matter as such, but rather
the reality of the emotive imagination, the satisfaction of the unlimited, supranaturalistic desire of happiness, to which the actual,
objective body is a limitation.

As to what the angels strictly are, whom heavenly souls will be
like, the Bible is as far from giving us any definite information as
on other weighty subjects ; it only calls them πνευματα, spirits, and

declares them to be higher than men. The later Christians expressed themselves more definitely on this subject ; more definitely, but variously. Some assigned bodies to the angels, others not ; a difference which, however, is only apparent, since the angelic body is only a phantasmal one. But concerning the human body of the resurrection, they had not only different, but even opposite, conceptions ; indeed, these contradictions lay in the nature of the case, necessarily resulted from the fundamental contradiction of the religious consciousness which, as we have shown, exhibits itself in the incompatible propositions that the body which is raised is the same individual body which we had before the resurrection, and that nevertheless it is another. It is the same body even to the hair, "cum nec periturus sit capillus, ut ait Dominus : Capillus de capite vestro non peribit."—Augustinus und Petrus, L. l. iv. dist. 44, c. 1. Nevertheless it is the same in such a way that everything burdensome, everything contradictory to transcendental feeling, is removed. "Immo sicut dicit Augustinus : Detrahentur vitia et remanebit natura. *Superexcrescentia autem capillorum et unguium est de superfluitate et vitio naturae. Si enim non peccasset homo, crescerent ungues et capilli ejus usque ad determinatam quantitatem.* sicut in leonibus et avibus."—(Addit. Henrici ab Vurimaria, ibid. edit. Basiliae, 1513.) What a specific, naïve, ingenuous, confident, harmonious faith! The risen body, as the same and yet another, a new body, has hair and nails, otherwise it would be a maimed body, deprived of an essential ornament, and consequently the resurrection would not be a *restitutio in integrum ;* moreover they are the same hair and nails as before, but yet so modified that they are in accordance with the body. Why do not the believing theologians of modern times enter into such specialities as occupied the older theologians? Because their faith is itself only general, indefinite, *i.e.*, a faith which they only suppose themselves to possess ; because, from fear of their understanding, which has long been at issue with their faith, from fear of risking their feeble faith by bringing it to the light, that is, considering it in detail, they suppress the consequences, the necessary determinations of their faith, and conceal them from their understanding.

§ 17.

What faith denies on earth it affirms in heaven ; what it renounces here it recovers a hundred-fold there. In this world, faith occupies itself with nullifying the body ; in the other world, with establishing it. Here the main point is the separation of the soul from the body, there the main point is the reunion of the body with the soul. " I would live not only according to the soul, but according to the body also. I would have the *corpus* with me ; I would that the body should return to the soul and be united with it."—Luther (Th. vii. p. 90). In that which is sensuous, Christ is supersensuous ; but for that reason, in the supersensuous he is sensuous. Heavenly bliss is therefore by no means merely spiritual, it is equally corporeal, sensuous—a state in which all wishes are fulfilled. "Whatever thy heart seeks joy and pleasure in, that shall be there in abundance. For it is said, God shall be all in all. And where God is, there must be all good things that can ever be desired." "Dost thou desire to see acutely, and to hear through walls, and to be so light that thou mayst be wherever thou wilt in a moment, whether here below on the earth, or above in the clouds, that shall all be, and what more thou canst conceive, which thou couldst have in body and soul, thou shalt have abundantly if thou hast him."—Luther (Th. x. pp. 380, 381). Certainly eating, drinking, and marriage find no place in the Christian heaven, as they do in the Mohammedan; but only because with these enjoyments want is associated, and with want matter, *i.e.*, passion, dependence, unhappiness. "Illic ipsa indigentia morietur. Tunc vere dives eris, quando nullius indigens eris."—Augustin. (Serm. ad Pop. p. 77, c. 9). The pleasures of this earth are only medicines, says the same writer; true health exists only in immortal life—"vera sanitas, nisi quando vera immortalitas." The heavenly life, the heavenly body, is as free and unlimited as wishes, as omnipotent as imagination. "Futurae ergo resurrectionis corpus imperfectae felicitatis erit, si cibos sumere *non potuerit*, imperfectae felicitatis, si cibus *eguerit*."—Augustin. (Epist. 102, § 6, edit. cit.). Nevertheless, existence in a body without fatigue, without heaviness, without disagreeables, without disease, without mortality, is associated with the highest corporeal well-being. Even the knowledge of God in heaven is free from any effort of thought or _faith, is sensational, immediate knowledge — intuition. The Christians are indeed not agreed whether God, as God, the *essentia Dei*, will be visible to bodily eyes. (See, for example, Augustin. Serm. ad Pop. p. 277, and Buddeus, Comp. Inst. Th. l. ii. c. 3, § 4.) But in this difference we again have only the contradiction between the abstract and the real God; the former is certainly not an object of vision, but the latter is so. "Flesh and blood is the wall between me and Christ, which will be torn away......There everything will be certain. For in that life the eyes will see, the mouth taste, and the nose smell it; the treasure will shine into the soul and life...... Faith will cease, and I shall behold with my eyes."—Luther (Th. ix. p. 595). It is clear from this again, that God, as he is an object of religious sentiment, is nothing else than a product of the imagination. The heavenly beings are supersensuous sensuous, immaterial material beings, *i.e.*, beings of the imagination; but they are like God, nay, identical with God, consequently God also is a supersensuous sensuous, an immaterial material being.

§ 18.

The contradiction in the Sacraments is the contradiction of naturalism and supernaturalism. In the first place the natural qualities of water are pronounced essential to Baptism. "Si quis dixerit *aquam veram* et *naturalem* non esse de necessitate Baptismi atque ideo verba illa domini nostri Jesu Christi: Nisi quis renatus fuerit *ex aqua* et Spiritu sancto, ad metamorpham aliquam detorserit, anathema sit.—Concil. Trident. (Sessio vii. Can. ii. de Bapt.) De

substantia hujus sacramenti sunt *verbum* et *elementum*......Non
ergo *in alio liquore* potest consecrari baptismus *nisi in aqua.—*
Petrus Lomb. (l. iv. dist. 3, c. 1. c. 5). Ad certitudinem baptismi
requiritur major quam *unius guttae* quantitas......Necesse est ad
valorem baptismi fieri *contactum physicum* inter aquam et corpus
baptizati, ita ut non sufficiat, vestes tantum ipsius aqua tingi......
Ad certitudinem baptismi requiritur, ut saltem *talis pars* corporis
abluatur, ratione cujus homo solet dici vere ablutus, v. 6, collum,
humeri, pectus et *praesertim caput.—*Theolog. Schol. (P. Mezger.
Aug. Vind. 1695, Th. iv. pp. 230, 231). *Aquam, eamque veram* ac
naturalem in baptismo adhibendam esse, exemplo Joannis......
non minus vero et Apostolorum Act. viii. 36, x. 47, patet.—F.
Buddeus (Com. Inst. Th. dog. l. iv. c. i. § 5)." Thus water is
essential. But now comes the *negation* of the natural qualities
of water. The significance of Baptism is not the natural power
of water, but the supernatural, almighty power of the Word of
God, who instituted the use of water as a sacrament, and now by
means of this element imparts himself to man in a supernatural,
miraculous manner, but who could just as well have chosen any
other element in order to produce the same effect. So Luther, for
example, says : "Understand the distinction, that Baptism is quite
another thing than all other water, not on account of its natural
quality, but because here something more noble is added. For
God himself brings hither his glory, power, and might..........as
St. Augustine also hath taught : 'accedat verbum ad elementum
et fit sacramentum.'" "Baptize them in the name of the Father,
&c. Water without these words is mere water..........Who will
call the baptism of the Father, Son, and Holy Ghost mere water?
Do we not see what sort of spice God puts into this water?
When sugar is thrown into water it is no longer water, but a
costly claret or other beverage. Why then do we here separate
the word from the water and say, it is mere water ; as if the word
of God, yea, God himself, were not with and in the water........
Therefore, the water of Baptism is such a water as takes away sin,
death, and unhappiness, helps us in heaven and to everlasting life.
It is become a precious sugared water, *aromaticum*, and restorative,
since God has mingled himself therewith."—Luther (Th. xvi. p.
105).

As with the water in Baptism, which sacrament is nothing
without water, though this water is nevertheless in itself indifferent, so is it with the wine and bread in the Eucharist, even
in Catholicism, where the substance of bread and wine is destroyed
by the power of the Almighty. "Accidentia eucharistica tamdiu
continent Christum, quamdiu retinent illud temperamentum, cum
quo connaturaliter panis et vini substantia permaneret : ut econtra,
quando tanta fit temperamenti dissolutio, illorumque corruptio, ut
sub iis substantia panis et vini naturaliter remanere non posset,
desinunt continere Christum." — Theol. Schol. (Mezger. l. c. p.
292). That is to say : so long as the bread remains bread, so long
does the bread remain flesh ; when the bread is gone, the flesh
is gone. Therefore a due portion of bread, at least enough to

render bread recognisable as such, must be present, for consecration to be possible.—(Ib. p. 284.) For the rest, Catholic tran-
sub-tantiation, the *conversio realis et physica totius panis in corpus
Christi*, is only a consistent continuation of the miracles of the
Old and New Testaments. By the transformation of water into
wine, of a staff into a serpent, of stones into brooks (Ps. cxiv.) by
these biblical transubstantiations the Catholics explained and
proved the turning of bread into flesh. He who does not stumble
at those transformations, has no right, no reason to hesitate at
accepting this. The Protestant doctrine of the Lord's Supper is
not less in contradiction with reason than the Catholic. "The
body of Christ cannot be partaken otherwise than in two ways,
spiritually or bodily. Again, this bodily partaking cannot be
visible or perceptible," *i.e.*, is not bodily, "else no bread would
remain. Again, it cannot be mere bread; otherwise it would not
be a bodily communion of the body of Christ, but of bread.
Therefore the bread broken must also be truly and corporeally
the body of Christ, although invisibly " (*i.e.*, incorporeally).—
Luther (Th. xix. p. 203). The difference is, that the Protestant
gives no explanation concerning the *mode* in which bread can be
flesh and wine blood. "Thereupon we stand, believe, and teach,
that the body of Christ is truly and corporeally taken and eaten
in the Lord's Supper. But how this takes place, or how he is in
the bread, we know not, and are not bound to know."—Id. (ut
sup. p. 393). "He who will be a Christian must not ask, as our
fanatics and factionaries do, how it can be that bread is the body
of Christ and wine the blood of Christ."—Id. (Th. xvi. p. 220).
"Cum retineamus doctrinam de praesentia corporis Christi, quid
opus est quaerere de modo?"—Melancthon (Vita Mel. Came-
rarius, ed. Strobel, Halae, 1777, p. 446). Hence the Protestants as well as the Catholics took refuge in Omnipotence, the
grand source of ideas contradictory to reason.—(Concord. Summ.
Beg. Art. 7, Aff. 3, Negat. 13. See also Luther, *e.g.*, Th. xix. p.
400.)

An instructive example of theological incomprehensibleness and
supernaturalness is afforded by the distinction, in relation to the
Eucharist (Concordienb. Summ. Beg. art. 7), between partaking
with the mouth and partaking in a fleshly or natural manner.
"We believe, teach, and confess that the body of Christ is taken
in the bread and wine, not alone spiritually by faith, but also
with the mouth, yet not in a Capernaitic, but a supernatural
heavenly manner, for the sake of sacramental union." "Probe
namque *discrimen* inter manducationem *oralem* et *naturalem*
tenendum est. Etsi enim oralem manducationem adseramus
atque propugnemus, naturalem tamen non admittimus..........
Omnis equidem manducatio naturalis etiam oralis est, sed non
vicissim *oralis manducatio* statim est *naturalis*..........Unicus
itaque licet sit actus, *unicumque organum*, quo panem et corpus
Christi, itemque vinum et sanguinem Christi accipimus, *modus*
(yes, truly, the *mode*) nihilominus maximopere differt, cum panem

et vinum modo naturali et sensibili, corpus et sanguinem Christi
simul equidem cum pane et vino, at *modo supernaturali* et *insen-
sibili,* qui adeo etiam a nemine mortalium (nor, assuredly, by any
God) explicare potest, *revera interim* et *ore corporis accipiamus."—*
Jo. Fr. Buddeus (l. c. Lib. v. c. i. § 15).

§ 19.

*Dogma and Morality, Faith and Love, contradict each other in
Christianity.* It is true that God, the object of faith, is in himself
the idea of the species in a mystical garb—the common Father of
men—and so far love to God is mystical love to man. But God is
not only the universal being; he is also a peculiar, personal being,
distinguished from love. Where the being is distinguished from
love arises *arbitrariness.* Love acts from necessity, personality from
will. Personality proves itself as such only by arbitrariness; personality seeks dominion, is greedy of glory; it desires only to assert
itself, to enforce its own authority. The highest worship of God
as a *personal* being is therefore the worship of God as an absolutely
unlimited, arbitrary being. Personality, as such, is indifferent to
all substantial determinations which lie in the nature of things;
inherent necessity, the coercion of natural qualities, appears to it a
constraint. Here we have the mystery of Christian love. The love
of God, as the predicate of a personal being, has here the significance of grace, favour : God is a gracious master, as in Judaism he
was a severe master. Grace is arbitrary love,—love which does
not act from an inward necessity of the nature, but which is equally
capable of *not* doing what it does, which could, if it would, condemn its object; thus it is a groundless, unessential, arbitrary,
absolutely subjective, merely personal love. "He hath mercy on
whom he will have mercy, and whom he will he hardeneth (Rom.
ix. 18)......The king does what he will. So is it with the will of
God. He has perfect right and full power to do with us and all
creatures as he will. And no wrong is done to us. If his will had
a measure or rule, a law, ground, or cause, it would not be the
divine will. For what he wills is right, because he wills it. Where
there is faith and the Holy Spirit......it is believed that God
would be good and kind even if he consigned all men to damnation.
'Is not Esau Jacob's brother? said the Lord. Yet I have loved
Jacob and hated Esau.' "—Luther (Th. xix. pp. 83, 87, 90, 91, 97).
Where love is understood in this sense, jealous watch is kept that
man attribute nothing to himself as merit, that the merit may lie
with the divine personality alone; there every idea of necessity is
carefully dismissed, in order, through the feeling of obligation and
gratitude, to be able to adore and glorify the personality exclusively.
The Jews deified the pride of ancestry; the Christians, on the other
hand, interpreted and transformed the Jewish aristocratic principle
of hereditary nobility into the democratic principle of nobility of
merit. The Jew makes salvation depend on birth, the Catholic on
the merit of works, the Protestant on the merit of faith. But the
idea of obligation and meritoriousness allies itself only with a deed,

a work, which cannot be demanded of me, or which does not necessarily proceed from my nature. The works of the poet, of the philosopher, can be regarded in the light of merit only as considered externally. They are works of genius—inevitable products : the poet *must* bring forth poetry, the philosopher *must* philosophise. They have the highest satisfaction in the activity of creation, apart from any collateral or ulterior purpose. And it is just so with a truly noble moral action. To the man of noble feeling, the noble action is natural : he does not hesitate whether he should do it or not, he does not place it in the scales of choice ; he *must* do it. Only he who so acts is a man to be confided in. Meritoriousness always involves the notion that a thing is done, so to speak, out of luxury, not out of necessity. The Christians indeed celebrated the highest act in their religion, the act of God becoming man, as a work of love. But Christian love in so far as it reposes on faith, on the idea of God as a master, a *Dominus*, has the significance of an act of grace, of a love in itself superfluous. A gracious master is one who foregoes his rights, a master who does out of graciousness what, as a master, he is not bound to do—what goes beyond the strict idea of a master. To God, as a master, it is not even a duty to do good to man ; he has even the right—for he is a master bound by no law—to annihilate man if he will. In fact, mercy is optional, non-necessary love, love in contradiction with the essence of love, love which is not an inevitable manifestation of the nature, love which the master, the subject, the person (personality is only an abstract, modern expression for sovereignty) distinguishes from himself as a predicate which he can either have or not have without ceasing to be himself. This internal contradiction necessarily manifested itself in the life, in the practice of Christianity ; it gave rise to the practical separation of the subject from the predicate, of faith from love. As the love of God to man was only an act of grace, so also the love of man to man was only an act of favour or grace on the part of faith. Christian love is the graciousness of faith, as the love of God is the graciousness of personality or supremacy. (On the divine arbitrariness, see also J. A. Ernesti's treatise previously cited : " Vindiciæ arbitrii divini.")

Faith has within it a malignant principle. Christian faith, and nothing else, is the ultimate ground of Christian persecution and destruction of heretics. Faith recognises man only on condition that he recognises God, *i.e.,* faith itself. Faith is the honour which man renders to God. And this honour is due unconditionally. To faith the basis of all duties is faith in God : faith is the absolute duty ; duties to men are only derivative, subordinate. The unbeliever is thus an outlaw *—a man worthy of extermination. That which denies God must be itself denied. The highest crime is the crime *laesae majestatis Dei.* To faith God is a personal being—the supremely personal, inviolable, privileged being. The acme of personality is honour ; hence an injury towards the highest personality

* " Haereticus usu omnium jurium destitutus est, ut deportatus."—J. H. Boehmer (l. c. l. v. Tit. vii. § 223. See also Tit. vi.)

is necessarily the highest crime. The *honour* of God cannot be disavowed as an accidental, rude, anthropomorphic conception. For is not the personality, even the existence of God, a sensuous, anthropomorphic conception? Let those who renounce the honour be consistent enough to renounce the personality. From the idea of personality results the idea of honour, and from this again the idea of religious offences. " Quicunque Magistratibus male precatus fuerit, pro eorum arbitrio poenas luito; quicunque vero idem scelus erga Deum admiserit......*lapidibus blasphemiae causa* obruitur." —(Lev. xxiv. 15, 16. See also Deut. xii., whence the Catholics deduce the right to kill heretics. Boehmer, l. c. l. v. Th. vii. § 44.) "Eos autem merito torqueri, qui Deum nesciunt, ut impios, ut injustos, nisi profanus nemo deliberat: quum parentem omnium et *dominum omnium non minus sceleris sit ignorare*, quam *laedere.*"— Minucii Fel. Oct. c. 35. " Ubi erunt legis praecepta divinae, quae dicunt: honora patrem et matrem, si vocabulum patris, quod in homine honorari praecipitur, *in Deo impune violatur?*"—Cypriani Epist. 73 (ed. Gersdorf). "Cur enim, cum datum sit divinitus homini liberum arbitrium, adulteria legibus puniantur et sacrilegia permittantur? An *fidem non servare levius est animam Deo, quam feminam viro?*"—Augustinus (de Correct. Donatist. lib. ad Bonifacium, c. 5). " Si hi qui nummos adulterant morte mulctantur, quid de *illis statuendum censemus, qui fidem pervertere conantur?*"—Paulus Cortesius (in Sententias (Petri L.) iii. l. dist. vii.). " Si enim illustrem ac praepotentem virum nequaquam exhonorari a quoquam licet, et si quisquam exhonoraverit, decretis legalibus reus sistitur et injuriarum auctor jure damnatur: *quanto utique majoris piaculi crimen est, injuriosum quempiam Deo* esse? Semper enim per dignitatem injuriam perferentis crescit culpa facientis, quia necesse est. quanto major est persona ejus qui contumeliam patitur, tanto major sit noxa ejus, qui facit." Thus speaks Salvianus (de Gubernat. Dei, l. vi. p. 218, edit. cit.)—Salvianus, who is called *Magistrum Episcoporum, sui saeculi Jeremiam, Scriptorem Christianissimum, Orbis christiani magistrum.* But heresy, unbelief in general—heresy is only a definite, limited unbelief—is blasphemy, and thus is the highest, the most flagitious crime. Thus to cite only one among innumerable examples, J. Oecolampadius writes to Servetus: "Dum non summam patientiam prae me fero, dolens Jesum Christum filium Dei sic dehonestari, parum christiane tibi agere videor. In aliis mansuetus ero: in *blasphemiis* quae in Christum, non item."—(Historia Mich. Serveti. H. ab Allwoerden Helmstadii, 1737, p. 13). For what is blasphemy? Every negation of an idea, of a definition, in which the honour of God, the honour of faith is concerned. Seryetus fell as a sacrifice to Christian faith. Calvin said to Servetus two hours before his death: " Ego vero ingenue praefatus, me nunquam *privatas injurias* fuisse persecutum," and parted from him with a sense of being thoroughly sustained by the Bible: " Ab haeretico homine, qui αὐτοκατάκριτος peccabat, *secundum Pauli praeceptum* discessi."—(Ibid. p. 120.) Thus it was by no means a personal hatred, though this may have been conjoined,—it was a *religious hatred* which brought Servetus to the stake—the hatred which springs from the nature of unchecked faith. Even Melancthon is known to have approved the execution of Servetus. The Swiss theologians, whose opinion was asked by the Genevans, very subtilely abstained, in their answer, from mentioning the punishment of death,* but agreed with the Genevans in this—"HorrendosServeti errores detestandos esse,severiusque idcirco in Servetum animadvertendum." Thus there is no difference as to the principle, only as to the mode of punishment. Even Calvin himself was so *Christian* as to desire to alleviate the horrible mode of death to which the Senate of Geneva condemned Servetus. (See on this subject, *e.g.*, M. Adami Vita Calvini, p. 90 ; Vita Bezae, p. 207 ; Vitae Theol. Exter. Francof. 1618.) We have, therefore, to consider this execution as an act of general significance—as a work of faith, and that not of Roman Catholic, but of reformed, biblical, evangelical faith. That heretics must not be compelled to a profession of the faith by force was certainly maintained by most of the lights of the Church, but there nevertheless lived in them the most malignant hatred of heretics. Thus, for example, St. Bernard says (Super Cantica, § 66) in relation to heretics : " Fides suadenda est, non imponenda," but he immediately adds : " Quamquam melius procul dubio gladio coercerentur, illius videlicet, qui non sine causa gladium portat,quam in suum errorem multos trajicere permittantur." If the faith of the present day no longer produces such flagrant deeds of horror, this is due only to the fact that the faith of this age is not an uncompromising, living faith, but a sceptical, eclectic, unbelieving faith, curtailed and maimed by the power of art and science. Where heretics are no longer burned either in the fires of this world or of the other, there faith itself has no longer any fire, any vitality. The faith which allows variety of belief renounces its divine origin and rank, degrades itself to a subjective opinion. *It is not to Christian faith, not to Christian love* (i.e., *love limited by faith*) ; *no! it is to doubt of Christian faith, to the victory of religious scepticism, to free-thinkers, to heretics, that we owe tolerance, freedom of opinion.* It was the heretics, persecuted by the Christian Church, who alone fought for freedom of conscience. Christian freedom is freedom in non-essentials only : on the fundamental articles of faith freedom is not allowed. When, however, Christian faith— faith considered in distinction from love, for faith is not one with love, " potestis habere fidem sine caritate" (Augustinus, Serm. ad Pop. § 90)—is pronounced to be the principle, the ultimate ground of the violent deeds of Christians towards heretics (that is, such deeds as arose from real believing zeal), it is obviously not meant that faith could have these consequences immediately and originally, but only in its historical development. Still, even to the earliest Christians the heretic was an antichrist, and necessarily so—"adversus Christum sunt haeretici " (Cyprianus, Epist. 76, § 14,

* Very many Christians rejected the punishment of death, but other criminal punishments of heretics, such as banishment, confiscation—punishments which deprive of life indirectly—they did not find in contradiction with their Christian faith. See on this subject J. H. Boehmer, Jus. Eccl. Protest. l. v. Tit. vii. *e.g.* §§ i. 155, 157, 162, 163.

edit. cit.)—accursed—"apostoli......in epistolis haereticos exsecrati
sunt " (Cyprianus, ib. § 6)—a lost being, doomed by God to hell
and everlasting death. "Thou hearest that the tares are already
condemne l and sentenced to the fire. Why then wilt thou lay
many sufferings on a heretic ? Dost thou not hear that he is already
judged to a punishment heavier than he can bear ? Who art thou,
that thou wilt interfere and punish him who has already fallen
under the punishment of a more powerful master ? What would I
do against a thief already sentenced to the gallows ?......God has
already commanded his angels, who in his own time will be the
executioners of heretics."—Luther (Th. xvi. p. 132). When therefore the State, the world, became Christian, and also, for that
reason, Christianity became worldly, the Christian religion a State
religion ; then it was a necessary consequence that the condemnation
of heretics, which was at first only religious or dogmatic, became a
political, practical condemnation, and the eternal punishment of
hell was anticipated by temporal punishment. If, therefore, the
definition and treatment of heresy as a punishable crime is in
contradiction with the Christian faith, it follows that a Christian
king, a Christian State, is in contradiction with it ; for a Christian
State is that which executes the Divine judgments of faith with
the sword, which makes earth a heaven to believers, a hell to unbelievers. "Docuimus......pertinere ad *reges religiosos*, non solum
adulteria vel homicidia vel hujusmodi alia flagitia seu facinora,
verum etiam *sacrilegia severitate congrua cohibere*."—Augustinus
(Epist. ad Dulcitium). "Kings ought thus to serve the Lord
Christ by helping with laws that his honour be furthered. Now
when the temporal magistracy finds scandalous errors, whereby the
honour of the Lord Christ is blasphemed and men's salvation
hindered, and a schism arises among the people......where such
false teachers will not be admonished and cease from preaching,
there ought the temporal magistracy confidently to arm itself, and
know that nothing else befits its office but to apply the sword and
all force, that doctrine may be pure and God's service genuine and
unperverted, and also that peace and unity may be preserved."—
Luther (Th. xv. pp. 110, 111). Let it be further remarked here,
that Augustine justifies the application of coercive measures for
the awaking of Christian faith by urging that the Apostle Paul
was converted to Christianity by a deed of force—a miracle. (De
Correct. Donat c. 6.) The intrinsic connection between temporal
and eternal, *i.e.*, political and spiritual punishment, is clear from
this, that the same reasons which have been urged against the
temporal punishment of heresy are equally valid against the
punishment of hell. If heresy or unbelief cannot be punished *here*
because it is a mere mistake, neither can it be punished by God in
hell. If coercion is in contradiction with the nature of faith, so
is hell ; for the fear of the terrible consequence of unbelief, the
torments of hell, urge to belief against knowledge and will. Boehmer, in his *Jus. Eccl.*, argues that heresy and unbelief should be
struck out of the category of crimes, that unbelief is only a *vitium
theologicum*, a *peccatum in Deum*. But God, in the view of faith,

is not only a religious, but a political, juridical being, the King of kings, the true head of the State. "There is no power but of God ......it is the minister of God"—Rom. xiii. 1, 4. If, therefore, the juridical idea of majesty, of kingly dignity and honour, applies to God, sin against God, unbelief, must by consequence come under the definition of crime. And as with God, so with faith. Where faith is still a truth, and a public truth, there no doubt is entertained that it can be demanded of every one, that every one is bound to believe. Be it further observed, that the Christian Church has gone so far in its hatred against heretics, that according to the canon law even the suspicion of heresy is a crime, "ita ut de jure canonico revera *crimen suspecti* detur, cujus *existentiam frustra in jure civili quaerimus.*"—Boehmer (l. c. v. Tit. vii. §§ 23–42).

The command to love enemies extends only to personal enemies, not to the enemies of God, the enemies of faith. "Does not the Lord Christ command that we should love even our enemies? How then does David here boast that he hates the assembly of the wicked, and sits not with the ungodly?......For the sake of the person I should love them; but for the sake of the doctrine I should hate them. And thus I must hate them or hate God, who commands and wills that we should cleave to his word alone......What I cannot love with God, I must hate; if they only preach something which is against God, all love and friendship is destroyed ;— thereupon I hate thee, and do thee no good. For faith must be uppermost, and where the word of God is attacked, hate takes the place of love......And so David means to say : I hate them, not because they have done injury and evil to me and led a bad and wicked life, but because they despise, revile, blaspheme, falsify, and persecute the word of God." "Faith and love are two things. Faith endures nothing, love endures all things. Faith curses, love blesses : faith seeks vengeance and punishment, love seeks forbearance and forgiveness." " Rather than God's word should fall and heresy stand, faith would wish all creatures to be destroyed ; for through heresy men lose God himself."—Luther (Th. vi. p. 94 ; Th. v. pp. 624, 630). See also, on this subject, my treatise in the *Deutsches Jahrb.* and Augustini Enarrat. in Psalm cxxxviii. (cxxxix.). As Luther distinguishes the *person* from the enemy of God, so Augustine here distinguishes the *man* from the enemy of God, from the unbeliever, and says : We should hate the ungodliness in the man, but love the humanity in him. But what, then, in the eyes of faith, is the man in distinction from faith, man without faith, *i.e.*, without God? Nothing : for the sum of all realities, of all that is worthy of love, of all that is good and essential, is faith, as that which alone apprehends and possesses God. It is true that man as man is the image of God, but only of the natural God, of God as the Creator of Nature. But the Creator is only God as he manifests himself outwardly ; the true God, God as he is in himself, the inward essence of God, is the *triune* God, is especially *Christ.* (See Luther, Th. xiv. pp. 2, 3, and Th. xvi. p. 581.) And the image of this true, essential, Christian God, is only the believer, the Christian. Moreover, man is not to be loved for his own sake, but for God's.

"Diligendus est propter Deum, Deus vero propter se ipsum."—
Augustinus (de Doctrina Chr. l. i. cc. 22, 27). How, then, should the
unbelieving man, who has no resemblance to the true God, be an
object of love ?

§ 20.

*Faith separates man from man, puts in the place of the natu-
ral unity founded in Nature and Love a supernatural unity—
the unity of Faith.* " Inter Christianum et gentilem *non fides
tantum* debet, sed etiam *vita* distinguere..........Nolite, ait Apostolus, jugum ducere cum infidelibus......Sit ergo *inter nos et illos
maxima separatio.*"—Hieronymus (Epist. Caelantiæ matronae)......
" Prope nihil gravius quam copulari alienigeniae.........Nam cum
ipsum conjugium velamine sacerdotali et benedictione sanctificari
oporteat : *quomodo potest conjugium dici, ubi non est fidei concordia?*
......Saepe plerique capti amore feminarum fidem suam prodiderunt."
—Ambrosius (Ep. 70, Lib. ix.). " Non enim licet christiano cum
gentili vel judaeo inire conjugium."—Petrus L. (l. iv. dist. 39, c. 1).
And this separation is by no means unbiblical. On the contrary,
we find that, in support of it, the Fathers appeal directly to the
Bible. The well-known passage of the Apostle Paul concerning
marriage between heathens and Christians relates only to marriages
which had taken place before conversion, not to those which were
yet to be contracted. Let the reader refer to what Peter Lombard says in the book already cited. " The first Christians did not
acknowledge, did not once listen to, all those relatives who sought
to turn them away from the hope of the heavenly reward. This
they did through the power of the Gospel, for the sake of which all
love of kindred was to be despised ; inasmuch as......the brotherhood of Christ far surpassed natural brotherhood. To us the
Fatherland and a common name is not so dear, but that we have a
horror even of our parents, if they seek to advise something against
the Lord.'—G. Arnold (Wahre Abbild. der ersten Christen. B. iv. c.
2). " Qui amat patrem et matrem plus quam me, non est me dignus
Matth. x.......in hoc vos non agnosco parentes, sed hostes.........
Alioquin quid mihi et vobis? *Quid a vobis habeo nisi peccatum et
miseriam ?*"—Bernardus (Epist. iii. Ex persona Heliae monachi
ad parentes suos). " Etsi impium est, contemnere matrem, contemnere tamen propter Christum piissimum est."—Bernardus (Ep.
104. See also Ep. 351, ad Hugonem novitium). " Audi sententiam
Isidori : multi canonicorum, monachorum.........temporali salute
suorum parentum perdunt animas suas......Servi Dei qui parentum suorum utilitatem procurant a Dei amore se separant."—*De
modo bene vivendi* (S. vii.). " Omnem hominem *fidelem* judica tuum
esse fratrem."—(Ibid. Sermo 13). " Ambrosius dicit, longe plus nos
debere diligere *filios quos de fonte levamus, quam quos carnaliter
genuimus.*"—Petrus L. (l. iv. dist. 6, c. 5, addit. Henr. ab Vurim.).
" Infantes nascuntur cum peccato, nec fiunt haeredes vitae aeternae
sine remissione peccati......Cum igitur dubium non sit in infan-
tibus esse peccatum, debet *aliquod esse discrimen infantium Ethni-*

corum, qui manent rei, et infantium in Ecclesia, qui recipiuntur a Deo per ministerium."—Melancthon (Loci de bapt. inf. Argum. II. Compare with this the passage above cited from Buddeus, as a proof of the narrowness of the true believer's love). " Ut Episcopi vel Clerici in eos, qui *Catholici Christiani non sunt,* etiam si *consanguinei* fuerint, nec per donationes rerum suarum aliquid conferant."— Concil. Carthag. III. can. 13 (Summa Carranza). " Cum *haereticis nec orandum, nec psallendum."*—Concil. Carthag. IV. can. 72 (ibid.). *Faith has the significance of religion, love only that of morality.* This has been declared very decidedly by Protestantism. The doctrine that love does not justify in the sight of God, but only faith, expresses nothing further than that love has no religious power and significance. (Apol. Augsb. Confess. art. 3. Of Love and the Fulfilment of the Law.) It is certainly here said : " What the scholastic writers teach concerning the love of God is a dream, and it is impossible to know and love God before we know and lay hold on mercy through faith. For then first does God become *objectum amabile,* a lovable, blissful object of contemplation." Thus here mercy, love is made the proper object of faith. And it is true that faith is immediately distinguished from love only in this, that faith places out of itself what love places in itself. " We believe that our justification, salvation, and consolation, lie out of ourselves."— Luther (Th. xvi. p. 497; see also Th. ix. p. 587). It is true that faith in the Protestant sense is faith in the forgiveness of sins, faith in mercy, faith in Christ, as the God who suffered and died for men, so that man, in order to attain everlasting salvation, has nothing further to do on his side than believingly to accept this sacrifice of God for him. But it is not as love only that God is an object of faith. On the contrary, the characteristic object of faith *as faith* is God as a subject, a person. And is a God who accords no merit to man, who claims all exclusively for himself, who watches jealously over his honour—is a self-interested, egoistic God like this a God of love ?

The morality which proceeds from faith has for its principle and criterion only the contradiction of Nature, of man. As the highest object of faith is that which most contradicts reason, the Eucharist, so necessarily the highest virtue of the morality which is true and obedient to faith is that which most contradicts Nature. *Dogmatic* miracles have therefore *moral* miracles as their *consequence.* Antinatural morality is the twin sister of supernatural faith. As faith vanquishes Nature outside of man, so the morality of faith vanquishes Nature within man. This practical supernaturalism, the summit of which is " virginity, the sister of the angels, the queen of virtues, the mother of all good " (see A. v. Buchers : Geistliches Suchverloren. (Sämmtl. W. B. vi. 151), has been specially developed by Catholicism ; for Protestantism has held fast only the principle of Christianity, and has arbitrarily eliminated its logical consequences ; it has embraced only Christian faith and not Christian morality. In faith, Protestantism has brought man back to the standpoint of primitive Christianity ; but in life, in practice, in morality, it has restored him to the pre-Christian, the Old Testament, the heathen, Adamitic, natural standpoint. God instituted marriage in paradise ; therefore even in the present day, even to Christians, the command Multiply ! is valid. Christ advises those only not to marry who "can receive" this higher rule. Chastity is a supernatural gift; it cannot therefore be expected of every one. But is not faith also a supernatural gift, a special gift of God, a miracle, as Luther says innumerable times, and is it not nevertheless commanded to us all ? Are not all men included in the command to mortify, blind, and contemn the natural reason ? Is not the tendency to believe and accept nothing which contradicts reason as natural, as strong, as necessary in us, as the sexual impulse ? If we ought to pray to God for faith because by ourselves we are too weak to believe, why should we not on the same ground entreat God for chastity ? Will he deny us this gift if we earnestly implore him for it ? Never ! Thus we may regard chastity as a universal command equally with faith, for what we cannot do of ourselves, we can do through God. What speaks against chastity speaks against faith also, and what speaks for faith speaks for chastity. One stands and falls with the other ; with a supernatural faith is necessarily associated a supernatural morality. Protestantism tore this bond asunder : in faith it affirmed Christianity ; in life, in practice, it denied Christianity, acknowledged the autonomy of natural reason, of man,—restored man to his original rights. Protestantism rejected celibacy, chastity, not because it contradicted the Bible, but because it contradicts man and nature. "He who will be single renounces the name of man, and proves or makes himself an angel or spirit.......It is pitiable folly to wonder that a man takes a wife, or for any one to be ashamed of doing so, since no one wonders that men are accustomed to eat and drink."—Luther (Th. xix. pp. 368, 369). Does this unbelief as to the possibility and reality of chastity accord with the Bible, where celibacy is eulogised as a laudable, and consequently a possible, attainable state ? No ! It is in direct contradiction with the Bible. Protestantism, in consequence of its practical spirit. and therefore by its own inherent force, repudiated Christian supranaturalism in the sphere of morality. Christianity exists for it only in faith—not in law, not in morality, not in the State. It is true that love (the compendium of morality) belongs essentially to the Christian, so that where there is no love, where faith does not attest itself by love, there is no faith, no Christianity. Nevertheless love is only the outward manifestation of faith, only a consequence, and only human. " Faith alone deals with God," " faith makes us gods ;" love makes us merely men, and as faith alone is for God, so God is for faith alone, *i.e.*, faith alone is the divine, the Christian in man. To faith belongs eternal life, to love only this temporal life. "Long before Christ came God gave this temporal, earthly life to the whole world, and said that man should love him and his neighbour. After that he gave the world to his Son Christ, that we through and by him should have eternal life.......Moses and the law belong to this life, but for the other life we must have the Lord."—Luther (Th. xvi. p. 459). Thus although love belongs to the Christian, yet is the

Christian a Christian only through this, that he believes in Christ. It is true that to serve one's neighbour, in whatever way, rank, or calling, is to serve God. But the God whom I serve in fulfilling a worldly or ·natural office is only the universal, mundane, natural, pre-Christian God. Government, the State, marriage, existed prior to Christianity, was an institution, an ordinance of God, in which he did not as yet reveal himself as the true God, as Christ. Christ has nothing to do with all these worldly things ; they are external, indifferent to him. But for this very reason, every worldly calling and rank is compatible with Christianity ; for the true, Christian service of God is faith alone, and this can be exercised everywhere. Protestantism binds men only in faith, all the rest it leaves free, but only because all the rest is external to faith.

It is true that we are bound by the commandments of Christian morality, as, for example, " Avenge not yourselves," &c., but they have validity for us only as private, not as public persons. The world is governed according to its own laws. Catholicism "mingled together the worldly and spiritual kingdoms," *i.e.,* it sought to govern the world by Christianity. But " Christ did net come on earth to interfere in the government of the Emperor Augustus and teach him how to reign."—Luther (Th. xvi. p. 49). Where worldly government begins Christianity ends ; there worldly justice, the sword, war, litigation, prevail. As a Christian I let my cloak be stolen from me without resistance, but as a citizen I seek to recover it by law. " Evangelium non abolet jus naturæ."—Melancthon (de Vindicta Loci. See also on this subject M. Chemnitii Loci Theol. de Vindicta). In fact, Protestantism is the practical negation of Christianity, the practical assertion of the natural man. It is true that Protestantism also commands the mortifying of the flesh, the negation of the natural man ; but apart from the fact that this negation has for Protestantism no religious significance and efficacy, does not justify, *i.e.,* make acceptable to God, procure salvation ; the negation of the flesh in Protestantism is not distinguished from that limitation of the flesh which natural reason and morality enjoin on man. The necessary practical consequences of the Christian faith Protestantism has relegated to the other world, to heaven— in other words, has denied them. In heaven first ceases the worldly standpoint of Protestantism ; there we no longer marry, there first we are new creatures; but here everything remains as of old "until that life ; there the external life will be changed, for Christ did not come to change the creature."—Luther (Th. xv. p. 62). Here we are half heathens, half Christians ; half citizens of the earth, half citizens of heaven. Of this division, this disunity, this chasm, Catholicism knows nothing. What it denies in heaven, *i.e.,* in faith, it denies. also, as far as possible, on earth, *i.e.,* in morality. " Grandis igitur virtutis est et sollicitate diligentiae, *superare quod nata sis : in carne non carnaliter vivere,* tecum pugnare quotidie."—Hieronymus (Ep. Furiae Rom. nobilique viduae). "Quanto igitur *natura amplius vincitur* et premitur, tanto major gratia infunditur."—Thomas à K. (Imit. l. iii. c. 54). " Esto robustus tam in agendo, quam in patiendo *naturae contraria.*"—(Ibid. c. 49.) " Beatus ille homo, qui propter te, Domine, omnibus creaturis licentiam abeundi tribuit, qui *naturae vim* facit et concupiscentias carnis fervore spiritus crucifigit" (c. 48). "Adhuc proh dolor! vivit in me *verus homo,* non est totus crucifixus."—(Ibid. c. 34, l. iii. c. 19, l. ii. c. 12.) And these dicta by no means emanate simply from the pious individuality of the author of the work *De Imitatione Christi;* they express the genuine morality of Catholicism, that morality which the saints attested by their lives, and which was sanctioned even by the Head of the Church, otherwise so worldly. Thus it is said, for example, in the Canonizatio S. Bernhardi Abbatis per Alexandrum papam III. anno Ch. 1164. Litt. apost......primo ad. Praelatos Eccles. Gallic. : "*In afflictione vero corporis sui* usque adeo sibi mundum, seque mundo reddidit crucifixum, ut confidamus martyrum quoque eum merita obtinere sanctorum, etc." It was owing to this purely negative moral principle that there could be enunciated within Catholicism itself the gross opinion that mere martyrdom, without the motive of love to God, obtains heavenly blessedness.

It is true that Catholicism also in practice denied the supra-naturalistic morality of Christianity; but its negation has an essentially different significance from that of Protestantism ; it is a negation *de facto* but not *de jure.* The Catholic denied in life what he ought to have affirmed in life,—as, for example, the vow of chastity,—what he desired to affirm, at least if he was a religious Catholic, but which in the nature of things he could not affirm. Thus he gave validity to the law of Nature, he gratified the flesh, in a word, he was a man, in contradiction with his essential character, his religious principle and conscience. *Adhuc proh dolor ! vivit in me verus homo.* Catholicism has proved to the world that the supernatural principle of faith in Christianity, applied to life, made a principle of morals, has immoral, radically corrupting consequences. This experience Protestantism made use of, or rather this experience called forth Protestantism. It made the illegitimate, practical negation of Christianity—illegitimate in the sense of true Catholicism, though not in that of the degenerate Church— the law, the *norm* of life. You *cannot* in life, at least in this life, be Christians, peculiar, superhuman beings, therefore ye ought not to be such. And it legitimised this negation of Christianity before its still Christian conscience, by Christianity itself, pronounced it to be Christian ;—no wonder, therefore, that now at last modern Christianity not only practically but theoretically represents the total negation of Christianity as Christianity. When, however, Protestantism is designated as the contradiction, Catholicism as the unity of faith and practice, it is obvious that in both cases we refer only to the essence, to the principle.

Faith sacrifices man to God. Human sacrifice belongs to the very idea of religion. Bloody human sacrifices only dramatise this idea. "By faith Abraham offered up Isaac."—Heb. xi. 17. "Quanto major Abraham, qui unicum filium *voluntate jugulavit......*Jepte obtulit virginem filiam et idcirco in enumeratione sanctorum ab Apostolo ponitur."—Hieronymus (Epist. Juliano). On the human sacrifices in the Jewish religion we refer the reader to the works of

Daumer and Ghillany. In the Christian religion also it is only blood, the sacrifice of the Son of Man, which allays God's anger and reconciles him to man. Therefore a pure, guiltless man must fall a sacrifice. Such blood alone is precious, such alone has reconciling power. And this blood, shed on the cross for the allaying of the divine anger, Christians partake in the Lord's Supper, for the strengthening and sealing of their faith. But why is the blood taken under the form of wine, the flesh under the form of bread? That it may not *appear* as if Christians ate real human flesh and drank human blood, that the natural man may not shrink from the mysteries of the Christian faith. "Etenim ne humana infirmitas esum carnis et potum sanguinis in sumptione *horreret,* Christus *velari et palliari illa duo voluit speciebus* panis et vini."— Bernard. (edit. cit. pp. 189–191). "Sub alia autem specie tribus de causis carnem et sanguinem tradit Christus et deinceps sumendum instituit. Ut fides scil. haberet meritum, quae est de his quae non videntur, quod *fides non habet meritum,* ubi humana ratio praebet experimentum. Et ideo etiam ne *abhorreret animus* quod cerneret oculus ; quod *non habemus in usu carnem crudam comedere et sanguinem bibere*......Et etiam ideo ne ab *incredulis religioni christianae insultaretur.* Unde Augustinus : Nihil rationabilius, quam ut sanguinis similitudinem sumamus, ut et ita veritas non desit et *ridiculum nullum fiat a paganis, quod* cruorem occisi hominis bibamus."—Petrus Lomb. (Sent. lib. iv. dist. ii. c. 4).

But as the bloody human sacrifice, while it expresses the utmost abnegation of man, is at the same time the highest assertion of his value ;—for only because human life is regarded as the highest, because the sacrifice of it is the most painful, costs the greatest conquest over feeling, is it offered to God ;—so the contradiction of the Eucharist with human nature is only apparent. Apart from the fact that flesh and blood are, as St. Bernard says, clothed with bread and wine, *i.e.,* that in truth it is not flesh but bread, not blood but wine, which is partaken,—the mystery of the Eucharist resolves itself into the mystery of eating and drinking. "All ancient Christian doctors......teach that the body of Christ is not taken spiritually alone by faith, which happens also *out of* the Sacraments, but also corporeally ; not alone by believers, by the pious, but also by unworthy, unbelieving, false and wicked Christians." "There are thus two ways of eating Christ's flesh, one spiritual......such spiritual eating however is nothing else than faith......The other way of eating the body of Christ is to eat it corporeally or sacramentally."—(Concordienb. Erkl. art. 7). "The mouth eats the body of Christ bodily." — Luther (against the "fanatics." Th. xix. p. 417). What then forms the specific difference of the Eucharist? Eating and drinking. Apart from the Sacrament, God is partaken of spiritually ; in the Sacrament he is partaken of materially, *i.e,* he is eaten and drunken, assimilated by the body. But how couldst thou receive God into thy body, if it were in thy esteem an organ unworthy of God ? Dost thou pour wine into a water-cask ? Dost thou not declare thy hands and lips

holy when by means of them thou comest in contact with the Holy
One? Thus if God is eaten and drunken, eating and drinking is
declared to be a divine act; and this is what the Eucharist expresses, though in a self-contradictory, mystical, covert manner.
But it is our task to express the mystery of religion, openly and
honourably, clearly and definitely. *Life is God; the enjoyment of
life is the enjoyment of God; true bliss in life is true religion.* But
to the enjoyment of life belongs the enjoyment of eating and
drinking. If therefore life in general is holy, eating and drinking
must be holy. Is this an irreligious creed? Let it be remembered
that this irreligion is the analysed, unfolded, unequivocally expressed mystery of religion itself. All the mysteries of religion
ultimately resolve themselves, as we have shown, into the mystery
of heavenly bliss. But heavenly bliss is nothing else than happiness
freed from the limits of reality. The Christians have happiness for
their object just as much as the heathens; the only difference is,
that the heathens place heaven on earth, the Christians place earth
in heaven. Whatever *is*, whatever is really enjoyed, is finite; that
which is *not*, which is believed in and hoped for, is infinite.

§ 21.

*The Christian religion is a contradiction. It is at once the re-
conciliation and the disunion, the unity and the opposition, of God
and man. This contradiction is personified in the God-man. The
unity of the Godhead and manhood is at once a truth and an untruth.*
We have already maintained that if Christ was God, if he was at
once man and another being conceived as incapable of suffering,
his suffering was an illusion. For his suffering as man was no
suffering to him as God. No! what he acknowledged as man he
denied as God. He suffered only outwardly, not inwardly, *i.e.*,
he suffered only apparently, not really; for he was man only in
appearance, in form, in the external; in truth, in essence, in which
alone he was an object to the believer, he was God. It would have
been true suffering only if he had suffered as God also. What he
did not experience in his nature as God, he did not experience in
truth, in substance. And, incredible as it is, the Christians themselves half directly, half indirectly, admit that their highest,
holiest mystery is only an illusion, a simulation. This simulation
indeed lies at the foundation of the thoroughly unhistorical,*
theatrical, illusory Gospel of John. One instance, among others,
in which this is especially evident, is the resurrection of Lazarus,
where the omnipotent arbiter of life and death evidently sheds
tears only in ostentation of his manhood, and expressly says:
"Father, I thank thee that thou hast heard me, and I know that

* On this subject I refer to Lützelberger's work: "Die Kirchliche Tradition
über den Apostel Johannes und seine Schriften in ihrer Grundlosigkeit nach-
gewiesen," and to Bruno Bauer's "Kritik der Evangelischen Geschichte der
Synoptiker und des Johannes" (B. iii.).

thou hearest me always, but for the sake of the people who stand
round I said it, that they may believe in thee." The simulation
thus indicated in the Gospel has been developed by the Church
into avowed delusion. " Si credas susceptionem corporis, adjungas
divinitatis compassionem, portionem utique perfidiae, non perfidiam
declinasti. Credis enim, quod tibi prodesse praesumis, non credis
quod *Deo dignum* est.......Idem enim patiebatur et non patiebatur.
......Patiebatur secundum corporis susceptionem, ut *suscepti corporis
veritas crederetur* et non patiebatur secundum verbi impassibilem
divinitatem.......Erat igitur immortalis in morte, impassibilis in
passione.......Cur *divinitati* attribuis aerumnas corporis et infirmum
doloris humani *divinae connectis naturae?*"—Ambrosius (de incarnat.
domin. sacr. cc. 4, 5). "Juxta hominis naturam proficiebat sapientia, non quod ipse sapientior esset ex tempore......sed eandem, qua
plenus erat, sapientiam caeteris ex tempore paulatim *demonstrabat.*
......In aliis ergo *non in se* proficiebat sapientia et gratia."—Gregorius in homil. quadam (ap. Petrus Lomb. l. iii. dist. 13, c. 1).
" Proficiebat ergo humanus sensus in eo *secundum ostensionem* et
aliorum hominum *opinionem.* Ita enim patrem et matrem dicitur
ignorasse in infantia, quia *ita se gerebat et habebat ac si agnitionis
expers esset.*"—Petrus L. (ibid. c. 2). " Ut homo ergo dubitat, ut
homo locutus est."—Ambrosius. " His verbis innui videtur, quod
Christus non inquantum Deus vel Dei filius, sed inquantum homo
dubitaverit affectu humano. Quod ea ratione dictum accipi potest :
non quod ipse dubitaverit, sed quod *modum gessit dubitantis* et
hominibus dubitare videbatur."—Petrus L. (ibid. dist. 17, c. 2).
In the first part of the present work we have exhibited the truth,
in the second part the untruth of religion, or rather of theology.
The truth is only the identity of God and man. Religion is truth
only when it affirms human attributes as divine, falsehood when, in
the form of theology, it denies these attributes, separating God
from man as a different being. Thus, in the first part we had to
show the truth of God's suffering ; here we have the proof of its
untruth, and not a proof which lies in our own subjective view, but
an objective proof—the admission of theology itself, that its highest
mystery, the Passion of God, is only a deception, an illusion. It is
therefore in the highest degree uncritical, untruthful, and arbitrary
to explain the Christian religion, as speculative philosophy has
done, only as the religion of reconciliation between God and man,
and not also as the religion of disunion between the divine and
human nature,—to find in the God-man only the unity, and not also
the contradiction of the divine and human nature. Christ suffered
only as man, not as God. Capability of suffering is the sign of real
humanity. It was not as God that he was born, that he increased
in wisdom, and was crucified ; *i.e.*, all human conditions remained
foreign to him as God. " Si quis non confitetur proprie et vere
substantialem differentiam naturarum post ineffabilem unionem,
ex quibus unus et solus extitit Christus, in ea salvatum, sit con-
demnatus."—Concil. Later. I. can. 7 (Carranza). The divine nature,
notwithstanding the position that Christ was at once God and
man, is just as much dissevered from the human nature *in* the

incarnation as *before* it, since each nature excludes the conditions of the other, although both are united in one personality, in an incomprehensible, miraculous, *i.e.*, untrue manner, in contradiction with the relation in which, according to their definition, they stand to each other. Even the Lutherans, nay, Luther himself, however strongly he expresses himself concerning the community and union of the human and divine nature in Christ, does not escape from the irreconcilable division between them. "God is man, and man is God, but thereby neither the natures nor their attributes are confounded, but each nature retains its essence and attributes." "The Son of God himself has truly suffered and truly died, but according to the human nature which he had assumed ; for the divine nature can neither suffer nor die." "It is truly said, the Son of God suffers. For although the one part (so to speak), as the Godhead, does not suffer, still the person who is God suffers in the other half, the manhood ; for in truth the Son of God was crucified for us, that is, the person who is God ; for the person is crucified according to his manhood." "It is the person that does and suffers all, one thing according to this nature, another according to that nature, all which the learned well know."—(Concordienb. Erklar. art. 8.) "The Son of God and God himself is killed and murdered, for God and man is one person. Therefore God was crucified, and died, and became man ; not God apart from humanity, but united with it ; not according to the Godhead, but according to the human nature which he had assumed."—Luther (Th. iii. p. 502). Thus only in the person, *i.e.*, only in a *nomen proprium*, not in essence, not in truth, are the two natures united. "Quando dicitur : Deus est homo vel homo est Deus, propositio ejusmodi vocatur personalis. Ratio est, quia unionem personalem in Christo supponit. Sine tali enim naturarum in Christo unione nunquam dicere potuissem, Deum esse hominem aut hominem esse Deum. ......Abstracta autem naturae de se invicem enuntiari non posse, longe est manifestissimum.........Dicere itaque non licet, divina natura est humana aut deitas est humanitas et vice versa."—J. F. Buddeus (Comp. Inst. Theol. Dogm. l. iv. c. ii. § 11). Thus the union of the divine and human natures in the incarnation is only a deception, an illusion. The old dissidence of God and man lies at the foundation of this dogma also, and operates all the more injuriously, is all the more odious, that it conceals itself behind the appearance, the imagination of unity. Hence Socinianism, far from being superficial when it denied the Trinity and the God-man, was only consistent, only truthful. God was a triune being, and yet he was to be held purely simple, absolute unity, an *ens simplicissimum ;* thus the Unity contradicted the Trinity. God was God-man, and yet the Godhead was not to be touched or annulled by the manhood, *i.e.*, it was to be essentially distinct ; thus the incompatibility of the divine and human attributes contradicted the unity of the two natures. According to this, we have in the very idea of the God-man the arch-enemy of the God-man,— *rationalism*, blended, however, with its opposite—mysticism. Thus Socinianism only denied what faith itself denied, and yet, in contradiction with itself, at the same time affirmed ; it only denied a contradiction, an untruth.

Nevertheless the Christians have celebrated the incarnation as a work of love, as a self-renunciation of God, an abnegation of his majesty—*Amor triumphat de Deo ;* for the love of God is an empty word if it is understood as a real abolition of the distinction between him and man. Thus we have, in the very central point of Christianity, the contradiction of Faith and Love developed in the close of the present work. Faith makes the suffering of God a mere appearance, love makes it a truth. Only on the truth of the suffering rests the true positive impression of the incarnation. Strongly, then, as we have insisted on the contradiction and division between the divine and the human nature in the God-man, we must equally insist on their community and unity, in virtue of which God is really man and man is really God. Here then we have the irrefragable and striking proof that the central point, the supreme object of Christianity, is nothing else than *man*, that Christians adore the human individual as God, and God as the human individual. "This man born of the Virgin Mary is God himself, who has created heaven and earth."—Luther (Th. ii. p. 671). "I point to the man Christ and say: That is the Son of God."—(Th. xix. p. 594.) "To give life, to have all power in heaven and earth, to have all things in his hands, all things put under his feet, to purify from sin, and so on, are divine, infinite attributes, which, according to the declaration of the Holy Scriptures, are given and imparted to the man Christ." "Therefore we believe, teach, and confess that the Son of Man......now not only as God, but also as man, knows all things, can do all things, is present with all creatures." "We reject and condemn the doctrine that he (the Son of God) is not capable *according to his human nature* of omnipotence and other attributes of the divine nature."—(Concordienb. Summar. Begr. u. Erklär. art. 8.) "Unde et sponte sua fluit, Christo etiam qua *humanam naturam spectato cultum religiosum deberi.*"—Buddeus (l. c. l. iv. c. ii. § 17). The same is expressly taught by the Fathers and the Catholics, *e.g.,* "Eadem *adoratione advranda* in Christo est divinitas et *humanitas......*Divinitas intrinsece inest humanitati per unionem hypostaticam : ergo *humanitas* Christi seu Christus ut *homo* potest adorari absoluto cultu latriae."—Theol. Schol. (sec. Thomam Aq. P. Metzger. iv. p. 124). It is certainly said that it is not man, not flesh and blood by itself, which is worshipped, but the flesh united with God, so that the cultus applies not to the flesh, or man, but to God. But it is here as with the worship of saints and images. As the saint is adored in the image and God in the saint, only because the image and the saint are themselves adored, so God is worshipped in the human body only because the human flesh is itself worshipped. God becomes flesh, man, because man is in truth already God. How could it enter into thy mind to bring the human flesh into so close a relation and contact with God if it were something impure, degrading, unworthy of God ? If the value, the dignity of the human flesh does not lie in itself, why dost thou not make other flesh—the flesh of brutes the habitation of the Divine Spirit? True it is said : Man is only the organ in, with, and by which the Godhead works, as the soul in the body. But this pretext also is refuted by what has been said above. God chose man as his organ, his body, because only in man did he find an organ worthy of him, suitable, pleasing to him. If the nature of man is indifferent, why did not God become incarnate in a brute? Thus God comes *into* man only *out of* man. The manifestation of God in man is only a manifestation of the divinity and glory of man. "Noscitur ex alio, qui non cognoscitur ex se"—this trivial saying is applicable here. God is known through man, whom he honours with his personal presence and indwelling, and known as a human being, for what any one prefers, selects, loves, in his *objective nature ;* and man is known through God, and known as a divine being, for only that which is worthy of God, which is divine, can be the object, organ, and habitation of God. True it is further said : It is Jesus Christ alone, and no other man, who is worshipped as God. But this argument also is idle and empty. Christ is indeed one only, but he is one who represents all. He is a man as we are, "our brother, and we are flesh of his flesh and bone of his bone." "In Jesus Christ our Lord every one of us is a portion of flesh and blood. Therefore where my body is, there I believe that I myself reign. Where my flesh is glorified, there I believe that I am myself glorious. Where my blood rules, there I hold that I myself rule."—Luther (Th. xvi. p. 534). This then is an undeniable fact : Christians worship the human individual as the supreme being, as God. Not indeed consciously, for it is the unconsciousness of this fact which constitutes the illusion of the religious principle. But in this sense it may be said that the heathens did not worship the statues of the gods : for to them also the statue was not a statue, but God himself. Nevertheless they *did* worship the statue ; just as Christians worship the human individual, though, naturally, they will not admit it.

§ 22.

Man is the God of Christianity, Anthropology the mystery of Christian Theology. The history of Christianity has had for its grand result the unveiling of this mystery—the realisation and recognition of theology as anthropology. The distinction between Protestantism and Catholicism—the old Catholicism, which now exists only in books, not in actuality—consists only in this, that the latter is Theology, the former Christology, *i.e.*, (religious) Anthropology. Catholicism has a supranaturalistic, abstract God, a God who is other than human, a not human, a superhuman being. The goal of Catholic morality, likeness to God, consists therefore in this, to be not a man, but more than a man—a heavenly abstract being, an angel. Only in its morality does the essence of a religion realise, reveal itself : morality alone is the criterion, whether a religious dogma is felt as a truth or is a mere chimera. Thus the doctrine of a superhuman, supernatural God is a truth only where it has as its consequence a superhuman, supernatural, or rather antinatural morality. Protestantism, on the contrary, has not a supranaturalistic but a human morality, a morality of and for flesh and blood ; consequently its God, at least its true, real God, is no longer an abstract, supranaturalistic being, but a being of flesh and blood. "This defiance the devil hears unwillingly, that our flesh and blood is the Son of God, yea, God himself, and reigns in heaven over all."—Luther (Th. xvi. p. 573). "Out of Christ there is no God, and where Christ is, there is the whole Godhead."—Id. (Th. xix. p. 403). Catholicism has, both in theory and practice, a God who, in spite of the predicate of love, exists for himself, to whom therefore man only comes by being against himself, denying himself, renouncing his existence for self ; Protestantism, on the contrary, has a God who, at least practically, virtually, has not an existence for himself, but exists only for man, for the welfare of man. Hence in Catholicism the highest act of the cultus, "the mass of Christ," is a sacrifice of man,—the same Christ, the same flesh and blood, is sacrificed to God in the Host as on the cross ; in Protestantism, on the contrary, it is a sacrifice, a gift of God : God sacrifices himself, surrenders himself to be partaken by man. (See Luther, e.g., Th. xx. p. 259 ; Th. xvii. p. 529.) In Catholicism manhood is the property, the predicate of the Godhead (of Christ)—God is man ; in Protestantism, on the contrary, Godhead is the property, the predicate of manhood (Christ)—man is God. "This, in time past, the greatest theologians have done—they have fled from the manhood of Christ to his Godhead, and attached themselves to that alone, and thought that we should not know the manhood of Christ. But we must so rise to the Godhead of Christ, and hold by it in such a way, as not to forsake the manhood of Christ and come to the Godhead alone. Thou shouldst know of no God, nor Son of God, save him who was born of the Virgin Mary and became man. He who receives his manhood has also his Godhead."—Luther (Th. ix. pp. 592, 598).* Or, briefly thus : in Catholicism, man exists for God ; in Protestantism, God exists for man.† "Jesus Christ our Lord was conceived for us, born for us, suffered for us, was crucified, died, and was buried for us. Our Lord rose from the dead for *our* consolation, sits for *our* good at the right hand of the Almighty Father, and is to judge the living and the dead for *our* comfort. This the holy Apostles and beloved Fathers intended to intimate in their confession by the words : Us and our Lord—namely, that Jesus Christ is ours, whose office and will it is to help us......so that we should not read or speak the words coldly, and interpret them. only of Christ, but of ourselves

* In another place Luther praises St. Bernard and Bonaventura because they laid so much stress on the manhood of Christ.
† It is true that in Catholicism also—in Christianity generally, God exists for man ; but it was Protestantism which first drew from this relativity of God its true result—the absoluteness of man.

also."—Luther (Th. xvi. p. 538). " I know of no God but him who
gave himself for me. Is not that a great thing that God is man,
that God gives himself to man and will be his, as man gives himself to his wife and is hers? But if God is ours, all things are
ours."—(Th. xii. p. 283.) " God cannot be a God of the dead, who are
nothing, but is a God of the living. If God were a God of the
dead, he would be as a husband who had no wife, or as a father
who had no son, or as a master who had no servant. For if he is
a husband, he must have a wife. If he is a father, he must have
a son. If he is a master, he must have a servant. Or he would
be a fictitious father, a fictitious master, that is, nothing. God is
not a God like the idols of the heathens, neither is he an imaginary
God, who exists for himself alone, and has none who call upon
him and worship him. A God is he from whom everything
is to be expected and received......If he were God for himself
alone in heaven, and we had no good to rely on from him, he
would be a God of stone or straw......If he sat alone in heaven
like a clod, he would not be God."—(Th. xvi. p. 465). "God says:
I the Almighty Creator of heaven and earth am thy God......To be
a God means to redeem us from all evil and trouble that oppresses
us, as sin, hell, death, &c."—(Th. ii. p. 327.) "All the world calls
that a God in whom man trusts in need and danger, on whom
he relies, from whom all good is to be had and who can help.
Thus reason describes God, that he affords help to man, and does
good to him, bestows benefits upon him. This thou seest also
in this text: 'I am the Lord thy God, who brought thee out
of the land of Egypt.' There we are taught what God is, what
is his nature, and what are his attributes,—namely, that he does
good, delivers from dangers, and helps out of trouble and all
calamities."—(Th. iv. pp. 236, 237.) But if God is a living, *i.e.*, real
God, is God in general, only in virtue of this—that he is a God to
man, a being who is useful, good, beneficent to man ; then, in truth,
man is the criterion, the measure of God, man is the absolute,
divine being. The proposition : A God existing only for himself
is no God—means nothing else than that God without man is not
God ; where there is no man there is no God ; if thou takest from
God the predicate of humanity, thou takest from him the predicate
of deity ; if his relation to man is done away with, so also is his
existence.

Nevertheless Protestantism, at least in theory, has retained in
the background of this human God the old supranaturalistic God.
Protestantism is the contradiction of theory and practice ; it has
emancipated the flesh, but not the reason. According to Protestantism, Christianity, *i.e.*, God, does not contradict the natural
impulses of man :—"Therefore we ought now to know that God
does not condemn or abolish the natural tendency in man which
was implanted in Nature at the creation, but that he awakens and
preserves it."—Luther (Th. iii. p. 290). But it contradicts reason,
and is therefore, theoretically, only an object of faith. We have
shown, however, that the nature of faith, the nature of God, is

itself nothing else than the nature of man placed out of man, conceived as external to man.   The reduction of the extrahuman, supernatural, and antirational nature of God to the natural, immanent, inborn nature of man, is therefore the liberation of Protestantism, of Christianity in general, from its fundamental contradiction, the reduction of it to its truth,—the result, the necessary, irrepressible, irrefragable result of Christianity.

COSIMO is a specialty publisher of books and publications that inspire, inform, and engage readers. Our mission is to offer unique books to niche audiences around the world.

COSIMO BOOKS publishes books and publications for innovative authors, nonprofit organizations, and businesses. COSIMO BOOKS specializes in bringing books back into print, publishing new books quickly and effectively, and making these publications available to readers around the world.

COSIMO CLASSICS offers a collection of distinctive titles by the great authors and thinkers throughout the ages. At COSIMO CLASSICS timeless works find new life as affordable books, covering a variety of subjects including: Business, Economics, History, Personal Development, Philosophy, Religion & Spirituality, and much more!

COSIMO REPORTS publishes public reports that affect your world, from global trends to the economy, and from health to geopolitics.

FOR MORE INFORMATION CONTACT US AT
INFO@COSIMOBOOKS.COM

➢ if you are a book lover interested in our current catalog of books

➢ if you represent a bookstore, book club, or anyone else interested in special discounts for bulk purchases

➢ if you are an author who wants to get published

➢ if you represent an organization or business seeking to publish books and other publications for your members, donors, or customers.

COSIMO BOOKS ARE ALWAYS
AVAILABLE AT ONLINE BOOKSTORES

VISIT COSIMOBOOKS.COM
BE INSPIRED, BE INFORMED

CPSIA information can be obtained
at www.ICGtesting.com
Printed in the USA
LVOW12s0907201116

513797LV00001B/178/P